The Logic

of HISTORICAL
EXPLANATION

The Logic
of HISTORICAL
EXPLANATION

Clayton Roberts

The Pennsylvania State University Press
University Park, Pennsylvania

Library of Congress Cataloging-in-Publication Data

Roberts, Clayton, 1923–
    The logic of historical explanation / by Clayton Roberts.

        p.   cm.
    Includes bibliographical references and index.
    ISBN 0-271-01442-3 (cloth)
    ISBN 0-271-01443-1 (paper)
    1. History—Philosophy. 2. Logic. I. Title.
    D16.9.R57   1996
    901—dc20   94-40822
                                                                    CIP

It is the policy of The Pennsylvania State University Press to use acid-free paper
for the first printing of all clothbound books. Publications on uncoated stock
satisfy the minimum requirements of American National Standard for Information Sciences—Permanence of Paper for Printed Library Materials, ANSI Z39.48–
1992.

Contents

Si les phénomènes ne sont pas enchaînés les uns aux autres, il n'y a point de philosophie.

— Diderot, *Pensées sur l'interprétation de la nature*

Preface

In 1935 R. G. Collingwood, in "Human Nature and Human History," declared that history is an autonomous form of thought, that history is unlike the natural sciences, that history is nothing but the reenactment of past thoughts in the historian's mind. Then in 1942 Carl Hempel, in "The Function of General Laws in History," declared that historians, like scientists, explain the occurrence of events by subsuming them under laws governing the occurrence of like events, a declaration that came to be called the covering-law model of historical explanation. These two essays polarized analytical philosophers of history into two schools: the Hempelians and the anti-Hempelians, the positivists and the humanists. Among the positivists can be numbered Carl Hempel himself, Ernest Nagel, Morton White, Patrick Gardiner, and Robert Stover; among the humanists, William Dray, Alan Donagan, Michael Scriven, R. F. Atkinson, and A. R. Louch. The positivists insisted that the covering-law model was central to an understanding of the nature of historical explanation; the humanists denied that it was. This debate flourished in the 1960s but reached an impasse in the 1970s. Since neither school was persuaded by the arguments of the other, the debate became increasingly sterile. By the end of the 1970s the debate was not so much resolved as shelved.

Confronted with this impasse and influenced by postmodernist thought, philosophers of history turned in different directions. They turned to Hayden White and the analysis of the structure of narrative, to Jacques Derrida and the deconstruction of texts, to Hans-Georg Gadamer and Continental hermeneutics. But though these scholars had many interesting things to say about the influence of literary tropes on the shape of a narrative, about the subjective nature of the interpretation of texts, and about the problem of "understanding" the past, they said little or nothing about the logic that guides the historian in determining why an event occurred. Where the analytical philosophy of history ultimately reached an impasse, the postmodernist philosophy of history promptly entered a *cul de sac*. When Richard Miller published *Fact and Method* in 1987 and when Raymond Martin published *The Past Within Us* in 1989, there was the merest mention of White and Derrida and none of Gadamer. And when in 1990 nine philosophers of history assembled at Trent University (or sent papers) to honor William Dray, only one followed the postmodernist path. Indeed, the old impasse was still present, with Miller attacking and Martin accepting the basic postulate of positivism.

But there is a path through that impasse, and it is the purpose of this book to describe it. What is that path? It is the recognition that the covering-law model, when applied to macro-events (that is, to events such as wars and revolutions), is invalid, unworkable, even absurd, but when applied to micro-events (that is, to the discrete events leading up to those wars and revolutions) is valid, useful, indeed indispensable. The debate over the covering-law model in the 1970s proved sterile because the positivists persisted in applying it to macro-events and for that reason ignored the explanatory power gained by tracing the course of events leading up to the macro-event—a process I have chosen to call colligation. It likewise proved sterile because the humanists, though they appreciated the explanatory power of tracing, persisted in denying that in order to trace one had to subsume these lesser events under laws governing the occurrence of like events—a process I have chosen to call correlation. Colligation and correlation are the warp and the woof from which historians weave their explanations. And it is the marriage of colligation and correlation that furnishes the key to a reconciliation between the positivists and the humanists. Thus in Chapters 1 and 2, I endeavor to show why the covering-law model is unworkable at the macro-level and why tracing how a complex event came about has great explanatory power. And thus in Chapter 3, I endeavor to show why the humanists are mistaken in believing that the historian can write an explanatory narrative without recourse to covering laws.

A second purpose arose out of the reading and study required to accomplish the first. I discovered that many tasks requisite to an adequate description of historical explanation had not been performed. For example, no philosopher had systematically described the nature of covering laws. I therefore seek to do so in Chapter 4. More seriously, no philosopher has discussed the logic of colligation, with its exploration of convergent and divergent colligation, of overdetermination and counterfactuals, of cumulative colligation and structure, and of repetitive colligation and theory. I therefore endeavor to do so in Chapters 6 and 7. Other philosophers have discussed purposive action, most notably William Dray and Karl Popper, but none has shown how three separate logics—the logic of the situation, the logic of dispositional traits, and the logic of subsequent actions—may be combined in order to elucidate the historical agent's purpose. In Chapter 8, I endeavor to do so. And, finally, I discovered that considerable confusion existed in the writings of philosophers about the meaning of "interpretation." Therefore, in Chapter 11, I define it as an abbreviation of a total explanation, an abbreviation that points to the more important causes. This definition may be more prescriptive than descriptive, but I found it necessary to stipulate such a definition in order to introduce clarity where there was confusion.

Gradually, as I carried out these tasks, a third purpose formed in my mind: to write as full, as accurate, as systematic, and as comprehensive a description of the logic of historical explanation as was possible. It should be the description of a total explanation, an explanation in which the historian first describes the complex event that is to be explained, then traces the discrete events leading up to it, discovers the authors of those events, elucidates their purposes, relates those purposes to their desires and beliefs, investigates the origins of those desires and beliefs, and, finally, abbreviates this total explanation into an interpretation, an interpretation that emphasizes the more important causes. It should be an explanation so comprehensive that any one part of it, say, rational explanation, should be seen to be only a part of it, even only a small part of it. To describe this total explanation became the third purpose of this book.

There is yet another purpose that led me to write this book: a desire to make the writings of the analytical philosophers of history accessible to historians. Regarding their discipline as a craft governed by common-sense, historians have notoriously eschewed methodology and ignored philosophy. But they may have done so to their loss. This does not mean that a concern for the writings of the analytical philosophers of history will suddenly transform incompetent historians into mediocre historians, or mediocre historians into brilliant historians. But a concern for the philosophy of history might add depth and bite to methods courses in colleges and universities. It might innoculate historians against the more extravagant claims of social-science history. It might teach historians how to separate the wheat from the chaff in postmodernist thought. It might show them the fallacies of Marxist functionalism. The problem, though, is to overcome some of the obstacles thrown up by philosophers to an easy access to their thought: an austere style, a remorseless logic, a want of examples, and a technical vocabulary. I have tried to overcome these obstacles in three ways: by frequently citing, quoting from, and summarizing the thought of these philosophers, by including innumerable historical illustrations of explanatory thought, and by placing at the end of the book a glossary of the technical terms used by philosophers (and the neologisms invented by myself). It is my hope that a historian who has spent a lifetime writing and professing history and a decade reading philosophy can help make the thought of analytical philosophy of history accessible to his colleagues.

Beneath these four purposes lies a profounder purpose, one that arises from a belief, indeed a passionate belief, that historical research is not hopelessly subjective, that historical truth is not irremediably relative, and that every man is not his own historian. This does not mean for a moment that I believe that complete objectivity can be attained in the writing of history. Long before Jacques Derrida and Paul Ricoeur put pen to paper, Charles Beard and Carl Becker had challenged Leopold von Ranke's naive belief that the historian described the past "as it actually was." They saw that the historian could only view the past from his or her particular point of view. But Beard and Becker, as well as Derrida and Ricoeur later, failed to see that the historian, having written his or her particular interpretation of the past, must submit that interpretation to the public, more particularly to other historians, who will review it, criticize it, debate over it, and judge it. And these critics will judge the historian's reconstruction of what happened in the past by canons of evidence that are widely, if not universally, accepted; and they will judge the historian's explanation of why it happened by rules of logic that are widely, if not universally, accepted. The objectivity of history lies in the fact that historians do widely agree upon the validity of these canons of evidence and rules of logic. Since the rise of professional historiography in the nineteenth century, countless writers have elucidated these canons of evidence, canons such as the rule that a diary written the evening after an event occurred will more accurately describe that event than a memoir written thirty years later. But far fewer writers have elucidated those rules of logic that govern, or should govern, the construction of a historical explanation. I regard this book as a contribution to that task. And it is not simply an academic venture to rescue history from a Pyrrhonistic subjectivism. If historians and philosophers glory in the relativity of truth and sink into an easeful subjectivism, if they ignore the constraints placed on thought by canons of evidence and rules of logic, then they may well raise up a generation of citizens who cannot distinguish between the *National Enquirer* and the *New York Times* or between the conspiracy theories of the Militia of Montana and the documented conclusions of a committee of Congress.

Since I find the view that history is merely a hobby, like philately, equally as abhorrent as the view that it is fundamentally subjective, I have added a final chapter on "Causal Explanation and the Uses of History."

Three scholars—a philosopher, a political scientist, and a historian— have been so kind as to read the entire book in typescript and to comment upon it. Professor William Dray of the University of Ottawa is the philosopher, Professor James Farr of the University of Minnesota is the political scientist, and Professor Douglas Bisson of Belmont College the historian. I owe a great debt of gratitude to these scholars. As a result of their criticisms my study contains fewer errors, obscurities, contradictions, and misspellings than it would otherwise have contained. Since, however, I exercised an author's prerogative to reject suggestions and criticisms thought to be unwarranted, none of these scholars is responsible for the arguments found in this study.

I owe a special obligation to Professor William Dray. It was over thirty years ago that I read his *Laws and Explanation in History* and had the pleasure of meeting him when he was a Visiting Professor at the Ohio State University. The reading of his book and that meeting (which arose from his inviting me to lunch at the Faculty Club) sowed in my mind seeds of interest in the analytical philosophy of history, seeds that have finally come to harvest in this book. Though I do on occasion differ from Professor Dray, his books and articles have been the indispensable foundation from which my thought has proceeded.

I also owe thanks to my wife, Anne, for patiently reading the proofs of this book, in both galley proof and page proof.

Clayton Roberts
Dyer's Bay, Ontario
1 July 1995

1 THE FAILURE OF MACROCORRELATION

> Collective events that are appreciably complex are thus not usually explained by subsuming them as single units under abstract concepts appearing in generalizations.
>
> — Ernest Nagel, *The Structure of Science*

In 1942, Carl Hempel, building upon foundations laid by David Hume, John Stuart Mill, and Karl Popper, set forth what he believed to be the correct model of historical explanation, a model he found applicable to all branches of empirical science. In later articles he refined and elaborated upon his original model, but did not basically alter it.[1]

Hempel begins by defining a universal hypothesis. A universal hypothesis, he writes, "may be assumed to assert a regularity of the following type: In every case where an event of a specified kind C occurs at a certain place and time, an event of a specified kind E will occur at a place and time which is related in a specified manner to the place and time of the occurrence of the first event." He then states:

1. Hempel, "The Function of General Laws in History," 344–56; Hempel and Oppenheim, "The Logic of Explanation," 319–52; Hempel, "Explanation in Science and in History," 96–124; idem, "Deductive-Nomological vs. Statistical Explanation," 98–167; idem, "Explanatory Incompleteness," 398–415; idem, "Reasons and Covering Laws in Historical Explanation," 143–46; idem, "Aspects of Scientific Explanation," 333–489.

The explanation of the occurrence of an event of some specific kind E at a certain place and time consists, as it is usually expressed, in indicating the causes or determining factors of E. Now the assertion that a set of events—say, of the kinds C_1, C_2, . . . , C_n—have caused the event to be explained, amounts to the statement that, according to certain general laws, a set of events of the kinds mentioned is regularly accompanied by an event of kind E. Thus the scientific explanation of the event in question consists of

(1) a set of statements asserting the occurrence of certain events C_1 . . . , C_n at certain times and places,
(2) a set of universal hypotheses, such that
    (a) the statements of both groups are reasonably well confirmed by empirical evidence,
    (b) from the two groups of statements the sentence asserting the occurrence of event E can be logically deduced.[2]

Hempel illustrates his model with the example of the cracked radiator of a car left on the street during a cold night. The initial conditions were a radiator of iron, completely filled with water, with the lid screwed on tightly, and the temperature falling to 25° F. The empirical laws concern the expansion of water as it turns to ice. The conclusion is that leaving the car out on a cold night caused the radiator to crack.[3]

In later articles Hempel diagrams the model thus (with L standing for laws, C for the initial conditions, and E for the event to be explained (see Diagram 1).

$$\left. \begin{array}{c} C_1, C_2, \ldots, C_k \\ \\ \underline{L_1, L_2, \ldots, L_r} \end{array} \right\} \quad \text{Explanans S}$$

$$\qquad\qquad E \qquad\qquad\qquad \text{Explanandum sentence}$$

Diagram 1.

And he adopts the traditional practice of calling the event to be explained the explanandum and the two premises (i.e., the statement of the initial conditions and the statement of laws) that explain it the explanans.[4]

2. Hempel, "The Function of General Laws in History," 345–46.
3. Ibid., 346.
4. Hempel, "Explanation in Science and in History," 96–97; idem, "Aspects of Scientific Explanation," 336.

This is the model (called by William Dray the covering-law model) that started a civil war among analytical philosophers and brought down upon Hempel an avalanche of criticism. These criticisms were of three principal types: that historians do not cite general laws in their narratives, that no deduction can be made from laws that are not universal (i.e., invariable), and that unique events cannot be subsumed under general laws. Are these criticisms valid, and do they destroy the validity of the covering law model?

The Absence of General Laws in Historical Explanation

It is an undeniable fact that historians rarely cite general laws in their narratives. In his 1942 article Hempel explained the absence of such laws by the fact that the laws employed in the writing of history are drawn from a knowledge of human nature and are therefore assumed to be familiar. Assumed to be familiar, they are tacitly assumed in any given explanation. Such words as "therefore," "hence," "consequently," and "because" indicate the tacit assumption of such general laws. Hempel likewise suggested that such laws were also often ambiguous, ambiguous in the sense that though one can say that "discontent causes revolutions," one cannot say just what specific forms the discontent must take. Such explanations, he suggested, should be called "explanation sketches."[5] This led R. F. Atkinson to declare that the concept of "the explanation sketch" is "either a damaging admission of the inappropriateness of the law theory to history or a harsh exposure of the standards of explanatory cogency observed in the subject."[6] Yet, Atkinson notwithstanding, there is much validity in what Hempel was seeking to say, which can be seen by an examination of his discussion of explanatory incompleteness.

When one explains that a lump of butter melted because it was put into a hot frying pan, one omits certain laws and particular facts that are tacitly taken for granted. One has formulated the explanation elliptically.[7] Such explanations, tacitly assuming the existence of laws, are commonplace in historical writing. Indeed, N. R. Hanson has shown that covering laws are built into the very fabric of our language, though

---

5. Hempel, "The Function of General Laws in History," 349–51.
6. Atkinson, *Knowledge and Explanation in History,* 108.
7. Hempel, "Aspects of Scientific Explanation," 415.

he uses the term "theory-laden" to describe this fact. He gives this example: "The scar on John's arm was caused by a wound he received in the defence of the kingdom." And then he comments: "The scar on John's arm is explained by reference to the wound which caused it because a wound is just the sort of deep incision that would leave a scar like that. (No surgeon could have left such an untidy trademark.) Simply to string the wound and the scar on the same causal lines as neighbours, however, fails to mark the respects in which scars are explained by wounds." He gives a second illustration: "The watch-repairman's retirement is explained by reference to his scarred finger-tips because this is precisely the sort of damage to one's digital dexterity that would make a man useless for delicate work on timepieces." And then he gives a long list of theory-laden words: "acid," "copper," "protein," "pawn," "rook," "trump," "offside." One states that sugar is "soluble," which is tantamount to saying that sugar will always dissolve when placed in one's coffee.[8]

An elliptical formulation of an explanation is, in fact, like an enthymeme. Just as an enthymeme is a syllogism in which one of the premises is implicit, so an elliptical formulation is an explanation in which some of the premises are implicit. It suffices to say that "a lighted cigarette carelessly thrown away caused the fire." There is no need to state the covering law that lighted cigarettes dropped in combustible material cause fires. "These universal laws," observes Karl Popper, "are very often so trivial . . . that as a rule we take them for granted instead of making conscious use of them." He then adds, referring specifically to historical explanations, "But these laws may be so trivial, so much part of our common knowledge, that we need not mention them and rarely notice them."[9]

Elliptically formulated explanations, believes Hempel, are incomplete only in a rather harmless way. Partial explanations offer a more serious kind of incompleteness. A partial explanation occurs when the explanans, even when fully written out, only partially explains the explanandum. Hempel offers the following illustration of a partial explanation.[10] In *The Psychopathology of Everyday Life* Sigmund Freud seeks to explain why he mistakenly wrote "Thursday, October 20th," on his calendar under the date "September 20th." The explanation he gives is that his mistake was an unconscious fulfillment of a wish. He had just received a letter from a patient announcing her arrival on 20 October;

8. Hanson, "Causal Chains," 294–99.
9. Popper, *The Poverty of Historicism,* 124, 145.
10. Hempel, "Aspects of Scientific Explanation," 415–17.

his keen wish that she would come a month earlier led him to enter the October date under September. Freud's explanation is based on a general law that when a person has a strong, though perhaps unconscious, wish, the person will fulfill that wish in a slip of the pen or tongue. But the explanans given here only allows one to deduce that the slip would take some form or other that would unconsciously fulfill Freud's wish. The explanans does not imply that the slip would take the specific form of writing "Thursday, October 20th," on the calendar under "September 20th." In short, no aspect of the explanandum not also present in the covering law contained in the explanans can be explained by that explanans. Making a mistake is part of both the explanans and the explanandum, and so can be explained. The specific form that mistake took—making an entry on the calendar under the wrong month—is indubitably part of the explanandum, but it is not part of the covering law contained in the explanans. It is therefore not explained by the explanation offered. To this extent it is a partial explanation. Yet all is not lost, surely. An important aspect of Freud's conduct has been explained, namely, why he made a mistake. The particular form that mistake took may be a trivial matter. A partial explanation can be a useful explanation.

Explanatory closure, the third kind of explanatory incompleteness, simply expresses the truth that every fact or law invoked in an explanation need not in turn be explained. To demand that they be so would be to invite an infinite regress in explanation.[11] For example, in order to explain Freud's mistake, one need not explain why Freud received a letter from the patient or why persons express wishes unconsciously through slips of the pen. The fact that he received the letter, and the law that mistakes unconsciously express wishes, are accepted as given and then used in the explanation.

Having discussed these three kinds of incompleteness, Hempel turns to a discussion of an explanation sketch, but he now seems to define an "explanation sketch" differently. In 1942 the concept seemed to express the fact that many explanations are elliptical and partial. Now, in "Aspects of Scientific Explanation," the concept seems to describe an explanation that is not explicit or specific enough to qualify either as an elliptically formulated explanation or a partial one. An explanation sketch is now seen as "the general outlines of what might well be developed, by gradual elaboration and supplementation, into a more closely reasoned explanatory argument, based on hypotheses which are stated more fully and which permit of a critical appraisal by reference to empirical evi-

---

11. Ibid., 423.

dence."[12] This is a far more shadowy creature than the 1942 explanation sketch, and it strikes me as an invitation to write bad history. The historian should surely "elaborate and supplement" his or her sketch as fully as possible before publishing it, even though the final form is elliptical and partial. But notwithstanding this criticism of Hempel's later use of the concept "explanation sketch," it is clear that his discussion of the various kinds of explanatory incompleteness does account for the apparent absence of laws in historical explanations.

The Want of Universal Laws from Which Deductions May Be Made

In 1943 Karl Popper proposed a model of explanation for the empirical sciences that closely resembled Carl Hempel's model. He wrote, "To give a causal explanation of an event means to deduce a statement which describes it, using as premises of the deduction one or more *universal laws*, together with certain singular statements, the *initial conditions.*" He went on to assert that the universal laws should be strictly universal statements, that is, that they permit of no exceptions.[13] In 1957 he applied this deductive model to the historical sciences.[14] In his first article Carl Hempel likewise spoke of "universal hypotheses" and likewise set forth a deductive model of explanation. Given the universal hypothesis and the initial conditions, one could deduce the cause of an event. But Hempel sensed, as presumably Karl Popper did not, that there were very few laws in history to which there were no exceptions. He therefore wrote: "And indeed it seems possible and justifiable to construe certain explanations offered in history as based on the assumption of probability hypotheses rather than of general 'deterministic' laws, i.e. laws in the form of universal conditions."[15] The obvious difference between a model employing universal laws and a model employing merely probabilistic laws forced Hempel in 1962 to distinguish two basic types of explanation: the deductive-nomological and the probabilistic-statistical. In the latter model the explanans does not logically imply the explanandum, but only confers a high likelihood upon it.[16]

12. Ibid., 424.
13. Popper, *The Logic of Scientific Discovery*, 59–60.
14. Popper, *The Poverty of Historicism*, 143–47.
15. Hempel, "The Function of General Laws in History," 350.
16. Hempel, "Explanation in Science and in History," 96–101.

Carl Hempel's introduction of and reliance upon probabilistic laws led Arthur Danto, Alan Donagan, and Michael Scriven to conclude that Hempel's model of explanation had collapsed. The laws being only probable, writes Danto, "we cannot, by appeal to these, ever succeed in explaining events."[17] Donagan admits that laws of probability allow us to explain mass events—that six million American smokers, for example, will develop lung cancer—but he insists that "Hempel's inductive-statistical model throws no light on causal explanations of individual events."[18] And Scriven agrees that the deductive model cannot be saved by the substitution of probability statements for universal hypotheses, "for one cannot *deduce* from any law of the form 'If C then probably E,' combined with the antecedent conditions C, that E occurs. One can only deduce that E probably occurs, and we are not trying to explain a probability but an event."[19]

Danto, Donagan, and Scriven are, of course, entirely correct in their belief that no explanation using probabilistic laws can be strictly deductive, but this does not mean that such an explanation cannot be nomological (i.e., rely upon a covering law). Hempel puts it this way: "Thus, probabilistic explanation . . . is nomological in that it presupposes general laws; but because these laws are of statistical rather than of strictly universal form, the resulting explanatory arguments are inductive rather than deductive in character. An inductive argument of this kind *explains* a given phenomenon by showing that, in view of certain particular events and certain statistical laws, its occurrence was to be expected with high logical, or inductive, probability."[20] In calling the resulting explanatory arguments inductive rather than deductive, Hempel is not wholly accurate. He had done better to say that the resulting explanatory arguments are both inductive and deductive. They are inductive in that the statistical laws employed in the explanans are established by induction. And the less the evidence for establishing the law, the shakier the law. It is deductive in that the explanation is deduced from the statistical law. It is not, however, *strictly* deduced from it; it is only *probabilistically* deduced. The lower the statistical probability of the law used in the explanans, the lower the probability that the explanation is true. The higher the statistical probability of the law (the closer it approaches one), the greater the likelihood that the explanation is true.

The essential question is this: are such probabilistic explanations

17. Danto, *Analytical Philosophy of History,* 211.
18. Donagan, "The Popper-Hempel Theory Reconsidered," 134–35.
19. Scriven, "Truisms as the Grounds for Historical Explanation," 457.
20. Hempel, "Explanation in Science and in History," 102.

found in history, and are they valid? The answer must be that historical works are replete with such explanations, just as everyday life is governed by them. That an insult led to a duel, that a tactical mistake led to defeat, that a victory led to a bestowal of an honor, that a betrayal led to a renewed enmity—these are some of the more commonplace explanations based upon probabilistic laws. As Oliver Wendell Holmes put it, "Every year, if not every day, we have to wager our salvation upon some prophecy based upon imperfect knowledge."[21]

The Unclassifiability of Concrete Events

Ever since the time of Wilhelm Windelband and Heinrich Rickert, the Idealists have argued that historical knowledge concerns the concrete, the particular, the unique. There is some merit to this doctrine. Historians study the battle of the Marne, not battles in general; they seek the causes of the Enlightenment, not of enlightenments in general; they study the rise of Hitler, not of dictators in general. Things in general they leave to the sociologists.

The Idealists also believe that historical events are too complex, too various, and too infinite in their aspects ever to be classified with other events, or even to be fully described. The assassination of Leon Trotsky, the crash of the stock market in 1929, and the abdication of Edward VIII were complex events, and therefore unclassifiable. Indeed, they cannot even be fully described, so numerous are the various aspects of these events. Should a historian attempt a complete description, he or she would surely omit some aspect. Given the uniqueness of such events, how can they be explained by subsuming them under a covering law?

To these objections Carl Hempel has replied by distinguishing a concrete event from sentential facts and events.[22] A concrete event is denominated by a noun phrase ("the assassination of Leon Trotsky") or a definite description ("the first solar eclipse of the twentieth century"). A concrete event has infinitely many different aspects and thus cannot be either completely described or completely explained. Sentential facts and events, however, are denominated by a sentence, the explanandum sentence. Such an explanandum sentence describes only that aspect of the concrete event that is classifiable and so can occur also in the covering law stated in the explanans. To explain Trotsky's assassination by

---

21. Quoted in Peter McClelland, *Causal Explanation and Model Building*, 240.
22. Hempel, "Aspects of Scientific Explanation," 421–23.

subsuming it under a covering law about assassinations, the historian can only explain those aspects of the occurrence that characterize it as an assassination. This does not mean that the historian is merely explaining a kind of event rather than an individual event. Rather, he is explaining the occurrence of a particular instance of a given kind of event. He is not explaining assassinations in general, but the assassination of Trotsky as a particular instance of assassinations in general.

Three conclusions emerge from this examination of the principal objections brought against the covering-law model. First, the fact that historical narratives do not contain explicitly stated covering laws does not invalidate the covering-law model. Such laws are contained elliptically in the narrative; and though the explanation is only partial, it is to that extent explanatory. Second, the fact that the laws implicit in historical narratives are probabilistic rather than deterministic likewise does not invalidate the model, since in the writing of history, as in the conduct of life, one must depend on probable truths. And third, though concrete events cannot be fully described or completely explained, aspects of those events can be described and explained. Hempel's reply to his critics does strike one as logically convincing. Yet notwithstanding this, ordinary historians find his model strange and irrelevant. Historians rarely apply it, and when they do apply it, it does not seem to work.

There is a clear reason this is so. The covering-law model cannot, as Ernest Nagel observes, explain "collective events that are appreciably complex,"[23] and it is with collective events that are appreciably complex that historians deal. Historians rarely seek to explain the occurrence of a complex event by subsuming it under a covering law, a process I have chosen to call macrocorrelation. That historians do not resort to macrocorrelation can be seen by looking at five typical examples. One concerns a single event, one an aggregate event, one a change in institutions, one a change in a statistical regularity, and one a change in ideas. When Peter Marshall, in *The Impeachment of Warren Hastings,* seeks to explain why the House of Commons impeached Warren Hastings, he does not, in order to discover what initial conditions precede an impeachment, investigate the dozens of earlier impeachments voted by the Commons. When Georges Lefebvre, in *The Coming of the French Revolution,* endeavors to explain why the French Revolution occurred, he does not subsume it under a covering law about revolutions. When A. F. Pollard, in *The Evolution of Parliament,* seeks to explain the rise of Parliament, he does not search out a law concerning the rise of representative assemblies. When J. D. Chambers, in *Population, Economy, and Society in Pre-*

23. Nagel, *The Structure of Science,* 574.

industrial England seeks to explain the decline in the death rate in England from 32.8 per thousand in 1701–50 to 22.5 per thousand in 1801–30, he does not set forth those conditions in other countries that had led to a similar decline. And when Keith Thomas, in *Religion and the Decline of Magic*, seeks to explain the decline in belief in witchcraft in England, he does not subsume the English experience under a covering law that correlates a decline in witchcraft with certain initial conditions.[24] Historians simply do not explain the occurrence of complex events by macrocorrelation, that is, by subsuming the complex event under a covering law. And those rash enough to try to do so invariably fail.

The Unclassifiability of Complex Events

One principal reason why attempts to explain complex events by macrocorrelation fail lies in the fact that complex events, such as impeachments, revolutions, the rise of parliaments, death rates, and changes in popular belief, are too complex, too varied in their aspects, too rich in detail, to be successfully subsumed under any covering law. One possible solution to this problem would be to eliminate all particular designations of the phenomenon to be explained, and to look for a common essence, a lowest common denominator. By means of this procedure Arthur Danto proposes to save the covering-law model. He writes:

> By Hempel's own criteria for a general law, a proposed law L must contain "no essential—i.e. no uneliminable—occurrences of designations for particular objects." Hence in so far as a description D of a phenomenon E contains such designations, it cannot, under D, be covered by a general law. Assuming we might eliminate from D all such designations and produce another description D_1 which contains none; still, E cannot be covered by such a general law under D—it being admitted that there are such descriptions—even though, under another description D_1, it can be so covered.[25]

In other words, a phenomenon E, say the Enlightenment, contains designations of particular objects, such as Montesquieu's defense of aristoc-

---

24. For full bibliographical information about these books, see the Bibliography at the end of this book.
25. Danto, *Analytical Philosophy of History*, 219–20.

racy, Voltaire's demand for justice, Rousseau's celebration of virtue, and Condorcet's belief in progress, that prevent the Enlightenment from being brought under a covering law. But redescribe the Enlightenment to mean "a reliance upon reason rather than faith," that is, move from D to D_1, and then one can subsume it under a law that also covers Periclean Athens, Confucian China, Unitarian Boston, and Victorian England.

Arthur Danto then concludes: "It immediately follows that any work of history will contain many descriptions of events under which the events cannot be explained if Hempel's model is correct. But it does *not* follow that the model is as such *incorrect* or that the events in question are unexplainable. Only unexplainable under the descriptions which have been given them."[26] In other words, in order to explain the event, one must redescribe it.

Two comments need to be made about Danto's insistence upon redescription. First, in doing so he does not really differ from Hempel, whose discussion of partial explanation makes it clear that he saw that a redescription of the event, omitting particular designations, was necessary. Second, neither Hempel nor Danto see that redescriptions are given at so high a level of generality as to make them useless to historians. When applied to complex events Hempel's partial explanation omits what is fundamental as well as what is trivial, and Danto's redescription washes out most of what the historian wants to explain. Danto appears to deny this, writing, "Indeed, to be able to redescribe the events is already, in a sense, to have explained them." But then he admits that to move from description to redescription, from D to D_1, from explananda to explanata, is to move from the concrete to the abstract.[27] He fails to see, however, that it is exactly the abstract nature of the explanatum, or redescription, that renders it useless in the explanation of complex events. As William Dray has rightly observed, "the historian, when he sets out to explain the French Revolution is just *not interested* in explaining it as *a* revolution—as an astronomer might be interested in explaining a certain eclipse as an instance of eclipses; he is almost invariably concerned with it as *different* from other members of its class."[28] Norman Hampson, speaking as an historian, not a philosopher, puts it this way: "There does not seem to me much point in attempting any general definition of the movement [the Enlightenment]. Such a

26. Ibid., 220.
27. Ibid., 220–21. Rex Martin (*Historical Explanation*, 109) likewise believes that Danto's analysis does not represent a basic alteration in the regularity-law model and does not succeed in saving that model.
28. Dray, *Laws and Explanation in History*, 47.

definition would have to include so many qualifications and contradictions as to be virtually meaningless, or else prove so constricting that logic would continually be trying to debar what common sense insisted on including."[29] Danto's proposal to save the covering-law model by means of redescription would be quite valid if one believed, as Aristotle believed, that there exists an essence of things (e.g., the essence of Enlightenment) and that one must penetrate to the essence of things in order to explain them. Karl Popper calls this view methodological essentialism, to which he opposes methodological nominalism. The methodological nominalist does not seek the essence of things; he seeks only to describe how things behave. Popper remarks that methodological nominalism has captured the natural sciences but that sociologists and historicists cling to methodological essentialism.[30] In this he is correct, but he might also have observed that the vast majority of historians are methodological nominalists. They do not seek the essence of conquests or revolutions or wars or enlightenments. They do not seek such essences, because, if they did exist, they would be but a faint simulacrum of what the historian wishes to explain. Historians wish to explain a particular revolution, not revolutions as a class of events.

Patrick Gardiner, in *The Nature of Historical Explanation*, argues otherwise, defending the study of classes of events. He treats the Norman Conquest as a conquest and asserts that there is a historical insight that can penetrate into the essence of things. He admits that "revolutions" cannot be tidily correlated, one with another, but declares "it is wrong to put this down to a recalcitrance inherent in the nature of the material of history."[31] For microevents, such as births, marriages, divorces, abortions, murders, voting, illness, and death, Gardiner is surely correct. Social historians do study classes of events. But for complex events such as conquests and revolutions he is surely wrong. As P. H. Nowell-Smith observes, "But it is not just that the historian is interested in the Revolution of 1688 for its own sake and not as a typical example of a revolution; rather it is that for him there is no such thing as a typical revolution."[32] He who would ask for proof of Nowell-Smith's contention can find it in Lawrence Stone's *Causes of the English Revolution*. In that book Stone devotes the first chapter to the sociological literature on revolutions in general and then ignores nearly all its findings in the following analysis of the English Revolution.

29. Hampson, *The Enlightenment*, 10.
30. Popper, *The Poverty of Historicism*, 26–34.
31. Gardiner, *The Nature of Historical Explanation*, 59.
32. Nowell-Smith, "Are Historical Events Unique?" 117.

There is a second reason why Stone ignored in his narrative the sociological literature discussed in the first chapter of his book. That literature failed to establish any law governing the causes of revolutions. Admit that by redescription one could find the essence of a revolution, say, that a revolution was any "rapid, fundamental, violent change in state or society." Could one find a law that correlated that phenomenon with a set of initial conditions? Could one find even a probabilistic law, one with a coefficient of correlation of more than .5? Attempts have been made, but they have not succeeded.[33] Thus there is a second principal reason complex events cannot be explained by subsuming them under a covering law: the laws are simply not there. Notwithstanding these considerations, a few bold scholars in the past have sought to find laws that explain the occurrence of complex events. It is worth looking at their attempts to see with what success they have met.

Attempts at Macrocorrelation

Prominent among those historians seeking universal laws is Henry Thomas Buckle, who in the nineteenth century sought to discover those physical and mental laws that governed the growth of civilization. But he merely imposed on the past his Victorian prejudices in favor of laissez-faire, free trade, religious toleration, science, and the iron law of wages.[34] Henry Adams, influenced by Auguste Comte, sought such laws but, finding none, fell into despair and wondered whether history could be a meaningful discipline.[35] The most notorious of the seekers after macroscopic laws in the twentieth century has been Arnold Toynbee. He sought to discover those laws that have governed the rise, growth, decay, and death of some twenty-one civilizations in the past, but his efforts only drew down upon him the wrath of historians such as Pieter Geyl.[36] Historians today do not cite or quote from *A Study of History.*

A more recent attempt to find laws that explain the occurrence of complex, or macroscopic, events is Barrington Moore's *Social Origins of*

33. For a discussion of these attempts, see the first chapter of Stone, *The Causes of the English Revolution.*
34. Buckle, *The History of Civilization in England.*
35. Dusinberre, *Henry Adams: The Myth of Failure*, 212–13, 220–21.
36. Toynbee, *A Study of History;* Pieter Geyl, *Debates with Historians*, 156–202.

Dictatorship and Democracy, in which he seeks to discover those historical conditions that lead to parliamentary democracy, those that lead to dictatorships of the right, and those that lead to dictatorships of the left. But historians have given his book a cool reception, largely because of his obsessive concern with economic factors to the neglect of others.[37] There have been other attempts to establish laws that govern macroscopic events, though not many. Quincy Wright in 1942 and Lewis Richardson in 1953 embarked on the scientific study of war; Walter Prescott Webb studied frontiers in North America, South America, Australia, and New Zealand; and Karl Wittfogel sought the laws that shape hydraulic societies.[38] All of these studies contain occasional perceptive insights and possess a heuristic value, but they have not led to the establishment of laws governing civilizations, dictatorships, wars, frontiers, and hydraulic societies.

The most explicit, self-conscious, confident, and naïve attempt to reduce history to a search for macrocorrelations was carried out by Frederick Teggart. In the preface to *Rome and China: A Study in Correlations in Historical Events,* he relates how he discovered that, though scholars held history to be a science, the results achieved by historical inquiry were wholly unlike those achieved in physics and biology. He came to the conclusion that this occurred because historians present "their results in a form of statement which is in the tradition of literature and has no relation to science." So he urged historians to cease composing narratives and to seek to solve problems. These problems should have reference to a class of events, and the historian's research "should be based on a comparison of events in different parts of the world or different areas." He took as his problem the recurrent barbarian invasions of the Roman Empire between 58 B.C. and A.D. 107. His results, he boasted, were beyond expectations: "Within these decades every barbarian uprising in Europe followed the outbreak of war either on the eastern frontiers of the Roman empire or in the 'Western Regions' of the Chinese. Moreover, the correspondence in events was discovered to be so precise that, whereas wars in the Roman East were followed uniformly and always by outbreaks on the lower Danube and the Rhine, wars in eastern T'ian Shan were followed uniformly and always by outbreaks on the Danube between Vienna and Budapest." He promptly proclaimed his success: "The primary result of the investigation has, therefore, been to

37. Moore, *Social Origins of Dictatorship and Democracy.* For criticisms and a defense of Moore, see Jonathan Wiener, "The Barrington Moore Thesis and Its Critics," 301–30.

38. Wright, *A Study of War;* Richardson, *Statistics of Deadly Quarrels;* Webb, *The Great Frontier;* Wittfogel, *Oriental Despotism.*

establish (for the first time) the existence of correlations in historical events."[39]

The only problem is that historians of the decline of Rome have ignored his correlations. They have found them neither convincing nor meaningful. Teggart's study has not entered into the mainstream of historical writing. His admonitions have been ignored and his book forgotten. He, as others before him, failed in an impossible task. If one defines macrocorrelation as seeking to explain the occurrence of complex events—an impeachment, a conquest, a revolution, the rise of parliament, a decrease in the death rates, a decline in belief in witchcraft—by subsuming them under a covering law that associates such events with certain initial conditions, then one must pronounce macrocorrelation a failure. The vast majority of historians do not use macrocorrelation to explain the occurrence of the events they are studying, and those who have attempted to use it have met with little success. Macrocorrelation is at best an irrelevance, at worst a disaster.

39. Teggart, *Rome and China: A Study of Correlations in Historical Events*, v–ix.

2 THE EXPLANATORY POWER OF COLLIGATION

The way it happened was this.

— Herodotus, *The Histories*

If historians do not explain the occurrence of complex historical events by subsuming them under covering laws, then how do they explain their occurrence? The answer is quite obvious: they explain their occurrence by tracing the sequence of events that brought them about. Peter Marshall begins his study by tracing the change of views about India that occurred in England from 1773 to 1783, continues it with an account of the triumph of the Opposition in 1784 and 1785, and concludes it with a day-by-day account of the voting of the impeachment in March and April 1787. Georges Lefebvre begins his narrative on 4 May 1789, when the Estates General assembled, and concludes it on 9 November 1789, when the National Assembly installed itself in a riding school near the Tuileries. A. F. Pollard traces the rise of parliament from its appearance in the thirteenth century, through its triumphs in the seventeenth, to its reform in the nineteenth. J. D. Chambers accounts for the declining death rate in the eighteenth century by tracing the decline in infanticide, the disappearance of the plague, the introduction of inoculation for smallpox, and the increasing use of cotton clothing and sheets (which reduced the incidence of typhus). Keith Thomas shows how disbelief in witchcraft began with the Lollards, who rejected belief in witchcraft for religious reasons, spread to grand jurors and petty jurors, who were perplexed by the problem of securing proofs of witchcraft, and was finally taken up by members of the Royal Society and adherents of the new mechanical philosophy, for whom witchcraft was an absurdity.[1]

I have chosen to call this process colligation, but other writers have given it other names. Ernest Nagel calls it "a genetic explanation," Louis Mink "a sequential explanation," William Dray "the model of the continuous series," Michael Scriven "a chain of causal explanations," R. F. Atkinson "narrative explanations," and Arthur Danto "the structure of a narrative explanation." Maurice Mandelbaum likewise speaks of structure, but distinguishes between an "explanatory structure," which looks backward toward a cause, and a "sequential structure," which proceeds forward in a narrative fashion.[2]

I have chosen to call this explanatory process colligation partly for reasons of economy of style—the expression is compact, it can easily be made into an adjective, and it neatly parallels correlation. But I have also chosen to call it colligation because I believe that tracing a sequence of events is what W. H. Walsh was endeavoring to describe when he borrowed the term from William Whewell. In *An Introduction to Philosophy of History*, Walsh writes:

> Ostensibly at least, historians do not attempt to illuminate particular situations by referring to other situations of the same type; their initial procedure at any rate is quite different. Thus when asked to explain a particular event—say, the British general strike in 1926— they will begin by tracing connections between that event and others with which it stands in inner relationship (in the case in question, certain previous events in the history of industrial relations in Great Britain). The underlying assumption here is that different historical events can be regarded as going together to constitute a single process, a whole of which they are all parts and in which they belong together in a specially intimate way. And the first aim of the historian, when he is asked to explain some event or

1. See the Bibliography at the end of this book for further bibliographical information.
2. Nagel, *The Structure of Science*, 368; Mink, "The Autonomy of Historical Understanding," 172–73; Dray, *Laws and Explanation in History*, 66; Scriven, "Causes, Connections, and Conditions in History," 241; Atkinson, *Knowledge and Explanation in History*, 128; Danto, *Analytical Philosophy of History*, 235–36; Mandelbaum, *Anatomy of Historical Knowledge*, 26.

other, is to see it as part of such a process, to locate it in its context by mentioning other events with which it is bound up.

Now this process of "colligation," as we may call it (following the usage of the nineteenth-century logician Whewell), is certainly a peculiarity of historical thinking, and is consequently of great importance when we are studying the nature of historical explanation.

Elsewhere he speaks of "the procedure of explaining an event by tracing its intrinsic relations to other events and locating it in its historical context."[3]

It is true that Walsh goes on to speak of colligation as the grouping of events under "appropriate conceptions,"[4] but such a procedure is very different from tracing a causal sequence of events. A historian does not explain the General Strike of 1926 by placing events under such conceptions as general strikes, or even under such conceptions as unions, economic demands, strikes, picketing, and syndicalism. Such terms are usefully employed in his explanation, but they are not the explanation. The confusion between two possible meanings of "colligation" may well be traced back to William Whewell, who defined "colligation" as the binding together of facts "by the aid of suitable Conceptions," but who went on to say, "This part of the Formation of our knowledge I have called the *Colligation of Facts:* and we may apply this term to every case in which, by an act of the intellect, we establish a precise connexion among the phenomenona which are presented to our senses."[5]

Walsh contributed to the confusion surrounding the term "colligation" by assigning to colligation a task—"explaining an event by tracing its intrinsic relations to other events"—that cannot be easily performed by grouping events under conceptions. Perceiving this, Walsh himself in 1967 suggested that colligation should be regarded as a form of interpretation rather than as a form of explanation. He added that William Dray's "explaining what" is likewise more concerned with interpretation than explanation. Dray has, in fact, called explanations of what happened "colligatory explanations."[6] This was a fruitful direction in which

3. Walsh, *Introduction to Philosophy of History,* 24–25, 59.

4. Ibid., 61.

5. Whewell, *The Philosophy of the Inductive Sciences,* 2:220. For a brief history of the term since Whewell's time, see the entry under "Colligation" in Ritter, *Dictionary of Concepts in History.*

6. Walsh, "Colligatory Concepts in History," 74–75; Dray, " 'Explaining What' in History," 407–8.

to move, for conceptions are far more useful in describing what happened—was it a revolution or an evolution, a depression or a recession?—than in explaining why it happened. But Walsh would not go that far; he continued to hold that colligation also meant the discovery of those ideas that explain a unique historical process—the rise of the bourgeoisie, for example.[7]

Behan McCullagh likewise takes both paths. He argues that colligation may be regarded as equivalent to classification. One may colligate, that is, give unity to, a number of events by calling them a revolution or an evolution or a polarization; and one does so on the basis of the form of the change, with no regard to the ideas that motivate the change. Such terms he calls "formal colligatory concepts." But he also holds that a set of ideas may explain historical change, though where Walsh holds that such a set of ideas and the change it causes is unique, happens but once, McCullagh believes such a set of ideas may recur as motivating forces at other times in history. Such a set of ideas he calls "dispositional concepts."[8] Unlike McCullagh, L. B. Cebik insists that colligation is simply a form of classification.[9] On the other hand, D. Thompson demands a complete divorce between colligation and classification.[10] The unmistakable tendency in Dray and Cebik is to make colligation a tool of description. Only Thompson insists that colligation be a tool for tracing a complex causal process, such as the sequence of events that leads to strikes, revolts, wars, or the scoring of a goal in a soccer match. It is Thompson's path I have chosen to follow.

This does not mean that I question the usefulness of colligating events under appropriate conceptions. In an article entitled "Colligation Under Appropriate Conceptions" William Dray has shown how such a procedure allows the historian to understand complex events such as the Renaissance.[11] It allows the historian to perceive a unity within an infinite number of facts. What allows a historian, for example, to decide what events make up the English Revolution? Surely he or she will not include every event, no matter how trivial, that took place between 1640 and 1660. Rather the historian will, accepting a definition of "revolution" as a rapid, fundamental, violent change in state or society, include all such changes: the destruction of the monarchy, the removal of the bishops from the Church, the abolition of the House of Lords, the sweeping away of the

7. Walsh, "Colligatory Concepts in History," p. 86.
8. McCullagh, "Colligation and Classification," 267–84.
9. Cebik, "Colligation and the Writing of History," 40–57.
10. Thompson, "Colligation and History Teaching," 88–94.
11. Dray, "Colligation Under Appropriate Conceptions," 156–69.

prerogative courts, and the emergence of radical ideas that challenged authority. Having isolated and defined the phenomena to be explained, the historian is in a better position to explain the occurrence of the English Revolution, but he or she has not yet explained why it occurred.

The term "colligation" has thus come to have two meanings: the tracing of the connections between events, and the grouping of events under appropriate conceptions. One could adopt the procedure of referring to colligation$_1$ and colligation$_2$ in order to distinguish between the two meanings, but this is an awkward and cumbersome procedure. Instead, throughout this book I use "colligation" to mean the tracing of the causal connections between events, and "classification" to mean the grouping of events under appropriate conceptions.

Whether under the name of "genetic explanation" or "sequential explanation" or "continuous series" or "causal chains" or "narrative explanation," philosophers have recognized the existence of colligatory explanations, but they have neither developed the logic nor admitted the explanatory power of such explanations. Yet their explanatory power is considerable, which can be illustrated using several examples drawn from everyday life.

The simplest illustration comes from the game of pool. Imagine that Steve Mizerak steps to the table, picks up the cue, strikes the cue ball so that it spins around the eight ball, runs across the table, hits the six ball, which then nudges the two ball into the pocket. What answer would one give to the question: why did the two ball go into the pocket? One might say, Because the six ball hit it, but that would be a truncated explanation. Or one might say that it went in because Steve Mizerak made the shot and he rarely misses. That would be macrocorrelation with a vengeance, and not very convincing, since even the great Mizerak does miss on occasions, even when just showing off. In truth, what one is most likely to do is to describe how Mizerak made the cue ball spin around the eight ball, how it then hit the six ball, which nudged the number two ball into the pocket.

Take a more complex example. Suppose one is a journalist and must explain why the Ohio State University defeated Wisconsin in football on Saturday. One might say, Because the two teams played in the Ohio State University stadium, where Ohio State always defeats Wisconsin. That law is indubitably true, but such a law has little explanatory power.[12] Or one might say, Because the Ohio State University line outweighed the Wisconsin line by an average of seven pounds a player (the

---

12. Since I wrote the first draft of this chapter, Wisconsin has finally defeated Ohio State in the Ohio State stadium.

team with the heavier line usually wins). This explanation, incidentally, is reminiscent of Karl Popper's explanation for the partition of Poland: the other armies had more men.[13] But teams with the heavier lines and armies with the most men do not always win. What the great majority of working journalists will do is to describe the four scoring drives engineered by Ohio State—giving the number of plays in each drive, analyzing further the crucial third-down plays, and describing with loving detail (if from Columbus) the touchdown plays.

A third example is Carl Hempel's cracked radiator. If he had been true to his model, he should not have mentioned laws about water under normal atmospheric pressure freezing at below 32° F, or about the pressure of a mass of water increasing with decreasing temperature below 39.2° F. He should, rather, have stated the covering law thus: radiators that are filled with water, that have caps tightly screwed on, and that are left on a street all night in freezing weather will crack. The correlation between cracked radiators and such conditions is very high, approaching one, yet the correlation offers no explanation. The explanation lies in tracing the events that led to the radiator's cracking. As the sun sets, the air grows cold. The cold iron in turn causes the water to grow cold. The drop in the temperature of the water causes it to expand. The expansion of the water cracks the radiator.

William Dray has rightly asked the proponents of the covering-law model whether one or many laws are required in their model.[14] They really ought to answer him. Hempel usually speaks of laws in the plural, yet it strikes me that logically there can be only one covering law, namely, that certain initial conditions regularly lead to the occurrence of a particular kind of event. Now, it is true, as Hempel sensed, that many laws are needed to explain why the radiator cracked, but this is true because the explanation has many steps, with each step requiring a covering law. To explain the cracked radiator one needs the law that hot air rises once the sun sets, the law that iron is a poor insulator, the law that freezing water expands, the law that the tensile strength of iron is such and such. Instead of diagramming his model as in Diagram 1, repeated here, he should have diagrammed it as in Diagram 2.

Hempel does recognize that there is a problem concerning the number of laws invoked in an explanation. He writes, "Incidentally, the notion of 'the number of laws' invoked in a given explanation is not as clear as it might seem, for one law may sometimes be quite plausibly rewritten as a

---

13. Popper, *The Open Society and Its Enemies*, 2:264–65.
14. Dray, *Laws and Explanation in History*, 52.

$$\left.\begin{array}{c} C_1, C_2, \ldots, C_k \\[1em] L_1, L_2, \ldots, L_r \end{array}\right\} \quad \text{Explanans S}$$

$$\overline{}$$

E   Explanandum sentence

Diagram 1.

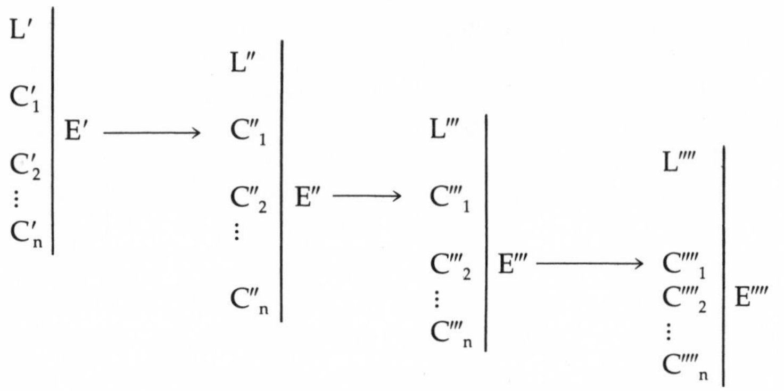

Diagram 2. L stands for law, C for conditions, and E for the event described in the explanandum sentence; the vertical line indicates the inference that the conditions to the left of the line caused the event to the right; the arrow indicates that an event becomes a condition in the next explanans.

conjunction of two or more, and conversely, several laws may sometimes be plausibly conjoined into one. But again it is not necessary for us to pursue this problem."[15] To the contrary, I believe it is necessary and important to pursue the problem, and in fact Hempel has. He offers two solutions to the problem.

The first is the concept of a minimal covering law. As he puts it, "If an explanation is of the form (D-N), then the laws $L_1, L_2, \ldots L_k$, invoked in its explanans logically imply a law L^* which by itself would suffice to explain the explanandum event by reference to the particular conditions noted in the sentence $C_1, C_2, \ldots, C_k$."[16] He goes on to call L^* a minimal covering law. An excellent example of such a law (though Hempel does not give it) is the law that radiators that are filled with water, that have caps tightly screwed on, and that are left on a street all night in freezing weather will crack.

15. Hempel, "Aspects of Scientific Explanation," 347.
16. Ibid., 346.

The second solution emerges rather shadowily from his discussion of genetic explanations. He writes, "Thus, schematically speaking, a genetic explanation will begin with a pure description of an initial stage; thence, it will proceed to an account of a second stage, part of which is nomologically linked to, and explained by, the characteristic feature of the initial stage, while the balance is simply added descriptively because of its relevance for the explanation of some parts of the third stage, and so forth" (Diagram 3).[17] This scheme traces successive events with a covering law bridging each step. One explains the cracked radiator by tracing how the setting sun caused the air to grow cold, how the cold air caused the iron to grow cold, how the cold iron caused the water to grow cold, how the cold water expanded, and how the expanding water cracked the radiator. This procedure is clearly more explanatory than reference to a minimal covering law.

$$S_1 \nearrow \begin{matrix} S'_2 \\ +D_2 \end{matrix} \Bigg\} \quad S_2 \nearrow \begin{matrix} S'_3 \\ +D_3 \end{matrix} \Bigg\} \quad S_3 \cdots \nearrow \nearrow \begin{matrix} S'_{n-1} \\ +D_{n-1} \end{matrix} \Bigg\} \quad S_{n-1} \rightarrow S_n$$

Diagram 3. Each arrow indicates a presumptive nomic connection between two successive stages: S, a set of sentences expressing all the information that the genetic account gives, information that, but for the initial stage, has been explained; and D, information adduced without explanation because of its explanatory significance for the next stage.

Ernest Nagel has given a similar analysis of a genetic explanation, replete with superscriptions and subscriptions (though neither Hempel nor Nagel lists initial conditions in the vertical manner I have, thereby obscuring the problem of assigning a weight to the different conditions). Nagel illustrates the working of his scheme with a passage, drawn from George Macaulay Trevelyan, in which Trevelyan explains why the Duke of Buckingham changed his mind about a Spanish marriage for Prince Charles. According to Nagel, Trevelyan explained Buckingham's change of mind by "intercalating a number of happenings" between his initial enthusiasm for the marriage and his final opposition to it. It is an acute analysis, particularly for its recognition that successive separate covering laws are needed to bridge the successive steps leading to Buckingham's change of mind.[18] Yet as acute as is Nagel's analysis, and as suggestive as

17. Ibid., 449–50.
18. Nagel, *The Structure of Science*, 564–68.

is Hempel's, neither fully appreciates the explanatory power of colligation. How great that power is can be seen by examining the two
principal functions it performs, that of turning correlation into explanation and that of validating an explanation.

The Transformation of Correlation into Explanation

It is a commonplace that there are many correlations that assert no
relation of cause and effect. In everyday life we know that night follows
day, storms a falling barometer, and rain a red sunset, yet we do not say
that night causes day, or a falling barometer a storm, or a red sunset rain.
Historians have likewise found correlations that are not causal. They
have discovered that the price of gasoline is correlated with the distance
of Halley's comet from the earth, that every hundred years (since 1490)
the decade of the nineties has brought harsh winters, and that every
American president since 1860 who was elected in a year divisible by
twenty has died in office.[19] Yet no one would suggest that the movement
of Halley's comet determines the price of gasoline or that the last decade
of a century causes harsh weather or that being elected in a year divisible
by twenty causes the death of a president. One cannot equate correlation
with causation; as Peter Strawson puts it, "mere regularities of succession do not of themselves satisfy us that we have found causes."[20]

Yet many philosophers are, rightly I think, uneasy at a complete divorce of correlation from causation. J. A. Passmore, for example, finds
"it quite arbitrary to say that an explanation by reference to a general
statement is 'not an explanation at all.' "[21] And heavy smokers would be
ill advised to conclude that smoking does not cause lung cancer, because
the connection between them is only a correlation. The best way to
approach this problem is to posit degrees of explanatory power. Different assertions have different degrees of explanatory power.

A mere statement of a correlation, such as that between smoking and
lung cancer, has some explanatory power, a power that increases with
the coefficient of correlation and with the number of instances surveyed.
It likewise increases, as William Dray has argued, if one can manipulate
a correlation, use it to control one's environment. He cites the example

19. President Reagan, by surviving two terms in office, brought this correlation to an
end (though John Hinkley nearly preserved it).
20. Strawson, "Causation and Explanation," 128.
21. Passmore, "Law and Explanation in History," 271.

of nurses who, influenced by Florence Nightingale, demonstrated that "dirt causes disease" by manipulating the dirt rate. By decreasing the amount of dirt, they decreased disease.[22] I am not sure that the element of control here is nearly as important as the fact that an increased number of instances are being recorded. The epidemiologist studying the figures recorded by the nurses manipulates nothing, yet he or she may well be led to believe dirt causes disease.

The greatest explanatory power, however, is gained neither by counting more instances nor by manipulation; it is gained by describing the connection between the two terms of the correlation. Historians and philosophers have given many names to that connection. David Hackett Fischer calls it "a presumptive agency," Peter McClelland "mechanisms at work," Carl Hempel and Paul Oppenheim "the inner mechanism of the phenomenon," William Dray "agency," R. M. MacIver the "causal series within the total conjuncture," H.L.A. Hart and A. M. Honoré "a description of its component stages," Maurice Mandelbaum "systematic connections," Michael Scriven "underlying process" and "inner workings," Theodore Abel "the inner-organic sequence," Peter Railton "mechanisms," and Peter Strawson "the minuter processes which underlie the grosser."[23] By whatever name one calls it, it is a series of connections between the two terms of the correlation.

Here a distinction must be made between a series of connections that happens only once and a series of connections that happens repeatedly. The former may be called a scenario, a scenario that explains the occurrence of an event; the latter a theory, a theory that explains a correlation (or law or regularity). Dray offers an illuminating example of the former.[24] He describes a center fielder's catching a fly ball from the scorekeeper's platform. Suppose, Dray suggests, one asks: why on that night in Victoria, B.C., was the fly ball, hit high up on the center field fence, caught? The answer that any journalist would give is that the center fielder saw where the ball was going, raced back, climbed the ladder to the scorekeeper's platform, stuck out his glove, and caught the ball in it. The scenario explains the event.

It is unlikely that the center fielder ever caught a fly ball again in that fashion. It was a singular event. On the other hand, every time I turn the

22. Dray, *Laws and Explanations in History*, 91–93.

23. Fischer, *Historians' Fallacies*, 169; McClelland, *Causal Explanation*, 67; Hempel and Oppenheim, "The Logic of Explanation," 332; Dray, *Laws and Explanation in History*, 95; MacIver, *Social Causation*, 254; Hart and Honoré, *Causation in the Law*, 46; Mandelbaum, *Anatomy of Historical Knowledge*, 72–73; Scriven, "Explanations, Predictions, and Laws," 212; Abel, "The Operation Called *Verstehen*," 682; Railton, "A Deductive-Nomological Model of Probabilistic Explanation," 207; Strawson, "Causation and Explanation," 122.

24. Dray, *Laws and Explanation in History*, 158–62.

key in the ignition of my car, it sets in train a series of events that leads to the motor starting. The turning of the key completes an electrical circuit; the completion of that circuit causes the battery to send juice to the starter and the distributor; the starter turns over the motor, causing several pistons to rise to the top of the cylinder and causing the fuel injection system to spray gasoline into the cylinder; the distributor sends a spark to the appropriate cylinder, which spark in turn causes an explosion driving the piston down; and the motor takes off (at which moment the sequence of events leading to the starting of the motor is replaced by a sequence of events, repeated as often as the rpm of the motor, that marks its running). To explain both the starting of the engine when the key is turned in the ignition and the subsequent running of the motor, one relies upon the theory of the internal combustion engine. It explains why every time one turns the key, the motor starts. Or, as P. H. Nowell-Smith writes, " 'Because it always happens so' is not an explanation. A constant conjunction is something to be explained. The explanation is provided by the construction of a theory."[25]

It might be asked, why construct a theory, why not just accept as an adequate explanation the correlation between turning the key and the motor starting? In science, where unobservable theoretical entities are often employed to establish the necessary series of connections, this would have the advantage of not requiring the use of such entities, entities like atoms or electricity. Carl Hempel calls this the paradox of theorizing: "It [the paradox] asserts that if the terms and the general principles of a scientific theory serve their purpose, i.e. if they establish definite connections among observable phenomena, then they can be dispensed with since any chain of laws and interpretative statements establishing such a connection should then be replaceable by a law which directly links observational antecedents to observational consequents."[26] But he promptly resolves the paradox by pointing out the advantages of establishing such connections. To begin with, establishing such connections obviates reliance upon action over extended space and time, which a phenomenalistically formulated account often requires. Why, for example, should turning a key in the ignition cause an engine several feet away to start? Second, it allows one to explain exceptions to the correlation being invoked. Suppose that, upon turning the key, the engine did not start. Knowing the theory of an internal combustion engine, I would at once investigate to see whether the battery was dead. Third, it can explain more than the observable symptoms. As Hempel

25. Nowell-Smith, "Are Historical Events Unique?" 111.
26. Hempel, "The Theoretician's Dilemma," 186.

writes, "when a scientist introduces theoretical entities such as electric current, magnetic fields, chemical valences, or subconscious mechanisms, he introduces them to serve as explanatory factors which have an existence independent of the observable symptoms by which they manifest themselves."[27] In other words, the theory of the internal-combustion engine can explain more than why turning the key starts the engine. What Hempel does not say is that establishing such connections explains the existence of the correlation. It is understandable why he does not, since he wrote "The Theoretician's Dilemma" to justify the use of theoretical terms in science, that is, terms that are not observable. Such hypothetical terms do not explain the existence of a correlation with the same explanatory power that connections that can be observed do. But implicit in his discussion is the belief that establishing such observed connections is explanatory of the correlation.

It is then a sequence of events that repeats itself over and over again that explains the existence of a correlation, and the appropriate term to describe this repeatable sequence is "theory." Thus Ernest Nagel explains the Boyle-Charles law for ideal gases by reference to the kinetic theory of gases; thus Theodore Abel explains the high correlation (r = .93) between good crops and the number of marriages by the theory that bad crops cause anxiety, that anxious people avoid commitments, and that people who avoid commitments do not marry; and thus R. M. MacIver sets forth the theory that explains the bends, namely, the absorption by the body of air under high pressure, the release of the oxygen and the retention of nitrogen under quick decompression, and the consequent formation of nitrogen bubbles in the bloodstream. MacIver perceptively calls this "the specific causal series" that explains "the bends."[28]

Nagel has observed that scientists constantly seek to reduce psychology to physiology, physiology to chemistry, chemistry to physics, and thermodynamics to mechanics.[29] Given the fact that a theory explains a correlation (say the correlation of temperature, pressure, and volume in a gas), it is not strange that scientists are wedded to reductionism. One can even imagine a molecular physicist, equipped with high-speed photographs, explaining to David Hume the manner in which the surface of one billiard ball impacted against the other, thus transferring its motion to it. But Hume, I imagine, would not have been impressed; he would simply have focused his puzzlement about causation on the smallest

27. Ibid., 205.
28. Nagel, *The Structure of Science*, 342; Abel, "The Operation Called *Verstehen*," 681; MacIver, *Social Causation*, 254.
29. Nagel, *The Structure of Science*, 359–66.

steps employed by the molecular physicist in his explanation. Ultimately there must be a correlation, or regular succession, or constant conjunction, that no theory can explain, a gap that no colligation can fill. Hume, as Karl Popper reminds us, regarded causation as both a relation between events and as a necessary connection. But when he looked for this necessary connection, he found only contiguity and succession. The necessary connection could not be observed. The nearest thing to it that could be observed was a constant conjunction.[30] This ineluctable fact led Bertrand Russell to argue that ultimately there can be no causation, only functional relations, and Karl Pearson to write that the "conception of correlation between two occurrences . . . is the wider category by which we have to replace the old idea of causation."[31]

But the weakness of Russell's and Pearson's position is patent. Only at the ultimately most microscopic level is this true. For the vast majority of phenomena, for the phenomena studied in chemistry, biology, psychology, sociology, history, and most of physics, it is quite meaningful to speak of cause, since one can trace the sequence of events, repeated again and again, that explains the existence of a correlation. This can be done either by direct observation or by theoretical models constructed from observed data by means of rules of correspondence. Strawson has shown convincingly how this sense of cause is gained and applied. A person can observe causation, the pushing of a pen, the pulling of a lever. (He might have added that one can observe a concatenation of events leading to an effect.) Nature presents to gross observation models of bringing something about, of the exercise of causal power. Strawson admits that one learns much about the operation of causality through the observation of regularities of succession, but insists that one can do so only because one already possesses the notion of causal efficacy, of effects being brought about in a variety of specific ways. Indeed, the very notion of mechanical power, of pushing or pulling, tells a person what is cause and what is effect, thus saving the notion of priority. We need not regard cause and effect as merely coordinate functions; cause does precede effect. No doubt a search for cause is often necessary, since cause does not usually present itself to gross observation. In such instances, by means of minuter observation or by theoretical constructions modeled on grosser models (as the model of subatomic structure is based on the model of the solar system), one can link the mere regularities of conjunction and so reach the level of explanation, discover the cause. Strawson recognizes that in sophisticated physical theory the utility of gross mod-

30. Popper, *Objective Knowledge*, 88.
31. Russell, *Mysticism and Logic*, 180–208; Pearson, *The Grammar of Science*, 157.

els diminishes and finally wears out altogether. "At this point," he writes, "also the notion of cause loses its role in theory; as Russell said that it would and should. But that is a point which none of us occupies for much of the time and few of us occupy at all."[32]

Michael Scriven makes much the same point:

> Deduction from a "mere empirical generalization" is very rarely explanatory, and it is only because laws usually involve more than this (as well as less) that they carry explanatory force. (The fact that they commonly reflect some underlying processes, albeit imprecisely, accounts for much of the inductive reliability we ascribe to them, and hence for much of our willingness to allow contrary-to-fact inferences from them.) Were it not for this fact, that what we call laws are usually thought to reflect the "inner workings" of the world, the deductive model would be singularly implausible.[33]

In other words, regularity of succession by itself does not satisfy us that we have discovered causes. We need first to discover the "inner workings." Put succinctly, colligation turns correlation into causation.

Even Frederick Teggart, the grand apostle of comparative history, admits that the discovery of correlation is no substitute for the investigation of causation. A thorough examination of dates led him to assert a correlation between wars in the East and invasions in the West, but to account for this correlation, "the focus of inquiry," in Teggart's words, "shifted from the critical examination of dates to an exploration of the possible linkages." And the investigation of these linkages led him to conclude "that the correspondence of wars in the East and invasions in the West was due to interruptions of trade."[34]

It is colligation that allows one to declare some correlations to be causal and some not, to distinguish between correlations that are only epiphenomenal and correlations that are genuinely causal. The falling barometer and the coming storm are only epiphenomena, both caused by the fall in air pressure. Likewise, inflation does not cause a recovery in the economy, but the easing of the money supply by the Federal Reserve may cause both the inflation and the recovery. A jingoistic press

32. Strawson, "Causation and Explanation," 121–34.
33. Scriven, "Explanations, Predictions, and Laws," 212. Morris R. Cohen ("Causation and Its Applicability to History," 18) likewise argues that natural science is never satisfied with statistical correlations between A and B but seeks "an intimate connection between A and B."
34. Teggart, "Causation in Historical Events," 9; *Rome and China*, lx.

did not cause the Spanish American war; a fervent nationalism produced both the war and the jingoistic press. What is needed to separate cause from epiphenomenon is a more microscopic examination of all the causal links involved, an examination that will show that the falling air pressure, not the falling barometer, caused the storm. In short, what is needed is colligation.

Colligation is closely related to description. Among analytical philosophers of history there is much dispute whether a description by itself is an explanation. Hempel and Oppenheim say it is not; Michael Scriven that it is.[35] B. Ellis, in an article entitled "On the Relation of Explanation to Description," provides an effective resolution of this dispute. He observes that historians and geologists often rely upon " 'process' explanations which answer the question 'What has happened (to bring this about)?' " "Such explanations," he continues, "consist of descriptions of the processes by which things have come to be in the states in which they are. They may therefore be called 'antecedent causal' explanations." In science there are similar "process" explanations, such as the earth's motion causing a shadow on the moon; but being "hidden processes" they demand a redescription to make the explanation evident. But whether a "hidden process" or an "antecedent causal" process, description becomes explanatory because it describes a process that is colligatory.[36]

The Validity of an Explanation

William Dray has argued that agency should be regarded as an alternative to theory in validating an alleged causal connection.[37] This is certainly true for a single instance of an event: the center fielder, for example, racing back, climbing the ladder, sticking up his glove, and catching the ball. But agency will not transform a correlation into an explanation unless that agency is repeated over and over again. If the center fielder repeatedly performs this scenario, then one could frame a theory to explain his repeatedly catching the ball high up on the wall. Or to put it another way, to transform the correlation "Dirt causes disease" into an explanation, one needs a theory; but one can explain why a single pa-

35. Hempel and Oppenheim, "The Logic of Explanation," 319; Scriven, "Explanation, Predictions, and Laws," 175–76.

36. Ellis, "On the Relation of Explanation to Description," 500, 504–5.

37. Dray, *Laws and Explanation in History*, 95.

tient died by tracing the path of the actual infection into the patient's lungs. Theories explain recurrent events; agency explains single events. Since historians spend most of their time explaining the occurrence of single events, Dray's emphasis on agency is entirely justified, especially since a careful attention to agency often destroys facile and erroneous explanations.

Take, for example, the explanation that historians for many years offered for the occurrence of the American Revolution—that it was in part a result of the Navigation Acts. Presumably they reached this conclusion by the use of a general law, such as "Revolutionaries always act upon the grievances they publish to the world"; and the Navigation Acts were declared to be a grievance. But Oliver Morton Dickerson, in *The Navigation Acts and the American Revolution*, minutely traced the response of the colonists to the Navigation Acts and discovered that the colonists welcomed the protection the acts offered more than they resented the restrictions imposed. At a conference on Philosophy and History held at New York University in 1970, Carl Degler referred to Dickerson's work as a splendid example of what a close "attention to evidence" will allow a historian to achieve.[38] Where Degler speaks of a close "attention to evidence," I prefer to speak of "a thorough tracing of the course of events"; but described either way, the process of colligation can be devastating to facile explanations based on dubious covering laws.

The fate of Max Weber's *Protestant Ethic and the Spirit of Capitalism* offers another instructive example. Influenced by a statistical survey carried out in 1900 by Max Offenbacher, a German sociologist, which showed that though Catholics made up 60 percent of the population of Baden, the Protestants of Baden owned a disproportionately large percentage of its capital assets, Weber posited a correlation between the appearance of Protestantism and the rise of capitalism. Historians, among them Henri Pirenne, promptly disputed this thesis. By tracing the growth of capitalism in late medieval Venice, Florence, Genoa, Augsburg, Nürnberg, Cádiz, Lisbon, Rouen, Antwerp, and Lübeck, all Catholic cities, they cast serious doubt on the validity of the thesis.[39] Yet there remained the curious correlation between Protestantism and commercial wealth in modern Europe, a correlation not limited to Baden. What explanation could the historian give for it? In an ingenious article, relying as heavily upon colligation as any of Weber's critics, Hugh

38. Degler, "Do Historians Use Covering Laws?" 207–8.
39. For an excellent discussion of Weber's thesis and its critics, see Leuthy, "Once Again: Calvinism and Capitalism," 26–38. See also Pirenne, *Economic and Social History of Medieval Europe*, esp. 160–66.

Trevor-Roper showed that the explanation lay in the hostility of Count-er-Reformation Catholicism to capitalism. This hostility drove capitalists from Antwerp, Liege, Lisbon, Augsburg, Milan, and other Catholic cities to Protestant lands. In the Catholic regions of Europe the spirit of capitalism withered.[40]

One can think of other examples. Nineteenth-century American historians of the War of 1812 attributed it solely to American anger at British Orders-in-Council, British violations of neutral rights, and British impressment of American seamen. Since it was about these grievances that American diplomats protested, then it must have been those grievances that caused the war. Then Louis Hacker in 1924 and Julius Pratt in 1925 analyzed the vote for war in the House of Representatives and in the Senate. They discovered that the maritime sections of New England were unanimous in opposition to war and that the inland and western states of Vermont, Ohio, Kentucky, and Tennessee were but one vote short of being unanimous for war. Westerners, many of whom had never seen the Atlantic ocean, voted for war; the New Englanders, whose ships were being boarded, voted against the war. Since 1925 no historian has argued that the maritime grievances were the sole cause of the war.[41]

Two British historians, Douglas Brunton and D. H. Pennington, similarly disposed of Christopher Hill's youthful argument that the English Civil War was caused by the determination of the bourgeoisie to seize power from a feudal landowning aristocracy. Their more microscopic investigations showed that many merchants supported the King, just as many landowners supported Parliament.[42] None of these attacks upon earlier explanations went unanswered, not Dickerson's, not Pirenne's, not Pratt's, not Brunton and Pennington's, but it is significant that those who answered the revisionists, as Brian Manning answered Brunton and Pennington, answered by tracing yet more minutely the course of events. Manning went beyond the members of the House of Commons to study the yeomen, craftsmen, and middling merchants of England who supported the parliamentary cause.[43]

It would be tedious to pile up further examples illustrating how colligation can expose facile and mistaken explanations, but a final comment must be made on David Hackett Fischer's rejection of causation. In

40. Trevor-Roper, "Religion, the Reformation, and Social Change."

41. The historiography of the War of 1812 is reviewed in Coles, *The War of 1812*, 27–33.

42. Brunton and Pennington, *Members of the Long Parliament*, 53–63; Hill, "The English Revolution."

43. Manning, *The English People and the English Revolution*, esp. 233–34.

Historians' Fallacies he writes, "Sometimes the question of causality can be by-passed by an investigator. In my opinion, whenever it can be avoided, it should be." He then quotes at length from A. L. Toole's *Elementary Practical Statistics:*

> In statistical work it is not necessary to prove that there are cause-and-effect relationships in every situation. Often the establishment of the fact that there exists an association, and the measurement of its degree or intensity are all that the investigator needs for the purposes of estimation and prediction. The statistician often is more interested in what he can accomplish by using observed associations or relationships than he is in assigning cause-and-effect or other explanations to them.

Fischer then comments, "This is surely true, and important."[44] Quite the contrary, it is surely false and misleading. The historian ought always to seek to discover the theory that explains a correlation and the agency that validates an explanation. The sociological imagination may be content with "observed association"; the historical imagination demands the discovery of agency. The many failures of macrocorrelation and the many successes of colligation demonstrate this.

In fairness to Fischer, it must be recorded that he immediately changed his mind, writing, "And yet, if an observer wishes to get beyond estimation and prediction to the problem of control, or to the problem of super- or extraregularistic explanation, then he must address himself to the problem of causality, however irritating it may be. And correlation, in conclusion, is only a necessary part of regularistic causal explanation. It is not sufficient, in itself, to resolve such issues."[45] Perhaps what he is trying to say is this: where the historical evidence does not permit the discovery of agency, one must do with an "observed association." This observation is true and important. But its truth and importance should not be permitted to overshadow a much greater truth, namely, that in history the drive should be to discover the theory that explains an "observed association" and the agency that validates an explanation. Indeed, there is reason to believe this is true in science as well. Sir Arthur Eddington once observed, "It is also a good rule not to put overmuch confidence in the observational results that are put forward until they are confirmed by theory."[46]

44. Fischer, *Historians' Fallacies*, 169.
45. Ibid., 169.
46. Quoted by Horace Freeland Judson, in the *New Yorker*, 4 December 1978, 132.

Where Fischer questions the explanatory power of colligation, Patrick Gardiner largely ignores it. In *The Nature of Historical Explanation*, Gardiner does, it is true, mention Hippolyte Taine's belief that the historian looks for tenuous threads that tie events together, and he does mention Maurice Mandelbaum's belief that history is "a descriptive narration of a particular series of events which has taken place," but he is so intent on showing to be muddle Taine's assertion that a causal connection is like an invisible thread and showing to be wrong Mandelbaum's assertion that causal connections can exist without reference to generalizations that he drops the idea of a series of events altogether. What he says about Taine and Mandelbaum is true, but it leads him to focus on the problem of establishing the connection between two events, to the neglect of investigating the explanatory power of tracing a series of events. It also leads him, since he ignores the tracing of events, into the realm of macrocorrelation. He seeks to explain the unpopularity of Louis XIV by subsuming his case under the covering law "Rulers are unpopular whenever their policies prove detrimental to the fortunes of their countries." He quickly sees, however, that historians would find this unconvincing, as indeed they would—what about the continued popularity of Henry VIII? So he suggests that it is only "a general precept" that the historian would seek to show to be true in this instance, an explanation the historian would not confirm (as scientists confirm a law) but justify, justify by telling more of the story, by assessing various factors involved (heavy taxation, curbing the nobility, religious persecution).[47] At this point Gardiner approaches the idea of colligation, but he does not reach it. What a historian would do, what Pierre Goubert does in *Louis XIV and Twenty Million Frenchmen*, is to trace the growing unpopularity of Louis XIV. When did it begin and where? Among what classes? To what other classes did it spread? What policies aroused the most opposition? When and where did his unpopularity deepen? By tracing how Louis XIV's unpopularity came about, the historian explains it.

In *The Nature of Historical Explanation*, Gardiner remarks on the simplicity of explanation in everyday life.[48] It might be useful, therefore, to illustrate the explanatory power of colligation by an example drawn from everyday life, though everyday life filtered through literature. In *Tom Jones*, Henry Fielding recounts the following episode:

> One day, when Mr. Allworthy and his whole family dined at Mr. Western's, Master Blifil, being in the garden with little Sophia,

47. Gardiner, *The Nature of Historical Explanation*, 81–97.
48. Gardiner, *The Nature of Historical Explanation*, 87.

and observing the extreme fondness that she showed for her little bird, desired her to trust it for a moment in his hands. Sophia presently complied with the young gentleman's request, and after some previous caution, delivered him her bird; of which he was no sooner in possession, then he slipt the string from its leg and tossed it into the air.

The foolish animal no sooner perceived itself set at liberty, than forgetting all the favors it had received from Sophia, it flew directly from her, and perched on a bough at some distance.

Sophia, seeing her bird gone, screamed out so loud that Tom Jones, who was at a distance, immediately ran to her assistance.

He was no sooner informed of what had happened, than he cursed Blifil for a pitiful rascal; and then immediately stripping off his coat he applied himself to climbing the tree to which the bird escaped.

Tom had almost recovered his little namesake, when the branch on which it was perched, and that hung over a canal, broke, and the poor lad plumped over head and ears into the water.[49]

Hearing the noise and confusion, Mr. Allworthy came to the scene and demanded an explanation why Tom was in the water. Master Blifil could have answered that Tom fell into the water because the branch broke. Such an answer would have been true, but truncated. It would not have explained very much. It would not have explained why Tom was on the branch. Or Master Blifil could have replied, "Adventurous boys fall into canals, and Tom is an adventurous boy." But do all adventurous boys fall into canals, or even very many of them? It would not have been a convincing answer. In fact, Blifil gave none of these answers. Instead he said, "I had Miss Sophia's bird in my hand, and . . . ," and he recounted the rest of the story. He might well have prefaced his explanation with the words of Herodotus, "The way it happened was this."

If further proof of the explanatory power of colligation is required, it can be found in the recent revival of narrative history. A narrative is the appropriate literary vehicle for colligation, since it is by narrative that one tells how it happened. Despite this fact narrative history fell into disrepute some twenty years ago. It was condemned as old-fashioned and superficial. Cliometricians proposed to replace it with quantification, model building, and the search for a body of lawlike generalizations. History would be merged into the social sciences, and analysis would replace narrative. But in recent years the charms of quantification and

49. ·Fielding, *Tom Jones*, 113–14.

model building have faded, and the writing of narrative history has revived.[50] Even so stalwart a proponent of social-science history as Samuel
Hays has admitted that systematic social history has failed in its main
purpose.[51] There is, of course, one solid reason it has failed. To explain the
complex events that historians study one must resort to colligation, to the
tracing of events, to the construction of a scenario. One cannot explain
such events by subsuming them under a covering law. And the most
appropriate literary form for constructing such a scenario is a narrative.

A narrative may, of course, have a purpose other than explanation.
Narration should not be identified with colligation, though it is the appropriate literary vehicle for colligation. Narration is a literary form,
colligation a logical procedure. A narrative may tell a dramatic story, may
portray a hero, may relate a comic tale, may unfold a tragedy, may
satirize society, may do many things other than explain how something
came about.

It is likewise important to distinguish colligation from emplotment, a
concept central to Hayden White's *Metahistory*.[52] Emplotment means the
construction of a plot structure within a historical narrative, with the
purpose of exhibiting the character, the pattern, the direction, the significance, and the ultimate goal of the events described. Colligation means
tracing the causal sequence of events leading up to a historical event,
with the purpose of explaining the occurrence of that event. Emplotment
is the appropriate strategy for revealing pattern in history, colligation for
discovering causation. A Hegelian might dispute this, might assert that
emplotment also discovers causation, that to locate an event in a plot
structure is to explain the occurrence of that event. There is some truth
in this assertion, but only if one accepts a teleological explanation for the
occurrence of an event as a valid explanation. President Kennedy's trip
to Dallas forms a significant episode in the larger story of his assassination, but his assassination does not explain why he went to Dallas—
unless, that is, one believes that God or Providence or Destiny or the
World Spirit sent him there that he might be assassinated. But for those
of us who cannot accept a teleological explanation, to emplot an event is
not to explain it. Indeed, Hayden White himself, in *Tropics of Discourse*,
declares that emplotment, though necessary in order to grasp the nature
of the whole field presented in a narrative, does not explain why a given

    50. Stone, "The Revival of Narrative," 74–96. For a useful account of the debate be-
tween narrative and analytical historians, see Dray, "Narrative Versus Analysis in History."
    51. Hays, "Scientific Versus Traditional History," 77.
    52. White, *Metahistory*, esp. 5, 7–10, 12, 141–42, 167, 211, 249, 251, 304, 343–45, 357,
403–4, 426–28.

event within that field occurred when it did.[53] White's *Metahistory*, in which the explanation of an event is regularly equated with the "meaning" of an event, is a brilliant contribution to the speculative philosophy of history, but it is not, and does not aspire to be, a contribution to the analytic philosophy of history, in which to explain an event means to discover the cause of its occurrence.[54]

One need not be a Hegelian, of course, to believe that there is pattern in history and that one of the tasks of the historian is to discover those patterns. As both Louis Mink and William Dray have shown, the historian by the configuration he gives to his narrative illuminates those patterns.[55] But to discover a pattern in historical events is not to explain why those events occurred. Quite the reverse. To discover a pattern in history is to discover a phenomenon that cries out for explanation. What explanation can be given for the occurrence of the pattern? The answer—unless one accepts teleological explanations—lies in the explanations for the occurrence of the particular events that form that pattern.

53. White, *Tropics of Discourse*, 67.

54. Though a brilliant contribution to the speculative philosophy of history, it has not gone unchallenged. David Carr (*Time, Narrative, and History*) has argued, most cogently, that a narrative is not an artificial construct imposed by the historian on a chaotic past. Quite the contrary, human experience is already structured narratively.

55. For a discussion of Louis Mink's concept of "configuration," with critical comments, see Dray, *On History and Philosophers of History*, 128–33, and idem, *Philosophy of History*, 100–105.

3 THE NECESSITY OF MICROCORRELATION

Explanation seems to require appeal to general principles, whether universal or statistical, serving to connect events in patterns.

— Israel Scheffler, *The Anatomy of Inquiry*

That colligation possesses explanatory power seems indisputable, but a fundamental problem remains: by what logic does the historian decide which events belong, and which do not belong, in the causal sequence that leads to the event to be explained? How, amidst a sea of simultaneous events and a score of possible motives, does the historian decide which events and which motives matter and which do not? How does the historian decide that Sophia gave the bird to Blifil because he asked for it and not because she was bored with it, or that Sophia screamed because the bird flew away and not because she then saw a rabbit, or that the limb broke because Tom climbed out upon it and not because the wind blew against it? In short, how does the historian steer a path through the forest of facts in the historical records?

Ernest Nagel and Carl Hempel have offered a solution to this problem: the historian uses a succession of covering laws to connect the successive steps in the sequence.[1] Peter Railton calls these successive covering

1. Nagel, *The Structure of Science*, 564–68; Hempel, "Aspects of Scientific Explanation," 449–50.

laws "nomic connections."[2] But this solution to the problem has met with the hostility of a whole host of philosophers, whose objections and alternative solutions deserve attention.

The most extreme among these philosophers is Michael Oakeshott, for whom there exists no problem and therefore no need for a solution. In four celebrated sentences he writes, "And the only explanation of change relevant or possible in history is simply a complete account of change. History accounts *for* change by means *of* a full account of change. The relation *between* events is always other events, and it is established in history by a full relation *of* the events. The conception of cause is thus replaced by the exhibition of a world of events intrinsically related to one another in which no lacuna is tolerated."[3] The error in this argument is obvious: the relation between events, as Hume saw, is not always other events. There is no event between the motion of the first billiard ball and the motion of the second, which it hits. The one event precedes the other event, with no event in between. There are similar lacunae in historical sequences, gaps that no other event bridges. Charles I attempts to arrest the five members. The members of the House of Commons then withdraw to Grocer's Hall, London. Oakeshott assumes that historians can intuitively grasp the intrinsic relation of one event to another, of Charles's attempt and the Commons's withdrawal; but alas, historians often differ in the sequences they trace. Intuition is hopelessly subjective. To achieve an objective explanation, that is, one that will convince not only oneself but others, a historian must offer some logical warrant for each step in the sequence he or she traces.

W. B. Gallie likewise believes that narratives are self-explanatory, that there can be a succession of incidents which, in fact, need no explanation at all.[4] But he admits that at times there occurs an obscure or baffling set of facts, a crux that needs removing. In such cases, historical explanation, which he regards as ancillary to narrative, must come to the rescue. The historian may need to point to some one condition that is necessary for the event to occur. "Thereupon," he writes, "we look for an antecedent event, the *explicans,* which can be accounted a necessary condition of the *explicandum,* on ordinarily inductive grounds (observation of analogous cases)."[5] In admitting this he moves halfway toward the covering-law model, but only halfway, since there is no obligation on the historian to give the sufficient conditions for the occurrence of the event. Gallie states this explicitly. In a genetic explana-

---

2. Railton, "A Deductive-Nomological Model of Probabilistic Explanation," 208.
3. Oakeshott, *Experience and Its Modes,* 143.
4. Gallie, *Philosophy and the Historical Understanding,* 23, 29, 107–9.
5. Gallie, "Explanations in History and the Genetic Sciences," 387, 390–91.

tion, he writes, "the prior event is not taken in conjunction with certain universal laws, to constitute a sufficient condition of the occurrence of the subsequent event."[6] In short, historians need only give necessary conditions. They are free to shop around among the necessary conditions that they like best—though Gallie does urge them to choose those that suggest a continuity with the causes of previous and subsequent events. This advice leaves the door open to subjectivism. Historians of the English Revolution, for example, who wish to make fear of popery the theme of their narratives will discover that fear of popery was a necessary condition for the occurrence of a long succession of events leading from the riot at St. Giles to the Grand Remonstrance, conveniently ignoring other necessary conditions. On the other hand, historians who would make hatred of arbitrary taxation their theme are free to choose it as the necessary condition in the same succession of events. Each historian may confirm whatever prejudices he or she brings to his or her research. This may serve the purpose of narration, but hardly that of explanation.

Where Gallie admits the covering-law model halfway, A. R. Louch repudiates it entirely. "The historian is able to repudiate the covering-law model," he writes, because "his object is to lay out a continuum of events related in such a way as to meet the condition of narrative smoothness." He illustrates such continuity with the example of a motion picture of the blossoming of a flower. This provides us with a smooth flow of change where widely separated glances provide only radical discontinuities. "The visual model," he writes, "suggests that explanation can be provided simply by filling in the gaps in perception." To the possible objection that the historian does not see a flower blossoming, he replies that narrative stands proxy for experience. In the absence of the ideal, *seeing* something change before one's eyes, one must rely on a narrative. By filling in the gaps in this narrative the historian explains the course of events. As Louch puts it, "to explain is to fill in the gaps." He admits that there are connections in this continuum, but they are not causal or statistical. Rather, the narrative is "constructed out of adjacent descriptions which closely resemble one another." The historian is seeking to discover a chain of similarities. Louch concludes, "The account that can convert the apparent discontinuities in human, biological, geological or cosmological history into the perceived evolution of earlier into later states is in that sense explanatory. The force of such explanation does not depend upon covering laws or theories, but rests instead on a covert assimilation of these

6. Ibid., 391.

accounts to what is directly perceived."[7] The fatal defect in Louch's visual model is that it describes rather than explains. If we watch, through time-lapse photography, the blossoming of a flower, we gain a description of its blossoming, a vivid one. We see it change, but we do not understand why it changes. We do not learn, for example, that without sunshine it will not blossom, or if denied water it will wither, or that without fertile soil it will be stunted. For millennia gardeners have known that flowers need sunlight in order to grow, and water and good soil. They have known this because when planted in the shade of a great tree, the flower did not blossom, but when placed in the sunlight, it did. Flowers that were not watered withered, and flowers grown in gravel were stunted. These are covering laws that the shrewd gardener soon discovers. Now, it is true that by colligation the plant biologist can show how the sun makes the flower grow, how chlorophyll assists in the formation of carbohydrates by photosynthesis. But in doing so, the biologist is not discovering a chain of similarities, but rather a chain of connected events, often quite dissimilar events. What connects them (the succession of events at the most microscopic level in the theory of photosynthesis) is regularity of succession or constant conjunction. Louch's visual model is most appropriate for narrative or description. Historians who wish to describe what happened will surely use it. But it is quite inappropriate for narrative as explanation. Historians who wish to explain why something happened will have to look to some other model.

Because Maurice Mandelbaum accepts the explanatory value of a continuous series of occurrences, he can be said to belong to the narrativist school, but he sees more clearly than Oakeshott or Gallie or Louch the difficulties that school confronts. Oakeshott's position, he asserts, is paradoxical only if what is to be explained is a single, isolated event, and not some continuous series of events. "However," he quickly adds, "it is by no means clear in his account how the events in any particular series of occurrences are related to each other, so that it may be said of them that they form a continuous series."[8] He then declares that he will correct this deficiency.

Rejecting Hume's analysis of causation, he asserts that a direct perception of causal relation and an immediate experience of causal power are possible.[9] Cause and effect are not to be construed as distinct events, but as components within a single ongoing process. A pregnancy, a death, a

7. Louch, "History as Narrative," esp. 55–59.
8. Mandelbaum, *The Anatomy of Historical Knowledge*, 119.
9. Mandelbaum, "The Distinguishable and the Separable," 253–57.

tackle in football, a light being switched on should not be regarded as separable from their causes, but as the terminable state of a single ongoing process. Events in a series of occurrences are related to one another as parts to a whole.[10]

One obvious difficulty to this analysis of causation immediately arises. By what criterion is one event said to be part of the process and another event not? Did the tackle bring down the halfback, or did a cry from the stands at the same moment bring down the halfback? Mandelbaum would answer that the tackle brought him down, because we see the tackler bring him down—and causation can be directly perceived. To Hume's principle of constant conjunction he opposes the principle of visibility. But the principle of visibility will not stand up to close scrutiny. An illusionist makes the pea appear to be under one cup, though it is actually under another. A magician appears to saw a woman in half, but the principle of regularity keeps us from rushing up to stop him. An electric eye opens a door, but we do not see it do so. A laser beam reads a label, a microwave oven heats up a hamburger, a bell hit by a hammer sends off sound waves, but we do not see these things happening. But there is no need to multiply instances, since Mandelbaum himself deserts the principle of visibility for that of regularity. Describing Michotte's demonstration that perception may deceive a person about causal relations, he writes, "It is here, of course, that regularity of sequence becomes important; it is a test that is used in everyday affairs when we check on the reliability of the causal attributions we make, and which others also make."[11]

Peter Strawson has likewise argued against separating cause and effect into different states of affairs. He writes, "There is no question of dissolving the transaction into a sequence of states of affairs—a sequence of 'distinct existences'—and wondering whether, or in virtue of what, the sequence constitutes a causal sequence."[12] Strawson is certainly right that when we observe a man pushing a door open we do not ordinarily dissolve the transaction into a sequence of states. But consider the following scenario. A doorman regularly pushes on a door that is in fact opened by a mechanism that is started when the doorman's hand breaks the beam of an electric eye. We see him pushing on the door; we do not see the electric eye. One day the electric eye breaks, freezing the

10. Mandelbaum, *The Anatomy of Historical Knowledge,* 51–69.

11. Ibid., 77. Behan McCullagh (*Justifying Historical Descriptions,* 174–75) has likewise criticized Mandelbaum for failing to see that two events need not be perceived to be distinct in order to be causally related.

12. Strawson, "Causation and Explanation," 121.

door shut. The doorman pushes, but the door does not open. We then conclude that we were in error to believe that the doorman's pushing on the door caused it to open, especially when we learn that the door always opens when the electric eye is working and its beam is broken. Here the principle of regularity—or, in Hume's language, of constant conjunction—has clearly triumphed over the principle of visibility. This does not mean that Strawson and Mandelbaum are wholly wrong. They are correct in asserting that on some occasions causation can be observed; where they go wrong is in believing that being observed makes the action a cause. Regularity of succession, or constant conjunction, makes it a cause. The fact that causation may on occasions be observed is a matter of practical importance. It gives us a shortcut to the conclusion that one event caused another. We see a person throw a rock through a window, and conclude immediately that the rock caused the window to break. We do not have to throw other rocks through other windows (or even have heard that it had been done) in order to establish the constant conjunction between thrown rocks and broken windows, a conjunction needed to support the conclusion that the rock broke the window. We saw the rock hit and go through the window. A single observed instance allows us to form the law that thrown rocks break windows. The doctrine of visibility affords a shortcut to the establishment of laws that otherwise could only be established by numerous observations of constant conjunction. (Though it might be remarked, parenthetically, that as we grow up we quickly learn from experience, that is, from a regularity of association, that visible physical contiguity is proof that there also exists a constant conjunction between action and result.) The doctrine of visibility deserves emphasis because I later urge that the doctrine of rationality furnishes for action explanations the same shortcut that the doctrine of visibility offers for explanations in nature.

Mandelbaum's admission that regularity of sequence is important is not the only retreat he makes to the Hempelian model. Repeatedly his argument leads him to the covering-law model. He observes that elements in a causal explanation form a strand. "Why just these occurrences," he asks, "and not others?" And he answers, "We must appeal to generalizations concerning how some aspect of one factor was dependent on some aspect of the other."[13] On another occasion he writes, "Except in cases involving the direct perception of causality in a particular instance, a strong admixture of theory is apt to enter into our everyday causal explanations, and this element may well be continuous with

13. Mandelbaum, *The Anatomy of Historical Knowledge*, 102–3.

the kinds of theoretical framework found in the sciences. Therefore, it should not be assumed that there are fundamental and irreconcilable differences between scientific generalizations and causal explanations in everyday life."[14] To which one may add, historical research uncovers remarkably few instances of "a direct perception of causality."

In fairness to Mandelbaum, it should be pointed out that his *Anatomy of Historical Knowledge* is in essence a sustained attack upon macrocorrelation and a vigorous celebration of colligation. His insistence that two events are not separable reflects a desire to trace the agency between a cause and an effect, and his distrust of generalizations is a distrust of those who would ignore agency. At one point he is explicit about this. "Thus," he writes, "the use of lawlike generalizations in history cannot be held to supplant sequential historical accounts, as Hempel believed they should."[15] How right, how true (though Hempel, in "Aspects of Scientific Explanation," allows for genetic explanations): general laws are not enough by themselves; colligation is indispensable. But this truth ought not to lead philosophers to deny the indispensability of covering laws as a bridge joining the steps in a historian's sequential account of events.

William Dray is as contemptuous of the covering-law model as is Mandelbaum, is as enthusiastic about the explanatory power of narrative as is Mandelbaum, and is equally perplexed by the problem of connecting the steps within a narrative. The covering-law model, writes Dray, "is, in fact, so misleading that it ought to be abandoned as a basic account of what it is to give an explanation." And he writes later, "But, as I have shown, to give and defend a causal explanation in history is scarcely ever to bring what is explained under a law, and almost always involves a descriptive account, a narrative, of the actual course of events, in order to justify the judgment that the condition indicated was the cause."[16] He calls the narrative model of explanation the "Model of the Continuous-Series," meaning a continuous series of happenings or subevents. Such a model inevitably poses the problem, how does one connect the links in the chain of events that make up the continuous series? To this problem Dray offers five different solutions. On one occasion he offers the Mandelbaumian solution of visibility: "In typical historical cases, too, the continuous series constructed by the historian's explanatory narrative will consist of observable happenings." But he does not develop this idea. Rather, in the same paragraph he proposes a second solution: "For to explain with the aid of a theory [which

14. Ibid., 78.
15. Ibid., 185. See also his acute criticism of Hempel in "Historical Explanation: The Problem of 'Covering Laws,'" 233–38.
16. Dray, *Laws and Explanation in History,* 19, 50.

the automobile mechanic does with the theory of the internal-combustion engine] is to do indirectly what the historian, perhaps painstakingly and piecemeal, does directly: reduce what is puzzling to what is not."[17] By what procedure, by what logic, the historian reduces what is puzzling to what is not, he does not say. There is a third solution, closely related to the second: "The point is rather that in offering a sum of sub-sequences to explain a gross one, the former must be *acceptable* to some person, investigator, craft, audience, &c." This leads into a fourth solution: "They [the sub-sequences] must themselves raise no further demand for explanation in that particular context"; and so a fifth and related solution: the sub-sequences "are—to use a convenient term of Dr. F. Waismann's—'hat-doffing' phenomena. They do not puzzle us; we ask no question of them; we just 'take off our hats to them.' "[18] Thus one has five possible criteria: observability, puzzle ending, acceptability, finality, and hat doffing.

Dray himself seems to recognize that these various solutions are unsatisfactory, for he entertains the idea that the covering-law model is, after all, needed to connect these subevents. Of his explanation of the seizure of the car engine, he writes:

> But reference to a series of facts constituting the story of what happened between the leakage of the oil and the seizure of the engine does explain the seizure. Even if it were true that these smaller scale events were each covered by law in the sense that in every case I would be prepared to assent to a law corresponding to a sub-sequence, the law involved would be, at most, part of the explanation of the gross event, not of the sub-event they cover; so that when they do function in an explanation they are not *covering* laws at all.[19]

I can agree that the sublaws are part of the explanation of the gross event, but I cannot agree that they are not part of the explanation of the subevent they cover. A law establishing a correlation between metal rubbing on metal and an increase in heat is explanatory. It may not be as powerfully explanatory as a molecular theory showing why friction causes heat, but it does have some explanatory power. But what matters far more is that the correlation, or law, offers a logical warrant for placing that link in the chain of circumstances leading to the seizure of the engine. None of Dray's alternatives offers any similar warrant.

17. Ibid., 81.
18. Ibid., 68–69.
19. Ibid., 70.

Arthur Danto's analysis of narrative explanation presents a complex case, since he initially accepts a Mandelbaumian connection of the part to the whole, rejects Nagel's causal chain, and adopts Gallie's belief that continuity renders the explanandum intelligible, yet he later retreats to a Nagelian solution. He begins by insisting that causation is about change and has the structure of a story. His model of a narrative explanation is this:

1. X is F at t−1.
2. H happens to X at t−2.
3. X is G at t−3.

To illustrate the model, he gives the following example:

1. The car is undented at t−1.
2. The car is struck by Y at t−2.
3. The car is dented at t−3.

At this point Danto, probably unconsciously, performs a sleight-of-hand trick. Instead of stating that Y is a truck that was seen to hit the car at t−2, he says that Y is unknown. Now, this raises an interesting problem (to which I return later), the problem of filling in the gaps in a historical narrative. But the problem of gaps is not the problem that Danto is discussing. The problem he is discussing is, how does the historian decide that it was the truck hitting the car and not the driver coughing at the same moment (an event Danto mentions) that caused the dent? Nagel would answer that a Humean analysis leads us to conclude that the truck, and not the cough, caused the dent, since there is a regularity of succession between trucks hitting cars and dents occurring but not between drivers coughing and dents occurring. Danto, in fact, agrees. "We can easily," he writes of this model, "fit it to Hume's paradigm."[20]

But he doubts if a more complex sequence can fit Hume's paradigm. The example of the dented fender presents only one causal episode, not a chain of them. Danto thus turns to a more complex example, which he borrows from Nagel, the example of Buckingham's changing his mind about Charles's marriage to the infanta. "The connection between the Duke's favoring the marriage," he writes, "and then opposing it is not a causal connection; they are end-points of a temporally extended change."[21] Where Nagel declares that there is no

20. Danto, *Analytical Philosophy of History*, 233–37.
21. Ibid., 235.

connection between C_0 (Buckingham's favoring the marriage) and C_{12} (Buckingham's opposing the marriage), but only a connection between C_0 and C_1 (Buckingham's frustration at delay), and C_1 and C_2, and so forth, Danto asserts that there is a connection between C_0 and C_{12}, that of the part to the whole. It has the structure of a story. A narrative is a form of explanation. But by what rules does the historian select certain episodes for the narrative and exclude others? Quoting Gallie on the importance of continuity (or the persistence of elements) in making a narrative intelligible, he gives these three rules: a narrative must be about the same subject; it must adequately explain the change that occurs; and it must contain only information that explains the change.[22]

These rules are unexceptionable, but too vague. One wishes to know how a narrative adequately explains the change that occurs. For a simple change, one involving but one step, subsumption under a single general law suffices. Danto calls such a sequence "an atomic narrative." But how does the historian explain a sequence of changes, a sequence that Danto calls a "molecular narrative"? Possibly influenced by Gallie's emphasis on the persistence of elements in a narrative, Danto demands a general law for the entire sequence. As he writes, "In a molecular narrative each unit is covered by a general law which covers the entire change." But surely the covering law that would connect Buckingham's enthusiasm for the marriage with his trip to Spain is different from the covering law that would connect his trip to Spain with his frustration, and so forth, through the whole sequence of events leading to his hostility to the marriage. Why not simply regard a molecular narrative as an end-to-end series of atomic narratives? We should not, replies Danto, "because we are interested in the larger change, of which the intermediating changes are parts."[23] What he fails to see is that they are not parts because they partake of some persistent element or share a general law; they are parts because they logically connect C_0 with C_{12}, Buckingham's favoring the marriage with his opposing it. To validate this connection one needs not one general law but twelve different laws.

Michael Scriven is yet another philosopher who believes that explanation is a description of a process; and like the others he is exercised by the problem of what counts as the right description. He answers that a right description is one that "fills in a particular gap in the understanding of the person or people to whom the explanation is directed." It

---

22. Ibid., 235, 249–51.
23. Ibid., 252.

provides "an appropriate piece of information," the appropriateness "being a matter of its relation to a particular context." And it locates the puzzling phenomenon "in a system of relations."[24]

Within such a system of relations, Scriven holds that "cause and effect are physically identical and only conceptually distinct." And he illustrates this identity by describing how the provision of subsidies, the supplying of British armies, the raising of government loans, the growth of British exports, and a similar growth in British shipping enhanced the role of the City of London as a financial center. Behan McCullagh has acutely observed that Scriven has described the growth of these various activities but has not explained why financial business increased as a result. Explaining *how* a change occurred, urges McCullagh, only helps to explain *why* it occurred when the stages of a change were causally related to one another. In such a causal chain cause and effect are distinct from one another.[25]

Where Scriven emphasizes understanding, John Passmore emphasizes familiarity. An explanation is intelligible, he writes, "provided that it relies upon a familiar sort of connection." The historian, he adds, "helps us to see how a change occurred, by showing it in process; in so doing he appeals to our sense of what connections are natural," not to unfamiliar principles. But what makes a connection familiar, natural? He answers, a generalization that no longer needs to be defended, generalizations such as "Influenza can cause death" and "Men seek power, wealth, and preferment for their family." Passmore speaks often of the need to make the explanation intelligible, but his examples suggest that what makes a connection intelligible is a familiar generalization, that is, a covering law.[26]

Where Passmore emphasizes familiarity, J. H. Hexter emphasizes credibility. Like the others he is reluctant to use covering laws to connect steps in a historical narrative. In its place he argues for the standard of credibility and for the use of a processive narrative. By a processive narrative he means a narrative that proceeds as a story, dramatically rather than chronologically. Two comments should be made about Hexter's rejection of what he calls "the logic of explanation by narration."[27]

First, for all the scorn he heaps on explanation by narration, he does on occasion accept it. He does admit that two events can be shown to be causally connected by subsuming them under the appropriate covering

24. Scriven, "Explanations, Predictions, and Laws," 175–76, 193.
25. McCullagh, *Justifying Historical Descriptions*, 174–75.
26. Passmore, "Explanation in Everyday Life, in Science and in History," 111–13, 120–21.
27. Hexter, *The History Primer*, 166–67, 192–93, 266.

law. The trouble, he argues, lies in the skeleton nature of such an explanation and in its tedious chronological sequences. Explanation by narration omits too much—the drama, the pivotal point of tension, personality, emotion—and includes too much—every link in every sequence, every pitch to every batter in every inning of a baseball game. The answer to these objections is apparent. A historian employing a narrative explanation is perfectly free to add color and drama to his narrative. There is no law, there is no injunction, against his doing so. On the contrary, he would fall short of his duty as a historian if he did not add to the logic of explanation the rhetoric of persuasion. Likewise there is no law saying that the historian must describe every link in a causal sequence. A historian must examine every link, true, and test its validity, but if he finds dozens of them to be routine, he need not burden his narrative with them.[28]

Second, the standard of credibility that Hexter proposes is far too vague. Nowhere does he define "credibility." In fact he explicitly declines to define it. He does, however, vouchsafe to give an illustration of what is incredible. In explaining how Willie got muddy pants, it is incredible to say he met with a witch who turned herself into a mud puddle. But surely the reason the reader finds this incredible is the absence of any instances of a witch turning herself into a puddle. It violates the laws of nature as we know them, laws that often act as covering laws in historical explanations. An assertion of causation is credible because one knows many instances of it; that is, there is a lawlike generalization justifying it.[29]

R. F. Atkinson denies any such role to covering laws in shaping a narrative. "I am quite sure," he writes, "that there is no conception of causation which could serve as the foundation of a true, general account of coherence in history." And he asserts that it is coherence that makes a "mere" narrative explanatory. By coherence he means "comprehensiveness with unity, nothing relevant omitted, everything irrelevant excluded." Other than declaring that coherence is relative to the question the historian asks, he does not elaborate upon the concept. He does not show how coherence is explanatory. He does, however, go on to say that historical writing can become explanatory without being brought closer to the covering-law model or to the rational model, and to declare that narrative "can be explanatory in itself." One can readily agree with Atkinson that the historian can give coherence to a narrative without employing the concept of causation, but such a

28. Ibid., 154–66, 170–74, 190–97, 266–67.
29. Ibid., 143–45, 267–69.

narrative would not be explanatory—dramatic, perhaps, or comic, but not explanatory.[30]

In this respect William Walsh is much nearer the truth. The duty of the historian, he writes, is to produce not just a narrative but a "significant narrative." "By this phrase," he continues, "I mean a narrative which is, in a sense, self-explanatory, which makes us see not only the order of the events but also their connections." He then gives three kinds of causation that can establish that connection: an antecedent event, a dispositional term, and a purpose. And he indicates his preference for the third as the main concern of historians (though allowing that the other two must supplement it). Admittedly, he does not show how these three kinds of causation shape a narrative, but turns instead in a direction that Atkinson would applaud. Events must be "put in a coherent whole." To explain is to render intelligible; it is to find meaning and point in material initially not seen to have meaning and point. No doubt to explain is to render intelligible, but what makes a causal sequence intelligible? Passmore is surely right to see that it is reliance upon lawlike generalizations, though Walsh wisely broadens this to include dispositional traits and purposes.[31]

In *Fact and Method*, Richard Miller has sought to show that causation is directly apprehended. Though he does not succeed in this, he does succeed magnificently in showing that correlation alone does not reveal causation. A falling barometer does not cause rain, the red shift an expanding universe. Nor does an increased frequency in a phenomenon (say, of heart attacks) when a new antecedent is introduced (say, smoking) show that the new antecedent caused the increased frequency. As Miller writes, "Notions of causing an event, bringing something about and the like are not dispensable in favor of notions of correlation and logical entailment, in any analysis of causation, including probabilistic ones. Rather, the notion of a particular causal connection is required to make it clear when correlations are relevant to causal claims."[32] He is certainly right to argue that the basic distinction between explanation and nonexplanation requires causal notions and that an acceptable generalization should reflect the operation of a causal mechanism bringing about the regularity. Or, as I express it in Chapter 2, colligation turns correlation into causation.

But how does one know when one has discovered a cause? Not by defining or analyzing the concept of cause, argues Miller, but by collect-

30. Atkinson, *Knowledge and Explanation in History,* 131–36.
31. Walsh, " 'Meaning' in History," 297–99.
32. Miller, *Fact and Method,* 46; see also 55, 58.

ing a core of robustly causal notions: of the wind's blowing leaves, of a sting's causing pain, of fear's causing flight. These elementary interpretations of events as causes, he argues, need no justification, no analysis. Neither does the use of empathy to discern motives. "On the face of it," writes Miller, "that normal humans with no special expertise have a special means of identifying motives is no more surprising than that they have special means of identifying shapes."[33]

But a close examination of Miller's robustly causal notions shows that it is the experience of constant conjunction, not visual apprehension, that leads one to call them causes. One does not see the wind blow the leaves; one feels the wind on one's cheeks and simultaneously sees the leaves move. One does not see a sting causing pain but records the fact that pain follows the sting. One does not see the fear that causes soldiers to flee the battlefield; one takes their flight as a sign of fear. In every case it is the experience of the constant conjunction between feeling wind and seeing the leaves move, between feeling the pain and finding the bee's stinger in one's arm, between the sight of fleeing soldiers and their confession of fright that leads one to assert that the one caused the other (with priority in time distinguishing cause from effect). If a constant conjunction, or something approaching it, were not present, one could not assert causation. One might see a bee sting a person yet wrongly conclude that it caused pain, if that person were a bee keeper who had grown immune to the sting of a bee.

To understand why constant conjunction indicates a cause in these instances, when correlation by itself does not normally reveal causation, one must make a distinction between elementary and complex causes. An elementary cause has only one link in the causal chain, say, the connection between a gust of wind and the motion of leaves. A complex cause has many links in a causal chain, say, the connections between smoke entering the lungs and the bloodstream taking up harmful chemicals, between the actions of these chemicals and the formation of plaque, between the buildup of plaque and the narrowing of the arteries, between the narrowing of the arteries and the failure of blood to reach the heart. It is the task of both natural scientists and historians to trace such causal chains. In doing so they will find themselves using covering laws to connect each link in the chain.

Indeed, throughout his book Richard Miller repeatedly falls back on the covering-law model—though in various different disguises. Thus there is an auxiliary principle that similar causes are apt to have similar effects. There is another auxiliary principle that entries in the secret

33. Ibid., 129; see also 14, 44, 74, 78, 82, 130.

diary of an intelligent, successful public figure are apt accurately to state the rationales producing his or her major strategic actions. There is a framework principle about the stability of adult character traits. Then there is the power of an indefinite variety of specific principles of causal similarity. These principles describe certain specific kinds of situations in which similarities in outcomes are apt to be due to similarities in causes. Thus data will confirm a hypothesis that C caused E if characteristic C', of other situations, matches with characteristics of respective sequels E'. Behind the operation of these principles lies a repertoire of truisms: for example, when an intelligent person regularly prefers one thing to another, the person is usually motivated by a desire or acts out of habit. These principles of stability and uniformity, argues Miller, even allow prediction and control, upon which the appeal of counterfactual analysis ultimately depends. Richard Miller would deny that these principles and truisms are covering laws, because they are topic-specific and because they do not apply to science as a whole, but only to history, say, or to physics. But his refusal to allow these principles and truisms to be called covering laws does not gainsay their close resemblance to covering laws.[34]

The principal conclusion that emerges from this survey of alternatives to Nagel's and Hempel's solution to the problem of selecting facts for an explanatory narrative is that none is convincing. Six alternatives to Nagel's and Hempel's covering-law solution are discernible: the criterion of visibility, the criterion of recognizability, the criterion of intelligibility, the criterion of credibility, the criterion of coherence, and the criterion of apprehensibility. None successfully bridges the steps in a causal sequence.

Mandelbaum's criterion of visibility fails because regularity, not visibility, validates a causal connection between two events. True, Mandelbaum's talk of spatial-temporal relations, of correspondence between cause and effect, of complex patterning, and of functional properties accurately describes why a person is led to look for causal connections in certain places, but the psychology of explanation is not the same thing as the logic of explanation.

Dray's hat doffing, which may be called the criterion of recognizability, fails because it is so unanalytical. Because a connection is obvious does not mean that it is true. Dray's position borders on the intuitionist's, since the hat doffer offers no reason why the connection he recognizes is true. Dray does speak often of judgment, but never analyzes what makes a judgment acceptable. His reliance on judgment led

34. Ibid., 51, 71, 79, 80, 201, 206, 208, 218–19, 340.

Strawson to observe that Dray's " 'judgment' appears as a slightly mysterious gift of nature to historians."[35]

The same objection can be brought against the criterion of intelligibility, a criterion that Walsh and Scriven, among others, favor. What makes a connection in a causal sequence intelligible? Why is it unintelligible to say that the driver's cough caused the dent in the fender, and yet intelligible to say that the truck hitting the car caused the dent? The answer demands an appeal to a generalization, to a covering law. What makes the assertion of a connection intelligible is the fact that it depends upon a generalization that our experience tells us is true. It is a matter of considerable significance that Mandelbaum, Danto, Dray, Passmore, and Walsh are all driven by their arguments to fall back on positions not too different from the covering-law model.

Hexter's criterion of credibility fails for want of a definition of what credibility means. One suspects that if Hexter were to define and describe its role in a historical explanation, it, too, would resemble a covering law.

The defect of the criterion of coherence is that neither Gallie nor Atkinson nor Walsh nor Danto have shown why coherence and unity and continuity are explanatory. Hugh Trevor-Roper has written a most coherent account of how the "mere" gentry, driven by their resentment at the court, caused the English Revolution, but his account is based on connections that are false.[36] The error that Gallie makes explicitly and Atkinson implicitly is to confuse narrative with colligation, the telling of a story with the establishment of a causal sequence. Coherence and unity and continuity are fundamental to a good story, but only incidental to a correct causal explanation (or explanatory narrative).

Richard Miller's criterion of apprehensibility fails because it allows a single event, that is, an event observed only once, to be judged a cause. Miller writes:

> Suppose I believe the lore that Aeschylus died because an eagle dropped a tortoise on his head. Then I believe that one event, the eagle's dropping the tortoise on Aeschylus' head, caused another, Aeschylus' death. I need not believe, however, that at every other time when an eagle's dropping a tortoise on a person's head occurred, death follows. Nor need I be committed to the existence, much less a sketch of a general law relating

35. Strawson, review of *Laws and Explanation in History*, 266.
36. Trevor-Roper, *The Gentry, 1540–1640*; for his errors, see Hexter, "Storm over the Gentry."

death to tortoise impacts when further general properties are realized.[37]

But what if another observer said that Aeschylus's death was caused by the sun's going behind a cloud at that very moment. One would certainly answer him by saying that a shadow has never been known to kill a man but that heavy objects falling upon a man often have. One would thereby appeal to two covering laws, that shadows do not kill and that heavy objects do. Indeed, where there are no covering laws but only singular observations, anything goes; any assertion illustrated by an anecdote is true. Testing atomic bombs causes cold winters; putting fluoride in the water causes colon cancer; sugar causes hyperactivity. Richard Miller should be reminded that *post hoc, ergo propter hoc* is a fallacy, not a rule of logic. And he might be reminded of the challenge thrown down by Robert Stover: "Has Dray, has any historian or philosopher, ever come forth with an analysis showing how it is possible for the historian to make 'independent' judgments of causal connections in particular cases involving events conceived of as *sui generis?*"[38]

The bottom line, then, is this: what I have chosen to call microcorrelation (to distinguish it from macrocorrelation) is indispensable to colligation. In order to connect the discrete steps in an explanatory narrative, covering laws are necessary. Mr. Allworthy found Blifil's story credible because young ladies do not scream when they see a rabbit, though they do when their pet bird flies away, and branches of a tree oftener break when a boy climbs out upon them than when the wind blows. Dispositional traits may also be used to connect events in an explanatory narrative, but they are a species of covering law. Similarly, the elucidation of purpose is a vital step in most causal sequences, but (as I argue later) something very much like a covering law is necessary in the elucidation of purpose.

37. Miller, *Fact and Method*, 31–32. As always, Miller retreats to something very like a covering law when he writes (p. 31) that the dropping of a tortoise on Aeschylus's head could be viewed as the realization of a general property at a certain time.

38. Stover, *The Nature of Historical Thinking*, 62.

4 THE NATURE OF COVERING LAWS

The historian is not fussier than his fellow-men. He will explain the Duke of Guise's death as being the result of an assassin's stab, although he knows that not all stab wounds kill.

— John Passmore, "Explanation in Everyday Life, in Science, and in History"

The indispensable role of covering laws in tracing a causal sequence raises the question: what is the nature of those laws? The answer is complex but takes on some order if one examines what they are and what they are not. Covering laws are

1. probable, not invariable;
2. parochial, not universal;
3. empirical, not analytical;
4. predictive, as well as explanatory;
5. inductive, not deductive;
6. implicit, not explicit.

Probable, Not Invariable

Upon one issue all analytical philosophers seem to agree: the laws historians actually use are probable, not invariable; statistical, not deterministic. In the natural sciences one finds strictly deterministic laws, that is, laws to which there are no exceptions, but not in the social sciences, or in history.

Does the fact that historians use probable and not strictly deterministic laws destroy the efficacy of the covering-law model? Michael Scriven answers quite emphatically, yes. "Weakening the universal [i.e., invariable] law to a probability assertion," he writes, "shatters the deductive model."[1] Alan Donagan likewise observes, "One objection [to the Hempelian model] seems to be decisive: an explanation which rests on an approximate generalization cannot entail what it explains, and so must fall short of the *a priori* condition that it may allow no alternative to what it explains."[2] Yet a distinction can be made—and Carl Hempel makes it— between deductive-nomological explanations and probabilistic-statistical explanations, both of which are species of the covering-law model.[3] The deductive-nomological model allows one to deduce with *certainty* that given the initial conditions and an invariable law, an event will occur. The probabilistic-statistical model only allows one to deduce from the initial conditions and a statistical law that the event *might* occur. But in both cases the procedure is the same: initial conditions are subsumed under a covering law. Thus, weakening an invariable law to a probability assertion does shatter the deductive-nomological model, but it does not shatter the probabilistic-statistical model, which is an important variant of the covering-law model.

But does the probabilistic-statistical model allow the historian to explain a singular event? Donagan is convinced it does not. Such explanations, he argues, do not explain individual events, they only explain mass events. That 6 percent of smokers develop lung cancer may explain why six million smokers will develop lung cancer, but says nothing about a particular cigarette smoker. If a man, blindfolded, draws a white marble from an urn, it is not an adequate explanation of his drawing a white marble to point out that the urn contains 999 white marbles and only one black marble. If a man purchases a lottery ticket and loses, it is no explanation of his loss to say that he had only one chance in 100,000 to win. Reasonable expectations and explanations, Donagan asserts, differ fundamentally.[4] Were his arguments valid, the historian might as well close up shop. There could be no possibility of offering explanations. But fortunately, Donagan's arguments are not valid. His error, a common one, is to confuse a perfect explanation with an imper-

1. Scriven, "Truisms as the Grounds for Historical Explanations," 455.
2. Donagan, "Explanations in History," 433.
3. Hempel, "Aspects of Scientific Explanation," 378–93.
4. Donagan, "The Popper-Hempel Theory Reconsidered," 131–34.

fect explanation. He is entirely right that the probabilistic-statistical model does not allow a strictly logical deduction, that is, a perfect explanation. But it does allow imperfect explanations, explanations that approach perfection as the coefficient of correlation approaches 1. In fairness to Donagan it must be said that he finally admits this, writing, "Inductive-probabilistic explanations approach genuine explanations, in a measure as the statistical probability of the micro-mass events whose occurrence a genuine explanation must exclude approaches zero."[5] Only, he ought to have modified "explanation" with "perfect," not "genuine." In history, as in everyday life, the overwhelming majority of explanations are imperfect, but surely not fraudulent.

Hempel's model of a probabilistic-statistical explanation likewise requires a high probability of the event occurring. He does not believe that one can give a precise figure, say a coefficient of .8, above which such an explanation is valid and below which it is not, yet it must be high. His model allows the historian to explain why a blindfolded person drew a white ball from an urn filled with 999 white balls and one black ball. It cannot offer an explanation of so improbable an event as the drawing of a black ball.[6] Peter Railton, however, has devised a model, which he calls the deductive-nomological-probabilistic model, that does explain the occurrence of even improbable events. He illustrates it with an explanation of alpha decay in the nucleus of radionuclide uranium^{238}. This is an extremely improbable event, but if it does occur, it can be explained. He begins with the establishment of the law that all nuclei of uranium^{238} have a certain probability of emitting an alpha particle during a certain interval of time. He then states that u was such a nucleus of uranium^{238}. From this he deduces that u had that particular probability of decaying. Lastly, he gives the fact that u did alpha-decay during the interval. The law about the decay of the nuclei of uranium^{238}, together with the fact that u is such a nucleus and that alpha decay did occur, explains the occurrence of this improbable event. One could apply this model to the blindfolded person's pulling a black ball from the urn filled with 999 white balls and one black ball. It was an improbable event but, given the law of the composition of the balls in the urn, an explicable one.[7]

Railton and Hempel appear to be arguing over the nature of a probabilistic model of explanation, with Railton calling it "deductive" because one can deduce with certainty the occurrence of the explanandum event, and Hempel calling it "inductive" because one cannot deduce with certainty the occurrence of the explanandum event but can only infer that it

5. Ibid., 135.
6. Hempel, "Aspects of Scientific Explanation," 388–91.
7. Railton, "A Deductive-Nomological Model of Probabilistic Explanation," 213–19.

will probably occur. But in fact they are simply describing different uses of the same model. Railton uses the model to explain with certainty why, given a sufficient interval of time, an event will occur (ultimately the blindfolded person, if he keeps pulling out balls, will pull out a black one), but not at all why it occurs exactly when it does during that interval of time. Hempel uses the model to explain why an event occurred when it did (the pulling out of a white ball the first time), but he cannot explain this with certainty, only with high probability (.999). Looked at either way, the model offers useful explanations.

Railton makes the important observation that such probabilistic explanations depend upon the existence of a propensity to certain actions in individual chance systems.[8] This allows one to see that the probabilistic model is applicable to human conduct as well as physical systems. Imagine that one is at a tennis match, where one of the players is raging at the umpire for not overruling a linesman who called the player's second serve a fault. One turns to a friend and asks, "Why is that player raging so?" To which the friend replies, "That's John McEnroe. He never plays a tournament without raging at a line call sooner or later." This is an explanation, an explanation based on a knowledge of John McEnroe's propensity to rage at umpires who do not overrule close line calls that go against him. One cannot predict with certainty when McEnroe will erupt, but given his known propensity to erupt, one can predict that he will—sooner or later.

There are, it should be remarked, two kinds of indeterministic processes. Railton calls them "genuinely indeterministic processes" and "pseudo-random processes." Genuinely indeterministic processes are those—like alpha decay—in which the chance is written into the very fabric of nature. Pseudo-random processes occur when from ignorance of the initial conditions one is unable to describe the deterministic process that is actually there. Railton gives the example of the connection between mononucleosis and the swelling of the lymph glands. In 99 percent of cases of mononucleosis swelling of the lymph glands occurs. This could be due to a process that randomly misfires 1 percent of the time, or it could arise from an unknown deterministic process—call it X—that works to inhibit swelling and is present in one out of every hundred patients.[9] In the latter case a doctor, if he knew that X was present, could predict that the lymph glands would not swell. Even more to the point, when the lymph glands do not swell, he will explain it by the presence of X. Further research may discover the nature of X, allowing a complete explanation,

8. Ibid., 222.
9. Ibid., 209.

but even if the nature of X remains unknown, the doctor has offered an explanation of sorts, and one that fits the deductive-nomological model. Similarly, the observer of John McEnroe's behavior might posit a factor X that causes him to burst into a rage at the umpire when the umpire fails to overrule a close line call. Further research might even show X to be frustration at losing the previous few games. Whenever McEnroe begins to lose, he soon has a fit of rage. In this way a probabilistic explanation comes to resemble a deductive one. This possibility led Israel Scheffler to argue that there is "no incompatibility between the provision of a statistical explanation and the search for a deductive account of the phenomenon in question." He goes on to write, "We may, in fact, wish to construe statistical explanations as a special case of pragmatically incomplete deductive explanation, where needed elements are missing through ignorance. Such a construction seems obviously available everywhere except in the case of modern physical theory, which offers special arguments against it."[10] The discipline of history, being far removed from that of physics, allows its practitioners to construe statistical explanations as a special case of pragmatically incomplete deductive explanations.

There is yet another distinction between probabilistic explanations that must be made, that between statistical and inductive probability. Statistical probability describes the probability that the explanans statement being true, the explanandum event will occur. Inductive probability describes the probability that the explanans statement is true. The one, in Scheffler's words, gives "the *ground of the event*," and the other, "*grounds for acceptance* of the explanans as true." Scheffler gives the example of Dr. Jones, who explains a patient's high fever by listing such symptoms as a particular blood count, certain pains, and a specific pulse rate. But, Scheffler observes, it seems clearly inappropriate to take the patient's blood count, pain, and pulse as providing a causal account of the fever. Rather, they give the doctor grounds for believing that the patient has disease D and that the presence of D accounts for the high fever. The symptoms listed do not explain the fever; rather, they support the diagnosis of D, which explains the fever.[11] Similarly, it might be that John McEnroe, shortly before his eruption into rage, exhibited symptoms of frustration—banging his racket on the ground, glaring at the ball boy, stomping his foot. They might be seen as symptoms of a frustration that would soon lead to rage. Yet they may not be symptoms of frustration, in which case one would be wrong to attribute frustration to McEnroe. Or it might be that frustration at losing did not always lead to

10. Scheffler, *The Anatomy of Inquiry*, 35.
11. Ibid., 39–40.

rage at the umpire, in which case one might be wrong to offer it as an explanation of his rage. As Hart and Honoré observe, "The knowledge may be incomplete either because the best generalization available is a statement of frequencies or because the evidence, either for a fact or for a generalization, is inconclusive."[12]

These considerations raise two important questions: What degree of confirmation is necessary to establish a valid generalization? And what degree of probability is necessary to make the generalization useful in an explanation?

To the first question no more definite answer can be given than this: the more instances built upon, the better. Suppose the generalization was the statement "Charles I often broke his word." The more instances both of Charles's breaking his word and of his keeping his word that are observed, the more dependable will be any generalization about his faithlessness. To which one may add that the more informed and perceptive the historian is, the more accurate will be the historian's generalizations. This explains why a historian of great perspecuity and experience, who reads widely and deeply in the archives of an age, can write better history than the fledgling graduate student, why a Maurice Powicke can formulate more assured generalizations about the conduct of thirteenth-century English bishops than can a beginner, or a Norman Gash write more assuredly about nineteenth-century English politicians. William Dray and Michael Scriven have spoken of the historian's judgment as though it were some mystical power. It is not. The excellence of a historian's judgment lies in the degree of his or her knowledge of the conduct of thirteenth-century bishops and nineteenth-century politicians. By immersing themselves in the archives of an age, historians can frame to themselves more dependable covering laws.

To the question, how probable must the probability be that a generalization asserts? William Alston has answered, at least "greater than would be expected on the basis of chance alone."[13] Nicholas Rescher has given a similar answer: "With a probabilistic explanation, the explanatory premises do not provide a guarantee of the conclusion, but merely render it relatively likely, and so endow it with a relatively substantial (conditional) probability, say, one in excess of one half, or perhaps some other specified value K in the interval $0.5 < k < 1$."[14] Thus Charles I's faithlessness need not have been exhibited every time he made a promise, or even over half the times, but surely more often than most men break their promises.

12. Hart and Honoré, *Causation in the Law*, 415.
13. Alston, "The Place of the Explanation of Particular Facts in Science," 27.
14. Rescher, *Scientific Explanation*, 37.

Clearly the explanatory premise must assert a probability greater than expected on the basis of chance, but how much greater? There can be no definite answer. Rather, the historian should think in terms of stronger and weaker explanations. All explanations could be placed on a gradient from the strongest to the weakest. That a particular explanation is weak should not cause historians to reject it, though it should cause them to label it weak. Indeed, historians often do, writing that "certainly he acted from anger," or "probably," or "possibly."

Though historians may have to accept a weak explanation, they ought to strive to discover stronger ones. Toward this end, historians have adopted at least five strategies: model building, quantification, redescription, elimination analysis, and microcorrelation. In my judgment the first two are blind alleys, the other three are not, but they all deserve discussion.

Economists and political scientists, through the building of models, have sought to find exact laws for "ideal" conditions and for "pure cases" of the phenomena they are investigating. To overcome the use of laws of low probability they create a model composed of lawful relations of high probability. But as Ernest Nagel has observed, the discrepancy between the assumed conditions for which the laws are stated and the actual circumstances of the marketplace or political arena are so great as to make this strategy of dubious value.[15] Nor have the typological concepts favored by Max Weber proved fruitful of explanations, since his "ideal types" are too abstract to be of use in explanations. Models and typologies have at most a heuristic value to the historian. "The importance of models for the historian," concludes Geoffrey Barraclough, "is not that they offer him solutions, but that they indicate relationships and patterns which he can profitably employ in interpreting historical evidence."[16]

May Brodbeck has pointed out that assertions of probability are of two kinds: statistical statements and nonquantified generalizations.[17] Demographers, psephologists, and economic historians use the former, since birth rates, electoral returns, and the volume of trade can be given a statistical expression. But most historians use nonquantified generalizations as covering laws. "Politicians are ambitious." "Parliaments resent violations of their privileges." "Baseball gloves stop fly balls." "Charles I often breaks his word." And so forth. Now, such statements, as the social-science historian urges, can be quantified. One could, for example, put the intensity of a politician's ambition on a scale from one to ten,

15. Nagel, *The Structure of Science*, 509.
16. Barraclough, *Main Trends in History*, 59.
17. Brodbeck, "Explanation, Prediction, and 'Imperfect' Knowledge," 245.

or even from one to a hundred. But if one used such a scale to give a more precise measurement of a politician's ambition than the evidence justified, one would have committed a grievous error. A physicist, working in a laboratory, will allow for a margin of error arising from the imprecision of the instruments. Thus, he or she might give an answer as $3.56 \pm .03$. A scrupulous historian who sought to rank a politician's ambition on a scale of 0 to 10 would, in order to allow for the imprecision of evidence, have to write 6 ± 3, at which point it might be more sensible to fall back on the English language and write that he was extremely ambitious. A spurious precision in expression cannot heighten the probability of a covering law.

A redescription of the event to be explained, however, often can. To redescribe an event means to describe it in a more abstract, less concrete manner. One example will suffice to illustrate how such a redescription can allow the historian to use a more credible covering law. Frederick George Maitland, in order to explain why Queen Elizabeth placed an "etc." in her title, states that she was being deliberately ambiguous in order to delay committing herself either to acknowledging Rome's authority or breaking from it.[18] But Maitland's explanation does not tell us why Elizabeth used the expression "etc." rather than the expression "and so forth." If it were the historian's duty to explain that particular detail, he or she would be hard put to it to find any law to cover the explanation. Historians possess little information about Elizabeth's proclivity for "etc." rather than "and so forth," but they possess folios of information about her proclivity for ambiguity and delay. Furthermore, a covering law that described Elizabeth's proclivity for "etc." rather than "and so forth" would not explain why she used one of them. Most difficult of all would it be to find a law that covered both her decision to delay by means of ambiguity and her decision to use "etc." rather than "and so forth" to express that ambiguity. Maitland wisely chose the more abstract path. By regarding (i.e., redescribing) "etc." as an act of ambiguity, he was able to offer an explanation that was supported by a covering law of heightened probability. In doing so he no doubt limited the range of what he explained, but what he lost in completeness he regained in certainty. Yet redescription cannot be pressed too far, or (as shown in Chapter 1) crucial aspects of the event to be explained will be lost. Rex Martin rightly chides Arthur Danto for redescribing Caesar's invasion of Britain as "levelling inhibiting sanctions," since it sacrifices the crucial idea of invasion.[19] But though redescribing has only a limited use, it has a real one.

18. The illustration is drawn from Nagel, *The Structure of Science*, 552–58.
19. Martin, *Historical Explanation*, 109–10.

In fact historians are constantly, though unconsciously, redescribing. One concludes that the truck, not the cough, caused the dent in the fender of the parked car, yet one may never have seen a truck dent a fender. But one has seen other cars dent fenders. One immediately brings the incident under the covering law that heavy objects colliding with a fender will cause a dent in the fender.

There is a final aspect of redescription that deserves attention. Though it sacrifices certain details, it allows the narrative to be carried on. The historian of the Elizabethan settlement in the Church will be able to carry forward an explanatory narrative from Elizabeth's accession to the throne to the Acts of Supremacy and Uniformity. A covering law need not explain everything in order to bridge the gaps in an explanatory sequence of events. Elizabeth's proclivity for ambiguity and delay explains the "etc." in her title. The "etc." in her title helps explain the slowness of Rome in opposing her accession to the throne.

More effective even than redescription in securing explanatory reliability is the elimination of other possible causes, a logical process that Scriven calls "elimination analysis." Scriven chooses as an illustration of such an analysis Merriman's explanation of Cortés's third expedition to Baja California. Cortés, argues Merriman, embarked upon the expedition out of cupidity and confidence. This assertion takes on more credibility if all other possible causes—such as that he acted from stupidity or from fear of recall—are eliminated.[20] His career until that moment had revealed a far greater disposition toward cupidity and confidence than toward stupidity and fear. Other illustrations make the logic of elimination analysis even clearer. What cause other than Charles I's attempt to arrest the Five Members in January 1642 could explain the anger and fear of members of the House of Commons? Surely not the forthcoming wedding of Charles's daughter to the Prince of Orange, or the nomination of Lord Falkland as secretary of state, or an early snow storm that year. For want of any other credible explanation, the explanation based upon the covering law about Parliament's resenting any violation of its privileges takes on greater certitude. The certitude created by the absence of any other remotely credible cause goes far toward explaining why historians feel so confident in their explanations, though based on covering laws that are only probable.

Scriven's insight into the role of elimination analysis in historical explanation is profound and important, but his assertion that elimination analysis "does not require deduction or general laws of the usual kind"

---

20. Scriven, "Truisms as the Grounds for Historical Explanations," 447–58, and idem, "Explanations, Predictions, and Laws," 219–24.

is mistaken. How does the historian decide that cupidity and confidence afford a more credible explanation of Cortés's behavior than stupidity or fear?[21] To this question Scriven answers, "By refusing to accept a covering law answer to such a question, I do not intend to deny a link between the particular case and our general experience." In short, under the name of "general experience" he smuggles covering laws back into his explanation. Seeing this, he rapidly retreats, writing, "It is the particular fact, not the general propositions or the derivation, which provides the explanations in such cases."[22] Therein he is likewise mistaken. It is the particular facts in conjunction with the general proposition that form the two premises of the explanans, and it is the explanans that explains the occurrence of the explanandum. Throughout his articles Scriven refers to truisms and to normic statements as if they were not covering laws; but they are covering laws. They are statements of regularities, statements that the historian uses to explain the course of events. The disposition of the House of Commons to resent violations of its privileges is a truism requisite to an explanation of its anger at Charles's attempt to arrest the Five Members.

Raymond Martin and Richard Miller have both taken up Michael Scriven's idea of elimination analysis and made it a central argument of their recent books. "A historian," writes Martin, "may be able to show that his favored explanation is better than the best competing explanations without defending a covering law for it."[23] And Miller writes, "The comparison of rival hypotheses is an aspect of testing that can also provide an empirical warrant for the explanations in the absence of covering-laws."[24] These confident assertions raise two questions: By what logic does the historian decide that one explanation is better than the other? And why would not that same logic allow him or her to assess the truth of a single explanation?

Martin answers the first question by declaring that explanation A is better than explanation B if the arguments for the explanans in A having occurred are stronger than the arguments for the explanans in B having occurred, and if the explanans in A is a more sufficient explanation of the explanandum than is the explanans in B. To determine which arguments are the stronger for the occurrence of the two explanans, historians of

21. There is another means, based on his subsequent actions, to decide upon Cortés's motives. See Chapter 8, "Purposive Action."

22. Scriven, "Explanations, Predictions, and Laws," 222; idem, "Causes, Connections, and Conditions in History," 250; idem, "Truisms as the Grounds for Historical Explanations," 462.

23. Martin, *The Past Within Us,* 22.

24. Miller, *Fact and Method,* 50.

every stripe will resort to the usual methods of historical research. But how do historians decide which explanans is more sufficient? Martin's answer is vague. On one page he speaks of "the explanatory relevance of the explanans to the explanandum"; on another page, of some facts in the explanans having "a lawful relationship to facts of the same sort" in the explanandum.[25] Though he does not speak of covering laws, surely he is referring to covering laws. Martin also remarks on the absence (in the historical literature he examined) of arguments *for* the sufficiency of the explanans, and he implies that this shows that an explanation can be shown to be better than another without the employment of covering laws.[26] But Martin found no such arguments, because he was searching for explanations based on macrolaws, and no macrolaw can survive the rigors of historical research. Had he recognized that historians explain by tracing, he would have looked for those microlaws that connect steps in a colligatory sequence. True, he would not then have found explicit arguments *for* the sufficiency of an explanans, since historians do not make explicit the covering laws that form the explanans. But if challenged they could offer explicit arguments *for* the sufficiency of the covering laws contained in the explanans.

Miller answers the first question by referring the reader to the earlier part of his book: "A hypothesis is confirmed if there is a fair argument that its approximate truth, and the basic falsehood of current rivals, is entailed by the best causal account of the history of the data-gathering and theorizing so far. The relevant notion of a causal account is that specified in the theory of explanation in the first third of this book."[27] The notion of a causal account given there requires the historian to rely upon framework principles and truisms, principles and truisms that closely resemble covering laws.

Neither Miller nor Martin poses or answers the second question: why can the same logic that is used to compare two explanations not be used to judge the sufficiency of one explanation? The answer is that there are no reasons, and that historians, unless a controversy arises, do not compare rival explanations. They seek to discover and to elucidate a single explanation. This is particularly true when they must trace a complex chain or cone of causation leading to the event to be explained, using many different covering laws to connect the many links in the chain or cone. But these observations are not meant to diminish the force of Scriven's elimination analysis. The fact that no credible covering law can

25. Martin, *The Past Within Us*, 40, 42.
26. Ibid., 43–44.
27. Miller, *Fact and Method*, 7.

be found to challenge the covering law being used greatly enhances its credibility.

More effective than either redescription or elimination analysis in strengthening an explanation is microcorrelation, that is, the minute tracing of the explanatory narrative to the point where the events to be explained are microscopic and the covering laws correspondingly more certain. Redescription applied to macroscopic phenomena, such as revolutions, reformations, wars, invasions, and enlightenments, leads (as has been argued) to vacuous explanations, since crucial detail must be excluded. In a like manner, elimination analysis of macroscopic phenomena is barren because all macro–covering laws are barren. There are no valid laws under which the historian can subsume a revolution or a reformation or a war or an invasion or an enlightenment. But if one pursues a causal sequence of events in sufficient detail, then one need only explain why Elizabeth used "etc." or Cortés decided to go to Baja California. The more microscopic the event to be explained, the more likely that the covering law will be a platitude—or, in Scriven's terminology, a truism. Scriven gives the example of a man reaching for a dictionary, whose knee catches the edge of the table, thus turning over an ink bottle, whose contents run across the table, fall onto the carpet, and ruin it.[28] Consider but one step in the causal sequence, the ink dropping from the table to the carpet. In this instance the covering law is a platitude, the law of gravitation. But though a platitude, it possesses the highest degree of probability. Or consider William Dray's account of the outfielder who caught the fly ball. The last step in this causal sequence was the outfielder's glove stopping the flight of the ball. That an outfielder's glove will stop the flight of a baseball is a truism, but in this instance it is also a covering law that allows one to assert that the glove, and not a simultaneous shout from the grandstand, stopped the ball. Furthermore, it is only a law of probability. Outfielders have dropped fly balls. The fact that we do not reason about it in no way contradicts the proposition that the high probability of the glove stopping the ball and the low probability of the shout stopping it give the explanation its logical warrant.

What truly gives strength to historical explanation is the combination of redescription, elimination analysis, and microcorrelation. The historian pursues to the most microscopic level possible the sequence of events leading to the phenomenon to be explained. He then redescribes those microscopic events so that he can subsume them under a covering law, and so bridge the gaps within the sequence. At the same time, he searches for other possible redescriptions and covering laws, but finding

28. Scriven, "Truisms as the Grounds for Historical Explanations," 456–57.

none that are credible, he returns to the original redescription and micro–covering laws. All this he probably does without regarding the logical nature of what he is doing, but the resulting conclusion is not weaker for that reason. It is the combined effect of these three operations that explains why historians, though they use laws that are only probable, can nevertheless give explanations that are convincing.

Parochial, Not Universal

The above analysis leads to a second characteristic of the covering laws employed by historians: they are parochial rather than universal, meaning that they apply to narrow groups, not broad ones. For example, a historian seeking to explain why Elizabeth used "etc." in her title would instinctively refer neither to a disposition to delay in all humankind nor to a disposition to delay in all monarchs, but to a disposition to delay in Queen Elizabeth. This fact escaped Ernest Nagel, who first propounded this example. To justify Maitland's explanation of Elizabeth's action, he offers a general law about the conduct of all individuals in her situation; then he admits that such a law would not be true of all persons, and thus must be probabilistic.[29] He fails to see that a law solely about Elizabeth's conduct would be less probabilistic. (Even if the majority of humankind were more prone to delay than Elizabeth, the historian would choose the parochial law as more accurately describing Elizabeth's behavior.) Arthur Danto makes a similar error in explaining how an observer could conclude that Princess Grace's being an American was the cause of the presence of American flags on the streets of Monaco on a public holiday. He offers the following covering law: "Whenever a nation has a sovereign of a different national origin than its own citizens, those citizens will, on the appropriate occasions, honor the sovereign in some acceptable fashion."[30] This is too universal. A historian would be more likely to write, On public holidays the citizens of Monaco customarily raise the flag of the Princess's country of origin. This does not mean that a historian never uses a universal law, only that he or she will prefer the more parochial law if available. Such a law may be parochial because it refers to a single person rather than to a type, or to a type rather than to all humankind. Or it may be parochial because it refers to a person in particular circumstances. Dray calls such laws "highly specified," Scriven "qualified," Frankel "restrictive," White

29. Nagel, *The Structure of Science*, 556.
30. Danto, *Analytical Philosophy of History*, 220–21.

"complex," and Donagan "closed"; but under whatever name, they are parochial in the sense that they are less all-encompassing, less universal.[31] The covering laws available to a historian are like a spectrum, ranging from the most universal, say, about human nature in all ages, to the most parochial, say, about the conduct of Queen Elizabeth during her first decade on the throne. And the historian habitually chooses the more parochial, if available.

Indeed, the scientist, too, will chose—must choose—the more parochial law in a probabilistic explanation. Carl Hempel calls this "the requirement of maximal specificity for inductive-statistical explanations." He illustrates it with an explanation of Jones's recovery from a streptococcal infection when treated with penicillin. His chances of recovery are high if he is regarded as a member of a group including all patients, but low if regarded as a member of a group of octogenerians with weak hearts. As Hempel puts it:

> Indeed, one would want an acceptable explanation to be based on a statistical probability statement pertaining to the narrowest reference class of which, according to our total information, the particular occurrence under consideration is a member. Thus if K [the total information] tells us not only that Jones had a streptococcus infection and was treated with penicillin, but also that he was an octogenerian with a weak heart (and if K provides no information more specific than that) then we would require that an acceptable explanation of Jones's response to the treatment be based on a statistical law stating the probability of that response in the narrowest reference class to which our total information assigns Jones's illness, i.e., the class of streptococcal infections suffered by octogenerians with weak hearts.[32]

Without knowing the technical term for it, historians have long accepted "the requirement of maximal specificity."

To this reliance on parochial laws in historical explanation some students of logic have objected. Dray suggests that a law so highly specified is trivial and serves no methodological purpose, since "it is, or very well may be, a 'law' with only a single case."[33] Mandelbaum, discussing the

31. Dray, *Laws and Explanation in History,* 39; Scriven, "Causes, Connections, and Conditions in History," 246; Frankel, "Explanation and Interpretation in History," 416; White, *Foundations of Historical Knowledge,* 22; Donagan, "Explanation History," 435.

32. Hempel, "Aspects of Scientific Explanation," 398.

33. Dray, *Laws and Explanation in History,* 39.

fact that ordinary wood floats and waterlogged wood sinks, concludes that the covering-law model fails to explain this phenomenon, since the need to define the law more narrowly defeats the attempt to establish correlation.[34] Scriven declares that one cannot include time or space in the description of an event, because then it would not be a "kind of event."[35] And Robert Stover maintains that "a causal account is incomplete if we cannot remove from the description of causes references to particular times, places, persons, and things."[36] These objections do have some validity. If historians push parochialism to the point where there is only a single case, where there are no other comparable cases, then they have defeated explanation. If the space and time encompassed by a covering law are shrunk to a single space, Queen Elizabeth in her closet, and a single moment in time, ten in the morning on 1 December 1558, then there can be no covering law at all, only the description of an event or state. But there is no statute that declares that historians must do this, nor do they do so. Historians do limit their covering laws in space and time, but they do not shrink them to a point. They, or more likely scientists, will establish one law for wood that is waterlogged and another law for wood that is not waterlogged, but they will not seek to establish a law for a single log found in Dyer's Bay and observed only once, on 15 July 1984.

These considerations raise the question: How many instances would a law be required to have? Hempel has posed this very question and answered it as follows. "To insist on some particular finite number would be arbitrary, and the requirement of an infinite number of actual instances raises obvious difficulties. Clearly, the concept of scientific law cannot reasonably be subjected to any condition concerning the number of instances, except for the requirement barring logical equivalence with singular statements."[37] Hempel is surely right. A law with only a single case is an impossibility. The logic of induction requires that there be a number of instances to establish a law. Indeed, if historians did seek to employ in an explanans statement a law based on a single instance, they would open themselves to the charge of committing the fallacy of *post hoc, ergo propter hoc*. And those who believe that explanation is possible without a covering law must needs show how one singular event can be shown to have caused another singular event.

The objection of the logicians to the use of highly specified laws are

34. Mandelbaum, *The Anatomy of Historical Knowledge*, 100.
35. Scriven, "Truisms as the Grounds for Historical Explanations," 474.
36. Stover, *The Nature of Historical Thinking*, 53.
37. Hempel, "Aspects of Scientific Explanation," 341.

largely theoretical, but two very practical considerations have arisen in this regard: Can the historian form covering laws about the conduct of a single individual? And are the laws of past ages different from those of the present?

To the first question Dray, Donagan, and Scriven appear to answer no. I say "appear" because they hedge their answers with qualifications. Dray declares that explanations based on the dispositions of individuals, because of their particularity, fall short of law-covered explanation, but then admits that to explain Disraeli's attack upon Peel by referring to his ambition does subsume his action under a regularity.[38] Donagan admits that to call Bertrand Barère a "political animal" is to make a dispositional statement about him, but then asserts that such a statement is a hypothetical proposition, not an empirical regularity. Later he declares that individual men and women have been known consistently to exhibit traits of character, and that historians have explained actions in terms of such traits, but he then adds that such traits are "logical constructions," not laws.[39] In "The Popper-Hempel Theory Reconsidered" Donagan is even more emphatic in denying that laws can be about individuals.

> Only when a singular hypothetical is presented as a special case of a universal hypothetical is it accepted by natural scientists as explanatory. Hence the true objection to recognizing as covering laws generalizations which apply only to named individuals is *not* that such generalizations cannot be scientifically substantiated. They can be. It is that scientists require an explanation to exhibit a connection between the initial conditions and the event to be explained, which generalizations applying only to named individuals cannot do. The connection between John's taking arsenic and John's having a pain in the throat is that John is a man; that between Mars and following an elliptical orbit is that Mars is a planet. It is because such connections can only be expressed by strictly universal statements, that the Popper-Hempel theory cannot recognize as a possible covering law any statement which is not strictly universal.[40]

Had Donagan taken as an example not John's taking arsenic but his taking aspirin when allergic to aspirin, then he would have seen the hollowness

---

38. Dray, *Laws and Explanation in History*, 146. In the second edition of his *Philosophy of History*, published in 1993, Dray accepts "limited-law explanations"; see 25.

39. Donagan, "Alternative Historical Explanations and Their Verification," 67–72.

40. Donagan, "The Popper-Hempel Theory Reconsidered," 140–41.

of his argument. If John suffered stomach pains every time he took aspirin, this would explain why, when he took aspirin on Friday, he developed stomach pains. This explanation remains valid even though the great majority of persons do not develop stomach pains on taking aspirin.

Scriven, in seeking to explain Cortés's actions, finds a law about his cupidity and confidence to be trivial and "possibly to have only one instance, viz., Cortés in this situation."[41] The addition of the words "in this situation" makes this assertion of singularity undoubtedly true, but the accusation of singularity would not apply to a display of Cortés's cupidity on many other occasions—a possible generalization that Scriven passes over in silence. The truth is that the conduct of an individual does exhibit regularity, a regularity historians observe empirically and use in explanation. As J. O. Wisdom has observed, "although the assertion of a disposition about a particular person, such as Hitler, may appear to be a particular, nonetheless its mode of operation is general."[42] Or as Henry Fielding said many years ago, a novelist should not only depict actions all humans may be likely to do, but actions an individual might be likely to do, "for what may be only wonderful and surprising in one man, may become improbable, or indeed impossible, when related of another." Then he adds, "I will venture to say, that for a man to act in direct contradiction to the dictates of his nature, is, if not impossible, as improbable and as miraculous as anything which can well be conceived."[43]

The question whether the laws of the past are different from the laws of the present has embarrassed both the Idealists and the Positivists, both R. G. Collingwood and Karl Popper. Collingwood faced the cruelest dilemma, for as heir to the historicist tradition he asserted that the past differed from the present, but as heir to an idealistic tradition he believed that historians were able to rethink the thoughts of past historical actors, a belief that implied a continuity between past and present.[44] Popper faced a less cruel dilemma, since he roundly denounced the historicist contention that the validity of historical generalizations is confined to the historical period in which they are observed. Yet even he had to admit that some laws, even scientific laws, have lost their validity.[45]

41. Scriven, "Truisms as the Grounds for Historical Explanations," 455.
42. Wisdom, "General Explanation in History," 259–60.
43. Fielding, *Tom Jones*, 337–38.
44. For a clear exposition of Collingwood's dilemma, see Martin, *Historical Explanation*, 44–47.
45. Popper, *The Poverty of Historicism*, 99–102. Yet in his *Objective Knowledge*, 193, Popper declares, "Only if we require that explanation shall make use of universal statements or laws of nature (supplemented by initial conditions) can we make progress towards realizing the idea of independent, or non–*ad hoc*, explanations."

Since the rise of historicism in the nineteenth century, historians have had no such doubts. They have insisted that one use the laws of a past age or of a different culture to explain that age or that culture. Mark Bloch observes that historians differ from sociologists in their attitude toward time, the historian seeing change, the sociologist continuity.[46] David Hackett Fischer castigates "the fallacy of the universal man."[47] And Isaiah Berlin regards it as absurd to blame Richelieu for not acting like Bismarck, since "the seventeenth century had its own character."[48] Indeed, Terence Ball maintains that what makes a historical explanation historical is its reliance on temporal, rather than universal, laws.[49]

The problem does arise, therefore: if the past is different from the present, then how is it accessible to historians today? The answer is twofold. First, the past is not wholly unlike the present—the languages of the past, for example, can be translated into modern languages. And, second, historians may learn that language, decipher it, and then immerse themselves in the records of the age. "The right way to understand history," runs a familiar adage, "is to go on reading till you can hear the people talking."

Many social scientists cling to the use of universal laws in explanation because they believe that universal laws carry greater explanatory strength than do parochial laws. Are they right in this contention? In order to answer this question one must first distinguish between the strength of a law to explain many events, or many steps in a narrative of events, and the strength of a law to explain a single event, or a single step in a narrative of events. The sociologist, the political scientist, and the economist strive for laws that explain many events, for which reason general laws do have, for them, greater explanatory strength. But few historians seek such laws. Most historians seek only that law which allows them to explain a single step in a sequence of events. To that purpose they seek the law that, having a higher probability, is more likely to explain that step; and it is the parochial law that has the higher probability.[50]

General laws certainly do have a role to play in historical explanation, though that role is subordinate to parochial laws. The subtle analysis of the projectivity of hypotheses by Nelson Goodman suggests both why

46. Bloch, *The Historian's Craft*, 27–29.

47. Fischer, *Historians' Fallacies*, 203–7.

48. Berlin, "The Concept of Scientific History," 10.

49. Ball, "On 'Historical' Explanation," 183–84.

50. Nicholas Rescher (*Scientific Explanation*, 65–66) draws a distinction between the explanatory strength and the explanatory power of an explanation. For a discussion of this distinction, see below, pages 99–100.

they do and why they are subordinate. He argues that information about a predicate (say, about a single soldier in the Twenty-sixth Division) increases the credibility of a hypothesis about that predicate more than information about the parent predicate (that is, about all soldiers in the Twenty-sixth Division). There are, of course, occasions when one has too little information to support a hypothesis and so must rely upon an overhypothesis (to use Goodman's term), but even then "the effect of overhypotheses varies inversely with their generality."[51] Nicholas Rescher gives an illuminating example of the tug-of-war between such hypotheses. He presents three explanatory accounts:[52]

1. Mr. X is an American rug dealer, and 90 percent of them are Armenian.
2. Mr. X is an Ohio rug dealer, and 70 percent of them are Armenian.
3. Mr. X is a Cleveland rug dealer, and 30 percent of them are Armenian.

He then observes that the third explanation why Mr. X might be thought to be an Armenian is the "worst" of the group because it endows the assertion that Mr. X is of Armenian descent with a lower conditional probability than do (1) or (2).[53] Herein he is in error. The third explanation is the "best" because it would lead to fewer errors in judging whether a Cleveland rug dealer is an Armenian. The fact that 90 percent of American rug dealers are Armenian would lead a historian confidently to predict that Mr. X was Armenian, but he would be in error 70 percent of the time. Knowing that Mr. X was from Ohio would make the historian less confident, but still far too confident. But knowing that Mr. X was a Cleveland rug dealer would lead the historian to say that there was only a 30 percent chance that he was Armenian.

One can also show that a law clogged with qualifications, far from being less explanatory, is more explanatory. Recently a lawyer in Chicago was shot in the parking lot of a supermarket. He was shot with a twenty-two caliber pistol, which led the police to suspect that he was shot by the Mafia, since the Mafia always uses twenty-two caliber pistols in gangland killings. Yet so do ordinary robbers, so there would exist only about a 10 percent probability that the Mafia murdered the lawyer. But no money was taken from the murdered lawyer, which is also characteristic of gangland killings. Yet an ordinary robber, frightened by what he had done, might run off without taking the money. The fact that the lawyer still had his wallet might lend a 30 percent probability to the

51. Goodman, *Fact, Fiction, and Forecast*, 108–19.
52. Rescher, *Scientific Explanation*, 59–60.
53. Ibid., 60.

hypothesis that the Mafia killed him. Furthermore, the lawyer was shot in the chest, which is also characteristic of gangland killings, not the back. That fact alone might lend a 30 percent probability to the hypothesis that the Mafia killed him. But the probability that the Mafia shot him becomes much higher if one uses a covering law clogged with all these qualifications, namely, that whenever a man is (1) shot by a twenty-two caliber revolver, (2) in the chest, and (3) his money is not taken, then it is about 70 percent likely that the Mafia shot him. Add the qualification that the lawyer had recently represented a rival branch of the Mafia in court, and the probability that the Mafia shot him soars to near 100 percent.

The important fact to remember is that a covering law in a historical explanation has one, and only one, function: to bridge the gap from one step to another in a narrative, thereby allowing the historian to trace the course of events leading to the phenomenon to be explained.

Empirical, Not Analytical

The belief that explanations need not rely on covering laws that are empirical owes much to Gilbert Ryle's discussion of dispositional statements in *The Concept of the Mind.* In that book he distinguishes between the assertion that the window broke because a stone hit it and the assertion that the window broke because it was brittle. The former assertion requires a causal law and fits the Hempelian model; the latter does not. It does not because dispositional statements (though lawlike) are not laws, do not report observable states of affairs, and narrate no incidents. Dispositional statements are "inference tickets," which license one, using "rules of inference," to connect the window's being brittle with the window's breaking.[54]

The difficulty with this analysis is that talk of inference tickets and rules of inference is quite unnecessary, a needless multiplication of entities. To say that the window broke because it was brittle is merely an elliptical way of saying that it broke because stones break brittle windows. Take the explanandum event to be a broken window. The explanans statement, following the Hempelian model, would be made up of two parts, the statement of a singular event and the statement of a regularity. The statement of the singular event is implied rather than explicitly stated, namely, that a stone hit the window. The statement of

54. Ryle, *The Concept of Mind,* 43–44, 88–89, 123–25.

the regularity is partly implied and partly stated explicitly, namely, windows that are both brittle and hit by stones nearly always break. The dispositional explanation that the window broke because brittle is merely an elliptical way of stating a causal explanation based on the empirical law that windows that are both brittle and hit by stones nearly always break. Or, as Carl Hempel expresses it, "there is no difference in the strength of the claims, but only in the mode of expressing them."[55] Or, as Israel Scheffler remarks, Ryle's "explanation *conforms* to the deductive pattern, rather than *diverging* from it."[56]

As is argued later, one event does not cause another; a match carelessly thrown away does not cause a fire. Rather, a set of conditions—a thrown away match, dry twigs, and the presence of oxygen—causes the fire. The brittleness of the glass was one aspect of the conditions that caused the window to break, so also was a thrown stone; and perhaps one should add other conditions, such as the fact that the stone was thrown at a speed of more than ten miles an hour. All statements of causation are elliptical, leaving something unsaid. To emphasize the brittleness of the glass as a cause is perfectly proper, but it does not allow one to dismiss as irrelevant the other, implied conditions. Indeed, the assertion Gilbert Ryle regards as satisfying the Hempelian model—the window broke because a stone hit it—leaves much unsaid, particularly that the glass was brittle. Stones do not break shatter-proof glass. W. W. Bartley, defending the Popper model, puts the matter most succinctly, "Where Ryle says there are two kinds of explanation, Popper would say there are two kinds of conditions."[57]

It is, of course, possible to make the dispositional trait analytical. One does so by making it part of the definition of the object or person who displays it. I may define "brittle glass" as any glass that breaks when hit by a stone. Then if I declare that the glass broke because it was brittle, I am making an analytical deduction, not an empirical explanation. But I am also stating a tautology that has no explanatory power, such as Moliere's remark that opium puts people to sleep because it has a dormitive power. "We expect the explanatory premises in a satisfactory explanation," observes Ernest Nagel, "to assert something more than what is asserted by the *explicandum*."[58] In other words, if the regularity asserted in the explanans ("brittle glass breaks when hit by a stone") is already asserted by definition in the explicandum, then nothing is really explained.

55. Hempel, "Aspects of Scientific Explanation," 355.
56. Scheffler, *The Anatomy of Inquiry*, 85.
57. Bartley, "Achilles, the Tortoise, and Explanation," 24.
58. Nagel, *The Structure of Science*, 36.

Even sentences can be made analytical. Thus I can rewrite the sentence "If a person fears change, he will vote Tory" to read "If it is true that a person who fears change will vote Tory and John fears change, then John will vote Tory." But little has been gained, because the historian must first show that it is true that a person who fears change will vote Tory. Perhaps it was because he saw this that Gilbert Ryle opposed moving from "If P, then Q" to "If 'If P, then Q' and P, then Q." By declining to move to the second sentence he in effect admits that dispositional statements are empirical, not analytical.[59]

In his concept of "normic statements" Michael Scriven advocates an analytical scheme of explanation. He regards normic statements as a hybrid, containing some universal features (meaning there can be no exceptions) and some statistical features (meaning there can be exceptions). He gives an example of such a statement, "Strict Orthodox Jews fast on the Day of Atonement." To this there might be an exception—a strict Orthodox Jew might not fast if ill. But if these exceptions are all listed, then the statement becomes norm defining, that is, will have "a selective immunity to apparent counterexamples."[60] In this way Scriven believes he has brought back the certainty that Hempel's statistical model surrenders. But in fact all he has done is to define "strict Orthodox Jew" more elaborately, leaving fewer traits in the world of reality and placing more traits in the world of language. That is to say, traits such as "fasting on the Day of Atonement but not when ill" are made defining characteristics of strict Orthodox Jews rather than traits that in the real world are often associated with those calling themselves strict Orthodox Jews. R. F. Atkinson takes the same position as Scriven, arguing that when a historian explains that persons gave to charity because they were generous, the historian does not refer to the fact that experience shows that generous persons usually give to charity, but to the fact that if the persons did not give to charity, they could not be called "generous," since by definition "generous" persons are ones who give to charity. "This is not something one has to learn from experience," concludes Atkinson, "it comes from an understanding of the meaning of the word 'generous.' "[61]

---

59. Ryle defends his not moving to the second sentence by insisting that to admit rules of logic (e.g., rules of inference) as premises of an explanation would be to invite an infinite regression (Ryle, " 'If', 'So' and 'Because,' " 327–28). For a refutation of Ryle's argument, see W. W. Bartley, "Achilles, the Tortoise, and Explanation," 28–30, where he distinguishes between rules establishing the validity of an argument and evidence supporting the truth of a conclusion, and May Brodbeck, "Explanation, Prediction, and 'Imperfect' Knowledge," 257, where she distinguishes between the use of a rule and the justification of a rule.

60. Scriven, "Truisms as the Grounds for Historical Explanations," 459–66.

61. Atkinson, *Knowledge and Explanation in History*, 117.

A person cannot be imprisoned for loading down definitions with more and more defining characteristics, but one may ask, as May Brodbeck has asked, where will it all end? Remarking on Jones's vanity, she writes, "If there are an infinite number of lawlike statements expressing Jones's 'kind of vanity,' then where do we draw the line between what we mean by vanity and what happens to be connected with it, like his ambition or his gregariousness."[62] The whole exercise seems to be tautological and futile, yet there is a kernel of truth in what Scriven and Atkinson are saying. Historians who have learned much about Orthodox Jews and much about generous persons have insensibly transferred this knowledge to their definitions of Orthodox Jews and generous persons. Students of these historians then learn the definitions and apply them to explaining the past. Scientists, observes Ernest Nagel, "at first discovered copper to be a good conductor of electricity; in time this quality was made part of the definition of copper."[63] But it was experience that taught historians and scientists that Orthodox Jews fast on the Day of Atonement and that generous persons give to charity and that copper is a good conductor of electricity.

Scriven lists truisms among his normic statements, and cites several truisms about William the Conqueror (that he was a reasonable man, that he saw that Scotland was more of a danger to England than England had been to Normandy, that he had ample land for his supporters). He then declares that these truisms are not like the laws that Hempel's deductive model requires, since they are not universal, that is, without possible exceptions. This can be readily granted. But he goes on to say that neither are they statistical.[64] This, too, can be granted if by "statistical" he means "quantifiable." But it cannot be granted if by "statistical" he means "probable." His truisms, in fact, are probable laws (inasmuch as they are more than a description of fact), just as Ryle's dispositional statements are probable laws. Ryle admits that dispositional statements are "lawlike," but seems reluctant to call them laws. It seems to me that circumlocutions such as "lawlike" and "truisms" are unnecessary once a person admits that probable laws are laws.

Scriven's hostility to the Hempelian model leads him to one further criticism of the belief that laws are a part of an explanation. Laws are not, he argues, part of the explanation; they are only grounds that justify the explanation. To ask that the justification of the explanation be part of the explanation is like asking that the grounds for thinking a descriptive

62. Brodbeck, "Explanation, Prediction, and 'Imperfect' Knowledge," 272.
63. Nagel, *The Structure of Science*, 54.
64. Scriven, "Truisms as the Grounds for Historical Explanations," 459.

statement to be true be part of the statement. "But surely," he writes, "an explanation does not have to contain its own justification any more than a statement about Gandhi's death has to contain the evidence on which it is based."[65]

The parallel that he draws, however, is false, and once that falsity is exposed, his argument falls to the ground. In the covering-law model there are three terms: the initial conditions, the covering law, and the event to be explained. Now, a skeptic might demand the evidence to show that the initial conditions did in fact exist. He might also ask for the evidence that the covering law under which the initial conditions are subsumed was in fact true. And were he a total skeptic, he might even demand evidence that the event to be explained actually occurred. In each case the evidence demanded justifies one part of the explanation but is not part of it. The evidence plays a secondary role, not a primary role, in the explanation. But the three terms themselves (initial conditions, covering law, and the event to be explained) are primary, that is, they are indispensable to it. Now, it is true that the law is often not expressed, just as it is true that in an enthymeme one of the premises is not expressed, but neither enthymeme nor explanation has logical force without the unexpressed term. Scriven notwithstanding, laws are an integral part of a causal explanation.

Roses by any other name smell just as sweet, and empirical laws by any other name are just as central to historical explanation. Whether disguised as dispositional traits or inference tickets or truisms or normic statements or justifying statements, laws that describe the regularities to be found in the real world are crucial to any explanation why an event occurred.

Predictive, as well as Explanatory

In describing his model of historical explanation, Carl Hempel has insisted upon the structural identity, or symmetry, of explanation and prediction. An explanation is not complete, he argues, unless it might also function as a prediction. More precisely, he urges that, "any rationally acceptable answer to the question 'Why did event X occur?' must offer information which shows that X was to be expected—if not definitely, as in the case of D-N explanation, then at least with reasonable probability.

---

65. Ibid., 445–46; idem, "Explanations, Predictions, and Laws," 196–97; idem, "New Issues in the Logic of Explanation," 351–53.

Thus, the explanatory information must provide good grounds for believing that X did in fact occur; otherwise, that information would give us no adequate reason for saying: 'That explains it—that does show why X occurred.' "[66] Thus, if we can state that the Duke of Guise died because stabbed, we could also have predicted that he would die if stabbed.

To the doctrine of the structural identity of explanation and prediction, Israel Scheffler and Michael Scriven have objected that there are many correlations that allow us to predict what will happen yet do not explain why it happened. Sunspots are followed by radio disturbances, and the symptoms of cancer allow us to predict its spread, but neither is explanatory.[67] To this exception to his doctrine Hempel readily assents, writing, "Reliance on general connecting principles [colligation, in my terminology], while not indispensable for prediction, is required in any explanation."[68] The structural identity Hempel asserts concerns not all predictions but all causal explanations. The covering law that allows a causal explanation must also allow a prediction.

A far more serious challenge to the symmetry of explanation and prediction is the fact that the Duke of Guise might not have died of the stab wounds. Assume for the moment that in the sixteenth century two out of every three persons stabbed survived. This makes the difficulty even greater, for the covering law used to explain the Duke's death might lead one to predict his survival. May Brodbeck has most satisfactorily explained this paradox with her distinction between the symmetry of explanation and prediction in principle and their asymmetry in practice. They are symmetrical in principle because, given a knowledge of the sufficient conditions for the occurrence of an event, one could predict it. Thus if one knew not only that the Duke of Guise would be stabbed but also that he would be stabbed in the chest immediately above the heart, three times, with the dagger piercing three inches deep, then one could predict the death of the Duke. In practice, however, historians often do not know all of the initial conditions needed to explain the occurrence of an event; therefore they cannot predict the occurrence of that event. Thus there is a practical asymmetry between explanation and prediction.[69]

What saves the writing of history from futility and gives to historians' explanations a greater certainty than could ever be attached to their predictions is the fact that the occurrence of the event demonstrates the

66. Hempel, "Aspects of Scientific Explanation," 367–68.
67. Scheffler, "Explanation, Prediction, and Abstraction," 277, 282; Scriven, "Truisms as the Grounds for Historical Explanations," 468.
68. Hempel, "Aspects of Scientific Explanation," 368–69.
69. Brodbeck, "Explanation, Prediction, and 'Imperfect' Knowledge," 249–52.

presence of the unobserved initial conditions. Hempel calls such explanations "self-evidencing explanations."[70] Take the simplest possible example. A pool player hits the cue ball toward the one ball, which is lying
toward the center of the pool table. If the cue ball hits the one ball at the
correct angle, the one ball will go into the side pocket. Spectators may
see the cue ball moving toward the one ball, but they cannot predict
whether the one ball will go into the side pocket, since they cannot
observe whether the cue ball will hit the one ball at exactly the correct
angle. But once the one ball has gone into the pocket, they can explain
the fact by saying, "The cue ball hit the one ball at the correct angle." Or
take Michael Scriven's illustration of the bridge that collapsed from metal
fatigue. It is true that historians could not have predicted when it would
fall, since they had no independent measure of the metal fatigue, but
once it fell, and in the absence of any other possible explanation, such as
a bomb falling on the bridge, they may validly assume the presence of
the necessary amount of metal fatigue. They will use the presence of that
fatigue in their explanations of the collapse of the bridge.[71]

There are, of course, phenomena, such as the emission of an alpha
particle by a radioactive substance, that are fundamentally probabilistic
and for which no complete explanation is possible. The laws describing
such phenomena, say the laws of quantum theory, "permit," writes
Hempel, "only a probabilistic explanation of a particular emission P
rather than a 'complete' explanation 'ex post facto.' "[72] But historians
rarely, if ever, write of such phenomena. The laws historians use are
probable because of the historians' ignorance of all the initial conditions
they need to know in order to predict.

It is important to establish the fact of the symmetry of prediction and
explanation in principle, for were this not so, historians could not use
counterfactuals in their explanations. Counterfactuals are of two kinds:
negative and positive. A negative counterfactual states that had something *not* happened that in fact did happen, something else that in fact
did happen would *not* have happened. For example, "Had he not lit a
match (which he did), the explosion would not have occurred." Or "Had
the Duke of Guise not been stabbed, he would not have died." A positive counterfactual states that had something happened that in fact did
not, something else that in fact did not happen would have happened.
For example, "Had he lit a match (which he did not do), an explosion
would have occurred (which in fact did not)." Or "Had Guy Fawkes set

70. Hempel, "Aspects of Scientific Explanation," 372–73.
71. Scriven, "Explanations, Predictions, and Laws," 182–84.
72. Hempel, "Aspects of Scientific Explanation," 407.

off his gun powder (which he did not), James would have died." Negative counterfactuals carry more conviction than positive counterfactuals because they posit only the removal of a necessary condition for the occurrence of an event—the lighting of the match, the stabbing of the Duke. The fact that the event did occur (the explosion, the death of the Duke) allows the historian, using self-evidencing information, to conclude that the other conditions were present (air, gas, dryness in one case; a deep wound, want of medical attention in the other) that were needed to transform a necessary condition into a sufficient condition. With a positive counterfactual, the historian cannot be certain (unless he or she had independent information) that there was gas in the room or that Guy Fawkes had gathered enough gun powder to blow through the heavy masonry of Westminster Hall.

Whether a counterfactual is given a negative or a positive expression, its truth depends upon the truth of the covering law employed (that a spark, air, gas, dryness will cause an explosion; that a deep stab wound will cause death). Thus the most convincing way to challenge the truth of such a counterfactual, and the explanation it supports, is to challenge the truth of the covering law employed. Find instances where a spark, air, gas, and dryness do not cause an explosion, or a deep stab wound death. Raymond Martin has observed that historians in their debates often make use of historical counterexamples. He defines a historical counterexample as follows: an argument "with one premise, which asserts that some event occurred or fact obtained that was not accompanied by another event or fact of a specified kind, and a conclusion, which asserts that some event or fact similar to the former was not a sufficient cause of some event or fact similar to the latter."[73] He then gives three examples of historical counterexamples: J. B. Bury's query, why, if depopulation, the Christian religion, and the fiscal system led to decline in the West (of the Roman Empire), did it not also lead to decline in the East? Richard Hofstadter's query, why, if the frontier led to democracy in the United States, did it not lead to democracy in South America and Siberia? and Lawrence Stone's query, why, if a Court/Country antithesis caused the breakdown of government in England in 1640, did it not cause a breakdown after 1660? In all three of these examples, instances are cited that negate the covering law employed in the proffered explanation. Martin sees that a historian could reply that the negative instances are drawn from different spatial and temporal locations, and thus from disanalogous situations, and so do not negate the covering law employed. But he also observes that historians possess no acceptable gen-

---

73. Martin, *The Past Within Us*, 128.

eral criterion for deciding whether another situation is analogous or
disanalogous.[74]

Martin rightly says that by employing historical counterexamples in
their debates historians provide "strong support for the central claim of
the positivist analysis." He also sees that the principal role of historical
counterexamples is negative, to disprove the covering laws employed by
other historians.[75] He could usefully have taken one further step and have
asserted that covering laws at the macro level—at the level of imperial
decline, growth of democracy, and breakdown of government—do not
exist at all or, if asserted, are probably untrue. Historians may use such
laws for heuristic purposes (directing their research to particular areas),
but historians do not explain complex events by subsuming them under
laws about depopulation and decline, about frontiers and democracy, or
about Court/Country conflicts and breakdowns. In actual practice, historians explain such complex events by tracing how they came about.

But in tracing how such events came about, the historian must connect each step in the sequence of events leading to the occurrence of the
complex event. To explain the occurrence of famine in a country where
there was a flood (to borrow an example from Martin) historians would
not subsume those events under a covering law that floods cause famine. They would realize that some floods enrich a land. Yet they would
also realize that some floods do cause famines, which realization would
lead them to study the effects of the flood. They would trace the course
of the flood waters; they would see what crops were submerged beneath
the flood waters; they would discover how important these crops were
to that country. Suppose they discovered that the flood waters submerged the corn crop for one week, thus ruining it. This particular step
in the narrative would be carried forward by a covering law: corn submerged in water for a week dies. There being no known instance of corn
surviving a week's inundation, such a covering law can withstand counterexamples. Furthermore, there being no sign of a drought or pests, one
could confidently voice the counterfactual statement that had there been
no flood, there would have been a corn crop.

This particular counterfactual statement forces one to qualify the assertion that a negative counterfactual is stronger than a positive one, since
the negative counterfactual statement here (had there been no flood
there would have been a corn crop) does seem weaker than the positive
counterfactual (were a flood to submerge the corn for a week, there
would be no crop). The reason for this is the fact that a flood submerging

74. Ibid., 129–39.
75. Ibid., 139.

corn for a week is a sufficient, as well as a necessary, cause of the ruin of the corn crop, whereas the negative counterfactual statement (had there been no flood, there would have been a corn crop), does not express a sufficient cause of a good corn crop, only a necessary one. In short, the stronger counterfactual is always that which posits the imagined removal or the imagined presence of a sufficient cause.

B. C. Hurst has written that the counterfactual cannot be a problem for the historian, since "for an historian if an event did not take place it cannot be the cause of another event"; and A.J.P. Taylor echoes this sentiment when he writes, "How can we decide about something that did not happen? Heaven knows, we have difficulty enough in deciding what did happen."[76] Both are wrong, for the simple reason that an assertion of causation (that igniting the match caused the explosion) carries with it the corresponding counterfactual prediction (had he not lit the match there would have been no explosion). The assertion of causation and the counterfactual prediction are the obverse and reverse side of the same coin. And both depend on the fact that a covering law allows both prediction and explanation.[77]

Inductive, Not Deductive

Carl Hempel has distinguished between deductive-nomological explanations, which are based on invariable laws, and statistical explanations, which are based on statistical laws. He has further divided statistical explanations into deductive-statistical explanations and inductive-statistical explanations. The former amounts to the subsumption of a narrower statistical uniformity under a more comprehensive one. Thus from the hypothesis that for atoms of every radioactive substance there is a characteristic probability of disintegrating during a given interval of time, other statistical aspects of radioactive decay may be deduced.

76. Hurst, "A Comment on the Possible Worlds of Climo and Howells," 54; Taylor, *The Trouble-Makers*, 16–17.

77. A counterfactual is dependent upon the ability of a historian to predict. In order to predict he relies upon his knowledge of certain regular, normal, predictable characteristics of reality, such as the fact that oxygen is necessary for combustion. Climo and Howells ("Possible Worlds in Historical Explanations," 1–20) make the same point, but in an unnecessarily cumbersome fashion. Instead of talking about predictable characteristics of the real world—which the historian must know in order to assert a counterfactual—they talk about possible worlds that resemble the real world. For a highly technical but illuminating discussion of the relation of causation to counterfactuals, see David Lewis, "Causation."

Ultimately, however, statistical laws are meant to apply to particular occurrences, which requires an inductive-statistical explanation. Hempel calls such an explanation inductive because the conclusion, say, that penicillin cured Jones's streptococcus infection, is not deductively implied but rather inductively supported by the law that penicillin effects a cure in a high percentage of cases. Hempel makes his meaning clear, but I find it clearer to envision the conclusion as deductively implied by the law, rather than as inductively supported by it. True, it is not a "deductive certainty," as Hempel says, but it is a deductive probability.[78] One is not confirming a law, invariable or probabilistic, with another instance; one is deducing a conclusion from a law already established by induction, that is, by observing many instances of its operation. It does seem to me more sensible to regard all nomological explanations as deductive in form. Where there is an invariable law, the conclusion deduced is certain; where there is a probabilistic law, the conclusion deduced is probable.

The covering-law model of explanation, therefore, is deductive in form. What is not deductive in historical explanations is the means by which the covering laws employed are established. Though scientists may deduce covering laws from more general laws and theories, historians rarely, if ever, do so. This raises the question: where then do historians find the laws they use in explanations? Three possible sources come immediately to mind. They may borrow them from other disciplines, they may gain them from personal experience, or they may form them as they pursue their researches.

That historians borrow from the natural sciences and medicine when necessary will hardly be disputed. Medical discoveries about the nature of porphyria allowed historians to explain George III's "madness." What is disputed is whether historians do borrow, or can profitably borrow, from the social sciences, that is, from sociology, anthropology, political science, and economics. Carey Joynt and Nicholas Rescher are confident that they do, describing the historian as "parasitic on the scientist, since the historian is not a producer of general laws, but a consumer of

78. Hempel, "Aspects of Scientific Explanation," 380–83. Abraham Kaplan writes (*The Conduct of Inquiry*, 344–45), "Hempel has acknowledged that explanations adducing statistical generalizations must be conceived as inductive arguments. These might still be fitted into the deductive model, however, with only slight emendations. For in modern developments of inductive logic, following Carnap, the circumstance that the conclusion has a certain degree of confirmation with respect to the evidence adduced follows deductively from the premises of the inductive inference. What is explained is then, not why the conclusion is true [I would say 'certainly true'], but why it is probable [I would say 'probably true']."

them."[79] But the examples they give of such laws lend little support to their argument. From sociology they cite the law that "cohesiveness in groups leads to greater conformity"; from anthropology, that all societies "recognize a system of culturally patterned relationship between kinsmen"; from political science, that "balance-of-power policies . . . have tended toward polarization of all states about the two most powerful"; and from economics, that "every economic society prescribes its own standards of conduct."[80] The fault with these laws is that they are so banal and vacuous as to be useless to the historian. They are macrolaws appropriate to explanation by macrocorrelation, but as shown in the first chapter, nearly all attempts at explanation by macrocorrelation have failed. Such laws are worthless when it comes to microcorrelation, as Lawrence Stone seems to have discovered when writing *The Causes of the English Revolution*. At one point he refers to a familiar sociological explanation of discontent, "the familiar 'J-curve' of a fairly long period of prosperity, which aroused expectations of continuing improvement, followed by a sharp downward turn," only to conclude later that "deteriorating financial conditions were definitely *not* a factor in arousing discontent among the landlord class, which was the main actor in the coming drama."[81] More recently Robert Ashton has remarked on the inappropriateness of employing sociological concepts designed to illuminate modern society to explain the radically different society that prevailed from 1603 to 1649.[82]

Psychology, particularly psychoanalysis, has furnished many concepts to the historian, but hardly with conspicuous success. Historians today look with considerable suspicion on psychoanalytic biographies, such as Erik Erikson's study of Martin Luther. They show more sympathy to studies in social psychology, such as Mark Bloch's *Les Roi Thaumaturges* or Georges Lefebvre's *La Grande Peur de 1789*, but it is difficult to show precisely how concepts drawn from psychology have contributed to the analysis of those phenomena. The facile use of psychological concepts such as inferiority complex, repression, subconscious, and introversion more often insults common sense than it illuminates the past. Consider the historian who explained the dedication of the early Chinese Communists by attributing to them a sense of guilt gained from having survived the Long March.[83] All of this does not mean that historians should not

79. Joynt and Rescher, "The Problem of Uniqueness in History," 154.
80. Joynt and Rescher, "On Explanation in History," 386–87.
81. Stone, *The Causes of the English Revolution*, 131.
82. Ashton, *The English Civil War*, 82.
83. I have drawn this example, as well as the comments on Bloch's and Lefebvre's books, from Geoffrey Barraclough, *Main Trends in History*, 66–67, 79–80.

look to psychology or to sociology for insights into human behavior, for the stimulus it gives them to look at human conduct in a different light. It only means that historians rarely draw the covering laws they employ from sociology and psychology.

It would be foolish to deny that historians draw many of their ideas about human nature (and it is with human nature that the historian is largely concerned) from their own experience, especially if one extends that experience to the reading of newspapers, novels, biographies, plays, and essays. The historian unavoidably approaches the past with a certain view of human nature, whether cynical or naïve, whether materialistic or idealistic, views that will color his or her explanation of human conduct in the past. What the historian gains from experience and observation and reading are not ready-made concepts so much as the material from which, by induction, the historian forms concepts about how human beings are likely to act in different situations. Just as historians learn from experience that ink spilled over the edge of a table falls to the ground, so they learn from experience that men and women asked to pay taxes will look for loopholes in order to avoid paying them.

But for the best historians the concepts they use as covering laws come from their own research, both research in the primary sources and reading in the secondary literature on their subject. Joynt and Rescher notwithstanding, historians do produce their own general laws (though fortunately they are parochial laws). Students of sixteenth-century England first read Elton and Neale, then the statutes and law reports, then diaries and letters, until they sense how Tudor prelates and privy councillors, Parliament men and merchants, seamen and soldiers, husbandmen and craftsmen, were likely to act. Why was Frances Yates so great an historian? She was great, observes E. H. Gombrich, because "she had come to understand the mentality of past ages with greater immediacy than most of us."[84]

What should be underlined is the fact that whether one gains one's covering laws from experience, observation, reading, or research, one establishes those laws (or one's fellow historian does) inductively, by generalizing from observed instances, which generalizations can be projected to unobserved instances. There must, of course, be unobserved instances, or there is no law. Generalizations based upon all known instances are not laws and play no role in explanation. R. F. Atkinson argues otherwise, asking, "Why should not a summary explain?" He then borrows an example from Michael Oakeshott—"All the Reformation parliaments were packed"—and concludes that "the individual case

---

84. Gombrich, "On Frances Yates," *New York Review of Books*, 3 March 1983, 11–13.

is accounted for by being presented as one of a number of similar cases."[85] Surely the individual case is sufficiently accounted for by the earlier research that showed that that parliament, and all others, were packed.

"All butter melts at 150° F" is a law, declares Nelson Goodman, and "All the coins in my pocket are silver" is a generalization. What makes the difference? he asks, and answers, "The fact that the first is accepted as true while many cases remain to be determined, the further, unexamined cases being predicted to conform with it. The second sentence, on the contrary, is accepted as a description of contingent fact *after* the determination of all cases, no prediction of any of its instances being based upon it."[86] Historians no doubt use summative generalizations, but they do not use them to explain why one event caused another. For that they need a covering law.

Implicit, Not Explicit

No fact works more strongly against the belief that historians use covering laws than the fact that such laws are not visible in historical narratives. They are not visible because they are implicit, not explicit. Murray Murphey finds historians at fault for not making the covering laws they employ explicit. The historian, he writes, should "present evidence to support his causal statements, and the only way he can present such evidence is to exhibit the covering law in question."[87] But Raymond Martin rightly observes that humanists cannot accept the injunction that historians justify the covering laws they employ, and that positivists overestimate the importance of justifying covering laws.[88] There are, I believe, two reasons why historians do not, and need not, make explicit the covering laws they employ. In the first place, many of these covering laws are platitudinous, and it would be tedious continually to assert

85. Atkinson, *Knowledge and Explanation in History,* 111.

86. Goodman, *Fact, Fiction, and Forecast,* 19. See also Hempel, "Aspects of Scientific Explanation," 340–43. The fact that a law, unlike a summative generalization, allows prediction raises the problem of induction, a problem David Hume first posed and with which philosophers have wrestled ever since. Few historians share Hume's skepticism about a possible logic of induction, but those who do should read Scheffler, *The Anatomy of Inquiry,* esp. 230, 291, 295, 299–302, and R. C. Jeffrey, *The Logic of Decision,* esp. 156, 177–78. Both authors defend the possibility of reaching truthful generalizations by means of induction.

87. Murphey, *Our Knowledge of the Historical Past,* 89–90.

88. Martin, *The Past Within Us,* 24, 48.

their truth. The historian who declares that the levying of ship money caused discontent need not state the generalization that Englishmen in the seventeenth century resented paying taxes, especially taxes to which they had not consented in parliament. Second, these covering laws are so numerous in a historical narrative that any attempt to justify each one would hopelessly clog the narrative. Such a history would be unreadable, and a history that is not read cannot explain anything. But the fact that historians need not make explicit the covering laws they employ does not excuse them from the necessity of making sure those laws are true. Indeed, the value of their histories depends as much on the truth of the covering laws they employ as on the truth of the assertion that the causal events in question occurred. Histories are profound and wise, rather than superficial and naïve, because the implicit covering laws in them are profoundly and wisely observed, rather than superficially and naïvely observed. Reviewers and perceptive readers can readily distinguish the difference between such histories. Occasionally, of course, historians will make their generalizations explicit. This occurs particularly when a controversy arises among historians over the truth of an explanation. Raymond Martin astutely observes that the widespread use of historical counterexamples in historical debates demonstrates that historians do use covering laws in their explanations and that they are concerned with the truth of those laws.[89] But until controversy impels historians to make their covering laws explicit, they will allow those laws to remain implicit. But the fact that they are implicit does not mean that they are unimportant. The truth of a narrative depends on their being true.

89. Ibid., 139.

5 THE PROBLEM OF INDISCRIMINATE PLURALISM

A gardener who fails to water the flowers causes them to die. But another person's failure to water them is not a cause. Because the first is abnormal, the latter normal.

—H.L.A. Hart and A.M. Honoré,
Causation in the Law

In the previous four chapters I have often referred to one event causing another event. This does not, of course, happen, and the expression is only an abbreviation for something more complex. An event X does not cause an event Y; rather, a set of conditions—$C_1, C_2, \ldots, C_n$—causes an event Y. Not a lighted match, but a lighted match and a pile of paper and the presence of oxygen causes a fire. Not the new liturgy, but the new liturgy and a volatile congregation and a planned resistance caused the riot in St. Giles. And the covering law employed asserts a regularity, not between event and event, but between a set of initial conditions and the event.

The substitution of a set of initial conditions for a single event raises the problem of indiscriminate pluralism. Are all of the conditions—the match, the paper, and the oxygen in the one instance, the liturgy, the congregation, and the organization in the other—to be given equal weight? Can one even enumerate all the conditions? What about the dryness of the paper or the fact that no person was present with a fire extinguisher? Or the weakness of the Scottish bishops and the absence of privy councillors? In fact if one allows the absence of certain conditions to be a necessary condition, then the number of conditions that must be enumerated is limited only by a person's imagination. One might even insist on including the fact that a comet did not destroy the earth a moment before the fire or the riot. Thus the problem of indiscriminate pluralism is a twofold problem: how to enumerate all the conditions that are part of the initial conditions and how to give greater weight to one condition than to another.

But the problem of indiscriminate pluralism is made even more complex by the fact that it has three different dimensions, which might usefully be labeled A, B, and C. In dimension A the problem is that sketched above, namely, to decide which of many initial conditions (lighted match, paper, oxygen) are the more important in bringing about the event (the fire) and therefore deserve mention. This problem arises whenever there is a single covering law under which the event to be explained is subsumed. Dimension B arises when a single event (the outbreak of the First World War, say) is explained by a colligatory narrative, the steps of which (the assassination at Sarajevo, the Austrian ultimatum to Serbia, the Serbian refusal, etc.) are joined by a series of different covering laws. The problem here is to decide which of the causes delineated are the more important. Dimension C arises when there are a large number of similar events to be explained (say, auto accidents), and the historian seeks to discover the more important factors in causing them (speed, mechanical failure, etc.). In dimension A philosophers and historians tend to speak of conditions, in dimension B of causes, and in dimension C of factors. But though philosophers and historians tend to speak in this way, they do not always distinguish between the three dimensions, with the result that confusion arises. In this chapter I focus on dimension A, leaving to the chapters on the logic of colligation and the logic of historical interpretation the other two.

To the problem of indiscriminate pluralism as presented by dimension A, philosophers of history have offered various solutions, among them the following:

1. Totalism
2. Minimalism
3. Pragmatism
4. Abnormalism
5. Metaphysicalism
6. Moralism
7. Probabilism

Totalism

Maurice Mandelbaum, citing Thomas Hobbes in his support, maintains that to explain the occurrence of a particular event one must discover the entire cause, or aggregate of all conditions. He favors abandoning the distinction between cause and conditions. It is not, he argues, "sufficient to single out some one factor and denominate it as 'the cause,' distinguishing it from what are merely 'conditions.' " To explain a fire one must mention not only that a lighted match was carelessly dropped into a wastebasket but also that the basket was near inflammable curtains, that the walls were easily combustible, that a draft came through an open window, that the house was not fireproof. Then he observes, "These conditions are all necessary to explain the series of events in this particular case."[1] Herein Mandelbaum reveals a confusion in his mind between the initial conditions that explain a single step in a process (the paper going up in flames) and all the conditions explaining all the steps in the process (the house burning). The problem of distinguishing the "more important" causes in a series of events leading to the macroevent to be explained is no doubt a difficult problem, but it is a different problem from that of enumerating and weighting the initial conditions that fall within a covering law and that, with that law, explain the occurrence of a single event.

William Alston avoids this confusion, yet he still argues that one must list all the sufficient conditions in order to explain the occurrence of an event. If one does not list them, there can be no complete explanation. As he puts it, "The open-endedness of a sufficient condition law in respect to possible disturbing factors prevents any logical derivation of an explanation of a particular fact from the law plus a report of the instance of the sufficient condition." If severe punishment, he writes, always led to increased dependency, then one would have a strict sufficiency law, a law that would allow one to explain a particular event. But if severe punishment leads to increased dependency only in conjunction with other unspecified conditions, then one has an open-ended sufficiency law, which cannot yield a complete explanation. The explanation of a particular event requires a total description of the conditions sufficient to cause it.[2]

Alston makes a shrewd point. All the conditions comprehended in the covering law must be present in the initial conditions. If the law states that whenever the flame of a match comes in contact with dry paper in the presence of oxygen, the paper will ignite, then the initial conditions

1. Mandelbaum, *Anatomy of Historical Knowledge*, 81–92, 140.
2. Alston, "The Place of the Explanation of Particular Facts in Science," 25–27.

must include flame, dry paper, and oxygen. But two observations must be made about this proposition. The first is that the covering law omits conditions such as that no gale occurred that night, that the temperature was not −70° F, that there was no fire fighter present with a fire extinguisher, and even that no comet plunged into that part of the earth at that moment. Second, even if the covering law contained all these conditions, the historian would not want to list them all among the initial conditions. Indeed, the historian would not even want to list oxygen and dry paper among the initial conditions. He or she would merely want to write that a match thrown into the wastepaper basket caused the fire. Totalism cannot explain why the historian is justified in doing this.

Hart and Honoré do urge that in many cases it is possible to give a full description of the positive initial conditions. But they immediately see the difficulty that arises when omission is regarded as a cause, as, for example, when the failure to consult a doctor leads to death.[3] On the whole, one must pronounce that totalism does not offer a workable solution to the problem of indiscriminate pluralism. R. F. Atkinson is surely right when he writes, "If causes have to be sufficient conditions they never are, nor could be, fully specified."[4]

Minimalism

Few philosophers explicitly advocate what I have chosen to call the minimalist position, namely, that in the writing of history one need not give a sufficient cause for an event, but only a necessary cause, but several have implied that this is so. William Dray, in commenting on A.J.P. Taylor's argument that Hitler did not cause the Second World War, because he would have "counted for nothing without the support and cooperation of the German people," asserts that this fact does not invalidate the claim that it was Hitler who caused the war. "For holding that a person causes what he intends need not commit us to the absurd idea that a causally significant intention must itself be a sufficient condition of what it causes. It is quite enough that it be a necessary one."[5] Michael Scriven hints at the same position when he writes,

3. Hart and Honoré, *Causation in the Law*, 395–98.

4. Atkinson, *Knowledge and Explanation in History*, 146. For a trenchant criticism of totalism, see Morton White, *Foundations of Historical Knowledge*, 109–15.

5. Dray, "Concepts of Causation in A.J.P. Taylor's Account of the Origins of the Second World War," 152. Yet Dray in *On History and Philosophers of History*, 100, taxes Norman A. Graebner for assuming that necessary causes are sufficient.

> An explanation tells us why something occurred if it tells us what factor or factors actually brought it about, i.e. what factor, in the circumstances, so tipped the balance of events as to produce the known outcome. Such a factor need not itself be a sufficient condition for the outcome; it may be simply one element in the set which is jointly sufficient. This far the covering law model can still go. But the crucial point is that the historian *does not* need to know what the other conditions are that make up the sufficient condition.[6]

The danger with this position (as remarked before) is that it opens the door to subjectivity. A historian may arbitrarily emphasize whatever necessary cause he or she wishes, say Hitler's role in causing the Second World War, and ignore all the others. Another historian may emphasize the role of the German people and ignore Hitler. And there is no criterion offered for determining which of several necessary causes is the most important, which tipped the balance of events. Furthermore, the minimalistic position assumes that the other conditions remain the same. To obviate this difficulty the minimalist must introduce the principle of *ceteris paribus*.

The principle of *ceteris paribus*, that is, "of other things being equal," most effectively solves what Hempel calls the quest for explanatory closure. The historian can close the list of conditions causing an event simply by stating a necessary condition or even several necessary conditions and then assuming that all other things are equal. The historian may declare that a carelessly thrown match caused the fire, assuming that oxygen and combustible material were always present. He or she may declare that the introduction of the new liturgy caused the riot at St. Giles, assuming that the Scots were zealous Presbyterians and their ministers active. All things being equal, the match caused the fire, and the liturgy the riot. Historians do in fact write history in this manner, especially narrative history. Indeed, it would be hard to imagine a narrative history that did not use such an abbreviated form of explanation.

Though the principle of *ceteris paribus* solves the problem of explanatory closure, it does not solve the problem of assigning weight to the many conditions that make up the sufficient conditions. Why should the historian not make the paper and cardboard thrown into the alley the cause of the fire, assuming that matches are always likely to be thrown there, or declare that the irrational zeal of the Presbyterians caused the

---

6. Scriven, "Causes, Connections, and Conditions in History," 248.

riot, and not the introduction of the new liturgy? The minimalist position, even reinforced by the principle of *ceteris paribus*, offers no guidance on this question.

To the vexed question whether historians should use necessary or sufficient causes to carry forward their narratives, Behan McCullagh offers a useful distinction. He distinguishes between a causal relation and an explanatory generalization.[7] Historians, he argues, need not be convinced that the occurrence of one event was sufficient for the occurrence of another event in order to believe that the two are causally related. It is enough that the first event is a necessary condition, and this can be done by showing that in its absence the explanandum event was unlikely to occur (as a cake is unlikely to rise if baking powder is left out). McCullagh is, of course, aware that there are other conditions, stable or normal or already revealed in the narrative, that, joined to the necessary condition, make up the sufficient conditions for the occurrence of the event. But he is surely right that historians need not describe these in order to carry on their narratives. Yet McCullagh is loath to abandon all reference to sufficiency. He recognizes that if causes are events or states of affairs that are merely necessary for the occurrence of another event, then for any given event there is a very large number of causes. This leads him to the conclusion that for a causal explanation to be satisfactory, there must be a generalization that states what usually suffices to produce events like the explanandum event. It is, indeed, a very useful distinction. Historians may use assertions of causal relation to carry on their narratives, but must use assertions of causal explanation when challenged to justify steps in their narratives. What this distinction does not do, however, is solve the problem, which of two or three necessary conditions is the historian to regard as the most important?

Pragmatism

William Dray has suggested that historians apply a pragmatic test in choosing between the various necessary causes of an event. They select "as causes those conditions which were humanly important because under human control." Such a causal explanation often focuses on what went wrong and ends in the assigning of blame.[8] Many other philosophers have concurred with this pragmatism. Patrick Gardiner asserts

---

7. McCullagh, *Justifying Historical Descriptions*, 166–67, 177–78, 190–94, 207–15.
8. Dray, *Laws and Explanation in History*, 98–99.

that one regards as the cause of an event what has practical value, what allows one to produce or prevent that event.[9] Charles Frankel declares that the historian, when imputing cause, is governed by an endeavor to control a specific situation—thus attributing a forest fire to human carelessness, not a dry summer.[10] R. F. Atkinson maintains that necessary conditions are likely to be regarded as causes where the concern is to eliminate an evil, such as cancer.[11] Hart and Honoré, whose concern is with the concept of responsibility in courts of law, naturally emphasize the contrast between a free, deliberate human action and all other conditions. Thus one concentrates on the delivery of the blow that broke a child's leg, not on the thinness of the bone in the leg.[12]

Closely allied to pragmatism is the recognition that the purpose of the historian will lead him or her to frame one question rather than another or to redescribe the explanandum event in one way rather than in another. Michael Scriven points out that the question, "Why has this man developed cancer?" may mean either "Why has he got cancer now, whereas a month ago he did not?" or "Why has he got cancer, whereas his brother, who works in the same job, has not?" Clearly, these different questions might elicit different necessary causes of the cancer.[13] As Hart and Honoré observe, the selection of causes from conditions is relative to the purpose of the inquiry: to the scientist gravitation is the cause of the stone falling, to the lawyer the act of letting it go.[14]

The key word in this last remark is "purpose." If the purpose of the court is to assign responsibility, it will look for a cause that assigns responsibility. If the doctor wishes to prevent cancer, he or she will look for a cause of cancer that can be controlled. If the traffic engineer wishes to prevent accidents, he or she will find the cause of an accident in the lack of a traffic light, not in the failure of a driver to look to the right. But what are the purposes of a historian? For a Lord Acton it will be to sit in judgment on the Napoleons of this world, and for a Marxist to make theory serve practice, but for most historians it is neither to judge nor to manipulate nor to prevent nor to promote; it is to understand. Historians are not judges or doctors or traffic engineers; they are scholars. This fact considerably limits the usefulness of the pragmatic test. Even Hart and Honoré see this. They criticize Collingwood for assuming that the cause of an event is equivalent to how we can produce or prevent it, and for

9. Gardiner, *The Nature of Historical Explanation*, 100–103.
10. Frankel, "Explanation and Interpretation in History," 417–18.
11. Atkinson, *Knowledge and Explanation in History*, 148.
12. Hart and Honoré, *Causation in the Law*, 31, 41–43.
13. Scriven, "Explanations, Predictions, and Laws," 255–56.
14. Hart and Honoré, *Causation in the Law*, 411–12.

writing that the identification of a cause is always dictated by practical interests. This is tantamount, they suggest, to making it improper to ask the cause of cancer if we cannot use that knowledge to prevent it.[15]

If totalism and minimalism fail, and if pragmatism has its limitations, what then will allow the historian to select the "more important" conditions or the "most important" condition, and so label them or it "the cause"?

Abnormalism

The doctrine of abnormalism holds that the "more important" conditions are those that depart more, and the "most important condition" is that one that departs most, from the normal course of events. Thus the presence of oxygen is not the most important cause of a fire, because oxygen is normally present. A carelessly thrown match is the most important cause because such an action is abnormal; it departs from the normal course of events. Similarly, the zeal of the Scottish Presbyterians, being always present, must be regarded as normal and so not the most important cause of the riot; the introduction of a new liturgy, being a departure from the familiar course of events, must be regarded as abnormal and so the most important cause.

Morton White, who named this doctrine abnormalism, has done more than any other philosopher to illuminate how central this doctrine is to historical explanation. But his account of abnormalism is in some ways flawed.

In the first place, as Murray Murphey has pointed out, he is inconsistent in first suggesting that the doctrine applies only to the explanation of abnormal events, then later stating that historians are also interested in the explanation of normal events. Does White mean to suggest, asks Murphey, that the doctrine of abnormalism only applies to a subset of events, those that are abnormal?[16] Whatever White may believe, it is clear that abnormalism applies both to normal and abnormal events. One explains a forest fire, an abnormal event, by the fact that a lighted cigarette was carelessly thrown away, in itself an abnormal event. One does not mention that the forest was dry and that oxygen was present. Similarly, one explains why the light in the living room came on, a

15. Ibid., 31, 33, 270.

16. Murphey, *Our Knowledge of the Historical Past*, 129; White, *Foundations of Historical Knowledge*, 115, 247–48.

perfectly normal event, by stating that John switched it on. In comparison to the fact that there was a constant source of electrical power in the house, John's act was abnormal. No one would answer the question, Why did the living room light go on? by saying that there was a constant source of electrical power in the house. That is accepted as normal. The fact that White uses this very illustration suggests that he does believe that the doctrine of abnormalism applies to ordinary events.[17]

The second flaw in White's account is more serious. He focuses so sharply on "the cause," meaning the "most important" condition, that he limits what can usefully be said. White is fully aware that in many situations there might be two initial conditions that are abnormal. Where that is the case, he suggests that historians can only be guided by their values and interests to prefer one to the other. He gives the example of a man's dying from imbibing arsenic. He then observes that if the amount of arsenic were too little to kill most men, one must say that the man died of a weak constitution.[18] Now, if historians must give a single condition among the initial conditions as the cause of the event, then they must choose either the arsenic or the weak constitution. But there is no reason they must. They may mention both the arsenic and the weak constitution. In fact one would be a poor historian if one did not. The number of abnormal conditions among the initial conditions are rarely so many that they cannot all be mentioned. The great majority of initial conditions—such as oxygen in the air, electricity in the house, the absorption of arsenic by the stomach—are so normal that they need not be mentioned. The remaining abnormal conditions are so few that they ought to be mentioned, all of them. Most historians will, believing that multicausal explanations are superior to unicausal explanations.

Furthermore, there is a scale of normality and abnormality. Thus the infrequency with which matches are thrown into alleys gives such an action a high degree of abnormality, while the nearly ubiquitous presence of oxygen gives it an overwhelming normality. But what of the debris left in the alley—the paper and boxes carelessly left in the alley? To leave debris in an alley is more common than throwing lighted matches into alleys, but less common than the presence of oxygen. The historian should probably mention it in an explanation of the fire, though not as prominently as the carelessly thrown match. Similarly, a private meeting of ministers of the Kirk is more common than the introduction of a new liturgy, but less common than the presence of Presbyterian zeal in the congregation. It, too, should be mentioned, though not

---

17. White, *Foundations of Historical Knowledge*, 165.
18. Ibid., 120–28, 132.

as prominently as the introduction of the liturgy. As there are degrees of normality and abnormality, so there must be a calculus of less and more important causes.

Though there exists a calculus of causes, with greater weight being given to some initial conditions than to others, there is little possibility of giving a statistical statement to such a calculus. This fact has led Ernest Nagel to suggest that historians must "rely on guesses and vague impressions in assigning weights to causal factors," with the result that there exists "wide divergences in judgments as to what are the main causes of a given event, and one historian's opinion may be no better grounds than another's."[19] But in concluding thus Nagel confuses a lack of precision with divergence in judgments. Ten observers at Fort Collins, Colorado, might differ in their estimates of the height of Long's Peak and Mount Meeker, expressed in feet, but they would all agree that Long's Peak is taller. Most historical judgments are not this obvious, but neither are they as subjective as Nagel suggests. The proper target of Nagel's strictures are those quantifiers who would give a more exact precision to their judgments than the facts warrant.

Morton White's most serious mistake is to apply abnormalism to macroevents. He applies it not only to a man with ulcers who eats parsnips and to a man of weak constitution who takes arsenic but also to the cause of the prosperity of the Dutch, the cause of the collapse of the Mediterranean commonwealth, and the cause of the American Civil War.[20] To these macroevents he applies the covering-law model (which he calls the regularist principle). But as I have sought to show in earlier chapters, this will not do. To explain phenomena such as the prosperity of the Dutch, the collapse of the Mediterranean commonwealth, and the outbreak of the American Civil War, one needs to trace how the complex and intricate events making up these phenomena came about. One must resort to colligation. At each step one must apply a covering law, with the appropriate initial conditions. Abnormalism quite properly belongs to selecting the more important initial conditions in each of these microsteps. Having worked through the myriad connected and parallel events leading to the final outcome, the historian has a wealth of causes. These causes would be bewildering in their scope and variety were it not for the fact that like causes repeat one another again and again. There is a common denominator. Certain causes are repeated more often than others. Historians, for example, who seek to explain the outbreak of the First World War will trace many events leading to the declaration of war

19. Nagel, *The Structure of Science*, 587.
20. White, *Foundations of Historical Knowledge*, 112, 117, 175.

in August 1914. In doing so they will find that nationalistic ambitions appeared as an important cause far more often than economic conflicts. They will then conclude that nationalistic ambitions, because they shaped events more often, were a more important cause of the outbreak of war than economic conflicts. What should be noted here is that the historian's reason for saying that nationalistic ambitions are more important than economic conflicts is the opposite of abnormalism. It is not the infrequency, but the frequency, with which nationalistic ambitions occur that makes the historian emphasize them.

Metaphysicalism

Morton White quite rightly dismisses the doctrine that the decisive cause of an event must fall into a specific metaphysical category. He lists such categories as event, state, voluntary action, and thought. And he argues that we cannot identify *the* cause by showing that it falls into one of these categories.[21] His is a very illuminating discussion because it shows that the desire of many historians to make the state or condition of things the fundamental cause, and not the triggering event, is misguided. Such a view, though White does not mention it, is widely held by the *Annales* school of historians, a school that looks with contempt on the event and with enthusiasm on structure. Though White does not mention the *Annales* school, he does quote Louis Gottschalk, who opposes explaining the First World War by the assassination of Archduke Ferdinand at Sarajevo. It was the state of Europe at the time that was the underlying cause of the war, not the assassination. It is common to dismiss such events as the triggers. But White sees that events as well as states might be the decisive cause. The following example (not White's) makes this clear. Imagine there is a bridge across a river, with a sign in front of it reading "Load Limit Five Tons." Imagine that a ten-ton truck drives across the bridge and it collapses. Surely the structure of the bridge is not the cause of its collapse. On the other hand, suppose that the fabric of the bridge through time decays, crumbles, and weakens. One day a four-ton truck drives across it, and it collapses. Clearly one would not select the event as the cause, but the state of the bridge. Likewise with Sarajevo. Assassinations were not that uncommon in the late nineteenth and early twentieth centuries. What was uncommon was the state of mind of the ministers in Vienna. They at once seized on

21. Ibid., 134–39.

the assassination as a pretext for sending an unacceptable ultimatum to Serbia. In deciding whether to emphasize event or structure, the doctrine of abnormalism is of great use.

White even more decisively rejects Collingwood's belief that the metaphysical category of thought should be the cause. "The mere fact that each of so many factors other than thoughts may be cited as *the* cause of an action—even an action of an ordinary person—makes it absurd to say, as Collingwood does, that when a historian asks, 'Why did Brutus do it?' he means, 'What did Brutus *think* which made him decide to do it?'"[22] But this takes one into the realm of action explanation, and so should be discussed in Chapter 8, "Purposive Action."

Moralism

Morton White likewise criticizes those who make moral values central to distinguishing *the* cause, though there cannot be many who do so. According to the moralistic theorists, *the* cause is the moral abnormality among the initial conditions. To illustrate this view, White quotes William Dray, who, commenting on Hart and Honoré remark that we blame the gardener, not another person, for not watering the flowers, writes, "We cite the omission as cause because flower-watering was to be expected of a gardener; it is what he ought to have done." Dray goes on to cite Avery Craven's belief that the American Civil War came about because statesmen did not do what they ought to have done.[23] White admits that historians do occasionally give such moralistic explanations, as when they refer to a man's failure to do something that was his moral duty to do. But he recommends that they abandon such practice and rely upon empirical judgments of what is abnormal, especially since one's colleagues might not share that moral judgment.[24]

At this point it is important to make a distinction between the gardener's not doing what his contemporaries thought he should do and the gardener's not doing what the historian thought he should do. There is no doubt that what is regarded as normal and abnormal can be established by moral judgments as well as by customary practices and laws of nature. If the gardener fails to water the flowers, he has failed to perform a duty. But who establishes that it is the gardener's duty to water the

22. Ibid., 148.
23. Ibid., 173.
24. Ibid., 174–78.

flowers? His contemporaries or the historian? If his contemporaries, then the task of the historian is merely *descriptive*, to describe what was the moral code of that time. But if the historian, then the task is *prescriptive*, to prescribe what is right and wrong. Which path should the historian take, the descriptive or the prescriptive?[25]

Or perhaps the question should be, which path can the historian take, for it is a commonplace that historians cannot rid themselves of their values, cannot attain complete objectivity. Indeed the very vocabulary they use is filled with value-laden words. But though they cannot attain complete objectivity, should they not seek to be as objective as possible? To this question Leopold von Ranke answered yes, Lord Acton no. Most practicing historians today would accept von Ranke's advice and seek to be as objective as possible. They would seek as accurately as possible to describe the values of the gardener's contemporaries and, relying upon that description, would judge the degree of abnormality of the gardener's dereliction of duty. But surely within the domain of history there is a place for the kind of history that Lord Acton urged historians to write, history that passes judgment on the malefactors of the past. Such histories, such passionate moral essays, though they may present a warped view of the past, teach important moral truths. They who do not believe there is a need for such histories should read Pieter Geyl's "Ranke in the Light of the Catastrophe."[26]

It is the desire to assign responsibility that leads the historian to focus on the wrongness of the gardener's action rather than its infrequency. It is likewise a desire to assign responsibility that leads one to place greater weight on voluntary rather than involuntary actions. Thus, in explaining the occurrence of a bank robbery (to borrow an example from Hart and Honoré), one gives greater weight to the robber who leveled the gun on the bank teller than to the hapless teller, who handed over the money. In a court of law the voluntary action of the robber and the coerced action of the teller point indubitably to the guilt of the robber. But the historian who eschews assigning blame may give greater weight to the robber's action than to the teller's because leveling a gun at a teller and demanding money is an abnormal act, one that few of us would do, while the teller's handing over the money is a normal act, one that most of us would do. Courts of law must assign responsibility; historians need not do so—and if they choose not to, they will probably write a truer account of the past.

25. For a valuable discussion of this issue, see Leon Pompa's criticisms of Dray and Dray's response, in Dussen and Rubinoff, *Objectivity, Method, and Point of View*, 112–31, 183–85; see also Dray, *Philosophy of History*, 78–79.
26. Geyl, *Debates with Historians*, 9–29.

Probabilism

Von Kries, quoted by Hart and Honoré, gives a succinct statement of the doctrine of probabilism. The cause of an event, he holds, is that condition which significantly increases the probability of the event occurring.[27] But this is really no solution to the problem of selecting the more important of many initial conditions. Rather, it is a solution to the problem of determining what initial conditions prevailed. For example, it is more probable that a carelessly thrown cigarette will cause a fire than will a carelessly thrown match. If both a lighted match and a lighted cigarette were known to have been thrown into a forest and a fire broke out, we would be more likely to decide that it was the cigarette that caused it. But if we did so decide, then the match would not be an initial condition. Von Kries's doctrine of probabilism is a doctrine for distinguishing between rival explanations.

Nicholas Rescher has discussed this problem with great discrimination and subtlety. He distinguishes two criteria that contribute to the "goodness" of an explanation, criteria he calls explanatory strength and explanatory power. Explanatory *strength* is determined by the extent to which an explanation renders the occurrence of an event more likely than do other alternative explanations. Thus an explanation that a carelessly thrown cigarette caused the forest fire is stronger than the explanation that a carelessly thrown match did, because a carelessly thrown cigarette is more likely to cause a forest fire than is a carelessly thrown match. Explanatory *power* is determined by the extent to which the explanation renders the occurrence of the event to be explained more likely than the occurrence of alternative events. Thus the explanatory power of the carelessly thrown cigarette is rather weak, since a carelessly thrown cigarette is more likely not to cause a forest fire than to cause it. Rescher then asks, what is the formal relation between the strength of explanations and their explanatory power? Usually, but not always, comparative strength coincides with the ranking of explanatory power, the stronger explanation is also the more powerful. Discord between the two can, however, arise when the most powerful available explanation merely predicts that a given event, say A, is more likely to occur than B is likely to occur, or C is likely to occur, or D is likely to occur, but not more likely to occur than B or C or D. Whenever the most powerful explanation renders all the other states impossible or renders them taken together less likely than A, then there can be no discord. Then the most powerful and the strongest are the same. For this reason the possibility of discord

27. Hart and Honoré, *Causation in the Law*, 412.

between explanatory strength and explanatory power is restricted to cases of explanation that are probabilistic, not deductive, and are very weak in terms of their explanatory power. Furthermore, any time that the historian considers only two possible outcomes (say, that the carelessly thrown cigarette did or did not cause a fire), then a conflict cannot occur between explanatory strength and explanatory power. They will always coincide. That is why, concludes Rescher, the two criteria of explanatory goodness have not been carefully distinguished in the past.[28]

Closely allied to the problem of determining the goodness of alternative explanations is the problem of overdetermination. Overdetermination occurs when a necessary condition is not truly necessary, because an alternative condition is present to take its place. The carelessly thrown cigarette ceases to be necessary if a carelessly thrown match started the fire at the same moment. Michael Scriven has distinguished between two kinds of overdetermination, simultaneous and independent. Simultaneous overdetermination occurs when either C or D could cause E and both C and D are present. Scriven gives the example of a firing squad executing a criminal.[29] Hart and Honoré also give examples: two men firing at the same time into a man's brain, and two men simultaneously approaching escaping gas with lighted candles.[30] The very examples Scriven, Hart, and Honoré choose indicate that simultaneous overdetermination occurs rarely in history and so presents no great problem in the logic of historical explanation. To this assertion there is one exception. When searching out the motives of a historical agent, simultaneous overdetermination may often occur. Thus hatred of arbitrary government, as likewise fear of rule by the army, may well have led members of the House of Commons to impeach the Earl of Strafford, each motive independently being sufficient to cause his impeachment. But the relation of motive to cause is a matter that is discussed later, in the chapter on purposive action.

Independent overdetermination occurs much oftener in practical life and in history than simultaneous overdetermination. Independent overdetermination occurs when either C or D could have brought about E but C brings it about before D can. Scriven gives the example of guerillas blowing up a bridge before an atomic bomb, released minutes before, detonates above the bridge.[31] Of this example of overdetermination Carl

28. Rescher, *Scientific Explanation*, 57–66.
29. Scriven, "Causes, Connections, and Conditions in History," 260.
30. Hart and Honoré, *Causation in the Law*, 117.
31. Scriven, "Explanations, Predictions, and Laws," 229.

Hempel observes that the atomic bomb is no explanation of the destruction of the bridge, because there was no bridge there when the bomb went off.[32] His observation is an acute one and suggests that independent overdetermination plays no role in the logic of correlation, that is, plays no role in analyzing the initial conditions that cause an event to occur. But independent overdetermination does play a major role in the logic of colligation, that is, in tracing the course of events that precede the event to be explained. Indeed, the problem of indiscriminate pluralism, as well as that of independent overdetermination, is far more complex when viewed as a problem in the logic of colligation, to which the next chapter is devoted.

Of the many solutions to the problem of selecting from numerous initial conditions those that should be called "the cause," the doctrine of abnormalism is the most useful to the historian. But this doctrine should not be viewed as the selection of a single condition as "the cause," but rather as the selection of several, perhaps even three or four, ranked by degree of abnormality. Armed with this tool, the historian can trace backward from a macroscopic event the web of sequences that led to its occurrence.

32. Hempel, "Explanatory Incompleteness," 405.

6 THE LOGIC OF COLLIGATION

For the want of a nail the shoe was lost, for the want of a shoe the horse was lost, for the want of a horse the rider was lost, for the want of a rider the message was lost, for the want of a message the regiment was lost, and for the want of a regiment the battle was lost.

— Military anecdote, quoted in Fischer, *Historians' Fallacies*

By the logic of colligation I mean those rules that guide, or ought to guide, the historian in tracing the course of events that leads up to the explanandum event and thereby explains why it occurred—or, to put it in another way, those rules that guide, or ought to guide, the historian in framing a colligatory chain. Philosophers of history have paid little attention to these rules, while historians have applied them instinctively rather than consciously. Yet they are important and deserve attention.

The first rule is to define the explanandum event exactly. As Georg von Wright observes, "Before explanation can begin, its object—the *explanandum*—must be described."[1] To the question, of what are explananda composed? most historians would answer "events," which only raises the question, what is the nature of "an event"? To this question Rolf Gruner and W. H. Walsh have given a clear and comprehensive answer. Events are not facts, since facts are "stated," whereas

---

1. Wright, *Explanation and Understanding*, 134–35.

events "occur" or "happen" or "take place." Neither is an event an object, since objects have an identity that persists. It is inappropriate, remark Gruner and Walsh, to say that Caesar was an event. What then is an event? An event, argue Gruner and Walsh, is a change in a state of affairs, or, put differently, a change in the state of an object. An object R is in state S_1; an event E happens; R's state S_1 is replaced by S_2.[2]

The emphasis on change, which is central to the definition of "an event," finds corroboration in the writings of Arthur Danto but is strongly opposed by Murray Murphey.[3] Murphey argues that history deals with particular facts, whether events or changes, and urges that history seeks to explain at least four different things: changes, laws, data, and facts. In doing so he introduces a profound confusion, a confusion that Gruner and Walsh carefully avoid. Murphey fails to see that data and facts are only the report of events. It is the events that historians seek to explain, not the data or facts (though they are, of course, concerned to see that the data and facts faithfully report the events). Murphey's reference to laws is a more valuable observation, though on closer examination a law turns out to be only a statement of the regularity with which events of a certain kind occur. That the historian needs to explain this regularity is indubitable, which is the reason Murphey's observation is valuable.

Gruner and Walsh are acutely aware of the complexity of "an event." In particular, they realize that an event may be conceived of as an object. They cite the example of a battle. A battle may be viewed as an object whose state changes. It was first slack, then fierce. Or it may be thought of as an event that changed the state of affairs of a country, as the Battle of Hastings changed the state of affairs in England. Similarly, the French Revolution can be viewed as an event or as an object: as an event it explains the end of the *Ancien Régime;* as an object it comprehends, among much else, the course of events in 1792—the fall of the monarchy, the September Massacres, the election to the Convention. An event, then, is made up of subevents. There is, however, a limit to this subdivision. We do not, observe Gruner and Walsh, speak of a horse happening.[4]

---

2. Gruner and Walsh, "The Notion of an Historical Event," 136–46. In "The Structure of States of Affairs," 107, Roderick Chisholm challenges Davidson's belief that events are particular things just as physical objects and persons are particular things. He holds that an event is an abstract object, which he calls a "state of affairs." Whatever the outcome of this ontological dispute, Gruner's description of an event remains useful in describing what historians actually study.

3. Danto, *Analytical Philosophy of History,* 233; Murphey, *Our Knowledge of the Historical Past,* 92–93.

4. Gruner and Walsh, "Historical Event," 149–52.

The multiplicity of subevents within an event makes it mandatory that the historian define the explanandum event precisely. "We do not explain events as such," remarks Danto, "but rather events under a certain description."[5] Historians who have ignored this maxim have created much needless controversy. R. H. Tawney, for example, attributed the English Revolution to the rise of the gentry. Hugh Trevor-Roper furiously opposed this view, attributing the English Revolution to the discontent of a declining gentry. In fact the two historians were talking about wholly different aspects of the English Revolution—Tawney about the parliamentary opposition to Charles I in 1641, Trevor-Roper about the Independents in 1648.[6]

Tawney and Trevor-Roper discuss different stages in an unfolding revolution; Lawrence Stone and Anthony Fletcher, different aspects of the revolution at the same stage in its development. Thus Stone entitles his work *The Causes of the English Revolution* and focuses on demands for changes in church and state, while Fletcher entitles his work *The Outbreak of the English Civil War* and focuses on the outbreak of fighting in August 1642. Both books are about the English Revolution, but they are about different aspects of it.

The fact that an event is often composed of subevents raises the problem of the relation of the subevents to the principal event. Peter Ossorio offers one solution: the subevents are constituents of the whole, as a carburetor is a constituent of an engine.[7] This, however, suggests an interconnectedness in historical affairs that is not there. Another possibility is that the relation is a causal one, but this hardly survives a moment's thought. Events do not cause the subevents, neither do the subevents cause the event. There may well have been many skirmishes at the Battle of Waterloo that did not contribute to Wellington's final victory but are regarded as part of the Battle of Waterloo. Indeed, one is driven back to the conclusion that complex events, such as the Battle of Waterloo or the English Revolution or the Protestant Reformation, are held together by nothing more than the fact that the events occurred in a certain place within a given time. Yet this is too loose. Much happened during the Protestant Reformation that would never fall within a history of the Protestant Reformation. It would be better to conclude that a subevent is related to an event by the fact that it contributed to the change in the state of affairs that the event is said to have caused. Thus

5. Danto, *Analytical Philosophy of History*, 250.

6. For an acute criticism of Tawney's and Trevor-Roper's views, see Perez Zagorin, "The Social Interpretation of the English Revolution," 381–87.

7. Ossorio, "*What Actually Happens*," 84–85.

any event that contributed to the replacement of the Catholic faith with the Protestant may be regarded as a subevent of the Protestant Reformation. Contributing to that change is the common denominator that holds the subevents together, as part of what may be called an aggregate event.

The second rule in the logic of colligation is to work backward from the event to be explained, or from that aspect of the event that is to be explained. Stylistically, historians carry their narratives forward through time, but logically they build their arguments backward through time. Historians who would explain the outbreak of civil war in August 1642 should begin with Charles I's raising his banner at Nottingham and with numerous royalists' flocking to that banner. They must then explain what caused Charles I to raise his standard and the royalists to flock to it. Few historians would doubt that it was the Militia Ordinance and the Nineteen Propositions, which placed military, executive, and ecclesiastical power in Parliament, that led the King to act and many Englishmen to support him. Nor would they doubt that it was Charles's refusal of the Ten Heads, his search for an army, and his attempted arrest of the Five Members that led Parliament to seek to seize military, executive, and ecclesiastical power. What led Charles to search for a military solution was his profound dissatisfaction with the political settlement of 1641 and his fear of the Root and Branch party. What led to the political settlement and the rise of the Root and Branch party was the summoning of the Long Parliament at a time when deeply felt political and religious grievances united Englishmen against the government of Laud and Strafford. Defeat in the two Bishops' Wars and bankruptcy forced Charles to summon the Long Parliament and so allow his subjects to demand the redress of grievances. Scottish zeal and English sullenness led to defeat in the two Bishops' Wars. And it was the introduction of a new Service Book in 1637 that precipitated the two Bishops' Wars.[8]

The colligatory chain becomes clearer if the steps are numbered, moving forward through time.

1. The introduction of the Service Book caused the Bishops' Wars.
2. The outbreak of war, joined with Scottish zeal and English sullenness, led to an English defeat.

8. I have drawn this colligatory chain from narratives written by Samuel Rawson Gardiner (*History of England,* vol. 10), C. V. Wedgwood (*The King's Peace*), Lawrence Stone (*The Causes of the English Revolution*), Anthony Fletcher (*The Outbreak of the English Civil War*), and Robert Ashton (*The English Civil War*). Though these authors differ in their interpretations of these events, they agree on what the course of events was.

3. Defeat, combined with the financial weakness of the Crown, led to bankruptcy and the summoning of the Long Parliament.
4. The summoning of the Long Parliament, combined with the existence of political and religious grievances, led to the political settlement of 1641 and the rise of the Root and Branch party.
5. The political settlement of 1641 and the rise of the Root and Branch party led Charles I to seek a military solution.
6. Charles's search for an army and rejection of the Ten Heads caused Parliament to pass the Nineteen Propositions and the Militia Ordinance.
7. The passage of the Nineteen Propositions and the Militia Ordinance led Charles to raise his standard at Nottingham and many royalists to flock to it.

One observation needs to be made at once: the above is not really a chain of events but a web of events. To be more precise, each link in the chain is made up of the initial conditions plus the covering law that connects these initial conditions to the event to be explained. This might be shown schematically as in Diagram 4. In the next link E_a becomes C_{b_1}, as in Diagram 5, and so forth through the chain, which now rather resembles a web of events.

$$
\begin{array}{c}
C_{a_1} \\
C_{a_2} \\
C_{a_3} \\
C_{a_4} \\
\vdots \\
C_{a_n}
\end{array}
\quad + \quad L_a \quad \text{explains} \quad E_a
$$

Diagram 4. C stands for conditions, L for law, and E for event.

$$
\begin{array}{c}
C_{b_1} \\
C_{b_2} \\
C_{b_3} \\
C_{b_4} \\
\vdots \\
C_{b_n}
\end{array}
\quad + \quad L_b \quad \text{explains} \quad E_b
$$

Diagram 5.

There is a strategy for making the web of events a straightforward chain of events: from the initial conditions select each time the most disruptive or abnormal condition and follow the most abnormal conditions through the web, ignoring all the others. One then has a chain, which may be shown schematically as

$$C_{a_1} \quad + \quad L_a \quad \text{explains} \quad E_a$$

E_a then becomes C_{b_1}, which leads to

$$C_{b_1} \quad + \quad L_b \quad \text{explains} \quad E_b$$

and so forth (in which a_1 and b_1 stand for the most abnormal condition among the initial conditions).

Applying this scheme to the outbreak of the civil war, one would have the following: the introduction of the Service Book led to the Bishops' Wars, the Bishops' Wars to defeat, defeat to the summoning of the Long Parliament, the summoning of the Long Parliament to the political settlement of 1641, the political settlement of 1641 to Charles's search for an army, Charles's search for an army to the Militia Ordinance, and the Militia Ordinance to Charles's raising the banner at Nottingham and the royalists' rallying around it. This form of colligation, the simplest form (perhaps too simple), may be called linear colligation, but colligation as a means of historical explanation is far more complex than this. In fact colligation may take, and should take, many forms, of which at least eight can be identified. They are

1. linear colligation,
2. convergent colligation,
3. divergent colligation,
4. microcolligation,
5. parallel colligation,
6. cumulative colligation,
7. repetitive colligation,
8. analytical colligation.

Linear Colligation

I have already described this form of colligation, but it raises one problem, that of infinite regress, which deserves attention. Benedetto Croce has stated the problem most explicitly. "It is very well known," he writes, "what happens when one fact is linked to another as its cause, forming a chain of causes and effects; we thus inaugurate an infinite regression, and we never succeed in finding the cause or causes to which we can finally attach the chain we have been so industriously putting together."[9] Or as Michael Oakeshott remarks, such a procedure "would resolve history into an infinite regress of abstractions in search of an absolute beginning, or limit its reference to whatever lay immediately behind the given event."[10] To this problem Hart and Honoré have offered one solution: a voluntary act puts an end to the search backward for the ultimate cause.[11] This doctrine no doubt has a place in law, but it has no place in history. Charles I's raising his standard at Nottingham in August 1642 was a voluntary act, but no historian would begin an account of the coming of the English Civil War with that act. A far better approach is that suggested by Arthur Danto and Michael Scriven.[12] Historians, they argue, seek to explain why change occurs. An explanandum event specifies the state of x, say A, before x changed into its present condition, say B. A man who died was once alive. Therefore the historian begins an explanation of the man's death, not with his birth, though that was a necessary condition of his being alive, but when he was last alive and healthy. (Though, as is shown in later chapters, if his possessing a weak constitution explains his death, the etiology of that weak constitution might be traced back to his birth.) Charles I in 1637 ruled a tranquil, prosperous kingdom; in August 1642 he did not. On 27 June 1914 Europe was at peace, its inhabitants drinking the waters of Ems and Baden Baden. On the 4 August Europe was at war. It is no accident that historians of the English Revolution begin their narratives with the introduction of a new Service Book into the Scottish church and that historians of the First World War begin with the assassination of the Archduke Ferdinand at Sarajevo on 28 June.

What changed on both occasions was a state of affairs. England was tranquil, it became troubled. Europe was at peace, it fell into war. Analytical philosophers dreamed up the problem of infinite regress, a problem that has never disturbed historians. Historians instinctively stop the backward search for the ultimate cause at the point where the state of affairs, whose alteration they seek to explain, flourished. To explain the death of a man one usually does not need to go beyond the last year when he was healthy and flourishing.

Far more serious than the problem of infinite regress is the problem of the simplicity and naïveté of linear colligation. It leaves out too much. To

9. As quoted in Patrick Gardiner, *The Nature of Historical Explanation*, 70–71.

10. Oakeshott, *Experience and Its Modes*, 127.

11. Hart and Honoré, *Causation in the Law*, 70. They do recognize that there are many exceptions to this doctrine of voluntarism.

12. Danto, *Analytical Philosophy of History*, 247–51; Scriven, "Causes, Connections, and Conditions in History," 257.

choose each time only one condition among the set of initial conditions is to ignore other conditions that might be significant. The celebrated story of the loss of a battle for the want of a nail rightly ridicules the simple-mindedness of linear colligation. "For the want of a nail the shoe was lost, for the want of a shoe the horse was lost, for the want of a horse the rider was lost, for the want of a rider the message was lost, for the want of a message the regiment was lost, and for the want of a regiment the battle was lost."[13]

More to the point, one cannot explain the origins of the two Bishops' Wars merely by referring to the imposition of a Service Book on the Scottish church; one must also mention that Charles threatened the Scottish nobility with the loss of their monastic lands. Similarly, one cannot explain the political settlement of 1641 simply by referring to the summoning of the Long Parliament; one must also mention the existence of (and trace the origins of) a sense of grievance throughout the kingdom. Anger at the service book converged with fear of losing monastic lands to produce the two Bishops' Wars. The summoning of the Long Parliament converged with a sense of grievances to produce the political settlement of 1641. The kind of colligation that represents what historians really do is convergent colligation.

Convergent Colligation

The nature of convergent colligation can be seen in diagram 6, drawn by R. M. MacIver.[14] It can be seen that A is the explanandum event, whose occurrence is explained by the convergence of B, B_1, and B_2, that the occurrence of B, B_1, and B_2 are in turn explained by the convergence, respectively, of C, C_1, C_2, of C_1, C_3, and C_5, and of C_2, C_4, and C_6, and so forth. "Clearly," writes MacIver, "there are many sequences that lead to A, and their number increases in a kind of geometrical ratio, the more links we add to the chain."[15] Hart and Honoré, borrowing from Glanville Williams, call this a "cone" of causation, so called because the series of

13. Fischer, *Historians' Fallacies*, 172. N. R. Hanson, in "Causal Chains," 289, gives a slightly different version of the anecdote: "For want of a nail a horseshoe was lost; for want of a horse a rider was lost; for want of a rider a battalion was lost; for want of a battalion a battle was lost; for want of a victory a kingdom was lost." Hanson's article, ostensibly an attack on colligation, is in fact an attack on simpleminded linear colligation.

14. MacIver, *Social Causation*, 190.

15. Ibid., 189.

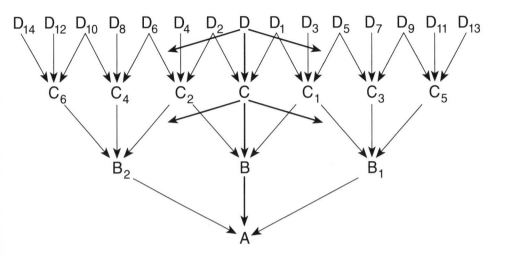

Diagram 6. Simplified Diagram of a Historical Sequence.

simultaneous conditions fans out as one goes back in time.[16] MacIver's diagram and Glanville Williams's image are helpful, but somewhat abstract. To understand convergent colligation in all of its complexity one needs to examine an example of it.

The outbreak of the English Civil War in August 1642 offers a convenient example. The first fact to observe is that not one condition but a set of conditions explains Charles's decision to raise his banner at Nottingham. True, his refusal to accept the Nineteen Propositions and the Militia Ordinance is the weightiest condition, but there were others, such as his determination to protect episcopacy, his exalted concept of kingship, his belief that he could win, the urgings of his wife, Henrietta Maria, even the fact that he did not die of small pox on the day before he raised his standard at Nottingham. The historian must also examine the conditions that led royalists to flock to his banner, conditions such as the illegality of Parliament's demands, fear of social anarchy, anger at proposals to alter the prayer book, loyalty to the King, and even the fact that they were still active in their counties and not prisoners in the Tower. And finally the historian must explain why the parliamentarians stuck to their demands to wrest military, executive, and ecclesiastical power from

16. Hart and Honoré, *Causation in the Law,* 64.

the king, an explanation that would include such conditions as the King's refusal to dissolve the Irish army, his plotting with the English army, his taking advice from gentlemen of the bedchamber, his favoring Catholics, the outbreak of the Irish Rebellion, and even the fact that the parliamentarians had not all emigrated to the colonies.

This analysis marks only the beginning of the historian's labors. He must then take each of these conditions as an explanandum event and discover.the set of conditions that caused its occurrence or appearance. In this fashion he must make his way back to the imposition of a new Service Book on the Scottish Church in 1637. The complexity of this cone of causation is daunting, and the historian who seeks to display it in its entirety may well lose his reader in a labyrinth of connections and inter-connections. To write a clear narrative, comprehensible to the reader, he obviously must find some strategies to guide himself and his reader through the labyrinth.

Of these strategies the most important is explanatory closure. Explana-tory closure can operate in two ways: vertically, by shortening the list of initial conditions that deserve inclusion, and horizontally, by not tracing a sequence backward in time. I call the first vertical because in my mind's eye I see a vertical list of initial conditions that, with the appropriate covering law, explain the occurrence of an event. Thus, the conditions leading Charles to raise his standard would appear as follows:

1. Determination not to accept the Militia Ordinance
2. Determination not to accept the Nineteen Propositions
3. Resolve to defend episcopacy
4. An exalted sense of kingship
5. The urgings of his wife, Henrietta Maria
6. That he had not died of smallpox the day before.

A historian could exercise closure after the first two; more likely he would exercise it after the first three. Yet he may choose to include four and five also. He would assuredly omit six, and all other necessary though utterly normal conditions.

The principles that guide the historian in the exercise of vertical ex-planatory closure are those described in the previous chapter, principally that of abnormalism. That Charles did not die of smallpox is in no way extraordinary—in no way did it disrupt the normal course of events— and therefore it does not deserve mention (though, had he died, the whole course of events would have been altered). Charles's exalted sense of kingship occupies a middle ground—he had always cherished such notions (as had Queen Elizabeth), yet they now assumed a new importance as Parliament made demands upon him that invaded his prerogative. The Nineteen Propositions require inclusion because they were an unprecedented demand upon the King, wholly disruptive of the accepted course of government.

I call a decision not to trace a sequence backward in time *horizontal closure* because in my mind's eye I see the cone of causation moving from left to right, horizontally, across a page, thus:

Scottish zeal $\searrow$
Prayer Book $\to$ Bishops' Wars $\to$ Defeat $\to$ Long Parliament $\to$ etc.
Financial weakness $\to$ Bankruptcy $\nearrow$

The historian of the English Civil War will surely trace the principal events that led from the introduction of the new Service Book to the outbreak of war, and he will surely include many subsidiary conditions that help to explain the course of events. But having introduced those subsidiary conditions, he need not trace them back in time (though he may if he wishes). He may argue that Scottish zeal, joined to the outbreak of the second Bishops' War, led to the defeat of England, yet he need not trace back to its source the zeal of the Scots. Or he may mention that the financial bankruptcy of the Crown, joined to defeat in the Bishops' War, led to the summoning of the Long Parliament. He may even show how that bankruptcy arose from the financial weakness of the Crown. But then he may exercise closure and not discuss the Tudor origins of that financial weakness. There is no law that says that the historian must pursue every sequence backward in time, especially those he believes less important than others; neither is there any law that says that other historians may not do so. History is a collective enterprise in which many historians explore numerous historical sequences.

The fact of horizontal explanatory closure raises the problem: how do historians determine which sequences in the cone of causation are more important than others and which steps within a sequence are more crucial than others? There are a number of ways they do this, among them (1) distinguishing causes from means, (2) detecting blind alleys, (3) discovering consequential sequences, and (4) excluding overdetermined sequences.

When a man shoots another man, the actual cause of death is the failure of oxygen to reach the brain of the victim. The sequence goes like this: the murderer aims the gun, he pulls the trigger, the gun fires, the bullet tears a hole in the victim's artery, the blood drains out of the wound, the blood is unable to reach the lungs to replenish its oxygen or to carry that oxygen to the brain, for want of oxygen the brain dies. Though this sequence of events indisputably occurs, the police report need not describe it; the report need only report that John Doe shot and killed Richard Roe with a handgun. What makes the pulling of the trigger the "cause" of the victim's death and the rest of the events "the means" of his death is the abnormality of the former and the normality of the latter, though perhaps a better expression would be the predictability of the latter. It is quite predictable, though not entirely so, that squeezing the trigger will cause the pistol to fire, that the bullet will tear an artery, that blood will flow out of a torn artery, that the want of blood will deprive the brain of oxygen, and that the want of oxygen will destroy the brain. The predictability of this sequence makes it a means by which the death comes about, not its cause, and so may be omitted from a discussion of its cause.

Historians often express this distinction with the phrase "the point of no return," meaning that a politician or statesman has taken an action that is as irrevocable as John Doe's squeezing the trigger. Anthony Fletcher comments thus on Parliament's passage of the Militia Ordinance: "There was no room for retreat."[17] In other words, the responses of the King and of Parliament were now so fixed, so predictable, that the events that occurred from March through August 1642 were rather the means by which the civil war came about than its cause. On another occasion Fletcher pushes the point of no return back to September 1641, writing, "The most important outcome of the politics of November 1640 to September 1641 was that Charles closed his mind to negotiation and so did Pym. The less they trusted the King the more they wanted the future guaranteed. . . . It is at least arguable that an insoluble political crisis was bound to follow."[18]

Or consider this example. The historian who would explain why the United States dropped an atomic bomb on Hiroshima would examine President Truman's motives for ordering the bombing but not the bombardier's decision to release the bomb.[19] Ordering the dropping of the bomb was an extraordinary event; obeying orders was a normal event.

17. Fletcher, *The Outbreak of the English Civil War*, 245.
18. Ibid., 89.
19. I have borrowed this example from Morton White (*Foundations of Historical Knowledge*, 144), who, curiously, does not use it to illustrate the doctrine of abnormalism, even though it follows directly after a discussion of horizontal and vertical multiplicity. It should be noted that in White's discussion of multiplicity of contributory causes (p. 142), his use of "vertical" and "horizontal" is the direct reverse of my use of them in discussing vertical and horizontal closure. Though we are using reverse terminology, we are saying the same thing.

Had the bombardier refused to release the bomb, historians would certainly have seized on that extraordinary event to explain why the bomb was not dropped on Hiroshima.

The distinction between cause and means can be abused by historians. E. B. Segal directs just such a criticism at A.J.P. Taylor's account of the coming of the Second World War. "By reducing all activism in German policy to the lowest possible point, Taylor has paradoxically reversed the ordinary chain of causal explanation. Hitler's bold enterprises have become simply reactions to British and French moves; and what were in part their response to positive German steps have been transformed into active initiatives which dropped concessions into Hitler's lap. . . . This is more than a misuse of evidence, it is a failure of conception."[20] Segal rightly speaks of Hitler's "bold enterprises" on the one hand and of Britain's and France's mere "responses" on the other, the former being more disruptive, more abnormal, the other more predictable, more normal. And Segal is certainly right that it was a failure of conception on the part of Taylor, for whatever one thinks of the international order in 1939, it was Hitler who disrupted it, not Britain and France.

At the other end of the spectrum from means, which do not deserve mention, are crucial events, which deserve emphasis. Historians often speak about "crucial actions," "decisive battles," "fatal decisions," "critical turning points." One characteristic that makes them crucial or decisive or fatal or critical is the fact that they are as unpredictable as the means of carrying forward a sequence are predictable. A football team, for example, may drive down the field to a touchdown in nine plays, yet the journalist describing the game will refer to only one crucial play, a completed pass on a third down with twenty yards to go for a first down. Driving off tackle for four yards is routine; completing a pass on third and twenty, to earn a first down, is not. Similarly, the historian of the Battle of Blenheim focuses not on the fierce fighting at Hochstadt and Blindheim during the morning but on the maneuver by which Marlborough in the afternoon moved his troops from the village of Blindheim to the center, thus outnumbering the French two to one at the decisive moment in the battle. Fierce fighting is normal in a battle; maneuvering one's troops so as to outnumber the enemy two to one is not. In a like manner, the voting of the Grand Remonstrance was a critical step in the coming of the civil war because earlier actions, such as the abolition of the Court of Star Chamber and the condemnation of ship money were seen by the majority of the Commons as legal and proper, but the demand in the Grand Remonstrance that the

20. As quoted in Dray, "Concepts of Causation in A.J.P. Taylor's Account of the Origins of the Second World War," 166 n.33.

King name advisers in whom Parliament could confide and that he summon a synod to reform the Church were seen by many as illegal and
improper. In the minds of historians there is a spectrum of events, ranging
from the ordinary, the normal, the predictable to the extraordinary, the
abnormal, the unpredictable. Just as they choose the more abnormal conditions from a set of initial conditions, so they choose the more abnormal
causes from a sequence of causes.

There are two other characteristics that make an event crucial or decisive or fatal or critical, namely, the fact that many consequences flow
from its occurrence and the fact that these consequences would not have
flowed from other possible sequences of events. These two characteristics may be called the principle of divergence and the principle of simple
determination.

Divergent Colligation

Divergent colligation is the opposite of convergent colligation. Rather
than diverse events leading to one event, one event leads to diverse
events. Thus the Grand Remonstrance was crucial as well for the consequences that flowed from its passage as for its abnormal character. It
provoked Charles into radical action. It helped create a royalist party. It
encouraged the opponents of episcopacy. It caused the parliamentarians
to bypass the Lords in their appeal to the people. It even kept Cromwell
from emigrating to the American colonies. These many consequences
later converged to help cause the outbreak of civil war in August 1642. The
principle of convergence and divergence can be depicted as in Diagram 7.

James Burke is one of the few historians to recognize explicitly the
existence of such a nexus. Writing of Francois Perier's discovery that
mercury in a tube was lower at the top of Puy le Dome than at the
bottom, he asserts: "The experiment on top of the mountain represents
another of those moments that occur in the process of change, in which
things come to a nexus. The invention of the barometer and the discovery of air pressure suddenly multiplied the number of possible routes
that the path of innovation could take."[21]

Burke's example shows that divergent sequences need not converge
once again to explain the occurrence of a single event, though of course
they may. In many instances such a sequence simply broadens out into a
web of events. When Charles Darwin and Alfred Russell Wallace formu-

---

21. Burke, *Connections*, 74–75.

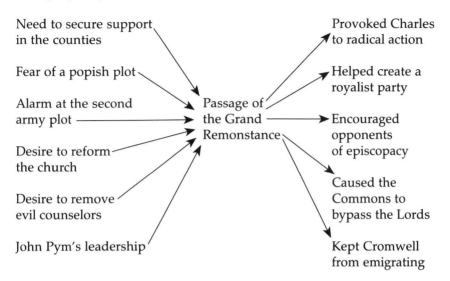

Diagram 7. The consequences listed on the right were caused in each case by the Grand Remonstrance plus other initial conditions; in all cases explanatory closure has been exercised.

lated the theory of evolution by natural selection, they set in motion a train of events that led to modern biology. Similarly when James Dewey Watson and Francis Crick discovered the structure of DNA, they set in motion a web of events leading to contemporary microbiology.

The very negation of divergence is a blind alley, that is, an event or a sequence of events that does not lead to the explanandum event. Imagine a baseball game in which in the first inning the shortstop for Cincinnati makes an error, allowing the batter to reach first base. But the pitcher then strikes out the next three men. Then in the bottom of the ninth, with Cincinnati leading Pittsburgh three to one, and with two outs, the second baseman makes an error, allowing the batter to reach first base. Upset by this, the pitcher walks the next man. The third batter then hits a home run. Pittsburgh wins four to three. The first error is of no consequence in explaining Pittsburgh's victory; it is a blind alley that no reporter would even mention. The second error was crucial, and any reporter who did not invoke it to explain Pittsburgh's victory would be derelict.

A familiar historical example of a blind alley is Andrew Jackson's victory over the British at New Orleans. The historian seeking to explain the Treaty of Ghent, which ended the War of 1812, need not mention Jackson's victory, since the negotiators at Ghent had completed their work before news of the victory reached Europe. Similarly, there is no need to evoke the Earl of Bedford's death in May 1641 to explain the failure of negotiations between the leaders of Parliament and the King, since those negotiations had already failed in April. Bedford's death and Jackson's victory might better be called empty alleys, since potential causal sequences were preempted by earlier sequences. One is dealing here with parallel, rather than convergent or divergent, colligation. T. A. Climo and P.G.A. Howells have shown that the historian must resort to counterfactual arguments of this kind to distinguish a genuine causal sequence from a preempted one.[22]

The existence of genuine and preempted causal sequences leads to a consideration of overdetermination and simple determination. When applied to the initial conditions that, with the appropriate covering law, explain the occurrence of a single event, overdetermination is rare— about as rare as two bullets simultaneously killing a man. But overdetermination, as applied to the existence of alternative possible sequences of events, is far more common. Many an assassin has discovered, upon the assassination of a leader, that there was another leader prepared to carry out the same program. Dutch resistance to Spain, for example, did not collapse with the assassination of William the Silent; Maurice of Nassau simply took over the leadership of the Dutch resistance to Spain.

An analogy drawn from farming can make vivid the relation between overdetermination and the crucial character of a sequence. Imagine a farmer intent on irrigating his fields. He plows furrows horizontally across his field, letting water flow from the irrigation ditch into the top furrow. In the piled-up soil separating the first furrow from the second, he digs three openings, so that the water may reach the second furrow. He likewise digs three openings between the second and third, and so forth. But between the third and fourth furrows he digs not three openings but only one (see Diagram 8). Now, it is obvious that if some accident occurred that caused one of the three openings between furrows one and two to become clogged, or between two and three, or between four and five, nothing would be lost. The water would flow through the other openings. But if the single opening between the third and fourth furrows became clogged, the most serious consequences would arise. Water would not reach the farther field. The opening between the third and fourth furrow is crucial, decisive, fatal. The three openings in the other furrows are not; they are not because they are overdetermined. The single opening between furrows three and four may, when open, be said to be simply determined; when clogged, underdetermined.

The summoning of the Long Parliament offers an excellent illustration

22. Climo and Howells, "Possible Worlds in Historical Explanation," 12–13.

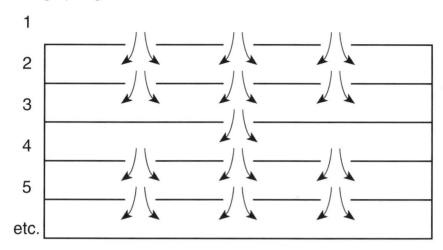

Diagram 8.

of an event that was crucial because it was simply determined. It may be called simply determined because there was no other institution in English public life for impeaching ministers, legislating against arbitrary taxation and prerogative courts, securing redress of grievances, and withholding supplies until those grievances were redressed. The English church, whose bishops Charles named, the courts of law, whose judges Charles appointed, the City of London, whose jurisdiction lay only in the City, the universities, which were far from London, could hardly organize resistance to the King. The only historical sequence that could have led to the outbreak of civil war had to pass through Parliament. It was quite otherwise in Scotland, where the Parliament was not the only possible organizer of resistance. In fact it was the General Assembly of the Scottish church, meeting at Glasgow, that organized resistance to Charles. In England, this was not so, and thus the historian may safely assert that the summoning of the Long Parliament was a crucial step in the coming of civil war.

To argue that the summoning of the Long Parliament was crucial is to appeal to a counterfactual, namely, that had it not been summoned, there would have been no civil war. There have been philosophers of history, Croce among them, who have insisted that historians are not at all concerned with what might have happened or could have happened. "It is curious," comments Morris Cohen about this fact, "that those most concerned with the close relation between history and practice should hold this dogma, when it is so obvious that all practical activity involves weighing the consequence of alternatives only one of which is realized. There is considerable evidence that if Alexander had been drowned crossing the Granicus none of his generals could have accomplished what he did."[23] George Eliot offers an even more arresting example. "Hamlet, Prince of Denmark, was speculative and irresolute, and we have a great tragedy in consequence. But if his father had lived to a good old age, and his uncle had died an early death, we can conceive Hamlet's having married Ophelia, and got through life with a reputation of sanity."[24]

Such appeals to the counterfactual are, however, dangerous. They may be safely made only where one step in a sequence is concerned, or where the succeeding steps are predictable, and when that first step is a negative counterfactual—for example, had the Long Parliament *not* been summoned, Strafford would not have been impeached. An appeal to a counterfactual can even be hazarded about a sequence of events, if the counterfactual is negative and is the crucial step in a sequence fruitful of many consequences. One can conclude that had the Long Parliament not been summoned, there would have been no impeachments, no abolition of Star Chamber, no attacks on the Church. Even this is a dangerous enterprise, if extended to the outbreak of war. The English in 1688 drove their King from the throne even though he had not summoned Parliament.

It is dangerous to appeal to counterfactuals that extend over a long sequence of events, because each step in that sequence multiplies the possibility of error. Any assertion of causation in history (the reverse of which is a counterfactual assertion) is only probable. Assume that there is a 4:5 chance that a person is correct in saying that A caused B (i.e., that had A not occurred, B would not have occurred). For simplicity's sake assume that the same probability holds for B causing C, for C causing D, and for D causing E. The probability of this linear colligatory chain holding true falls from 4:5 to 16:25 to 64:125 to 256:625, or from 80 percent to 64 percent to 51 percent to 41 percent. If the counterfactual were positive (i.e., had X occurred, Y would have occurred, and so forth) the probabilities would be lower, say 2:5, and the aggregate probability would drop correspondingly lower at each step. This fact explains why Pascal's remark that the Roman Empire would not have fallen had Cleopatra's nose been an inch longer strikes the historian as ridiculous. Yet historians do make similar assertions. Recently Hugh Trevor-Roper wrote: "If a left-wing government had prevailed in Spain [after the Spanish Civil War], Hitler, in 1940 would not have stopped at the Pyrenees. He would have sent his army into Spain to overturn it and would have

23. Cohen, "Causation and Its Application," 20.
24. Eliot, *The Mill on the Floss*, 353.

taken Gibraltar by force. Thereby he would have closed the Mediterranean, transformed the position in the Near East, and won the war."[25] Each of these counterfactuals raises doubts. Hitler's plans were centered on the invasion of Russia, not Spain, whatever the nature of its government. Furthermore, he could not agree with Mussolini and Petain on what to do with Spain. Had he invaded Spain, the Spanish might have resisted (as they resisted Napoleon), and Churchill would surely not have meekly surrendered Gibraltar. British sea power might have struck back at the Canary Islands or Ceuta. Were Gibraltar taken, the Mediterranean might still have been supplied through Suez. Were the Mediterranean closed, the Near East might still have been maintained through the Red Sea and the Persian Gulf. But the Near East was only a peripheral theater of war, the principal theater being in Europe.[26] Allow Trevor-Roper a 4:5 chance of being right each time (which is an extremely generous allowance), yet the chance that the whole sequence would hold true is only, by my calculation, 1:5. One can only conclude that in making this statement Trevor-Roper elected to be clever rather than right.

The improbability that a long series of counterfactuals will hold true suggests yet another strategy for judging what is crucial in historical narrative: a historian should emphasize proximate rather than remote causes. This has long been a principle in law, where the maxim prevails, "In jure non remota causa sed proxima spectatur." The reason for the maxim lies in the fact that the more remote the cause, the greater the difficulty of proving that the accused person realized what the effect of his or her action would be. Hart and Honoré cite the case of a plaintiff who sought damages from defendants who were late in delivering four gallons of whiskey. For want of the whiskey, the plaintiff's lumberjacks would not go into the water to construct a raft; for want of their labor, the raft was not constructed by the time of the rains; for want of being constructed by the time of the rains, the raft could not be taken to market for a profitable sale. The judge ruled against the plaintiff, concluding that "whiskey is very potential at times, but it cannot be relied upon to produce such beneficent results as are claimed for it in this case."[27]

What makes a remote cause undependable is the fact that at every step in the chain there must be concurrent causes, about whose presence or absence the historian may be ignorant. Nor is it conceivable, given the

25. "The Acts of the Apostles," *New York Review of Books*, 31 March 1983, 6–7.

26. I have drawn these criticisms of Trevor-Roper's assertion from Robert H. Whealey's letter to the *New York Review of Books*, 12 May 1983, 60–61.

27. Hart and Honoré, *Causation in the Law*, 23, 349, 372.

role of chance in history, that the historian could know about all of them. Many years ago J. B. Bury defined chance as "the valuable collision of two or more independent chains of causes."[28] Ernest Nagel gives a similar definition—"An event occurring at the intersection of two independent causal series"—and gives the example of a man going to a store to purchase tobacco and being hit on the head by a falling brick.[29] The movements of the man, once he resolved to get tobacco, are predictable: his rising from the chair, his getting his wallet, his opening the door, his going down the walk, his turning left, his walking under the wall. Similarly, the fall of the brick is predictable: the buffeting of the wall by rain and wind and ice, the weakening of the mortar, its gradual erosion, the final gust of wind, the acceleration of the brick downward at thirty-two feet per second. What was unpredictable was that these two sequences should intersect at this moment in space and time. History is replete with such unpredictable intersections; hence the role of chance, of the contingent, of the accidental in history.

Given the historian's ignorance of concurrent causes and given the role of chance in history, it becomes manifest why the historian cannot predict the future course of events. There is no way that a historian could have predicted that the brick would fall just as the man walked under the wall—unless the historian were as omniscient as God and could foresee the infinite concatenation of events within the universe. Yet, after the event, the historian can explain why the man was hit by a brick, can say that he was hit by the brick because he went for tobacco at that moment. May Brodbeck has rightly argued that in an explanation by a covering law there is in principle a symmetry between prediction and explanation, though often not in practice. The same is true of explanation by colligation, though here the gap between practice and principle is immense. In principle a person as omniscient as God could know that the brick would fall as the man walked by. But this presumes an omniscience so great that one is tempted to say that in colligatory explanations there is an asymmetry in principle as well as in practice between prediction and explanation. Historians do not predict, or if they do, they soon look ridiculous. This is no accident. Our ignorance of concurrent causes and the role of chance make it impossible to predict. Yet historians do explain why what happened happened, often very thoroughly and convincingly. Because colligation is such an essential part of historical explanation, historians can explain even though they cannot predict.

---

28. As quoted in Gardiner, *The Nature of Historical Explanation,* 111.
29. Nagel, *The Structure of Science,* 326–27. Hart and Honoré give a similar definition (*Causation in the Law,* 74).

There are two exceptions to this gloomy picture of the possibility of prediction. Where there are predictable causal chains and where there are many alternative paths to an event, prediction is possible. Tobacco is so addictive that we can predict that the man who went for tobacco, had the brick spared him, would most likely not have given up smoking. One might even predict that he would die of lung cancer, though here the probability of the prediction being true is less. Where one is explaining an aggregate event—say, the sale of cigarettes in America—there are often alternative paths to an event. Though some adult men do give up smoking, young girls are taking up the habit. Thus wherever there is overdetermination in a colligatory chain, prediction becomes possible. Though one hole in the farmer's furrow becomes clogged, the water can go through others. Nicholas Rescher has shown how this can occur for indeterministic physical systems. He has shown how in some systems the near-term future is more predictable than the long-term future, while in other systems the long-term future is more predictable than the near-term future.[30] The latter occurs when A may cause B or may cause C, but B will always cause D, and C will always cause D. Thus, though we cannot be sure that A will cause B, we can be sure that it will cause D. Clearly, for this to happen there must be alternative chains of causation ending in the explanandum event, D, which we seek both to explain and predict. In fact, if we are ignorant whether the causal path went through B or C, we can predict better than explain. Or more exactly, our explanation would be a macroexplanation, that is, that A caused D, but not a microexplanation, that is, that A caused B which caused D.

Microcolligation

Earlier in this chapter I listed seven steps leading from the introduction of the Service Book at St. Giles to the outbreak of civil war in August 1642 and suggested that each step was connected to the next by a set of initial conditions and a covering law. Thus a set of initial conditions (including the introduction of the Service Book) plus a covering law connect the first and second steps, that is, explain the occurrence of the Bishops' Wars. But this is not what historians really do, at least it is not what Samuel Gardiner and C. V. Wedgwood do. They do not employ a covering law to explain the outbreak of the Bishops' Wars. They explain their

30. Rescher, *Scientific Explanation*, 51–57.

outbreak by tracing how they came about. In fact a careful reading of
Gardiner and Wedgwood shows that there were at least seven steps
from the introduction of the Service Book on 23 July 1637 to the outbreak
of the first Bishops' War.

1. The introduction of the Service Book led to the riot in St. Giles.
2. The riot in St. Giles led to the drawing up of the Supplication and
   Tables, that is, to resistance.
3. The drawing up of the Supplication and Tables led to the Royal Proclamation of 20 February 1638.
4. The Royal Proclamation led to the swearing of the National Covenant
   on 28 February 1638.
5. The swearing of the National Covenant led Charles to demand the
   repudiation of the Covenant, to threaten force if it was not repudi-
   ated, and to order Hamilton to declare the signatories of the Covenant traitors.
6. Charles's threat led the Glasgow Assembly to abolish episcopacy and
   prepare for war.
7. The abolition of episcopacy caused Charles to send an army to
   Scotland.

This more detailed examination of the course of events may usefully
be called microcolligation. It does not, however, stop here. The gap
between each of the above steps may be subjected to further microcolligation. Historians are as remorseless in their pursuit of ever more
microscopic explanations as sociologists are zealous in their pursuit of
ever broader laws. Historians will trace the daily, even the hourly, events
of history. Thus they might fill the gap between the first and second
steps above with the following sequence:

1. Charles's intention to issue on Easter a proclamation that the new
   Service Book be read the next week led Henderson and Dickson, two
   Presbyterian ministers, to meet at Nicholas Balfour's house in Edinburgh to plan resistance and draw in the disaffected nobility.
2. The possibility of resistance led the Earl of Traquair to persuade the
   King to postpone the introduction of the new Service Book to July.
3. The announcement on 16 July that the new Service Book would be
   used the next week in Edinburgh churches led to murmuring and
   complaint in Edinburgh and to Henderson's and Dickson's advising
   the women to give the first affront and the townsmen to leave when
   the new Service Book was read.

4. On 23 July the Dean of St. Giles entered the pulpit and began to read from the new Service Book, which led a multitude of wives and serving women to shout abuses and to hurl objects at the Dean.
5. The tumult led the Bishop of Edinburgh to enter the pulpit, seeking to restore order, but failing.
6. The Bishop's failure led him to summon the Chancellor, who ordered the magistrates to clear the church of rioters.
7. The ejection of the rioters led them to pelt the doors and break windows with stone, and to attack the Bishop as he walked back to his home.

The ultimate end of this microcolligation is the discovery of the single, discrete event and the author or authors of that event.

Historians, however, soon confront a problem, a problem that may be called the problem of gaps. For want of evidence, they often cannot pursue the sequence of events through all the intervening single, discrete events, and so to the authors of those events. They may find months and years for which there is no evidence. At some steps in the sequence they may have much information, at others some, at others none. J. A. Passmore has given a vivid example of the problem of gaps drawn from everyday life. He supposes that he had ten miles to go in order to get home. He then explains to a listener that he traveled five miles by bus and three miles by taxi. That is all the information he gives. There is a gap of two miles in the explanation how he got home. What does the listener do to fill the gap?[31]

The answer is that the listener must, in order to explain how Passmore got home, invoke a covering law of greater generality. He might say that Passmore "either walked or found some other means of transportation"—it being improbable that he crawled or flew. In a similar manner historians who compose historical narratives must move up and down a ladder of generality. If the available evidence is sparse they must use covering laws of greater generality and often of less probability. If the evidence available is rich, they will trace the minute connections between events, using covering laws of greater particularity and therefore often of greater probability. The lawyer, as well as the historian, prefers to trace the connections between events rather than employ more general covering laws. A distinction must be made, write Hart and Honoré, "between statements of causal connexion and statements of probability; for the use of the latter is to argue from one event

31. Passmore, "Explanation in Everyday Life, in Science, and in History," 111.

to the other on the basis of limited knowledge, not to argue from one to another in the light of 'complete' knowledge."[32]

Since historians of medieval Europe confront these gaps in explanation more often than historians of modern Europe, it is appropriate to take an example from medieval history. In his *Anglo-Saxon England and the Norman Conquest* Henry Royston Loyn seeks to explain the freedom enjoyed by the sokemen in the Danelaw in 1086. There are those historians, he writes, who explain the freedom of the sokemen by the fact that they were Danish and brought that freedom with them from Denmark in the ninth century. But other historians argue that they were free not because they were Danish but because, while residing in East Anglia, they adopted the freedom of the society that existed there. If historians possessed a description of these sokemen (1) before they invaded England in the ninth century, (2) at the time of the invasion, (3) shortly after the invasion, and (4) a century later, they could soon put the problem to rest by tracing the history of the freedom of the sokemen. But historians do not have such evidence. Instead they must rely upon a covering law of greater generality. Loyn points out that free sokemen are found also in Mercia, where the freedom found in East Anglia never existed. He also notes that in Danish Leicestershire there were two thousand sokemen in the late eleventh century, while across Watling Street in English Warwickshire there was none.[33] The appeal here is to correlation, not colligation. The correlation between the existence of sokemen and a Danish population is high; the correlation between the existence of sokemen and an earlier English free society is low. So the historian concludes that the Danes brought their freedom with them. For want of immediate evidence to show that the Danish brought their freedom with them, the historian must appeal to a covering law that asserts that where there is a high correlation between a given trait and a particular people (and a low correlation between that trait and a particular section of the country), the customs of that particular people must explain the existence of the trait.

David Fischer and J. H. Hexter seem to believe that historical sequences are nearly always concealed. Thus Fischer writes:

> Narrative also involves the idea of connectedness among relevant events. But what is the nature of connections in a narrative series? "Tended, grew out of, developed, evolved, trend, development, tendency, evolution, growth," J. H. Hexter has written. "Such words are like sealed junction boxes on the complex circuits of

32. Hart and Honoré, *Causation in the Law*, 432.
33. Loyn, *Anglo-Saxon England and the Norman Conquest*, 54–55.

history. One knows that inside the boxes there are connections which induce the currents of history to change direction; but the boxes conceal rather than reveal how these connections are made."[34]

A quite different image occurs to me. It is the image of the Clapham railway junction, in which a dozen or more exposed wires run along the tracks from the signal operator's tower to various signals alongside the track. By pulling a lever the signal operator causes a signal hundreds of yards away to read "go" or "caution" or "stop." Suppose for a moment that the signal operator pulled a lever and two hundred yards down the track a signal moved to "stop." One could prove that the signal operator's pulling the lever caused the signal to move to "stop" by having the operator repeatedly perform the same act, with the same result, thus establishing an ever higher correlation between a pulled lever and a "stop" signal. This would be an exercise in correlation. But one could also examine where the lever was attached to the wire, follow the wire through a series of pulleys down the track and along it, and note where the wire was attached to the arm of the signal. This would be an exercise in colligation. It would also explain why the correlation existed; that is, it would transform correlation into causation. It is the proper image for the writing of narrative history.

Where Hexter's image is helpful is in explaining how historians bridge the gaps in their narratives, gaps caused by the want of evidence. Faced with a want of evidence describing part of a historical sequence, faced, that is, with a sealed junction box, historians must resort to more general covering laws. In this way they solve the problem of gaps. Yet it should be remarked that far more of the connections in history are open to inspection than Hexter seems to think. There are Clapham junctions as well as sealed junction boxes.

Parallel Colligation

The relentless pursuit of microcolligation often leads to parallel colligation. Parallel colligation is the description of a group of related events that occur simultaneously. To trace how a football team drives down the field in nine plays to score a touchdown is linear colligation. To describe in detail one of those plays is microcolligation. That description might

34. Fischer, *Historians' Fallacies*, 162–63.

have some linear elements—the center hands the football off to the quarterback who passes to the wide receiver—but it would have far more parallel elements, since twenty-two different players would be in motion simultaneously. Some would charge the passer, some would block for him, some feint and cut, others defend against the pass; one player might even trip and fall down. To explain why a play succeeded a reporter must describe the actions of many, if not all, the players. This is parallel colligation (though there may be some convergence in it), so called because the historian traces the separate but parallel actions of many persons.

This is particularly true of those who write about aggregate events, that is, about elections, battles, demonstrations, riots, legislative votes, migrations, and economic recessions. W. R. Fryer asks, "Did a swing in public opinion or John Robinson's management win the election of 1784?"[35] Now, no amount of linear colligation could answer this. To answer this question the historian must examine one constituency after another in order to discover whether in each constituency it was Robinson's management or a swing in public opinion that explained the result. What this resort to parallel colligation explains is an aggregate event, namely, the composition of the House of Commons—so many Whigs, so many Tories, so many independents. In this case the explanandum event is an aggregate event, and the explanation demands the exploration of many separate events. Such parallel colligation can be likened to a fiber-optic bundle, in which each fiber transmits only the light that enters into it and in which the whole bundle transmits an image formed by an array of closely packed dots, differing in brightness and color, coming from each fiber. In like manner separate elections give rise to the political coloration of a House of Commons.

On other occasions, in a legislative vote, for example, the separate simultaneous events converge on a single event. Parallel colligation now becomes convergent colligation, and the actions of the separate actors become concurrent causes of the passage of a bill. To explain why the Grand Remonstrance passed, the historian must explain why 159 members voted for it and 148 against it, though the explanandum event, the passage of the Grand Remonstrance, is a single event. Military history affords many examples of parallel colligation in which the explanandum event lies somewhere between an aggregate event and a discrete event. Consider the Battle of Borodino, about which Tolstoy wrote so movingly in *War and Peace*. He protests vehemently against attributing that victory

---

35. Fryer, "The Study of British Politics Between the Revolution and the Reform Act," 109.

to the genius of Napoleon. Such events, he argues, were the result of "the homogeneous, infinitesimal elements by which masses are led."[36] Though the evidence is wanting to examine every infinitesimal element, the historian would certainly wish to discover what happened on every part of the field of battle and to assess how it contributed to the final victory of Napoleon's army. The explanandum event becomes an aggregate event if one chooses to explain the disposition of troops on the battlefield immediately before General Kutuzov ordered his troops to retreat; it becomes a single event if one chooses to explain why the General ordered that retreat.

Though Tolstoy would abominate the thought, the historian might wish to investigate the influence of Napoleon's reputation, rhetoric, and orders upon each soldier in his army. This would be an exercise in divergent colligation. The historian soon learns that historical research requires a reliance upon divergent, parallel, and convergent colligation. Nothing less will capture the complex interplay of those many historical actors who have shaped the past.

Tolstoy favored a search for the infinitesimally small element, but historians more often speak in terms of armies, parties, classes, factions, states, and nations. Do they do this simply because there is a want of evidence about the infinitesimally small elements or because the reduction of societal facts (to use Maurice Mandelbaum's term) to their individual elements brings with it a loss of explanatory power? This question has divided philosophers into two camps, the methodological individualists and the methodological holists. The methodological individualists hold that *in principle* statements about society can be reduced to statements about the individuals who compose society. The methodological holists hold that this cannot be done without there being some remainder, some characteristics of society, that are not described or explained. In this controversy there are many issues upon which the opposing parties do in fact agree. In the first place, they agree that if one took away all the individuals in a nation, there would no longer be a nation. Ontologically, reduction is possible.[37] Second, they agree that one can-

---

36. Tolstoy, *War and Peace*, 776.
37. Maurice Mandelbaum, a proponent of methodological holism writes ("Societal Laws," 486), "The admission that all societal facts depend upon the existence of human beings who possess certain capacities for thought and for action by no means precludes the contention that these facts are irreducible to facts concerning those individuals." Ernest Gellner, another holist, writes ("Holism Versus Individualism in History and Sociology," 502), "At this point the Individualist will no doubt protest that despite the absence of explicit mention of individual dispositions, implicitly they are present; ultimately every social event must have its habitat in the individual psyche. Now this must be conceded."

not simply add up the individuals in a society but must take into account their relations to one another. The parts of a watch spread out on a table do not make a watch; they must first be put together. In a like manner, individuals do not make up a society until they are joined together by institutions, customs, conventions, rules, and practices. For there to be a banking system, there must be an individual who deposits money, an individual who receives the deposit, and rules, which both accept, governing the transactions.[38] Third, the reduction of societal facts to facts about individuals is often impossible *in practice*.[39] For want of information, the historian must rest content with societal facts. Not knowing what each member of a political party thought, not even possessing a record of debates within the party, the historian must rely on the party platform. Fourth, all agree that individuals do not exist in a vacuum. The society into which they are born shapes and forms them—though it should not be forgotten that the society that forms them is itself composed of individuals, of parents, school teachers, friends, preachers, authors, singers, police, and judges. Upon all these truths the two parties agree.[40] Wherein, then, do they differ?

Probably only on this: that *in principle* (as well as *in practice*) there are characteristics of society, "societal facts," that an entire knowledge about the individuals concerned cannot explain. Economists know that the forces of supply and demand determine the price of wheat on the Chi-

38. Ernest Nagel, a cautious supporter of methodological individualism, accepts the fact of "dynamically interrelated parts" (*The Structure of Science*, 397), and "Mechanistic Explanation and Organismic Biology," 303); May Brodbeck, also a cautious supporter of methodological individualism, accepts the fact of relations between individuals within a group ("Methodological Individualism: Definition and Reduction," 299).

39. It is this fact that makes Nagel (*The Structure of Science*, 435, and "Mechanistic Explanation and Organismic Biology," 304) and Brodbeck ("Methodological Individualism: Definition and Reduction," 304) cautious.

40. Mandelbaum's chief contention seems to be that society creates the setting within which the individual acts, determines the individual's place within that setting, and shapes individual choices, but he fails to see that the society that does this is composed of other individuals (*Anatomy of Historical Knowledge*, 137). Arthur Danto also sees that methodological individualists and methodological holists agree on more issues than they disagree upon (*Analytical Philosophy of History*, 267–71). Richard Miller ("Methodological Individualism and Social Explanation," 387–413) attacks methodological individualism for failing to distinguish between an agent's subjective reasons for acting and objective interests in so acting. By having the objective interests automatically shape the agent's actions, Miller removes the individual from the causal sequence. Thus a person's social role as a capitalist will automatically cause that person to assert that "what is good for General Motors is good for America." Miller assumes that all individuals who are capitalists will be of that same opinion; hence there is no need to look at the individual. It is unlikely that Mandelbaum and Gellner would agree to this reduction of the individual to an automaton.

cago commodity market. They know that a drought in Kansas will raise the price of wheat in Chicago and that a bumper crop will drive it down. They know, from Gresham's law, that bad money will drive good money out of circulation. This knowledge they do not gain, and cannot gain (say the methodological holists), by interviewing every wheat producer and buyer who uses the Chicago market or by interviewing every Elizabethan who uses shillings. That economists do not gain this knowledge from such interviews is certain, but that they could not is doubtful. In fact, if they seek to explain why prices rise after a drought or why bad money drives out good, they have to interview farmers, purchasers, and users of shillings. They will find that a farmer in North Dakota sold wheat to broker A rather than broker B because A offered more money than B; and they will find that A offered more money because he feared he could not secure from Kansas the wheat he needed for a client, the owner of a flour mill in St. Louis. And a customer in an Elizabethan shop will readily confess that when he pulled a worn, clipped shilling from his purse, and also a shiny, new shilling, he chose to give the shopkeeper the worn, clipped coin for fear it might be refused later, whereas he knew that the shiny, new shilling would always be accepted. So he took the new shilling home and locked it in a drawer. These interviews, examples of microcolligation, explain why the correlations expressed by the law of supply and demand and by Gresham's law exist.

The recognition that colligation explains why a correlation exists, that it transforms correlation into causation, reveals the fruitfulness of methodological individualism. There are no doubt immense problems in practice to the task of explaining by colligation many of the observed regularities in society. There is too little knowledge and there are labyrinthine complexities. But in principle it can be done, and in practice most historians continually strive to do it. Historians are not content until they reach the individual author of an event. At that point they confront problems that can only be solved by what I have chosen to call analytical colligation. Analytical colligation describes the historian's move from a description of an event to the discovery of the authors of the event, from the discovery of the authors of the event to an elucidation of their purposes, and from an elucidation of their purposes to the etiology of those purposes. Who was the author of an event, what were his or her purposes, and why did he or she have those purposes? In Chapter 8, "Purposive Action," I discuss analytical colligation, but first it is necessary to explore two other forms of colligation, cumulative and repetitive.

7 STRUCTURE AND THEORY IN HISTORY

> The function of the historian, aware of the three *durées*, is to discern and set forth the dialectic that takes place among them.
>
> — J. H. Hexter (summarizing Fernand Braudel's thought), *On Historians*

Consider for a moment the following (by now familiar) story: a person walks by an alley filled with trash, throws a lighted cigarette into the alley, thereby setting the trash on fire. There are at least three initial conditions causing the fire: the lighted cigarette, the accumulated trash, and the presence of oxygen in the air. The historian of the event may well choose to omit any mention of the presence of oxygen in the air, its presence being so normal. But he would be remiss not to mention the accumulation of trash in the alley, since many alleys are clear of trash. A lighted cigarette thrown into them would cause no fire. Suppose further that the historian was a curious person, who asked himself why was there trash in the alley. Digging into the records he discovers that a month ago a nearby shopkeeper put several cardboard cartons there, that several weeks ago a housewife threw some empty shopping bags there, that last week a salesman dumped some old brochures in the alley, and that just a day before a newspaper delivery boy left some old newspapers in the alley. B. Ellis calls this "process explanation," and

Arthur Stinchcombe "cumulative causation."[1] I have chosen to call it cumulative colligation.

Cumulative colligation differs from other forms of colligation in that the process it describes permanently alters the structure of society. Thus Arthur Stinchcombe divides the causes of social phenomena into two classes: those that cumulate or grow and those that are random turbulences that quickly sink back into the general flow of events, leaving no permanent effects.[2] Many a riot in the eighteenth century was suppressed, leaving the structure of society unchanged. Indeed, had the riot at St. Giles not led to the meeting of the General Assembly at Glasgow and to the abolition of bishops, it would have been merely a turbulent event. But it did lead to the abolition of bishops, an event that permanently changed the structure of the Scottish church. Linear, converging, diverging, and parallel colligation serve to explain the occurrence of an event, perhaps an aggregate event. But to explain changes in the structure of society one needs to study not so much the actions and reactions of men and women as the cumulative changes that those actions and reactions ultimately bring about. The actions of the shopkeeper, housewife, salesman, and newspaper boy changed the structure of the alley, as did, for that matter, the fire, which burnt up the trash, leaving an alley strewn with ashes.

By "structure" I do not mean those universal, ahistorical, collective structures that Claude Levi-Strauss finds in the unconscious of all persons and that form autonomous and objective systems of meaning. Since Levi-Strauss offers no independent means to penetrate into the unconscious, his structuralism is a purely formal system, devoid of empirical content. Nor do I mean the structuralism advocated by Michel Foucault, who is concerned with the structure that shapes how men think and their modes of discourse, structures that he believes determine everything else.[3] What I mean by "structure" is simply the organization of church and state, of society and the economy, of the county and the parish, of the schools and universities, of ideas and beliefs, of customs and practices. Sir Lewis Namier writes of the structure of politics at the accession of George III, and Thomas Kuhn writes of the structure of scientific revolutions. Most historians, however, write about the structure of government or society or education or the economy or beliefs

1. Ellis, "On the Relation of Explanation to Description," 504; Stinchcombe, *Theoretical Methods in Social History,* 61
2. Stinchcombe, *Theoretical Method in Social History,* 61.
3. For a searching critique of Levi-Strauss and the structuralist movement (i.e., Althusser, Lacan, and Foucault), see Clarke, *The Foundations of Structuralism,* esp. 96–109.

without using the word "structure." Wallace MacCaffrey, for example, illuminates the structure of politics at the Court of Elizabeth, and E.M.W. Tillyard describes the structure of the Elizabethan worldview without recourse to the word "structure."[4] What must be emphasized is that these structures are not just geographical and demographical features but also ideas, beliefs, habits, laws, customs, conventions, rules, and practices. Thus in 1580 the English held similar views about the rights and duties of government that belonged to the monarch, to the courts of law, to the House of Lords, to the House of Commons, to the justices of the peace, to the Corporation of London, to the boroughs of England, to the constables in the villages, and to the church wardens in their parishes. These views made up the structure of politics in England in 1580.

No group of historians has done more to point to the importance of structure than the *Annales* school in France. Led by Fernand Braudel and Emmanuel Le Roy Ladurie, they have studied those stable elements in society that have endured for many generations—the climate, the population, trade routes, methods of agriculture, and economic institutions. Braudel is particularly fascinated with structure, as readers of *The Mediterranean and the Mediterranean World in the Age of Philip II* will know. He there describes the mountains, plateaus, plains, peninsulas, and seas of the Mediterranean world, the movement of sheep and shepherds from high summer pasture to low winter pasture, the progress of caravans across the hot deserts of Africa, the shipment of broadcloth and silks from Spain to North Africa, the flow of gold from the Sudan to the Maghreb, the role of the Genoese in banking, the flooding of Venice, the havoc wrought by corsairs in the Mediterranean, the want of wood for building ships, the refusal of Jews to assimilate, and much else. Braudel is more interested in material structures than psychological ones, but other scholars in the *Annales* school have written of collective *mentalités*—that is, of habits of mind, shared beliefs, rituals, traditions, customs, fashions, and conventions.[5]

The emphasis placed on structure by the *Annales* school has greatly enriched historiography, but the *Annales* school has never seriously confronted the problem of the relation of structure to event. This arises in large part from their contempt for *histoire événementielle*, that is, for the history of events. Braudel regards events as trivial, superficial "crests of

4. Namier, *The Structure of Politics at the Accession of George III;* Kuhn, *The Structure of Scientific Revolutions;* MacCaffrey, *The Shaping of the Elizabethan Regime;* Tillyard, *The Elizabethan World Picture.*

5. Braudel, *The Mediterranean and the Mediterranean World in the Age of Philip II.* For a comprehensive description of works by the *Annales* school, see Stoianovich, *French Historical Method.*

foam" carried on the tides of history.[6] But, as W. H. Walsh has written, "history without events is logically inconceivable."[7] He is surely correct, since structures shape events and events undermine structures.

It would help to define exactly what structures are. To begin with, there are geological, geographic, and climatic structures, such as mountains, seas, soils, and rainfall, structures that explain why shepherds take their sheep across certain passes, why the Sudan exports gold, and why Venice is flooded. But such material structures can explain only a small part of the history of a people. Far more important are institutional, legal, moral, and psychological structures. There exist laws, rules, moral injunctions, and ethical codes and conventions that society enforces with a variety of sanctions. There are also customs, practices, habits, roles, opinions, and fashions that members of society learn from parents and peers. These structures lead to lawful acts, to customary behavior, to rule- and role-governed activities, and to standardized events. These structures shape manifold recurring events. In the seventeenth century an English lord sat in Parliament because the institution existed; a French lord ceased to sit in the Estates General, because the institution had fallen into desuetude. A French villager attended mass on a Sunday morning; an English villager did not. In modern Britain a person drives down the left side of the road; in America, down the right. The number of examples of rule- and role-governed activities could be multiplied indefinitely, but what deserves attention is the fact that they are all recurring events. They are repeated in much the same way by many persons on many occasions. In this they differ from a singular event, such as the assassination of the Archduke Ferdinand, or an aggregate event, such as the French Revolution, both of which are unique. It is surely no accident that when historians of the *Annales* school turned to the study of the lives of ordinary villagers, to social and economic history, they found themselves studying recurring events and the structures that shaped those recurring events.

It is implicit in the works of the *Annales* school that once the historian has described a structure, he or she has explained the occurrence of those events that the structure shapes. But is this so? And if so, by what logic does a description of a structure explain the occurrence of such repeated events? Though no writer of the *Annales* school (to my knowledge) has wrestled with this question, Murray Murphey has. In his book *Our Knowledge of the Historical Past*, he describes some typical examples of customary behavior—the handshake as a greeting, driving on the right side of the

6. Trevor-Roper, "Fernand Braudel, the *Annales,* and the Mediterranean," 475.
7. Walsh, "The Notion of an Historical Event," 15.

road, a professor's recognizing a student who has raised his hand—and he asks whether such customary patterns of behavior are to be regarded as laws? And he answers that they are lawlike, since from them one could have predicted the action and from them one can support a counterfactual. One could have predicted that the professor would recognize the student when he raised his hand; and one can support the counterfactual that if the student had not raised his hand, the professor would not have recognized him. "In short," Murphey concludes, "these customs are law-like and they can and do serve as the generalizations upon which explanations of human behavior are based."[8]

From such a conclusion P. H. Nowell-Smith dissents, arguing that normative language cannot be reduced to descriptive language, a normative rule to an empirical law. We do not, he argues, treat a red light as a sign that drivers will in fact stop, but only as a sign that they should stop. He is surely right in arguing thus. He is likewise right to see that to achieve formal completeness it is necessary to add empirical premises about the individual concerned. Thus we can explain the actions of a driver who stops at a red light by citing both the existence of the rule that drivers should stop and the fact that past experience has shown this driver to be conscientious. Nowell-Smith maintains that adding this empirical premise is trivial. Herein I believe he errs. It may be trivial in a practical sense—a historian may not bother to state that the driver was conscientious—but it is not trivial in a logical sense. The initial conditions, which make up the first part of the explanation of the driver's having stopped, must include both the rule about red lights and the fact that the driver was conscientious about obeying rules; similarly, the covering law employed in the second part of the explanation must state that conscientious drivers stop at stop signs.[9]

Nowell-Smith talks about rule-governed behavior. When seeking to explain role-governed behavior one is not concerned with normative statements but only with descriptive ones. Americans shake hands when they greet another person; Japanese bow. These are certainly lawlike statements, and they allow one to say, "He shook hands because he was an American" or "He bowed because he was a Japanese."

The role of structure in explaining recurring events should not blind one to its role in explaining singular events. The existence of trash in the alley (part of its structure at that moment) is nearly as important as the throwing of a lighted cigarette in explaining the subsequent fire. The role of structure is equally important in explaining the occurrence of aggregate

8. Murphey, *Our Knowledge of the Historical Past*, 77–79.
9. Nowell-Smith, "History as Patterns of Thought and Action," 148–49.

events, such as the English Revolution. Thus in his *Causes of the English Revolution* Lawrence Stone does not merely recite the events leading up to the revolution, he likewise analyzes the weaknesses in the structure of the monarchy at that time, weaknesses that help to explain the coming of the revolution. Among them were financial insolvency, the want of a standing army, and the want of a professional bureaucracy.[10]

But Stone does not leave the matter here. He also endeavors to show why the Crown in the previous century had grown so weak. He seeks to show why the structure of the English monarchy changed, which raises a fundamental problem that Fernand Braudel would rather ignore: how does the historian explain changes in the structure of society? Braudel would rather ignore this problem because of his infatuation with structure, which he views as unchanging and which he places in the realm of the *longue durée*. But he has found it impossible totally to ignore change in society. He therefore speaks of *conjunctures*, changes (often seen as cyclical) that occur every twenty or thirty or fifty years and that occupy the realm of the *moyenne durée*. Finally there are events, acts of individuals, often political, which are brief and evanescent and thereby occupy the *courte durée*. Of these three layers, or strata, of history Braudel regards structures as fundamental, *conjunctures* as fascinating, and events as trivial and unimportant.[11]

Lawrence Stone employs a similar tripartite, though otherwise different, scheme in his *Causes of the English Revolution*. He distinguishes between preconditions, precipitants, and triggers. Preconditions are clearly those weaknesses in the structure of government and society that made the English Revolution possible, weaknesses such as the want of a standing army and the lack of a professional bureaucracy. He is less clear on what defines a precipitant. On one occasion he makes a precipitant identical with a trigger, but in section 3 of chapter 3 he uses "precipitants" to describe those irritants (ship money, fines for refusing knighthood, fines for encroaching on royal forests, the trebling of wardships, etc.) that explain the growth of opposition during the 1630s. Triggers clearly belong to the realm of events, events such as the attempt to impose an English liturgy on the Scottish church, defeat in war, financial collapse, the death of Bedford, the Irish rebellion, the attempted arrest of the Five Members, and the passage of the Nineteen Propositions.[12]

One question immediately leaps to mind: by what logic does one

---

10. Stone, *The Causes of the English Revolution*, 60–64.
11. Braudel, *On History*, esp. 3–4, 13, 27–38, 48.
12. Stone, *The Causes of the English Revolution;* see p. 8 for the identification of precipitants with triggers.

distinguish the *longue durée* from the *moyenne durée* and the *moyenne durée* from the *courte durée*, structure from *conjuncture* from event? Or, in the case of Lawrence Stone, how does one distinguish preconditions from precipitants from triggers? Neither Fernand Braudel nor Lawrence Stone offers an answer to this question. Braudel, in fact, makes a shambles of his own scheme by positing the existence of numerous *durées*. He speaks of "three, ten, a hundred diverse *durées*."[13] There is, therefore, no logic by which one can establish a tripartite division of historical time.

The solution to this problem lies in not trying to divide up historical time at all, but rather in establishing two distinct kinds of colligation, the linear and the cumulative. Take the story of the careless cigarette smoker who throws a lighted cigarette into the alley. There is a linear series of events—lighting the cigarette, smoking it, walking by the alley, throwing the cigarette into the air, its landing on a pile of paper, its smouldering there, its being fanned into flame by a gust of wind, the flame spreading to other papers and cartons. Then there is cumulative colligation—the piling up of trash in the alley, first by the shopkeeper, then by the housewife, then by the salesman, finally by the newspaper boy. The historian, if sufficiently obsessed with the importance of structure, might even, by cumulative colligation, explain the presence of oxygen in the air. He might point out that millions of years ago there was no oxygen in the atmosphere, but that green plants appeared, which ever since have absorbed carbon dioxide, retained the carbon, and given off oxygen. He might even find it a clever taxonomy to place the appearance of oxygen in the *longue durée* and the accumulation of trash in the *moyenne durée*, but where then would he place the construction of the buildings that gave to the alley its configuration? In truth, it is a meaningless exercise to seek to classify the features of the alley by the length of time they existed. It is far more fruitful to seek to explain how those abnormal features that caused the fire to break out came into existence. The presence of oxygen in the air is normal, and so requires no explanation, hardly even mention; the presence of the trash is abnormal, and thus requires mention, perhaps explanation also. Certainly only that part of the structure that explains what happened needs in turn to be explained.

It is just this that Lawrence Stone does in his *Causes of the English Revolution*. He does not explain why there was an English monarchy in 1640, though no doubt he could have reached back into Anglo-Saxon history in order to describe the origins of that monarchy. Instead he explains why the English monarchy was weak in 1640 and why the

---

13. As quoted in Hexter, *On Historians*, 99. Hexter's appreciation of, and critique of, Braudel is acute, fair-minded, and brilliant.

English had grown hostile to the policies of the Crown. Between 1580 and 1640 the English monarchy, from being strong and popular, became weak and distrusted (just as the alley, from being empty, became littered). The structure of the monarchy and the structure of public opinion had altered.

The question then arises, one that Braudel never truly faces: how does the historian explain a change in structure, the appearance of a new institution, for example, or a new pattern of behavior? The answer is by tracing those events which cumulatively caused the institution to change or the new pattern of behavior to appear, an answer that reveals why Braudel never faced the problem. His contempt for the event was too deep to permit him either to recognize or to admit its importance in altering structure. But the story of the fire in the alley illustrates how events can cumulatively alter structure—the shopkeeper's dumping the cartons there, then the housewife her shopping bags, the salesman his brochures, the newspaper boy his newspapers. Lawrence Stone, too, examines events in order to explain why the English monarchy grew weak. Henry VIII's decision to go to war against France in 1544 meant that monastic lands that would have made the Crown financially independent were sold off to pay for the war. An adverse decision by the common-law judges in 1568 deprived the Crown of a chance to profit from England's reserves of coal. Elizabeth's decision to put political goodwill before fiscal efficiency resulted in a failure to adjust revenues to meet the rising costs engendered by inflation. The government failed to alter the Book of Rates to reflect the steady rise in import prices. In 1551, as an economy measure, the government dismissed those Italian and German mercenaries who might have formed the core of a standing army. In order to weaken the local power of great territorial magnates, the early Tudors deliberately built up the authority of the gentry. The Crown was thus in no position later to replace the local gentry with paid officials sent down from London. The break from Rome unleashed forces that weakened the Crown's control of the Church. "The pressure of events," writes Stone, "inexorably carried England towards a fragmentation of religious unity."[14]

Even scholars of the *Annales* school have come to see that structures change and that the historian must be concerned with such changes. They have learned to distinguish between "diachronic change," which has no history, since it maintains a constant rhythm, and "historical change," which involves the transformation of one or more structures. Today they speak of "structuring," "destructuring," and "restructuring."

14. Stone, *The Causes of the English Revolution*, 61–63.

Events may reinforce a particular structure or undermine an existing structure or initiate a new structure.[15] They even recognize that there is development and evolution in history. Michel Foucault, whose epistemic structuralism is so rigid, now speaks of "the process which . . . after a century and half set up psychiatry," and of "the slow evolution from one form of confinement, intended mainly for the poor, into a confinement involving medical treatment."[16] Jacques Le Goff, though he seeks to link the tripartite structure of heaven, hell, and purgatory to other tripartitite structures in medieval society, in fact explains the origin of the idea of purgatory by tracing its spread from Augustine to Gregory the Great, and so to the Cluniac order, to the cathedral schools and Cistercians in the twelfth century, and finally to the universities and preaching friars in the thirteenth century.[17] And Emmanuel Le Roy Ladurie talks of "the spiritual and intellectual development of various sectors of the bourgeoisie." He even speaks of "the accumulation of a 'critical mass' " during the eighteenth century, a critical mass that exploded in the French Revolution, leading to the creation of new structures. Though he nowhere explicitly speaks of events leading cumulatively to a change in structure, he does illustrate this process. In his study of Retif de la Bretonne he describes how the habit of eating fruit and vegetables arose in the French countryside during the eighteenth century. At one point he descends to the most particular of events, to Barbe, a country girl who accepts service in town, learns to eat fruit and vegetables while in town, and brings the custom back to her village. "Here was by no means an isolated case," he writes. "Many other young women went into service in the town as a sort of transitional vocation before returning to the land."[18] Though he would not recognize the vocabulary, Ladurie explains this change in dietary structure by linear colligation (Barbe's entering service, learning to eat fruit and vegetables, returning to her village, influencing other villagers), by parallel colligation ("hers was by no means an isolated case"), and by cumulative colligation (the new habit persisted).

Historians of the *Annales* school are particularly fascinated with any event that initiates a new structure, called by Charles Peguy "a critical event" and by Ladurie "a matrix-event."[19] Ladurie offers a splendid example of a critical event that initiates a change in structure. Trade

15. Stoianovich, *French Historical Method*, 38–39, 133.

16. Foucault, "An Exchange with Michel Foucault," *New York Review of Books*, 31 March 1983, 42.

17. See Natalie Zemon Davis's review of *The Birth of Purgatory*, by Jacques Le Goff, *New York Review of Books*, 18 July 1985.

18. Ladurie, *The Mind and Method of the Historian*, 237–38, 281–82.

19. Stoianovich, *French Historical Method*, 228–29.

caravans in the fourteenth century exchanged not only goods with the Asians, but viruses. One of these viruses was that of the plague. The plague brought death and depopulation to Europe. Depopulation ended the subsistence crisis of the early fourteenth century. The end of the obsession with subsistence, in turn, released those energies that led to the Renaissance, the invention of printing, and the discovery of America. (Whether Ladurie could justify these assertions of causation is doubtful, but it is certain that if he sought to do so, he would resort to linear, parallel, and cumulative colligation.) The virus was an initiating event, but Ladurie is equally fascinated with the idea of a "critical event." As he sees it, a crisis, such as that of the seventeenth century, encourages "the accumulation of a 'critical mass,' whose explosion then destroys the existing structure. Thus the years from 1600 to 1750 saw the spiritual and intellectual development of the bourgeoisie, the intellectual evolution of the nobility, and the development of a peasant elite, all of which phenomena came together to form a critical mass and that explosion which was the French Revolution."[20]

Marxists, such as Lucien Goldman, prefer to speak of "genetic structuralism," of functional structures that become dysfunctional, of internal contradictions that are an integral part of the structure yet eventually destroy it.[21] With such scholars, Ladurie would probably not quarrel. Indeed, he gives an excellent example of an internal contradiction destroying a structure when he shows how the custom of dividing the land equally among all one's children, prevalent among peasants in northern France, encouraged subdivision and undermined the land tenure there.[22] In this instance one part of the structure of society undermined another. But the principal conclusion that arises from this review of the methods of the *Annales* school is the fact that once one has cut through the rhetoric of the *Annales* school, one finds that they write history much as traditional historians do. When actually writing history, historians of the *Annales* school recognize the role of events in sustaining, undermining, and creating new structures, just as traditional historians (though they may not have trumpeted the fact) have always written about structure, about institutions, laws, morals, and customs. What is clear is that there is a continuing dialectic between event and structure, which no historian can afford to ignore. Structures shape events, especially the myriad events of daily life; events in turn sustain, then ultimately undermine, structures, creating new ones. The logic by which the historian shows how structure shapes

20. Ladurie, *The Mind and Method of the Historian*, 7, 275.
21. Stoianovich, *French Historical Method*, 131–32.
22. Ladurie, *The Mind and Method of the Historian*, 110–11.

events requires resort to covering laws and initial conditions, both of which include reference to structure. The logic by which the historian shows how events sustain or undermine or create structure is a combination of linear, parallel, and cumulative colligation, with each step in the cone of causation justified by a covering law. One does have to justify, by a covering law, the assertion that Barbe learned in town—and not from the promptings of the devil—to eat fruit and vegetables.

If one wished, one could even make the dialectic of event and structure a tripartite one, as Braudel and Stone sought to do. One could divide the elements of any historical situation into background, preconditions, and precipitants. The background to any historical situation is that part of the structure of society that is commonplace, normal, accepted. Had there been no Parliament in 1640, there would have been no civil war between Parliament and King. But the fact that Parliament existed no more requires comment by the historian than the fact that oxygen exists in the air. Indeed, there were many features of English society in 1640 that the historian simply assumes to have existed, such as manors, boroughs, commissions of the peace, lord lieutenancies, assizes, county elections, cathedral chapters, departments of state, not to speak of such *mentalités* as Protestant prejudices, respect for the law, and xenophobia. Braudel heaps scorn on earlier historians for neglecting such features, the structures of society, but in fact earlier historians had only chosen to leave to other historians in other books the task of explaining the origins of Parliament, of manors, of boroughs, and of other structures.

But not all the structures of society can be left in the background. Those changes in the structure that are essential to explaining the course of events—the preconditions for the occurrence of the event—must be examined and discussed. The English monarchy fell in the mid–seventeenth century in part because of structural defects—financial insolvency, the lack of a bureaucracy, the want of a standing army. The historian who would explain its fall must, by cumulative colligation, show how those defects came about. Similarly, the historian of the outbreak of the First World War must investigate those defects in the European state system that allowed the assassination of the Archduke Ferdinand at Sarajevo to lead to war—the armaments race, entangling alliances, German *Weltpolitik*, Russian Pan-Slavism, and Serbian pride. These preconditions are as necessary to an explanation of the outbreak of World War I as the presence of trash in the alley is necessary to an explanation of the outbreak of the fire there.

But it took a spark to set off the train of events that led both to war and to the fire. The assassination of the Archduke set off a train of events that led to the declaration of war in August, just as the riot in St. Giles set off a train of events that led to the outbreak of civil war in August 1642, and the throwing of the cigarette to a fire in the alley. The events in such a sequence are the triggers or precipitants of the catastrophe that follows. It is the conjuncture of this series of events with structural defects already present that explains the occurrence of the catastrophe.

Whether in the dialectic between event and structure the historian should give greater weight to the event or to the preconditions depends upon which is the more abnormal. If a truck of normal size drives across an ancient bridge whose fabric has crumbled, causing it to collapse, the crumbling of the fabric deserves attention. If a ten-ton truck drives across a bridge with a five-ton limit, causing it to collapse, it is the event that deserves emphasis. And if the bridge were originally built too weak to hold the traffic expected to use it, then the original structure deserves attention.

Understood in this way there is a *dialectique des durées*, a dialectic based on the conjuncture of permanent structure, changing structure, and event. To this extent there is truth in Braudel's claim (as summarized by J. H. Hexter) that "the function of the historian, aware of the three *durées*, is to discern and set forth the dialectic that takes place among them."[23]

But the distinction between permanent structure and changing structure is an artificial one. There is no sharp boundary that distinguishes a permanent structure from a changing one. There is only a continuum of more or less permanent and more or less changing structures. When an event occurs it occurs in a situation compounded of many structures. Some of those structures are of ancient origin, some of less ancient origin, others of recent origin, yet others of even more recent origin. There is a whole continuum of *durées*. Largely guided by the principle of abnormalism, the historian must decide which of those structures he or she regards as central to an explanation of the explanandum event that follows from a conjuncture of another event with those structures. The true function of the historian, therefore, is to discern and set forth the dialectic that takes place, not among the three *durées*, but between event and structure.

Theory in History

Where cumulative colligation leads to a consideration of structure in history, repetitive colligation leads to a consideration of theory in history.

23. Hexter, "Fernand Braudel and the Monde Braudellien," 505.

Rule-governed and role-governed behavior is learned behavior. One is taught rules and learns a role. But some regularities of behavior are neither taught nor learned, but occur spontaneously. In similar situations, men and women act similarly. Finding two different shilling pieces in their purses, Elizabethan ladies and gentlemen regularly handed over the worn, clipped coin and took the newly minted coin home to put in their lockboxes. Hence Gresham's law, that bad money drives out good. Inasmuch as history discovers such behavioral regularities, it can aspire to the status of a science, that is, to be a discipline that studies classes of events rather than unique events, assassinations in general rather than the assassination of Henry IV, revolutions in general rather than the English Revolution. The purpose of a science is to discover the laws governing the behavior of phenomena, not to search for the cause of a single event.

Science, then, is distinguished by the search for laws, laws such as Gresham's law, the law of gravitation, Boyle's law, Snell's law. Though such laws are used in the covering-law model of explanation in order to explain the occurrence of a single event, they are not in themselves an explanation. Rather, they are a description of a correlation. But asserting the existence of a correlation does not explain it. To explain why a law exists, why a correlation occurs, one needs a theory. Murray Murphey has rightly pointed out that laws need explaining, just as the occurrence of an event does.[24] What explains a law is a theory.

Though philosophers of science agree that a theory is an explanation of a law, Gilbert Ryle proposes a different definition. "An historian's account of the course of a battle," he writes, "is his theory."[25] Herein he departs too far from customary usage, for a theory must concern battles in general, not an account of a single battle. A theory might explain General Forest's celebrated law that victory goes to the general who "is there fustest with the mostest," but it does not explain victory in a single battle. What theory seeks to explain is recurrent phenomena.

As to how a theory explains a recurrent phenomenon, or law, there are two schools of thought. One school of thought, which we may call the deductive school, holds that a theory explains a law if that law can be logically deduced from the more general laws making up the theories, as Kepler's laws may be deduced from Newton's. Abraham Kaplan calls such theories "hierarchical theories," and P. H. Nowell-Smith likens them to a pyramid with the most general laws at the top.[26] The opposing

24. Murphey, *Our Knowledge of the Historical Past,* 93–94.
25. Ryle, *The Concept of Mind,* 289.
26. Kaplan, *The Conduct of Inquiry,* 298; Nowell-Smith, "Are Historical Events Unique?" 111–12. Other commentators who emphasize the deductive nature of theories are Gor-

school, which may be called the microscopic school, doubts that anything has been explained when a law is deduced from a more general
law, since the same question—why should such a uniformity exist?—
arises concerning the more general law as arose concerning the first law.
Laws, no matter how general, only describe uniformities; they do not
explain them. To explain a law a theory must contain a model that shows
how the system works, the system that gives rise to the uniformities
observed. As N. R. Campbell observes, such models "are an utterly
essential part of theories," and he goes on to show how the model of
elastic particles colliding with the sides of a box explains Boyle's and
Gay-Lussac's laws.[27] Ernest Nagel agrees, asserting that a model that
puts flesh on the skeletal structure of a theory is an inseparable part of
that theory. He argues that a model of electrons spinning in various
elliptical orbits around a nucleus is indispensable to Bohr's theory explaining the lines in the spectrum.[28] Abraham Kaplan calls such theories
"concatenated theories."[29]

What the microscopic school nearly glimpses, but does not quite do
so, is the role of repetitive colligation in the establishment of a theory.
What that role is can best be illustrated by repeating and elaborating
upon an illustration used in Chapter 2. Imagine that a man steps into his
car, puts a key into the ignition, turns it, and the motor starts. And
suppose his son, who is with him, asks, "Why did the motor start when
you turned the key?" The father might answer, "Because the motor
always starts when I turn the key." But this would hardly satisfy his son,
who would then ask, "Well, why does the motor always start when you
turn the key?" If the father were of the hierarchical school, he might say,
Because this car is a Chevrolet and all Chevrolets start when the key is
turned in the ignition. But it is unlikely that he would. More likely he
would proceed to describe the sequence of events that caused the motor
to start. By turning the key he caused two pieces of metal to come
together. Their coming together completed an electrical circuit, causing

don Graham, *Historical Explanation Reconsidered*, 49, and Arthur Danto and Sidney
Morgenbesser, eds., *Philosophy of Science*, 178.

27. Campbell, "What Is a Theory?" 258–66.

28. Nagel, *The Structure of Science*, 94–114.

29. Kaplan, *The Conduct of Inquiry*, 298. Herman Helmholtz once wrote, "To understand
a phenomenon means nothing else than to reduce it to the Newtonian laws." Commenting
on this, Philip Frank has observed, "It was completely forgotten that in Newton's own day
his theory was looked upon as a set of abstract mathematical formulas, which needed a
mechanical explanation to satisfy man's desire for causality. Newton himself recognized
this need." (Ibid., 343.)

electricity to run through it. The electricity flowed from the battery to the starter and to the spark plugs. The starter turned over the crankshaft, which caused the pistons to compress a vapor of gas that had come from the fuel-injection system. The electrical current also flowed through the distributor to spark plugs, which at the appropriate moment caused the gas vapor to explode, thus driving down the piston, turning the crank shaft, forcing up other pistons, and driving the fuel pump. There are several sequences here that come together (an example of convergence): the fuel pump pumping gas, the air filter cleaning the air, the fuel-injection system mixing the gas and air, the alternator generating electricity, the electricity going to the distributor to be distributed to the spark plugs. Laws are involved here, as covering laws connecting each step in the colligatory sequences, but the law stating that the motor will start when the key is turned is not deduced from some more general law about all motor cars. It is explained by tracing the repetitive colligatory sequence of events that occurs when the key is turned—a repetitive sequence because it always occurs when the key is turned. One can say in general that a theory explains a law by tracing a colligatory chain that exactly repeats itself over and over again. Every time the key is turned the same chain of events is set in motion, resulting in the motor starting. Repetitive colligation lies at the heart of a theory.

The above illustration is drawn from mechanics, but theories likewise explain correlations in history. Historians have long known that there existed a correlation between the age of members of Parliament and their support for either King or Parliament. In the House of Commons in 1642, members of Parliament in their twenties were royalists rather than parliamentarians by a factor of two to one; members of Parliament in their fifties were parliamentarians rather than royalists by a factor of two to one. How does one explain this correlation? Lawrence Stone does so in the following manner: "The most plausible explanation of this generation gap in reverse is that for men to be driven to revolution they need to have had personal experience first of the corruption of Buckingham in the 1620s and then of the tyranny of Charles, Laud and Strafford in the 1630s. If both experiences were necessary, but neither by itself was sufficient, this would explain both why the Revolution did not occur in the 1620s and why the old were more radical than the young in the 1640s."[30] The repetitive colligation in Stone's theory is parallel rather than linear, but it is there. Numerous men experienced the corruption of Buckingham, then the tyranny of Charles, Laud, and Strafford, and were then elected to Parliament, where, remembering this corruption and tyranny,

30. Stone, *The Causes of the English Revolution*, 133.

they supported Parliament against the King. This concatenation of events—experience of corruption, experience of tyranny, election to Parliament, opposition to the King—occurred separately to many men and explains the observed correlation.

It might be objected that the observed correlation is only a probability, and not a very high one at that. To which it can be answered that the correlation between turning the key in the ignition and the motor starting is only a probability, though a much higher one. There are occasions when, because the battery is dead or the solenoid burned out, the motor does not start. A theory can explain a probable law as well as an invariable law. Indeed, a theory is useful in explaining why a law is only probable. The theory of the internal-combustion engine, known to mechanics, allows them to test the battery and the solenoid, to see whether they are functioning.

In the physical sciences many of the entities, properties, and relations that make up a theory are hypothetical. They are, as Nagel observes, "the logical skeleton of the explanatory system." This abstract calculus, in turn, is given empirical content by rules of correspondence, rules that relate these hypothetical concepts (say, an electron) to the concrete materials of observation (the disturbance in a cloud chamber).[31] The nature of these hypothetical concepts has given rise to a fierce controversy between the instrumentalists, who hold that they are fictions, and the realists, who hold that they possess a reality. This controversy has little relevance to the social sciences, since, as Campbell suggests, in disciplines other than the physical sciences the theoretical and the observed properties have the same features.[32] But though no battle rages in the social sciences between instrumentalists and realists, there does rage an analogous battle between the functionalists and their critics.

The word "function" has two quite separate meanings, the confusion of which can promote misunderstanding. In ordinary usage, "function" simply means the purpose for which an institution exists, as in the sentence "The function of the post office is to deliver letters." In this sense historians, especially those concerned with the structure of society, have long used the term. The function of the medieval exchequer was to receive money from the sheriffs. The function of the Court of Common Pleas was to hear suits between the King's subjects. The function of Parliament was to pass statutes. The use of the term in this sense is quite unexceptionable, particularly because it does not contradict the analysis of society in terms of motives, desires, and purposes.

31. Nagel, *The Structure of Science*, 90.
32. Campbell, "What Is a Theory?" 252–53.

Then in the 1920s anthropologists and sociologists began to use "function" in a more technical sense. It now came to mean the role that an institution, custom, or myth played in maintaining the equilibrium of a system, much as a thermostat maintains the temperature of a room at 70° F. Two properties or events were said to be functionally related if there existed a nonaccidental covariance between them. Thus the function of feuds among the Zulus was, by acting as a safety valve, to maintain order. And the fishermen of Venice were allowed to elect their own doge, "a ritual with the function of persuading the ordinary people that they participated in the political system."[33]

In its more extreme form, a form favored by the anthropologist Bronislaw Malinowski, functionalism is an explanatory principle according to which the characteristics of a phenomenon can be explained by showing how that phenomenon is related to other phenomena in the same culture. The various elements in a culture are held to be what they are because of their interconnectedness.[34] As G. A. Cohen expresses it, functionalism is "a distinctive explanatory procedure, in which references to the effects of a phenomenon contributes to explaining it." Cohen puts forth this definition in a book defending Karl Marx's heavy reliance on functional explanation. Appropriately he chooses an illustration from Marx: "When Marx says that 'Protestantism, by changing almost all traditional holidays into workdays, plays an important role in the genesis of capital' he is not just assigning a certain effect to the new religion, but proposing a (partial) explanation of its rise in terms of that effect."[35]

Functionalism becomes even more extreme when these interrelated practices, customs, and institutions are seen as acting independently of the individuals involved. Sociologists and anthropologists came to speak of "manifest" and "latent" functions, and to focus on the "latent" functions of customs, myths, and institutions. The functionalists among them assumed that society cannot be understood simply by investigating the intentions of its members, at least not over the long run. "As a sociologist might say," writes Peter Burke, "explanations in terms of individual motives may work perfectly well at the micro-level, the level of face-to-face interaction, but they do not explain what happens at the macro-level, the level of the whole society."[36] This is so, the functionalists maintain, be-

---

33. Both illustrations are drawn from Burke, *Sociology and History*, 43, 46.
34. Mandelbaum, "Functionalism in Social Anthropology," 230.
35. Quoted in Mandelbaum, "G. A. Cohen's Defense of Functional Explanation," 247–48.
36. Burke, *Sociology and History*, 47.

cause the exploration of motives cannot account for the unintended consequences of the actions of men and women.

Two principal problems emerge from this kind of functionalism: Can
such assertions be tested? And are they explanatory?

The first problem is a difficult one. How can one demonstrate that
the feud acted as a safety valve that preserved Zulu society from disrup-
tion, or prove that the ritual election of a doge by the fishermen persuaded the ordinary people to acquiesce in the Venetian oligarchy? To
have explanatory value, a functional statement must, as Robert Brown
has argued, assert that the institution or custom is a *necessary* condition
to the maintenance of the system, or that the maintenance of the system is a *sufficient* condition to demonstrate the presence of the institution or custom.[37] This point can be made clearer by referring to the
theory of the internal-combustion engine. The function of the fuel-
injection system is to furnish a gas vapor to the cylinders and so keep
the motor running. That the fuel-injection system is *necessary* to the
running of the motor can be demonstrated by removing it. The motor
then stops. That the running of the motor is a *sufficient* condition proving the presence of a fuel-injection system can be demonstrated by
showing that all running motors have such systems. But there is no
way to test whether the feud was *necessary* to the maintenance of order
in Zulu society or whether the continuance of the Venetian state was a
sufficient condition to demonstrate the existence of a doge elected by the
fishermen of Venice. Social anthropologists cannot abolish the feud or
the election and observe what follows. They might look for comparative situations where there were no feuds or elections, but even then
they would face another difficulty, one discerned by Maurice Mandelbaum. If the principle of interrelatedness is expressed as a law stating
that all elements within a culture are related to all other elements in
such a way that none would be as it is if the other elements were
different from what they are, then the principle appears obviously to be
false. Yet if the law is weakened to state only that many elements in a
culture have some effect on one another, the principle becomes so weak
as to lack explanatory power.[38]

Jon Elster has shown, with his usual clarity, why a functionalist statement lacks explanatory power. The functionalist seeks to explain the
occurrence of a set of repeated actions (feuds among the Zulus, elections
of a doge) by the favorable unintended consequences of those actions (in

37. Brown, *Explanation in Social Science*, 122–23.
38. Mandelbaum, "Functionalism in Social Anthropology," 229–30.

maintaining order in Zulu society, in preserving the Venetian oligarchy). Elster then presents a model of such an explanation:[39]

1. Y is an effect of X;
2. Y is beneficial to Z;
3. Y is unintended by the actors producing X;
4. Y is unrecognized by the actors in Z;
5. Y maintains X by a causal feedback passing through Z.

Since Y is unintended by the actors producing X, and since Y is unrecognized by the actors in Z, one cannot discover a causal feedback mechanism by which Y maintains X. There is no explanation.

Elster, however, does not reject all consequence explanations. Behavior can be explained by its consequence if the consequence is intended by the actor or if some other agent who benefits from the behavior is able to maintain the behavior.[40] He even allows a full-fledged functionalist explanation if a causal feedback mechanism can be shown. But he has found only one such case in the literature of the social sciences (the survival of profit-maximizing firms), and it is a case of natural selection operating at the social level. In the rest of the literature of the social sciences, and especially in Marxist literature, he finds no such causal feedback. All he finds are functionalist explanations, such as the assertion that the bourgeoisie exist in order to bring about capitalism, or that capital, by expropriating the surplus value created by workers, "fulfills an historical and social function." The words in quotation marks are Karl Marx's. In such explanations the beliefs and intentions of individuals are overlooked. They are subordinated to the needs and demands of the system. It is no wonder that Elster concludes that functionalist explanations are "extremely unsatisfactory" and have no place in the social sciences.[41]

Elster does admit that a consequence explanation might dispense with intention, recognition, and feedback altogether if it rested on a well-established, testable consequence law, such as the law declaring that chlorophyll is essential to photosynthesis. But he is dubious that there are such laws in the social sciences.[42]

For want of such laws one must fall back on colligation, that is, on tracing the sequence of events from an action to its consequence, and possibly from the consequence through a feedback mechanism to the

39. Elster, *Logic and Society*, 121.
40. Elster, *Sour Grapes*, 105.
41. Elster, *Making Sense of Marx*, 27–37, 115; idem, *Ulysses and the Sirens*, ix.
42. Elster, *Sour Grapes*, 105.

author of the action. Christopher Peacocke calls this "a complete physical account" and contrasts it to a functional explanation.

> It is true that for any particular x, y, and G [x has the functional end of placing or keeping object y in state G] we may manage to state a complete physical account that is of exactly the same (or greater) predictive power as the functional account; in the case of the thermostat [x is a thermostat, y a room, and G the state of being at 70° F] operated by a bimetallic strip, this would involve a nonfunctional account of how the different coefficients of expansion of the two metals composing the strip operate to close or break the circuit at different temperatures.[43]

Though he prefers a complete physical account, Peacocke is aware that it is not always possible to give one. We know, he observes, the general functions of DNA, but we are ignorant of how it achieves them. But, one must add, we only know the functions of DNA because of the existence of consequence laws. In the social sciences, where such laws are rare, and particularly in history, where they are nonexistent, one must fall back on a complete account.

Most historians, unlike their cousins in sociology and anthropology, eschew functional explanations. It also appears that they eschew theoretical explanations. The corpus of historical writings contains few if any theories, at any rate of theories of the magnitude of Darwin's theory of natural selection. The reason this is so is not hard to discover. Historians have found few laws requiring explanation by a theory. Neither Vico nor Comte nor Marx nor Spengler nor Toynbee has found any laws that have stood the test of time, nor have lesser historians such as Henry Thomas Buckle or Frederick Teggart found any, though they have searched diligently. True, John Stuart Mill found a law of progress, and Auguste Comte a law of successive stages of civilization, and Karl Marx a law of the evolution of society, but in fact these supposed laws are no laws at all. They are merely a description and interpretation of the development of a single civilization, that of Western Europe. Such laws of succession, as Karl Popper has shown, are not truly laws, since they describe the evolution of a "unique historical process."[44] In order to be truly laws they would have to apply to many societies. Ever since Plato, philosophers have speculated that all societies pass through similar stages and that the laws governing the life cycle of societies can be studied as the

43. Peacocke, *Holistic Explanation*, 28–29.
44. Popper, *The Poverty of Historicism*, 108–11.

botanist studies the stages by which the caterpillar becomes the butter-
fly. Vico, Spengler, and Toynbee have sought to discover the laws governing such life cycles, but with little success. It does appear that the
history of a society or a civilization or a state is the history of a unique
process. Comparisons can be made, which are illuminating. Broad generalizations can be made, such as that ultimately all civilizations disappear.
But no laws have been established that govern the development of these
civilizations.

Nor have the social scientists themselves succeeded in finding important laws and the theories that explain them. As J. O. Wisdom has observed, the natural sciences are rich in the theory-type of explanation; in
the social sciences "examples are extremely hard to come by."[45] Where in
the social sciences are the comparable laws to Kepler's cube law, Newton's
laws of motion, Boyle's and Charles's laws, Snell's law of refraction, and
Mendel's first law? Indeed, one is struck when reading books by advocates of the social sciences at the paucity of laws cited for illustrative
purposes.[46] The one exception to this is economics, from which discipline
many laws are cited. But these laws apply mostly to an age of numerous
producers and numerous consumers, numerous enough to create by their
behavior observable regularities. In an age of giant corporations and powerful trade unions, this situation no longer prevails. As Peter McClelland
observes, "There is no oligopoly theory."[47] This has not been for want of
trying. In order to preserve the scientific character of their discipline,
economists have turned to model building. If the real world does not
furnish the regularities and uniformities required to sustain laws and
theories, then devise models that do. But, as Andrew Kamarck has
shown, the pursuit of models has led economic thought to become less
and less relevant to the real world.[48]

Where economists seek refuge in models, sociologists seek refuge in
"ideal types," but ideal types have the same defect as models: they
often bear little resemblance to the real world. A second refuge for
sociologists is the analytical generalization. If one cannot discover an

45. Wisdom, "General Explanation in History," 262. Other writers who concur with this
judgment are Ernest Nagel, *The Structure of Science,* 448; Carl Hempel, "The Logic of
Functional Analysis," 199; Gordon Graham, *Historical Explanation Reconsidered,* 71; R. B.
Braithwaite, "Models in the Empirical Sciences," 269; and Richard Hofstadter, "History
and Sociology in the United States," 9.

46. See particularly Stinchcombe, *Theoretical Methods in Social History;* Benson, *Toward
the Scientific Study of History;* Brown, *The Nature of Social Laws;* and Burke, *Sociology and
History.*

47. McClelland, *Causal Explanation and Model Building,* 122.

48. Kamarck, *Economics and the Real World,* 1–7, 71–73, 116–25.

empirical generalization, create one that is true by definition, such as the assertion that people who show a high ability to empathize do so because they participate in high-involvement relationships, and that all people who participate in high-involvement relationships show such ability. This example is drawn from Robert Brown's *Explanation in Social Science*. Brown goes on to observe that "the social sciences are filled with instances of analytical statements (one whose denials can be shown to be self-contradictory) that have been unwittingly treated as empirical assertions."[49] Historians themselves are not innocent of this misdemeanor. Toynbee's law of challenge and response is an analytical truth masquerading as an empirical truth (since the failure of a society to prosper is taken as proof that the challenge was too weak or too strong, while at the same time the fact that the challenge was too weak or too strong is offered as the explanation of its failure to prosper).[50]

The failure of social scientists to find meaningful laws has led Elster to conclude "that the basic concept in the social sciences should be that of a *mechanism* rather than of a *theory*." To which he adds the comment, "In my opinion, the social sciences are light-years away from the stage at which it will be possible to formulate general-law-like regularities about human behaviour."[51] And in his book *Nuts and Bolts* he describes what he means by mechanism. "A causal mechanism," he writes, "has a finite number of links. Each link will have to be described by a general law, and in that sense by a 'black box' about whose internal gears and wheels we remain ignorant." In short, he sees that explanation must be, in the words I have employed in this book, a marriage of colligation and correlation. He likewise sees that covering laws at the macro level cannot be sustained; the general-law-like regularities are not there. "Social scientists," he writes, "are rarely able to state necessary and sufficient conditions under which the various mechanisms are switched on. This is another reason for emphasizing mechanisms rather than laws."[52] But presumably, though he fails to elaborate upon this, he does accept the validity of those general laws that join the links within the mechanism, including those laws "about whose internal gears and wheels we remain ignorant."

Undeterred by the failure of past historians and social scientists to find laws, a group of historians has arisen within the historical profession

49. Brown, *Explanation in Social Science*, 136, 139.
50. Pieter Geyl (*Debates with Historians*, 165–80) has exposed the aprioristic, unempirical nature of Toynbee's laws.
51. Elster, *The Cement of Society*, viii.
52. Elster, *Nuts and Bolts*, see esp. 7–9.

who call themselves social-science historians. They believe that they can, by applying the methods of quantification, transform the study of history into a social science. The more vocal among them, like Lee Benson and Robert Berkhofer, hold that history should become a science, seeking laws and employing theories.[53] Armed with Personian coefficients, Spearman's rho, the Guttman scalogram, and the chi-square test, and employing factor analysis, cluster analysis, and multiple regression analysis, they have sought by the most refined statistical methods to discover behavioral regularities in the past. They have sought to correlate every kind of variable; the dichotomous (Catholic v. non-Catholic), the nominal categorical (poor, middling, rich), the ranked (richest, second richest, etc.), and the interval (75¢ a bushel, 79¢ a bushel).[54] They have sought to correlate mobility patterns with ethnic groups, fertility with the business cycle, voting behavior with class, aggression with child-rearing practices, the quality of housing with income, congressional votes with sectional loyalties, and voting Republican with high incomes. But they have found no laws that are not commonplace and have produced no theories that are acceptable. Indeed, the principal achievement of quantification has been to destroy earlier theories. Thus quantitative studies have shown that Turner's thesis that Whigs were planters and merchants, and Democrats poor farmers, is wrong for Alabama, that Rostow's take-off thesis is invalid, that David Rieseman's thesis that status decline turned middle-class persons into reformers is not true, that Diamond's thesis of an urban-rural conflict in presidential votes from 1860 to 1900 is false, that Daniel Lerner's model of modernization does not fit the facts, and that Morison and Commager were wrong to say that German Americans in 1860 moved from the Democratic party to the Republican in greater numbers than other ethnic groups.[55] The search for laws and theories by the social-science historians has proved a search for a will-o'-the-wisp. As Samuel Hays, the doyen of social science historians, recently admitted, "The explosion of monographic works displays considerable variety but has generated little integrated theory—the main promise of systematic social history."[56]

53. Benson, *Toward the Scientific Study of History;* Berkhofer, *A Behavioral Approach to Historical Analysis.* The more conservative advocates of quantification, such as William Aydelotte ("Quantification in History") and Stephen Thernstrom ("Quantitative Methods in History"), are skeptical about the possibility of a scientific history.

54. For a clear and concise description of these methods, see Dollar and Jensen, *Historian's Guide to Statistics,* esp. chaps. 2 and 3.

55. Benson, *Toward the Scientific Study of History,* 64–67, 70–77; Dollar and Jensen, *Historian's Guide to Statistics,* 18, 19, 136, 195–97.

56. Hays, "Scientific Versus Traditional History," 77.

Lee Benson has suggested that the reason the social-science historian has failed to transform history into a science lies in the present organization of the historical profession and the newness of the effort.[57] This is doubtful. Ever since the time of Henry Thomas Buckle historians have aspired to make history a science, only to fail. They have failed because the behavior of human beings does not exhibit the regularity necessary to establish laws governing their behavior. People do not always vote according to their economic status in the way that a rock always accelerates toward the ground at thirty-two feet per second per second. Most historians, Nowell-Smith remarks, do not "search for regularities because their subject matter does not in fact supply them; the search is simply unrewarding. And the reason for this is that their subject matter fails, contingently, to exhibit a certain characteristic that is a necessary condition of success in the natural sciences." The law of uniformity, which allows the scientist to speak of all sulphuric acid or all beetles, does not operate in the sphere of human action. There just are not enough similar battles, wars, and revolutions.[58] Historians are not less profound than scientists; they are simply studying behavior that exhibits far less regularity.

There is another reason quantification, hailed with such enthusiasm fifteen years ago, has faded into the background. The methods of quantification are chiefly designed to unearth correlations. To this end multiple regression analysis and other sophisticated tools have proved invaluable. But historical explanation rests only in part on the discovery of correlations. It also rests on colligation, that is, on tracing the sequence of events that leads to the event to be explained. The sophisticated tools of quantification are of no relevance here. Indeed the drive of the historian to trace the course of events ever more microscopically—a drive so alien to the sociologist's impulse to find macrolaws—runs counter to the search for laws. To explain the origins of the English Revolution by tracing the complicated web of events that extends from the riot at St. Giles to the raising of the royal standard at Nottingham makes redundant any recourse to the laws of revolutions. Inasmuch as historical explanation rests on colligation, quantification is irrelevant, and historical explanation does rest to a great extent on colligation.

The above arguments, however, pose an embarrassing question. If laws in history are few and theories nearly nonexistent, what becomes of the covering-law model of historical explanation? Does not the want of laws in history destroy the covering-law model? The solution to this

---

57. Benson, *Toward the Scientific Study of History,* 310, 314 n. 140, 327, 330–33.
58. Nowell-Smith, "Are Historical Events Unique?" 115.

paradox lies in a distinction, a distinction between macrolaws and microlaws. Social-science historians have found some laws, parochial and minor. What they have not found are macrolaws, whose validity extends over many years and to most humans. Consider, for example, the following example of a parochial and minor law. A historian seeking to account for the growth of population in Great Britain from 1760 to 1830 will notice that there was a great increase in population in those parts of Britain where there existed labor-intensive industries. This could be called the labor-intensive law of population growth: wherever there were labor-intensive industries, there occurred a growth in population. Further, a theory could be suggested to explain this law. Where there existed labor-intensive industries, young men could find employment. When young men could find employment, they could earn the money needed to establish a household. Possessing the money to establish a household, they would have the means to marry. Having the means to marry, they would do so. Because they married early, their wives would have more years in which to bear more children. Having more years in which to bear more children, they would bear them, and so the population would increase. What makes this law parochial and minor is the fact that the presence of labor-intensive industries does not explain the increase in population in Latin America, where they are generally absent; nor does the presence of labor-intensive industries invariably lead to an increase in population.

The above illustration points to an important truth: the laws historians have established concern events of which there are many instances. They concern births, marriages, divorces, deaths, crimes, arrests, convictions, hospitalizations, employment, juvenile delinquency, alcoholism, and so forth; the list could be indefinitely continued. They do not concern reformations, wars, revolutions, geographical discoveries, artistic innovations, religious awakenings, industrial revolutions, scientific revolutions, changes in literary styles, and so forth. Thus it is no accident that when historians broadened the field of history to include births, deaths, marriages, employment, crime, disease, and migrations, they found correlations. The many instances of such events allow them to correlate the occurrence of such events—say recidivism—with a number of explanatory variables, such as age at earliest arrest, age at release, financial aid, number of convictions for crimes against persons, and so forth. Paul Allison has shown how sophisticated such an analysis can be.[59] But such an analysis cannot be applied to wars, revolutions, and reformations, since there are too few of them and they are profoundly

59. Allison, *Event History Analysis;* see esp. 47–57.

dissimilar. Here explanation must be by colligation, by tracing the myriad events leading up to the war or revolution or reformation.

But here again laws appear, since each step in the complicated web of events leading to the war or revolution or reformation has to be connected with an earlier event by a covering law. And if there is a law, must there not be some theory to explain that law? There well may be, but often the covering law is so platitudinous that the historian feels no need to find a theory to explain it. Take Ladurie's explanation of the spread of the custom of eating fruit and vegetables to the countryside in eighteenth-century France. Relying on the diary of Retif de la Bretonne, he traces it to country girls like Barbe, who took service in town, learned the habit, and returned to the countryside.[60] To justify his assertion that Barbe learned the habit in town, he would have to employ a commonplace as a covering law, say, "All persons who returned from a town with a new habit, a habit prevalent there, learned that habit there." A psychologist might proffer some kind of learning theory to explain that law, though it is possible that Jon Elster is right and that we have here a "black box" about whose internal gears and wheels we remain ignorant. And ultimately we can have no theory. In this respect Bertrand Russell's speculation that ultimately causation has no place in science has a relevance to history. The physicist pursues analysis until there is no theory to explain a correlation, no mechanism to transform correlation into causation; there are only functional relations. Similarly, historians pursue analysis until they reach covering laws that are so commonplace that they see no need for a theory to explain them. The result is that in the writing of history there is almost no theory. In social and economic history, devoted to the study of comparable events of which there are a multitude of instances, there may be some parochial and meaningful theories, but in history devoted to the study of large, complex events there is none. Here there is only unrelenting tracing, pursued as minutely as possible, and so employing covering laws that are commonplace and require no theory to explain them.

This unrelenting tracing leads inexorably to the individual author or authors of an event, and to the study of their actions.

---

60. Ladurie, *The Mind and Method of the Historian*, 237–38.

8 PURPOSIVE ACTION

The prediction of the future from the past belongs to the theory of causality; the determination of the past from the present belongs to the theory of purpose.

> — Arturo Rosenblueth and Norbert Wiener,
> "Purposeful and Non-purposeful Behavior"

It is a truth universally acknowledged by philosophers of history that actions differ from events. Even though some philosophers, such as Carl Hempel and Paul Churchland, argue that the logical character of an action explanation is the same as that of a scientific explanation, they do acknowledge that actions differ from events.[1] Events occur; actions are performed by an agent, an agent who has a purpose. One gives a reason for the occurrence of an action, a cause for the occurrence of an event. One explains the occurrence of an event by asserting, Whenever X then Y. One explains the occurrence of an action by citing the desires and beliefs that led the agent to perform it. In explaining an event, one discovers the previous initial conditions that caused the occurrence of the event. In explaining an action, one discovers the subsequent actions that reveal the earlier purposes of the agent. In this sense even a machine can exhibit purpose. The actions of a guided torpedo in altering its

---

1. Hempel, "Explanation in Science and in History," 115–24; Churchland, "The Logical Character of Action-Explanations," 215–16.

course in order to hit its target, actions carried out subsequent to its firing, reveal its purpose.

The same impulse that leads scientists to seek to reduce psychology to physiology, physiology to chemistry, and chemistry to physics leads historians to explain aggregate events by tracing ever more minutely the sequence of events that led to them, and to elucidate those microevents by discovering the authors of them, and to explain the actions of those authors by discovering their purposes. But just as psychologists cannot always reduce their explanations to physiology, or physiologists theirs to chemistry, or chemists theirs to physics, so historians often cannot reduce their explanations to actions or choose not to reduce their explanations to actions. Historians can, and often do, explain why an event occurred by having one event cause another: a drought in Kansas caused the price of wheat to rise in Chicago; Barbe's residing in town caused her to learn to eat fruit and vegetables; finding little to do in London, nobles fell into dissipation; and (to borrow an example from Collingwood) "Mr. Baldwin's speech caused the adjournment of the House." Historians do so because it would be impossible to discover the purposes of all those who sold or bought wheat, unnecessary to discover whether Barbe first tasted fruit out of curiosity or because of peer pressure, impracticable to find out the reasons nobles in London fell into dissipation, and difficult to ascertain the Speaker's reasons for adjourning the House. The Speaker may have died, leaving the historian no clue why he adjourned the House. The historian therefore falls back on a covering law that whenever a prime minister makes such a speech as Baldwin made, the speaker adjourns the House.

But though historians often state that one event caused another, they would prefer to discover the purposes or intentions or motives or reasons or desires of the author or authors of an action. Philosophers who write about the logical character of action explanations use all of these terms, with the result that there is considerable disarray in their discussions. Some speak of purpose, some of intention, others of motive, yet others of reasons, desires, and wants.[2] To bring some order into this

2. Rex Martin (*Historical Explanation,* 159), Charles Taylor (*The Explanation of Behaviour,* 3), Arturo Rosenblueth, Norbert Wiener, and Julian Bigelow ("Behavior, Purpose, and Teleology," 221), and Richard Taylor ("Comments on a Mechanistic Conception of Purposefulness," 226) prefer "purpose"; G.E.M. Anscombe (*Intention,* 1), Georg Henrich von Wright (*Explanation and Understanding,* 89), John R. Searle (*Intentionality,* 112), Myles Brand (*Intending and Acting,* 23–32), and D. C. Dennet ("Mechanism and Responsibility," 160) prefer "intention"; Peter Winch (*The Idea of a Social Science,* 45), William H. Dray (*Laws and Explanation in History,* 123–24), and Kai Nielsen ("Rational Explanation in History," 307) prefer "reasons"; N. S. Sutherland ("Motives as Explanations," 145), Richard S. Peters (*The Concept of Motivation,* 27), and Abraham Irwin Melden (*Free Action,* 86) prefer "motive"; and Christopher Peacocke (*Holistic Explanation,* 3) prefers "desire."

disarray, it would be wise to make purpose the central concept and to relate the other concepts to it.

I have chosen to make purpose and not intention the central concept because "intention" has an ambivalent meaning that can obscure any analysis of how actions are explained. "Intention" may suggest "deliberate," that is, the opposite of accidental. One can say, "He intentionally took down the gun," meaning he did not do so accidentally or absent-mindedly. But one may also say, "His intention in taking down the gun was to shoot rabbits." In this case "intention" refers to his purpose in taking down the gun. The ambivalent character of the word "intention" has led Jack Meiland to use the terms "intention$_1$" and "intention$_2$," G.E.M. Anscombe to distinguish between an "intention *of*" and an "intention *in*," Christopher Peacocke to speak of "intentional" in a primary and in a secondary sense, and D. C. Dennet to capitalize "intentional" in order to avoid confusion with intent.[3] For the philosopher analyzing the nature of intentions, such a double usage may well be necessary; for the historian interested in the role that purpose plays in actions, it would be better to distinguish the two meanings of intention by using "intentional" to mean "deliberate" and "purpose" to mean "future intent."

"Purpose" is likewise superior to the expression "reasons for an action." Its great advantage here is the fact that it is not narrowly confined to rational action. There is no doubt that historical agents frequently perform actions for reasons that are eminently rational. William Dray has done the historical profession a service in emphasizing this.[4] But historical agents also perform actions out of habit, impulse, dispositions, emotions, and desires, many of which are not notably rational. The term "purpose" has the advantage that it covers both the rational and the irrational in behavior. The same reasoning that leads me to reject "reasons for" an action leads me to reject R. G. Collingwood's "thought" exhibited by an action. It, also, is too narrowly rational, though Louis Mink denies this, arguing that Collingwood's concept of thought encompasses, or can be modified to encompass, both emotions and unconscious motives. In reenacting thought the historian thereby reenacts the emotion that survives in the thought. Thus the emotion of ambition survives in Caesar's "ambitious decision" to cross the Rubicon. Unconscious motives, urges Mink, can be encompassed in thought by enlarging upon Collingwood's distinction between capricious and rational choice.[5] Louis Mink's elaboration upon

---

3. Meiland, *The Nature of Intention*, 8–10; Anscombe, *Intention*, 9; Peacocke, *Holistic Explanation*, 72; Dennet, "Mechanism and Responsibility," 160.

4. Dray, *Laws and Explanation in History*, 122–37.

5. Mink, *Mind, History, and Dialectic*, 164–70.

Collingwood's concept of thought is ingenious, but in the end unconvincing. It is unconvincing because Mink's tenuous, involuted, and speculative assertions are so at variance with the direct, succinct, and dogmatic utterances of Collingwood in *The Idea of History.*

Central to Collingwood's argument in *The Idea of History* is the metaphor of the "inside" and the "outside" of an action, with the thought expressed by the action being its "inside" and the physical description of the action its "outside." The historian, asserts Collingwood, explains an action by reenacting the thought that led to it. This metaphor has given rise to an extensive literature, with Collingwood's critics accusing him of mysticism and his apologists replying that reenactment is merely inference from what is known about the agent's situation.[6] The apologists are probably correct, but the whole controversy would have been unnecessary had Collingwood simply spoken of the purpose of an agent and the problem of ascertaining what that purpose was.

With "motive" and "desire" the question is not whether "motive" and "desire" are better terms to use than "purpose." The question, rather, is, what is the relation of "motive" and "desire" to "purpose"?

The relation of a motive to a purpose can be exemplified by the following illustration. A man puts his name up for election to Parliament. His choice is intentional; his purpose is to secure election to Parliament; his motive is to gain reputation, to enjoy the exercise of power, and to secure membership in the smartest club in London. As Anscombe has observed, "A man's intention is *what* he aims at or chooses; his motive is what determines the aim or choice."[7] But the motive need not be forward-looking, though it often is. It might be backward-looking, as is the motive of a man who kills another out of revenge. But the role of the motive remains the same, it is what determines the choice of a purpose. In this instance a desire for revenge determined the choice of the purpose, namely, to kill an enemy. Motives are aimed less at definite goals, which purposes always are, than at the satisfaction of emotions, emotions such as ambition, greed, pity, affection, or revenge. Motives may, of course, be mixed, as were those of the man who desired to enter Parliament equally for the reputation it brought, for the enjoyment of exercising power, and for its social amenities. Motives need not always be given for an action, as Richard Peters has observed. One does not attribute a motive to a person who performs a habitual or a conventional

6. Among critics, see esp. Gardiner, *The Nature of Historical Explanation*, 39; among apologists see Donagan, *The Later Philosophy of R. G. Collingwood*, 175–209, and Dray, "R. G. Collingwood and the Understanding of Actions in History," 9–26.

7. Anscombe, *Intention*, 18.

action, nor does one attribute a motive to an action arising from a well-known disposition. One seeks a motive only where the action seems to demand some justification.[8]

Concerning the relation of desire (or wanting) to purpose, there is a broad consensus among philosophers. Charles Taylor observes that desire gives rise to purpose, a formula that Peacocke makes more exact by asserting that beliefs and desires together underlie intention (or purpose), the beliefs being those concerned with the proposition that doing x will lead to y, which is the desired goal.[9] It is true, as Meiland has observed, that a person might, out of a sense of duty, perform an action he or she does not want to do. But this fact does not undermine, as Meiland argues it does, the assertion that desire plus belief leads to purpose. It merely places the agent's desire to do his or her duty above all other desires.[10] Abraham Melden has also questioned the formula that desire plus belief underlies intention or purpose. He has done so by making wanting parallel to intention, so that instead of "wanting" contributing to the formation of intention, it is a concept that can replace it. He reaches this conclusion because he is persuaded that wanting, just like intention, is only demonstrated by action. He believes that the connection between wanting and doing is a logical connection, not a causal one.[11] It is an ingenious argument, but it runs counter to the fact that one can, notwithstanding his assertions to the contrary, desire something but not believe that one can obtain it—and therefore take no action to obtain it. Both desire and belief are requisite to the formation of a purpose. Peacocke's scheme remains a useful one.

To the historian the critical question is not, What is the nature of purpose? Rather, it is, How can one determine what the agent's purpose was? By what logic does the historian decide that this purpose, and not that, led the agent to act? The obvious first step is to ask the agent, which for the historian of past generations means unearthing the purposes that the agent avowed at the time. But this obvious procedure has fallen into disrepute before the onslaught of behavioristic psychology and Rylean philosophy. Introspection is out and self-avowal suspect. Gilbert Ryle holds that persons discover their own long-term motives in the same way they discover the motives of others, namely, by applying lawlike propositions to overt behavior.[12] But in practice historians always

8. Peters, *The Concept of Motivation*, 27, 34, 49–50.
9. Taylor, *The Explanation of Behaviour*, 36; Peacocke, *Holistic Explanation*, 3, 16.
10. Meiland, *The Nature of Intention*, 115–17.
11. Melden, *Free Action*, 123, 125, 166, 176–77.
12. Ryle, *The Concept of Mind*, 90–92.

have—and probably always will—use the avowals and disavowals of historical agents. They plunder diaries, letters, speeches, interviews, memoirs, memoranda, and confessions for such self-reports. They even draw on such modern techniques as exit polls, in which journalists ask voters for their reasons for voting Labour or Conservative. Even the critics of self-reporting have come to admit its validity. Ryle himself admits that "open avowals let us know the explanation without research," that is, without having to ascertain the agent's personal capacities and propensities.[13]

The most interesting case of a critic of self-reporting retreating from his critique is that of Collingwood. At one point in his career he came close to rejecting introspective knowledge. A person's knowledge of his or her own thoughts, he contended, had to be obtained as others obtained it, by inference from his or her actions. But later in his career he wrote that there could be a private expression of thought. William Dray shrewdly sees that this concession ought to have led Collingwood to revise his metaphor of "inside" and "outside." He should now have declared that the "inside" represented the agent's expression of purpose and the "outside" the expression of that purpose by the event.[14] The metaphor would then truly have distinguished the natural sciences from history, since no stone has ever told the physicist why it fell, no tropistic plant told the botanist why it turned to the sun, and no cell told the physiologist why it divided. Yet countless historical agents have avowed why they acted as they did. In this respect, if in no other, history differs from the natural sciences.

But there are severe limitations to the value of self-reporting. Persons occasionally lie; they also occasionally delude themselves. It is not merely that they lie; they insensibly place their own motives in the best light. And they may well be ignorant of the deeper motives that guide their actions. Since the writings of Sigmund Freud no historian can ignore such hidden motives. But the historian is not helpless before such lies, biases, and self-delusions. There are rules for assessing when persons can be believed and when they cannot, rules that all historians learn in their professional training. Unguarded expressions are more trustworthy than carefully crafted speeches. Private diaries are more trustworthy than published memoirs. A letter from Marlborough to his friend Godolphin will be more frank than a letter from Marlborough to the Queen. Strafford's answer to his impeachment will be less truthful

13. Ibid., 172.
14. I have drawn on Dray, "R. G. Collingwood and the Understanding of Actions in History," 13–14, for this account of Collingwood's thought.

than his utterance at the council table. A memoir written thirty years after the event will be less accurate than an entry in a diary written the next day. The rules could be multiplied, but what deserves attention is the fact that these rules are gained from experience. They are generalizations about human conduct, laws drawn from the study of men and women in the past. Kai Nielsen once observed that by relying on self-knowledge or reasons, William Dray had successfully escaped the covering-law model.[15] There is much truth in this observation. A historical agent's avowing his or her purposes hardly fits into the Hempelian scheme. Yet it is also undeniably true that historians use rules based upon lawlike generalizations for deciding when they can believe an avowal. These rules do fit into the Hempelian scheme, inasmuch as such rules, like covering laws, arise from the principle of regularity, and not from a single instance. In other words, they are based on generalizations about human behavior, not on a single instance of an avowal being true.

In assessing the value of self-reporting in the determination of purpose, one fact should not be overlooked. Such reports, however biased, however deluded, furnish data upon which the historian can reason. Even the behaviorists now admit that introspective reports by experimental subjects furnish valuable data for their studies. The data provided to the historian by self-reports is equally rich. *Mein Kampf* and the Hossbach Memorandum are no models of verity, but we would know less about the origins of the Second World War if we did not possess them. Once again, it is obvious that such documents must be interpreted and that such interpretation will be based on rules of interpretation, rules based in turn on generalizations about the conduct of Adolph Hitler and of other Germans. But at this point the historian leaves the domain of self-reporting for that of deduction from the actions of the agent. And though one should not ignore the fact of self-reporting, it is indisputable that the chief means by which the historian establishes the purposes of historical agents is by deducing those purposes from their actions.

One of the most elementary ways in which one deduces purpose from actions is the interpretation of gestures, grimaces, sudden cries, tones of voice, and slips of the tongue. A baby's crying tells us that he wants his bottle; a dog's barking, that a stranger is approaching. Wilhelm Dilthey calls these "life-expressions" and asserts that we understand such expressions by intuition, by transposing ourselves into the state of mind of the person observed. He calls this "understanding," or, in German, *Verstehen*.[16] But Theodore Abel has argued that *Verstehen* is at bottom

---

15. Nielsen, "Rational Explanation in History," 315–16.
16. Dilthey, "The Understanding of Other Persons," 212–24.

nothing more than applying generalizations to observed behavior, generalizations learned from experience. We cry out when we stub our toes, so can readily interpret the cry of others who stub their toes. Ernest Nagel is not even sure that we need learn such generalizations from personal experience or that observers need exhibit empathy with persons they are observing in order to understand them.[17] We need never have been livid with rage in order to interpret others' lividness as rage. With this extreme view David Hume (as interpreted by James Farr) and Arthur Danto disagree.[18] They both regard the process Dilthey called *Verstehen* as taking part in two stages. First, one must decode the sign, that is, interpret the gesture or countenance or expression. Such gestures, countenances, and expressions are external signs of mental states, mental states such as anger, fear, love, hope, ecstasy, boredom, regret, and sorrow. One decodes these signs in the manner described by Abel. The second stage is to associate the idea, say, of fear, with the feeling of fear. As Hume observed, "we never remark any passion or principle in others in which, in some degree or other, we may not find a parallel in ourselves."[19] Or as Danto puts it, "The blind do not call up images of red."[20] In Hume's judgment, through sympathy we associate the idea of fear with the feeling of fear, though he came to doubt that one could describe the mechanism by which sympathy worked.[21] Danto puts it this way: only on the basis of right experience can a person make a correct sympathetic ascription of a mental predicate (say, of fear) to another person. And he defines *Verstehen* as the correct ascription of mental predicates.[22]

Most historians, I suspect, would agree that the description of the first stage of *Verstehen* by Abel, Hume, and Danto has sufficiently demystified the concept as to make it a useful and acceptable one. They would likewise probably agree that the debate about the second stage is an academic one, whose resolution one way or the other would not affect how they reasoned about the past. Danto, however, would probably disagree with this judgment, since he believes a right understanding of the second stage shows that *Verstehen* cannot take us into the interior of other periods. *Verstehen* can only capture in the past what the past has in common with the present.[23] This seems to contradict what historicists

17. Abel, "The Operation Called *Verstehen*," 682–84; Nagel, *The Structure of Science*, 484.
18. Farr, "Hume, Hermeneutics, and History," 290–307; Danto, *Narration and Knowledge*, 285–97, 337–40.
19. Quoted in Farr, "Hume, Hermeneutics, and History," 300.
20. Danto, *Narration and Knowledge*, 290–91.
21. Farr, "Hume, Hermeneutics, and History," 294–95.
22. Danto, *Narration and Knowledge*, 290.
23. Ibid., 285–86.

have long taught, namely, that only by immersing themselves in the records, and therefore in the life, of a different society can historians hope to understand it. The resolution of the contradiction, I believe, lies in this: The basic mental predicates of which Danto talks—anger, fear, love, hope, ecstasy, boredom, regret, and sorrow—are common to humanity in all ages. What is not common are the situations that occasion them and the gestures and countenances that express them. Danto speaks of a stone that to a Roman is a makeweight in a balance and to a medieval Christian a sacred object (because part of the fabric of a church). Each regards the stone (the identical stone) differently, and each lives in his own world. Danto goes on to conclude:

> Verstehen is, after all, understanding, not knowledge. Knowledge entails the truth of what is known, whereas understanding entails nothing so far as concerns truth or falsity of what is understood. Understanding, however it is achieved, gives us entry into the world of another in the sense that it opens up the beliefs of others when these define that world. But to understand the world of another is not to understand the world, unless those beliefs are also *our* beliefs, at which point they become transparent.[24]

What Danto fails to see here is that only by immersing themselves in Roman history can historians learn that a stone can serve as a makeweight in a balance. No experience in contemporary America would teach them this (I assume that all makeweights in America are made of metal). The historicists are, in my judgment, correct. The way to understand a different society is to immerse oneself in its records until one thinks and speaks like a denizen of that society. This fact follows from emphasizing the first stage in *Verstehen*, that described by Abel and Nagel. Indeed, Danto is certainly correct to imply that an emphasis on the second stage cuts us off from other societies. If their passions were truly different from ours, we could not understand them. But it is likely that their passions are not that different from ours—we, as well as medieval Christians, experience sacredness. What we have to learn is that in medieval Italy a Christian can direct that feeling to a stone from the fabric of a church. Just as the historian who immerses himself in a past society learns countless parochial covering laws that make him a better historian, so he learns countless small generalizations that allow him to decode the gestures, expressions, and demeanor of men and women who lived in that past age.

The interpretation of gestures, exclamations, and other life-expressions

---

24. Ibid., 337–40.

has a particular significance because it explains how we can distinguish action from movement. If a man picks up a lamp and dashes it to the floor, breaking it, we know that he did so intentionally, that the movements we observed were an "action." On the other hand, if a man rises from a chair, knocks over the lamp with his shoulder, thus breaking it, we know that the movement of his shoulder is a mere movement, an accident, not an "action." Actions, as Charles Taylor remarks, cannot be observed. We observe the movements of Jones's hand as he shakes hands with Smith, but to interpret those movements as a handshake we must classify them.[25] Experience has taught us that such movements are a handshake. To interpret such movements as an intentional action of a particular kind, we must subsume it under a law that connects certain movements with particular actions.

A skeptic might admit that all this is true but wonder if it is relevant to historical explanation. The historian does not see the gestures, countenances, bearing, and grimaces of the historical actors he or she is studying. This is usually true (portraits being the exception), but though the historian cannot witness these gestures, countenances, bearing, and grimaces, contemporaries did, and occasionally recorded their observations. We know something more about Charles I's character because Andrew Marvell wrote of his demeanor on the scaffold.

> He nothing common did or mean
> Upon that memorable scene.

If historians rarely deduce purpose from gesture and countenance, how do they deduce it? The answer: from the actions of the historical agent, as the following three scenarios should make clear. A housewife leaves her house, drives off, and returns. To her husband's query, "Where have you been?" she replies, "To the grocery store to buy milk." This is only a self-report, but the husband decides that she is telling the truth, since he remembers that they had run out of milk at breakfast. He rightly deduces that the need for milk had led his wife to go for milk. The second scenario is somewhat similar. A housewife leaves her house, drives off, and returns. To her husband's query, "Where have you been?" she replies, "To the grocery store to buy milk." But the husband in this case did not notice that they were out of milk. He does, however, remember that every Wednesday at four o'clock his wife goes to the grocery store to buy milk, in order to tide them over until her weekly shopping on Saturday; and he observes that it is now Wednesday at

---

25. Taylor, *The Explanation of Behaviour*, 90–94.

four. The third scenario is likewise similar but not identical. The house-wife leaves the house, drives off, and returns. To her husband's query, "Where have you been?" she replies, "To the grocery store to buy milk." The husband in this case is not aware that they needed milk or that his wife regularly goes shopping at this time, but he does watch her take two cartons of milk from a brown shopping bag and put them in the refrigerator. From this he decides that she is telling the truth. Each of these scenarios illustrates a characteristic way in which a person deduces a purpose (to get milk) from an action (driving off from the house and returning). The three methods may be called the logic of the situation, the logic of dispositional traits, and the logic of subsequent actions.

The Logic of the Situation

One sees a man leap from a burning building and deduces that he wishes to save his life. One sees a husband attack his wife's lover and deduces that he is seeking revenge. One sees a man thread his way across a street, dodging the cars, and deduces that he wishes to reach the other side safely. One sees a soldier insert a bayonet upon the com-mand of his officer to do so, and deduces that he wishes to obey his officer. In all these instances the observer deduces the purpose of the action from the situation that gives rise to it. The observer does not do this in any mysterious way; he or she does not do it by entering into the mind of the leaping, attacking, dodging, or obeying man. Rather, as R. M. MacIver observes, "we relate the action of one individual to the actions of others in similar situations."[26] We subsume the action we are witnessing under a generalization gained from observing (or, more likely, from reading about, hearing about, or viewing on film) similar situations and actions.

Most situations that the historian studies are far more complex than a man leaping from a burning building. Caesar deciding to cross the Rubicon or Brutus resolving to assassinate Caesar represent more compli-cated situations. Nevertheless, those situations, coupled with the ac-tions taken, help the historian to explain those actions. The two philoso-phers who have done the most to illuminate this model of explanation are Karl Popper and William Dray.

Popper calls his model the logic of the situation or situational analysis. The basic premise of this model is that the historian should and can

---

26. MacIver, *Social Causation*, 211.

interpret an action as an attempt to solve a problem. The historian's task is to reconstruct the problem situation as it appeared to the agent, thereby showing that the actions of the agent were adequate or appropriate to the situation. The one animating law for this model is the principle of acting appropriately to the situation, a principle Popper calls the rationality principle. He does not suggest that agents always act in a manner appropriate to the situation, that is, rationally. He merely suggests that when they do, the historian can, by reconstructing the situation, understand their actions. What Popper regards as essential is not the reenactment of the thoughts of the agent, but rather the careful analysis of the situation.[27]

Under the name "rational explanation" William Dray puts forward a similar model, though he places greater emphasis on the reenactment of the thoughts of the agent. "The historian," he writes, "must *penetrate* behind appearances, achieve *insight* into the situation, *identify* himself sympathetically with the protagonist, *project* himself imaginatively into his situation."[28] But in the discussion that follows he emphasizes the reconstruction of the agent's calculations in the light of the circumstances. We understand an action when we see that it is the thing to do in view of the agent's peculiar circumstances. What we want to know when we ask to have an action explained is in what way it was appropriate. We can understand an action when we can agree that it was the thing to do in view of the agent's circumstances. Such an account permits the construction of a calculation that certifies the action as appropriate. Only by putting him- or herself in the agent's position can the historian understand why the agent did what he or she did.[29] Nothing in this account of rational explanation would offend Popper, the positivist.

There is, however, a fatal defect in both Popper's and Dray's accounts of situational analysis: they fail to show how the historian discovers the purpose or purposes of the agent. Indeed, they assume that a knowledge of those purposes is part of the situation. Popper writes that the situation "already contains all the relevant aims and all the available relevant knowledge, especially that of possible means for realizing these aims."[30] And Dray writes, "It may also be necessary, at times, to take note explicitly of the agent's purposes, which may be quite different from the one's which the investigator would have had in the same

---

27. Popper, *The Poverty of Historicism*, 147–50; idem, *The Open Society*, 2:97; idem, "The Rationality Principle," 359–65; idem, *Objective Knowledge*, 179–89. For a useful exposition of Popper's views, see Farr, "Situational Analysis," 1085–1107.
28. Dray, *Laws and Explanation in History*, 119.
29. Ibid., 122–26.
30. Popper, "The Rationality Principle," 359.

circumstances, or even in the circumstances the agent envisaged."[31] Nowhere do they show how the historian gains a knowledge of these aims
and purposes. The reason for this defect lies in their preoccupation with
"understanding" and in their equating of "understanding" with "explanation." But understanding and explanation are two different things, as
the following example makes clear. Imagine a motorist driving along a
highway. Suddenly a car coming in the opposite direction crosses the
center line and starts down the wrong lane, straight at the motorist. The
motorist swerves off the highway into the ditch. One observer says to
the other, "Why did he swerve off the highway?" To which the other
observer replies, "In order not to be hit by the other car and killed." The
second observer has reconstructed the purpose of the motorist from the
situation and the action. The first observer then comments, "Ah, now I
understand why he swerved." Or perhaps, "Ah, now his swerving is
intelligible." What has made his swerving intelligible is the knowledge
of the motorist's purpose. We "understand" an action when we know
both the agent's purposes and his situation and find his action appropriate to those purposes. But first we must discover his purposes. Indeed,
in action explanation, as contrasted to event explanation, the first obligation is to find the purposes that led to the action. There is nothing wrong
with a historian seeking to "understand" an agent's actions, that is, to
make them intelligible. That is a legitimate task among the many tasks
allotted to the historian. But it is not explanation. It does not answer the
question, Why did the motorist swerve? That question is answered by
the discovery of his purposes. "He swerved in order to avoid a head-on
collision and save his life."

In fairness to Dray it must be said that under the rubric "reasons" he
sees this. Thus he writes, "Since the calculating gives what we should
normally call the agent's *reasons* for acting as he did, I shall refer here-
after to this broad class of explanations as 'rational.' "[32] Or again, "It is
not necessary for the historian to show that the agent had reason for
what he did; it is sufficient for explanation to show that he had reasons."[33] Dray's model makes good sense if one equates his reasons for
an action with the purposes that lay behind the action. The goal of
situational analysis then becomes the discovery of those reasons, or
purposes.

It must be allowed that an agent's larger purposes have a place in a
description of the agent's situation. The larger purpose of the motorist

31. Dray, *Laws and Explanation in History*, 125.
32. Ibid., 123–24.
33. Ibid., 126.

was to continue living; he was not suicidal. The historian discovers this by talking to the motorist's friends, who came to this conclusion both from the motorist's own remarks and from his exhibiting a relish for life. Knowing that the motorist's larger purpose was to continue living, the historian concludes that his immediate purpose in swerving was to save his life. Suppose that the historian knew that the motorist was suicidal, that his larger purpose was to end his life. In this case the historian might attribute his swerving to a desire to spare the lives of those in the other car (or perhaps not to die in a particularly violent manner). If the historian has no independent knowledge of the agent's larger purposes, then it can be no part of the description of the situation, and the ensuing analysis will be less certain. The historian, therefore, who searches out the agent's larger purposes will certainly make a more accurate deduction of the agent's immediate purpose than the historian who does not.

The example of the motorist is drawn from everyday life; it might be well to draw one from history. Consider the question, Why did Cardinal Wolsey advise Henry VIII to ally with Charles V? A. F. Pollard asserts that he did so in order to become pope through Charles's assistance.[34] Pollard no doubt came to this conclusion from an examination of the situation. Wolsey was known to be ambitious to become pope, and Charles V had promised to support his candidacy. The appropriate action for Wolsey was to advise Henry to ally with Charles. But it is essential in situational analysis to discover all the facts, down to the smallest detail, of the situation. R. B. Wernham, who has done this, doubts that Wolsey, in order to become pope, advised Henry VIII to ally with Charles V, pointing out that Francis I also had promised to favor Wolsey's candidacy.[35] Pollard might reply that Charles V was in a far stronger position to influence the College of Cardinals than was Francis I. All of this illustrates the point that both Popper and Dray emphasize, that one must know the agent's desires and the situation thoroughly.

But Wolsey's case presents another problem. He may well have advised Henry VIII to ally with Charles V because he knew that it would be welcome advice. Given Wolsey's situation—dependent on Henry's favor, ambitious for wealth and power, eager for more offices and titles— the giving of such welcome advice would be an appropriate, a rational action. How is the historian to decide which purpose guided Wolsey's actions? Or if both did, which was the preeminent motive? Two strategies immediately present themselves. The first is to ask which purpose, given the situation, would be the more appropriate. Given Wolsey's far

34. Pollard, *Henry VIII*, 122.
35. Wernham, *Before the Armada*, 98.

greater dependence on Henry, his immediate master, than on Charles V, residing at a distant court, the answer probably would be that the desire to curry Henry's favor was a more appropriate purpose than the desire to secure Charles's aid in a quest for the papacy. The second strategy is to fall back on the dispositional traits of Cardinal Wolsey. Did his past conduct show him to be more disposed to please Henry VIII than to pursue intrigues in Rome? Had he risen to greatness by serving his monarch or by serving the Church? Few historians would doubt that he had risen to greatness by serving his monarch, and would probably conclude that the purpose of pleasing Henry was the preeminent purpose. Thus both strategies favor Wernham's position.

I discuss the second strategy in the following section, on dispositional traits. What concerns me now is how the historian reaches the conclusion that the purpose of pleasing Henry was a more appropriate purpose in that situation than the purpose of seeking Charles V's aid in a bid for the papacy. He does so, as Dray has rightly observed, by placing himself in Wolsey's situation. He asks himself, were I Wolsey, were I ambitious to be pope, were I also determined to please Henry, did I know all that he knew about Henry's immediate power and Charles's remote concerns, what purpose would be uppermost in my mind? He assumes that Wolsey is a rational person. It follows that his reasoning would be Wolsey's reasoning. This is the rationality principle that both Popper and Dray place at the center of their models. This does not mean that Popper and Dray believe that men and women always act rationally. Not for a moment. It merely means that when they do act rationally, the historian (who presumably always acts rationally) can discover their purposes by placing himself in their situation, by observing their actions, and by asking, What purpose would make that action appropriate?

But here an important point must be made. The rationality principle is only a shortcut to the establishment of the law that gives validity to our deducing the purpose from the action and the situation. We place ourselves in the position of the motorist who swerved in order to avoid a head-on collision. We conclude that we would swerve in order to save our lives. We then conclude that the motorist swerved for that same purpose. But what logical warrant do we have for reaching this conclusion? Only the lawlike generalization that all, or nearly all, rational (not suicidal) motorists do in fact swerve for that purpose, a law that years of experience has shown to be true. But how can we personally know there is such a law? We have not counted all the instances in which rational motorists have swerved in order to save their lives. The answer is that the rationality principle takes us there by a shortcut. We regard ourselves as rational. We know that we would swerve in order to save our lives. We therefore conclude that all rational persons would swerve in order to save their lives. But suppose they did not. Suppose half of them swerved in order to save the life of the oncoming motorist. Then the shortcut we took would have led us into error. There being no lawlike generalization that all rational motorists would swerve to save their lives, our explanation would have no logical warrant, though reached by the rationality principle. Fortunately for the rationality principle, the supposition made above is an implausible one. In practice the rationality principle often allows the historian to take a shortcut to a valid lawlike generalization.

The function of the rationality principle is very like the function of the visibility principle in the causation of physical events. David Hume argued that merely seeing one billiard ball hit another does not justify our believing that the first ball caused the second ball to roll across the table. We need to subsume the event under a generalization about such events, to appeal to the constant conjunction between the two events. Maurice Mandelbaum has endeavored to deny this, but what he has really shown is that seeing one billiard ball cause another to fly across the table is only a shortcut to establishing a law about the constant conjunction of the two events.[36] Similarly, the historian's rational calculation about the purpose that arises from a particular situation and the ensuing action is only a shortcut to a law connecting that purpose with the particular situation and action. The rationality principle is to action explanation what the visibility principle is to event explanation.

Carl Hempel has rightly observed that any attempt to ascertain an agent's purpose from his actions must be done conjointly with a hypothesis about his beliefs regarding the most appropriate means to achieve that purpose. The driver's purpose is to avoid a collision; his belief is that swerving to the right is the best way to do so. If he thought that swerving to the left was the better way, he would have done so. "Hence," writes Hempel, "strictly speaking an examination of an agent's behavior can serve to test assumptions about his beliefs or about his objectives, not separately, but only in suitable pairs. That is, belief attributions and goal attributions are *epistemically interdependent*."[37] Thus from the situation and the action, the historian must deduce both the purpose to avoid a collision and the belief that the best way to do so was by swerving right.

Carl Hempel has also raised the question whether the logic of rational explanation differs decisively from that of covering-law explanation.

36. See above, pages 40–42.
37. Hempel, "Aspects of Scientific Explanation," 475.

And he answered that if conceived rightly it does not. He begins by giving Dray's scheme of a rational explanation:

Agent A was in a situation of kind C.
When in a situation of kind C, the thing to do is X.
Therefore, agent A did X.

Hempel, however, believes if rightly conceived rational explanation should take the following form:[38]

Agent A was in a situation of kind C.
A was a rational agent at the time.
Any rational agent, when in a situation of kind C, will invariably (or with high probability) do X.
A did X.

What Hempel has done is to remove a normative statement, "The thing to do is X," and replace it with an empirical statement, "Any rational agent will invariably (or with high probability) do X." This change seems to me entirely warranted,[39] but I would like to propose a further change in this scheme of rational explanation:

Agent A was in a situation of type C.
A did X.
All rational agents who do X in a situation of kind C have (or are likely to have) the purpose Y.
A was a rational agent.
Therefore, agent A had the purpose Y.

This restatement transforms the scheme from an assertion of causation to a description of purpose. The problem now becomes one of interpretation, not explanation. The historian must now interpret the meaning of a situation and an action in order to discover purpose. He or she acts like a doctor who discovers what a patient's disease is by interpreting the meaning of four or five symptoms. That historians must act in this man-

---

38. Hempel, "Reasons and Covering Laws in Historical Explanation," 154–55. In "Aspects of Scientific Explanation" Hempel words his scheme without reference to high probability (see 470–71).

39. Ruth Macklin ("Norm and Law in the Theory of Action," 400–408) has sought to restore normative statements to action explanations, but can do so only by identifying the assertion that an agent "should" act in a certain way if he or she is to be thought to have acted rationally with the normative "should," that is, with an ethical prescription.

ner does not mean that they can dispense with laws, can act upon a single observation. It merely means that instead of relying upon those covering laws that form part of the explanans statement in a causal explanation, they rely upon generalizations that connect a given situation and action with a particular purpose. Such lawlike generalizations can be likened to those rules of correspondence that connect observational terms with theoretical terms in science, or with the laws that allow a doctor to deduce from a set of symptoms that a patient has a particular disease. The falling barometer does not cause the rain that soon comes, but it tells us that there is a low-pressure system present, which will bring rain. The symptoms the doctor observes do not cause the disease, but they tell the doctor that a particular disease is present. Hempel asks the question, why not dispense with the intermediate term, with, for example, the "low-pressure system"? Why not simply make an operational connection between the falling barometer and rain?[40] In terms of historical explanation, one could ask, why bother about identifying the purpose? Why not just say that certain situations will cause rational persons to do certain actions? The answer is that thereby one has deserted an action explanation for an event explanation. And by deserting an action explanation one loses the valuable information that the argument from dispositional traits and the argument from subsequent actions can bring to the elucidation of purpose and so ultimately to a better explanation of the event. The wiser procedure is to focus on the discovery of the agent's purpose, to which end the historian should use the logic of the situation, the agent's dispositional traits, deductions from the subsequent actions, even self-avowals. Using all these means, the historian will be less likely to err.

It is often said that the historical method differs from the scientific in that the historical method emphasizes interpretation rather than causal analysis. The above exposition of the nature of situational analysis shows that there is some truth in this characterization of the historical method (though not of the scientific, since scientists also interpret observational data in order to arrive at the theoretical terms needed for their explanations). Historians do interpret situations and actions in order to discover agents' purposes. They do not, however, interpret such situations and actions by intuitively entering into the mind of agents or by imaginatively reenacting their thoughts. Rather, they interpret such situations and actions by gaining a thorough knowledge of the situation and by employing empirical rules of correspondence that connect a situation and an action with a particular purpose. Inasmuch as this proce-

40. Hempel, "The Theoretician's Dilemma," 185–87.

dure involves interpretation, it is an example of hermeneutics, hermeneutics being the science or art of interpretation. And to this extent
James Farr is correct when he writes that Karl Popper is less a positivist
than a hermeneutic philosopher.[41]

The Logic of Dispositional Traits

By itself, a knowledge of the objective situations in which persons find
themselves is inadequate to elucidate the purposes of the actions they
perform. If the housewife and her husband are allergic to milk, a refrigerator empty of milk would not lead us to conclude that the housewife
had driven off to get milk. If a suicidal driver swerved to avoid a collision, we would have to conclude that he did so for some reason other
than a desire to save his life. If Sir Thomas More, rather than Cardinal
Wolsey, had advised Henry VIII to ally with Charles V, we would conclude that he did so, not out of ambition, but out of a concern for true
religion and the welfare of the English people. The purpose of a vain
person will be different from that of a modest person, those of a phleg-
matic person different from those of a hot-tempered person, those of a
rational person from those of an irrational person.

The following scenario illustrates the inadequacy of situational analysis by itself. Imagine that there are two congressmen from constituencies
where the voters heavily favor capital punishment. Imagine further that
a bill comes before Congress to impose capital punishment on those who
murder police officers. The two congressmen vote for the bill. Why?
Situational analysis would lead us to conclude that they did so in order
to please their constituents and assure their reelection. But suppose
further inquiries showed that one of the congressman was the son of a
murdered policeman, had always voted for law-and-order bills, and had
on many other occasions voted against the wishes of his constituents.
The second congressman, however, had often spoken privately against
capital punishment and had never voted against any measure favored by
his constituents, or for any measure opposed by them. Clearly, the two
congressmen voted for the bill from different motives, with different
purposes in mind, a truth that could not be elucidated by the method of
situational analysis alone.

It follows that in order to discover a person's purpose in performing
an action, one needs to know about that person's character, beliefs,

41. Farr, "Situational Analysis," 1087; Farr, "Popper's Hermeneutics," 157–76.

habits, temperament, and predilections. How does one gain such knowledge? One gains it by induction. One gains it by observing the conduct of the agent during his or her life. How does he or she act, react, speak, and behave in countless, varied situations? From these observations one establishes that the agent has certain dispositional traits. She likes milk. He is suicidal. One person is rational, another irrational—for rationality is a dispositional trait in the same way that vanity is, or having a hot temper.

Dispositional traits are generalizations about individuals or groups— even about nations. When they are about an individual they are called a singular hypothetical. Though about a single person, a singular hypothetical is a generalization, a generalization from which we can reason syllogistically. Behan McCullagh gives this example of a statistical syllogism:[42]

1. In thousands of cases, the letters V.S.L.M., appearing at the end of a Latin inscription on a tombstone, stand for *Vatum Solvit Libens Merito.*
2. From all appearances the letters V.S.L.M. are on this tombstone at the end of a Latin inscription.
3. Therefore these letters on this tombstone stand for *Vatum Solvit Libens Merito.*

Though this example concerns the meaning of letters in an inscription, other statistical generalizations cited by McCullagh concern the dispositional traits of individuals. "Napoleon was dictatorial"; "Huskisson was concerned to rationalize the tariff system." Indeed, McCullagh emphasizes the statistical nature of these generalizations by roughly translating the historian's ordinary vocabulary into a statistical statement:[43]

extremely probable	=	in 100–95% of cases
very probable	=	in 95–80% of cases
quite or fairly probable	=	in 80–65% of cases
more probable than not	=	in 65–50% of causes
hardly or scarcely probable	=	in 50–35% or cases
fairly improbable	=	in 35–30% of cases
very improbable	=	in 20–5% of cases
extremely improbable	=	in 5–0% of cases.

The two philosophers who have emphasized most the role of dispositional traits in their models of historical explanation are Patrick Gardiner

---

42. McCullagh, *Justifying Historical Descriptions,* 47.
43. Ibid., 52.

and Gilbert Ryle. To say "John hit you with a hammer because he is bad-tempered" is not, argues Gardiner, to assert that his bad temper caused him to hit you. Yet it is explanatory, since it represents an instance of how John can be expected to behave under certain conditions.[44] We explain a particular action, argues Ryle, by applying to it the relevant dispositional trait that the agent possesses. As glass is brittle, so the agent is ambitious or vain or greedy or cowardly or indifferent to money. The agent's motives in performing an act cannot be regarded as the cause of the act, since motives are not happenings and therefore cannot be causes. Motives are generalized dispositions to act in a certain way in certain situations. To explain an action by reference to its motive is to classify it under a general disposition. To say that an agent's ambition explains an action is analogous to saying that the brittleness of the glass explains why it broke.[45]

The most obvious weakness of this model of explanation is that it overlooks the objective situation that precipitated the display of the dispositional trait. It overlooks the stone that caused the brittle window to break or the provocation that caused John to swing his hammer. In justice to Ryle, it must be said that he recognizes this weakness, writing, "But the general fact that a person is disposed to act in such and such ways in such and such circumstances does not by itself account for his doing a particular thing at a particular moment; any more than the fact that the glass was brittle accounts for its fracture at 10 P.M. As the impact of the stone at 10 P.M. caused the glass to break, so some antecedent of an action causes or occasions the agent to perform it when and where he does so."[46] Once one regards both the dispositional trait and the antecedent of an action as initial conditions in a deductive-nomological explanation, it becomes evident, as Israel Scheffler has observed, that dispositional explanation "conforms to the deductive pattern, rather than diverging from it."[47]

A second weakness arises when two dispositional traits oppose each other. The French revolutionary Barère, writes Alan Donagan, "had in the months before June 1793 exhibited both a disposition to support the Revolution and a disposition to discharge his obligations as a friend to the Girondins." From his conduct before June 1793 an observer would be hard put to predict whether, if a choice were forced upon Barère, he would support the Revolution or defend his friends. In June 1793 the choice was forced upon him, and he chose to support the Revolution

44. Gardiner, *The Nature of Historical Explanation,* 124–25.
45. Ryle, *The Concept of Mind,* 43, 86–93, 113–15, 167–73.
46. Ibid., 113.
47. Scheffler, *The Anatomy of Inquiry,* 84–85.

and turn on his friends. If a thorough examination of Barère's past showed that on most occasions he placed friendship above politics or placed an equal emphasis on both, then in this instance a dispositional explanation would fail to explain his action. What did determine his choice, it appears, was the objective situation. His life was in danger if he opposed the Revolution. This is how Thomas Babington Macaulay explains Barère's choice. Barère made the motion to prosecute the Girondins in order to save his life. Leo Gershoy, however, differs, asserting that Barère made the motion in order to support the Revolution. What Macaulay and Gershoy fail to see is that Barère may well have acted from both purposes, just as Wolsey may have advised Henry to ally with Charles both to gain the papacy and to curry favor with his master. Historians here face the problem of deciding what weight to give to two dispositional traits working to the same end. To solve this problem they must fall back on a generalization. Did Barère during his life act more often as a careerist or more often as a zealot? Did Wolsey during his career act more often as a son of the Church or more often as a servant of the King?[48]

The source of this weakness in dispositional explanations is the fact that dispositional traits are only probabilities. "A cowardly man," observes R. B. Brandt, "does not always do cowardly things."[49] People, as we commonly say, "act out of character." One cannot, writes Donagan, hold "that what a man does on a given occasion is necessarily determined by the disposition he exhibits on other occasions."[50] But this skepticism should not be carried too far. No doubt it is true that a person occasionally acts out of character, but the very phrase suggests that on many occasions the person does act in character, that is, in a predictable manner. Yet the nature of this conduct will surely vary with the nature of the circumstances. The true challenge to the historian is to learn how the agent is disposed to act in a great variety of circumstances. Perhaps what is needed is a law that "people of disposition X, in situation Y, will act in such and such manner." This is not a wholly unrealizable ideal. It was said of Bishop Stubbs, "His historical insight was such as to enable him not only to judge men and the course of events, but to make him capable of predicting with remarkable precision how a man would act in certain circumstances."[51]

48. The material concerning Barère in this paragraph has been taken from Donagan, "Alternative Historical Explanations," 58–89.
49. Brandt, "Personality Traits as Causal Explanations in Biography," 194.
50. Donagan, "Alternative Historical Explanations," 70.
51. Hutton, *William Stubbs, Bishop of Oxford*, 169.

Donald Davidson has suggested that there are two ways in which to increase the probability of the "very rough low-grade statistical tendency statements implied by attributions of desires and beliefs."[52] One way is to describe more exactly the objective situation in which rational agents find themselves. He attributes this approach to Carl Hempel, who would introduce laws of greater generality about what all agents would do under certain conditions. Davidson himself takes the opposite tack. He is less interested in what all rational persons would do. "The line I have been developing," he writes, "suggests that the laws implicit in reason explanations are simply the generalizations implied by attributions of dispositions."[53] He illustrates this with President Ford's compromising on an energy bill, which Davidson explains by Ford's desire to curry favor with the voters. The existence of such a desire cannot be proved by any single action, but only by a knowledge of the dispositional traits of President Ford. Davidson concludes, "This is the point, I suggest, where general knowledge of the nature of agents is important, general knowledge of how persistent various preferences and beliefs are apt to be, and what causes them to grow, alter, and decay. . . . The laws that are implicit in reason explanations seem to me to concern only individuals—they are the generalizations embedded in attributions of attitudes, beliefs and traits."[54] Davidson is unduly dismissive of Hempel's approach. Historians must, whenever they have no knowledge of the dispositional traits of an agent, fall back on calculations concerning what any and all rational persons would do in a certain situation. Rational explanation and dispositional explanation, Hempel's approach and Davidson's, are complementary rather than contradictory.

What is even more illuminating is the conjunction of the logic of the objective situation with the logic of dispositional traits. The housewife's refrigerator is empty. She is known to love milk. It is Wednesday, and she regularly shops on Wednesday. She drives away in her car. The observer, therefore, concludes that her purpose is to buy milk. Knowing the situation in which the housewife finds herself, knowing her desires and habits, and observing her actions, the historian can deduce the purpose of her actions.

No one has seen more acutely than Jon Elster the necessity of supplementing the logic of situation with the logic of disposition. In his earlier works he emphasizes the logic of situation, which he calls the rational-

52. Davidson, "Hempel on Explaining Action," 243.
53. Ibid., 243.
54. Ibid., 251.

choice model.[55] In order to explain human behavior by this model one must first determine what a rational person would do in the circumstances. The next step is to ascertain what the person actually did. "If," Elster writes, "a person says that he wants X and yet deliberately refrains from using the means that he knows to be the most conducive to X, we usually conclude not that he is irrational but that he does not really want X."[56] To be rational an action must be the best means of realizing a person's desire, given his or her beliefs. But as Jon Elster studied human behavior, especially collective bargaining in Sweden, he found that this rational-choice model had its limitations. It might fail through indeterminacy (several actions might seem equally good) or through irrationality (people fail to follow its prescriptions). He soon saw that it must be supplemented with a logic of dispositions, which he calls a theory of social norms. Social norms may be moral, religious, legal, traditional, role-defined; they may be found in the workplace, in the marketplace, in codes of honor. They have a firm grip on the mind because of the strong emotions their violation triggers. Sociologists, asserts Elster (and one can well add historians), explain behavior by invoking these norms. But Elster does not, therefore, jettison his belief in the rational-choice model. People's motives are determined both by self-interest and by the norms to which they subscribe. Eventually, he concludes, the social sciences must construct a general theory of action that encompasses both rational action and norm-driven action.[57]

The Logic of Subsequent Actions

If the conjunction of situational analysis and dispositional explanation is illuminating, even more illuminating is the conjunction of three logics: the logic of the situation, the logic of dispositional traits, and the logic of subsequent actions.

In exploring the logic of subsequent actions one must first of all distinguish subsequent actions from immediate actions. The housewife's immediate action was to drive off in the car; her subsequent actions were to purchase the milk, return home, take the milk cartons from her grocery bag, and put them in the refrigerator. Clearly, her purpose could hardly be deduced from her action in driving off in the car—she might be

55. Elster, *Ulysses and the Sirens*, 116.
56. Elster, *Solomonic Judgments*, 28; Elster, *Nuts and Bolts*, 11–31.
57. Elster, *Solomonic Judgments*, 1–35; Elster, *The Cement of Society*, 97–151.

leaving for the hair dresser's or to visit a friend or to fill up the gas tank of the car. This fact creates an embarrassment for those who believe with Collingwood that an action is the outward expression of an inward thought. In one sense, of course, an action is. The housewife's driving off in the car was the outward expression of her intention to drive off in the car. Given that her action was deliberate, and not done somnambulistically or in a drunken stupor, then her driving off was an expression of her intention to drive off. But such a conclusion is trivial and as an explanation circular. If we deduce her intention from her action, we cannot then use her intention to explain her action.

This might lead a follower of Collingwood to redescribe the action so as to include bringing the milk home, in much the same way that Donald Davidson sought to describe as one action both a person's turning on the light and his thereby alerting a burglar. Both Michael Cohen and Charles Landesman have shown the logical absurdities that arise from such a procedure.[58] William Dray contemplated such a maneuver when he wrote that one might want to say that Caesar's crossing of the Rubicon expressed both the thought that he wanted to reach the other shore and the thought that he wished to oust Pompey from the capital. But he quickly saw that if one did that, one could no longer claim that Caesar's wanting to oust Pompey explained "the action," since "the action" to be explained had now become "the crossing of the Rubicon to oust Pompey."[59] Clearly, there is no warrant in logic or reason for lumping together the action to be explained and subsequent actions.

This poses the question, What can be deduced from the immediate action itself? First, as has been remarked, the intention to do that particular act. Caesar's crossing the Rubicon in a deliberate fashion tells us that he harbored that intention. Second, if it is an action of a familiar type, which nearly always brings about a certain end, we can deduce that it was done to bring about that end. If we see a man push the button of a doorbell, we can deduce that he did so in order to make it ring. Or, in a less trivial sense, if we see a hunter take down his gun from the rack in a deliberate manner, we can deduce that his purpose is to go pheasant shooting, since it is well known that whenever he takes down his gun, he goes pheasant shooting. In the case of the doorbell we deduce the purpose from the situation, and in the case of the hunter, from a dispositional trait. In truth, one can deduce very little about an agent's purpose from a knowledge of his or her immediate action, Collingwood notwithstanding.

58. Davidson, "Actions, Reasons, and Causes," 686; Cohen, "The Same Action," 75–89; Landesman, "Actions as Universals," 251–52.

59. Dray, "Historical Understanding as Re-Thinking," 208.

In order to deduce an agent's purpose, therefore, historians must investigate, not the agent's immediate action, but his or her subsequent actions. They must, as Rosenblueth and Wiener say, determine past purposes from present actions. Thus historians can deduce Caesar's purpose in crossing the Rubicon from his subsequent action of driving Pompey from Rome. Similarly, historians can deduce Oliver Cromwell's purpose in seizing power from his later actions promoting religious liberty for Protestants and maintaining order in England. Or consider General Monck, whose silence and inscrutable demeanor as he marched south in 1660 puzzled all the English. Historians now conclude that his purpose was to secure the election of a free parliament. They conclude this because his every action in London in the next months was consonant with this purpose and none inconsonant with it. It is usually not a single subsequent action but a succession of them that allows the historian to deduce the purposes of the agent. The historian must carefully examine an entire scenario. Abraham Melden calls such a scenario "the whole character of the proceedings"; P. H. Nowell-Smith calls it "the implementations of a general plan"; Charles Taylor, "the function of the state of the system in its environment"; and Arthur Rosenblueth and Norbert Wiener, the behavior of "the system" when "exposed to different initial and subsequent conditions."[60] Rosenblueth and Wiener illustrate their observation with the example of a guided torpedo. One can deduce the goal of such a torpedo by observing that when a ship veers to the left to avoid it, it alters its course to the left, and when the ship then turns to the right, it too turns to the right.

The careful examination of the whole scenario allows the historian to solve some of the problems arising from explanation by purpose. Gilbert Ryle has observed that similar actions may be done for quite different motives.[61] Consider the following scenario, which is of my invention, not Ryle's. One man goes to the ice rink in order to skate; another goes to the ice rink in order to make the acquaintance of a beautiful woman whom he has seen there. A detailed chronicle of their actions at the rink would show whether they spent their time skating or talking with the young lady, thereby revealing the purpose of each. The scenario might also show that the same man had two or more purposes in going to the rink, both to skate and to purchase shoelaces for his skates. A more detailed scenario can also reveal hidden purposes. The housewife who

---

60. Melden, *Free Action*, 100; Nowell-Smith, "History as Patterns of Thought and Action," 150; Taylor, *The Explanation of Behaviour*, 9; Rosenblueth and Wiener, "Purposeful and Non-purposeful Behavior," 236.

61. Ryle, *The Concept of Mind*, 60.

went to the store to buy milk might really have gone there to see the manager, with whom she was having an affair. Her behavior in the store would soon make this evident, as would her later action in pouring some of the milk down the drain in order to have a pretext for returning to the store.

A more detailed scenario, however, could not help detecting a change in purpose. Consider the hunter who went hunting for pheasants. Finding none, he changed his mind, shot some rabbits, and returned home with them. An observer watching him return could only conclude that his purpose had been to shoot rabbits—and in the end it was. A more detailed scenario is most powerful when it confirms an avowed intention. In November 1937 Adolph Hitler, according to the Hossbach Memorandum, announced to his generals his intention of occupying first Austria, then Czechoslovakia. A.J.P. Taylor doubted that Hitler meant what he said; he was only seeking to win over his generals to a program of increased armaments. But Alan Bullock, by tracing Hitler's subsequent actions, demonstrated convincingly that Hitler meant what he said.[62]

The chief advantage to be gained by making the scenario as detailed as possible is to increase the certainty that one has deduced the purpose of the agent correctly. Take the case of Jack, who goes ice-skating regularly. Is his purpose to improve his ability to skate or to get better acquainted with Karen? It depends. If the scenario shows that Jack arrives early, works on his figures for half an hour, skates the whole two hours, practices mohawks and three-turns, and leaves only when the rink closed, then we have many reasons to conclude that his purpose is to improve his ability to skate. But if he arrives late, waits until Karen arrives to put on his skates, sits by her side while doing so, talks with her when on the ice, leaves the ice when she does, follows her to the coffee machine, and departs from the rink promptly after she does, then we should conclude that his purpose in going to the rink is to get to know Karen better. Now, each item in this scenario offers a clue to his purpose. His waiting until she arrives gives a hint of his purpose, since we know from experience that individuals who do so are probably more interested in the young lady than in skating. Talking with her on the ice offers another generalization from which to make a deduction: a young man who talks with a young lady is probably interested in her, though this is not always true. Yet he follows her off the ice and drinks coffee with her—a third typical act from which to draw a deduction. Finally, he leaves promptly after she does, a fourth act typical of the actions of a young man whose purpose is less to improve his skating than to get to

62. This controversy is discussed in McCullagh, *Justifying Historical Descriptions*, 121.

know Karen better. The important point is this: each action heightens the probability that our deduction of his purpose is correct. That he waits until she arrives to put on his skates might give us a 25 percent chance of having deduced his purpose correctly. But each subsequent act heightens that probability.

It is often difficult, and perhaps unimportant, to distinguish motive from purpose. One can say that Cromwell's purpose in seizing power was to promote religious liberty for all Protestants, but it might be better to say that it was his motive. His purpose might have been more immediate—to defeat the efforts of the Presbyterians to drive the sectarians from the army. Where the goal is immediate, singular, and particular, historians tend to speak of the agent's purpose; where the goal is more remote, plural, and diffuse, they tend to speak of the agent's motive. In either case, historians are helped in identifying purpose or motive by the subsequent actions of the agent.

At this point in my argument the discerning reader might want to cry out that all this smacks of teleology. Surely historians had long ago given up the Aristotelian concept of a final cause. To this objection there are two answers.

First, I have deliberately sought in the above discussion to avoid any assertion of causation. I have simply addressed the question, How does one determine what the agent's purpose was? I leave to the following section, devoted to action schemes, to determine whether purpose can be considered the cause of an action. For the moment, the one question calling for attention is how to determine agents' purposes. To this task deduction from their subsequent actions are as useful as deductions from their situations and from their dispositional traits. In every case the historian is interpreting signs, seeking the meaning of those signs. Certain actions in particular situations are signs of the agent's purpose, as are observed dispositional traits and subsequent actions. The historian's task is to decode, to interpret, these signs. Hence it is quite correct to describe the historian as a hermeneuticist. And though hermeneutics has to do with interpretation, not explanation, this does not mean that it is not deductive. Experience teaches historians those generalizations that allow them to recognize the meaning of actions, whether in a certain situation or by a particular person or followed by other actions. The particular instance is subsumed under the generalization. People who are out of milk usually drive off to get milk. A person who regularly shops for milk on Wednesday tends to drive off for milk on Wednesdays. A person who brings home milk has probably driven off to get milk. Under these generalizations the historian subsumes the particular event that occurred that Wednesday when the housewife drove off. James Farr calls this pattern of reasoning the hermeneutic circle. "By means of the experience gained in a long life we mount up to the knowledge of men's inclinations and motives from their actions, expressions, and even gestures, and again descend to the interpretation of their actions from our knowledge of their motives and inclinations. Motives and actions are mutually informing. Not verification and causal analysis; but interpretation and the hermeneutic circle."[63]

Since in the next section I argue that purpose is explanatory when incorporated in an action scheme, the above answer to the charge of teleology is a bit of a dodge. Thus a second answer to the charge is necessary. Briefly it is this: when applied to the actions of a person, teleological explanations are legitimate. What has given teleology a bad name is its application to biological and historical processes, behind which there is no recognizable conscious person, nothing capable of having a goal. Thus historians are deeply distrustful of Hegel's Absolute Spirit and Marx's dialectical materialism. Unless one believes in a personal deity who is controlling history, it is meaningless to explain the entire historical process in terms of a final goal. Pattern one might find in history, but not a conscious goal. C. J. Ducasse sees this clearly:

> The disrepute into which teleological explanations have fallen is doubtless due to their having been so frequently . . . put forth in cases where the existence of the agent appealed to and of his beliefs and desires was not already known, but invented outright and purely *ad hoc.* . . . But when antecedent evidence for their existence is present (e.g., when the hypothetical agent is a human being) a teleological explanation is methodologically quite respectable, although like any other, it may in a given case not happen to be the correct one.[64]

Ducasse is quite right. When applied to an agent who is a human being, a teleological explanation is quite legitimate.

There remains one last problem: what does the historian do when deductions from the objective situation, from dispositional traits, and from subsequent actions differ, even prove contradictory? Behan McCullagh has provided the most thoughtful answer to this problem. Where there is no contradiction, a valid statistical syllogism warrants a reasonable degree of belief in the conclusion. Where several statistical syllogisms favor a conclusion, its probable truth is heightened. Where they point in different directions one must seek a balance of probabilities. But more satisfactory

63. Farr, "Hume, Hermeneutics, and History," 293.
64. Quoted in Scheffler, *The Anatomy of Inquiry,* 90.

than this procedure is the argument to the best explanation. The historian should let each of the different hypotheses that the evidence makes probable become part of a separate explanation of the total relevant evidence. The historian then asks which explanation best accounts for all the available evidence. Thus McCullagh finds Gershoy's explanation of Barère's behavior (that he sought to sustain the authority and unity of the revolutionary government) superior to Macaulay's (that he acted from self-interest) because Gershoy's explanation made intelligible a far greater number of Barère's actions. And thus Collingwood's explanation of Caesar's actions in 54 B.C.—that he sought to conquer Britain—is superior to the explanation that he only intended a punitive expedition. It is superior because a punitive expedition is incompatible with the fact that he took an army comparable in size to that used by Claudius to conquer the island a century later. But though McCullagh recognizes the importance of the argument to the best explanation, he also sees that the arguments historians use are a hybrid form, partly statistical and partly an argument to the best explanation.[65]

Action-Explanation Schemes

In the pages above I have focused on a single question: how do historians discover the purpose or purposes of the historical agent? The answer I developed is that historians do so by a combination of means, by heeding the agent's self-avowals, by using situational analysis, by generalizing from dispositional traits, and by reasoning from subsequent acts. But having discovered the agent's purpose or purposes, can historians say that such a purpose or purposes caused the agent's actions? The answer is no. Historians cannot because many persons have purposes that they do not fulfill in action. A man may desire to vacation in Bermuda. He may even resolve to vacation there next spring. But for want of money and time he does not go to Bermuda next spring, or any spring. Conceivably he may have the money and the time but does not know how to get to Bermuda. To translate a purpose into action, one needs a knowledge of the means to fulfill that purpose, the ability to carry out those means, and the opportunity to do so. As well as a purpose to vacation in Bermuda, one needs the knowledge where to buy a plane ticket and to secure hotel accommodations, the money to pay for them, and two weeks off from work.

The fact that a purpose, in order to be said to cause an action, must be

65. McCullagh, *Justifying Historical Descriptions*, 55, 62–64, 67–68, 122–24.

allied with a belief in the appropriate means to fulfill it and with the ability and opportunity to carry out those means has given rise to a plethora of action schemes.

In 1959 Christopher Peacocke put forward a scheme based on what he calls E-concepts, that is, "explanatory concepts." He identifies three E-concepts: desire, belief, and intention. Desire includes motivation, goals, and reasons for acting. Belief comprehends the belief that a given action will lead to the fulfillment of one's purpose, which Peacocke expresses by the phrase "if he Ø's then P." Desire joined to belief gives rise to intention, namely, the intention to Ø. Peacocke adds that the above will lead to action only in conditions C, with "conditions C" standing for the agent's physical and psychological conditions.[66]

Paul Churchland in 1970 proposed a scheme with six premises:

1. Wanting Ø.
2. Believing that A-ing would achieve Ø.
3. Believing that no other means was preferable.
4. Having no want that overrode wanting Ø.
5. Possessing the ability to do A.
6. Knowing how to do A.

If all these premises are true, then the agent A's.[67]

A year later Georg von Wright published his "practical inference" scheme, or P-I. It states that if A intends to bring about P and A considers that he cannot bring about P unless he does a, then A sets himself to do a. Later Wright rewrote the scheme in a more complex way in order to allow for the agent's changing his mind or being prevented from acting. He also stated that the agent must believe himself capable of doing the action required.[68]

In 1977 Rex Martin published his scheme, which included seven premises:[69]

1. If a person x is in a particular situation which he proposes to deal with in a certain way, and
2. one of the courses of action he might take is A, although alternatively he might take courses B, C, or D, and
3. his purpose is to handle the situation by accomplishing such and such thing, and

66. Peacocke, *Holistic Explanation*, 11–12, 14, 37, 53, 113.
67. Churchland, "The Logical Character of Action-Explanations," 216.
68. Wright, *Explanation and Understanding*, 96, 106–7.
69. Martin, *Historical Explanation*, 157.

4. this purpose, or end in view, is not overridden by any other purpose that he has, and
5. he does not prefer any of the alternative courses of action—B, C, or D—to doing A, and
6. doing A is judged by him to be a means to, or part of, accomplishing his purpose, and
7. he is able, personally and situationally, to do A,
   then x does A.

It is evident that these various schemes have much in common. If one conflates them, one arrives at six necessary premises. The first premise, obviously, is a statement of the agent's purpose, since it is the agent's purpose that is invoked to explain his actions. But one must add the proviso, as a second premise, that it is his overriding purpose. If a person who desires to vacation in Bermuda suddenly has a more powerful desire to buy a Porsche and has only enough money for the one or the other, that person will buy the Porsche. A third premise must be a belief that the means will accomplish the ends, that flying to Bermuda and securing hotel accommodations there is an efficacious means to accomplish the purpose of vacationing in Bermuda. But here one needs to add a fourth premise, namely, that the specific means are the most efficacious or preferable means to accomplish the purpose. If a man preferred to go to Bermuda by boat, he would not take the plane—and it is his flying to Bermuda that one is seeking to explain. The fifth premise is that the agent has the ability to employ the means, for example, to fly to Bermuda and reside in a hotel there. A man cannot fly to Bermuda if he is bankrupt or in jail. The sixth premise is that the agent has the opportunity. However wealthy and free, a man could not fly to Bermuda if there was an airline strike. One might lump the fifth and sixth premises together, namely, ability with opportunity, but it promotes clarity to treat them separately. The one characterizes the agent; the other characterizes the situation.

Before I turn to an examination of the nature of an action scheme, it is worth inquiring into the relation of such a scheme to Carl Hempel's model of rational explanation. Hempel's model seeks to formulate Dray's rational explanation in a covering-law form:[70]

Agent A was in a situation of kind C.
A was a rational agent at the time.

70. Hempel, "Reasons and Covering Laws in Historical Explanation," 154–55.

Any rational agent, when in a situation of kind C, will invariably (or
with high probability) do X.
A did X.

Alan Donagan takes exception to this formulation, arguing that explanations in terms of the logic of the situation are fundamentally different
from covering-law explanations. According to Donagan an explanation
by situational logic has the following form:[71]

A was resolved to achieve the end E at all costs.
A judged his situation to be C.
A judged that E could only be achieved in C if he did X.
Therefore, A did X.

And he gives this example:[72]

Brutus was resolved to preserve the Republic at all costs.
Brutus judged that to preserve the Republic it would be necessary to join
Cassius' conspiracy.
Brutus joined Cassius' conspiracy.

James Leach and Michael Martin, in separate articles, voiced some
trenchant criticisms of Donagan's scheme. Both observed that Donagan's scheme does not meet the deductive requirement, since Brutus
might resolve to join the conspiracy yet not do so. He might die before
the conspiracy took place, or the conspiracy might dissolve away before
he could join it. Clearly, Donagan (to use my language) failed to include a premise concerning ability and opportunity. Both also criticized
Donagan for using a singular statement ("If Brutus judged that to preserve the Republic it was necessary to perform a certain act, he would
perform that act") to connect the agent's beliefs with his actions. He
ought, they argue, to have used a lawlike premise to bridge the gap
between beliefs, goals, values, and external circumstance, on the one
hand, and the action, on the other. Leach proposes the law "Any man
resolved to achieve an end E at all costs when in circumstances of kind
C, will with high probability do X."[73] Martin proposes, "In situations of
type C^1 (normal conditions) a rational agent in sense Z who has resolved to pursue goal E at all costs and judges that his situation is C

71. Donagan, "The Popper-Hempel Theory," 24.
72. Ibid., 20–21.
73. Leach, "The Logic of the Situation," 265.

and judges that E could be achieved in C if he did X and has certain other beliefs about his situation, does X."[74]

There is some validity in these criticisms, but what both Leach and Martin fail to see is that they are no longer talking about Hempel's scheme. Leach talks of assimilating Donagan's scheme to Hempel's,[75] and Martin writes that once Donagan's scheme is corrected, it begins to look like Hempel's.[76] But both are mistaken. The corrected schemes proposed by Leach and Martin resemble Donagan's more than Hempel's. Hempel's scheme makes no reference whatever to purpose; Donagan's scheme treats the situation as an irrelevancy. In fact when he gives his example, he drops any reference to the situation. He speaks only of Brutus's resolve and of his judgment of what is necessary to carry out that resolve. In fact one can remove from Leach's and Martin's amended versions of Donagan's scheme all references to situation, and they remain just as valid. The premise that the agent has the opportunity to act comprehends anything that a description of the situation would offer. Hempel's scheme, on the other hand, depends fundamentally on a description of the situation and makes no mention of purpose. Hempel goes straight from the premises of a rational agent in a particular situation to the action performed by the agent. Hempel is concerned with the logic of the situation. Donagan, Leach, and Martin are concerned with the logic of purpose. Though the two logics are different, they can be wedded together. Situational logic gives the historian the means to elicit the agent's purpose. Having elicited that purpose, the historian can then move to the logic of purpose.

By the logic of purpose I mean simply this: by what logic can an agent's purpose be shown to be the cause of his or her action? How can one show that a man's purpose to vacation in Bermuda was the cause of his flying to Bermuda? Clearly, as the previous discussion shows, this can only be done if the statement of his purpose is allied to five other conditions. These six conditions may usefully be regarded as the initial conditions that caused the action. The six are as follows.

1. The agent's purpose.
2. The fact that it is an overriding purpose.
3. The agent's belief that a certain action will lead to the achievement of that purpose.
4. The fact that that action is the most preferable action to achieve the purpose.

74. Martin, "Situational Logic and Covering Law Explanations in History," 394.
75. Leach, "The Logic of the Situation," 267.
76. Martin, "Situational Logic and Covering Law Explanations in History," 389–90.

5. The fact that the agent has the ability to perform that action.
6. The fact that the situation gives the agent the opportunity to perform that action.

But initial conditions can only be said to cause an action if they are subsumed under a covering law that correlates the occurrence of the initial conditions with the occurrence of the action. Therefore a covering law is required. It would take the following form:

> An agent whose overriding purpose is P, who believes that X is the preferable means to achieve P, and who has the ability and opportunity to do X will do X.

The question then arises, Is this action scheme explanatory? And the answer depends upon the question whether the law establishing the connection between the initial conditions and the action is analytical or empirical. As Peacocke repeatedly insists, "explanation must either cite or rest upon *a posteriori* facts." They must not be a priori.[77] Or as Donagan remarks, "no proposition that is true by definition states an empirical regularity."[78] The empirical regularity "Stones thrown at windows break windows" is explanatory. But if a stone is not thrown hard enough, it might not break the window. So one adds, "Stones thrown hard enough to break windows will break windows." But this is analytical, is true by definition, and so is not explanatory. To be explanatory one should say that stones of a certain weight thrown at a certain velocity will break windows of a certain tensile strength. If less heavy or thrown less hard they will not break such windows.

The question now becomes, Is the action scheme above analytical or empirical? And the answer lies in an examination of each of the six premises.

The establishment of the agent's purpose is certainly not analytical. One cannot determine from the fact that a man boarded a plane for Bermuda that his purpose was to vacation there. He might be going on business or to connect with a flight to Cuba or to buy a pound of cocaine. The agent's purpose has to be determined a posteriori, not a priori, has to be determined by looking at his action in the light of his situation, his dispositional traits, and his subsequent actions, not to speak of his self-avowals.

The second item—that his purpose to vacation in Bermuda was an

---

77. Peacocke, *Holistic Explanation*, 144.
78. Donagan, "Alternative Historical Explanations," 68.

overriding purpose—is just as clearly analytical. His very acting upon that purpose defines it as overriding, as overriding at that moment any other purpose. It is a priori true.

The third item—that he believed flying to Bermuda was the appropriate means to fulfill that purpose—is a more complex matter. It is more complex because belief in the appropriate means is so inextricably linked with purpose. As Hempel has remarked, purpose and belief in the appropriate means to fulfill that purpose are epistemically interdependent. The agent's action in a particular situation tells us both about his purpose and about his belief in means. If we see a car swerve right to avoid a head-on collision, we conclude both that the driver's purpose was to save his life and that he believed that the means to do so was to swerve right. The means could be different. An experienced race-car driver might swerve to the left, into the now empty opposite lane. Observing this, we would conclude that he swerved left in order to save his life. Situational analysis (allied to dispositional traits and subsequent actions) tells us about the combination, purpose/belief, not about purpose alone or belief alone. If Brutus joins Cassius's conspiracy, then the historian concludes both that his purpose was to save the Republic and that he thought joining the conspiracy the appropriate means to do so. Belief then is an a posteriori element in the scheme. We cannot deduce it by definition from the fact of the agent's actions. We must deduce it hermeneutically from what we know about the agent's situation, disposition, and subsequent actions. It is true that in this combined entity, purpose/belief, belief in the appropriate means seems to occupy a subordinate position. As Immanuel Kant observed, "who wills the end, wills (so far as reason has decisive influence on his actions) also the means which are indispensably necessary and in his power. So far as willing [the means] is concerned this proposition is analytical."[79] Were the purpose known but not the means, this would be true. If one knew that the agent's purpose was to vacation in Bermuda for the next two weeks, one could (assuming the agent to be rational) deduce analytically from his boarding a plane for Bermuda that he believed this the appropriate means to carry out his purpose. But in fact the historian of this event deduced the purpose and the belief in means simultaneously—deduced them by means of the hermeneutical circle described in the previous section. That purpose and belief in the appropriate means are inextricably connected is vividly illustrated by Rex Martin's story of the native who accidently wounded himself with his knife and then proceeded to wipe off his knife (rather than clean his wound), believing that wiping off his knife would

79. Quoted in ibid., 76.

cure his wound.[80] Such a means of curing a wound would be opaque to us, until we learned by experience that in such a culture the natives believed that cleaning the knife cured the wound. Indeed, until we knew of this belief, we could not deduce the native's purpose in cleaning the knife. It does appear that purpose and belief are inextricably joined and that hermeneutical analysis gives us a knowledge of both. Thus a belief in means is an empirical, not an analytical, truth.

The fourth item is clearly analytical. One can deduce from the very fact that he took the plane to Bermuda that he believed this the preferable means to reach Bermuda. Had he believed that going by ship was preferable, he would have gone by ship. The very action he took defines his preference. Now, one might ask why he preferred to go by plane rather than by ship, but this is to ask a different question from the one that the action scheme seeks to answer. The action scheme seeks to answer the question, why did he board a plane for Bermuda? The etiology of his preference for a plane is a legitimate problem to solve; so too is the etiology of his purpose to vacation in Bermuda. But the historian should ask these questions later, once he or she has answered the immediate question, why was the person boarding the plane for Bermuda?

The fifth item—the ability to perform the means necessary to fulfill the purpose—is likewise analytical. The fact that the agent was able to board the plane with a ticket in his hand demonstrates that he had the ability to do so. Obviously he was neither bankrupt nor in jail. Barère's making the motion to prosecute the Girondins in itself demonstrated that he had the ability to do so. The same holds true for the sixth item—opportunity. The fact that the vacationer was able to board the flight demonstrated that the opportunity was there. The fact that Barère made the motion to prosecute the Girondins demonstrated that the opportunity existed.

Reviewing all six items, it appears that four of them are true a priori and therefore are not explanatory. This might lead one to propose removing them from the scheme entirely. But this would be a mistake for two reasons. First, their presence is necessary to ensure that purpose/belief is in fact the cause of an action. For reasons that James Leach and Michael Martin have made clear, the occurrence of the action cannot be deduced from the purpose and belief alone. Other, incompatible purposes might intrude. Other means might be preferred. The agent may be unable to carry out his purpose. Or he might not have the opportunity.

Second, inquiring, inquisitive historians, historians who would press their explanations to the uttermost, may well wish to explain why the

---

80. Martin, *Historical Explanation*, 88.

agent's purpose was overriding, or why he preferred one means to another, or why he had the ability, or why he had the opportunity. To ignore the a priori premises would be to cut off these inquiries. Why, for instance, was Barère in a position to make the motion? How did he come to be a member of the Convention and of the Committee of Public Safety? These are important historical questions, and the historian arrives at them by what I have chosen to call analytical colligation. The historian starts with the event, seeks its authors, discovers their motives, beliefs, abilities, and opportunities, and then investigates the etiology of those motives, beliefs, abilities, and opportunities. If one omitted ability and opportunity from the scheme, questions about their etiology might be neglected.

Action schemes, thus, are in part analytical and in part empirical. Inasmuch as they are analytical, they cannot be said to be explanatory. Paul Churchland ends up calling the law employed in such schemes "a theoretical nomological" and defends the law on the grounds that it has proved "explanatorily successful."[81] It has proved explanatorily successful for this reason: it allows the historian to state that a particular purpose and a particular belief in the appropriate means to achieve that purpose did in fact *cause* the action that the historian seeks to explain. What is truly explanatory, therefore, is the particular purpose and the particular means. What these are the historian discovers by means that I have described as hermeneutical.

One final question remains: can mental events, such as purpose and beliefs, cause a physical action? The answer is obviously yes; purposes and beliefs do lead to actions. I know from experience that I intended to go to the store to buy some groceries and did. No great mystery surrounds the fact that mental events such as purposes *do* cause physical actions. The mystery surrounds the *manner* in which mental attitudes cause physical actions. Donald Davidson has wrestled with this, only to conclude that his search for a solution was a failure.[82] Peacocke, though he makes the realization of intentions in physical states a necessary part of the holistic explanation, declares that these physical states do not need to be known. But this does not entail a rejection of causation. "The agent's attitudes," he writes, "do indeed *cause* his actions."[83] One can see why Robert Cummins has observed that the doctrine that reasons are not causes has fallen on hard times. "What's more," he writes, "it has fallen on hard times mainly because it seems clear that reasons do

---

81. Churchland, "The Logical Character of Action-Explanations," 225–26.
82. Davidson, "Freedom to Act," 155.
83. Peacocke, *Holistic Explanation*, 153, 162.

explain action, and the underlying assumption here, once again, is surely that explanation is causal subsumption."[84]

Not only has the doctrine that reasons are not causes fallen on hard times, but so has behaviorist psychology, which would replace "reasons" for actions with "drives." A reduction of purpose to some neural state is not only impracticable but unnecessary. With the rise of cognitive psychology it has become apparent that the brain, like the computer, is an information-processing system. To explain the contents of a print-out one does not take the computer apart and examine the chips from which it is made. Rather, one asks to see the program that was fed into the computer. "Intentional characterized capacities," writes Cummins, "are instantiated as capacities to execute information-processing programs." And he adds, "The only alternatives are dualism, which is not an alternative theory but the claim that theory is impossible, and 'neuronalism'— i.e. the doctrine that intentionally characterized capacities are realizable only as neurophysiological capacities." Neuronalism he finds implausible because it ties purpose to the chemistry-physics of the brain.[85] Rather, it is the task of psychology to show how the brain executes information-processing programs. And one can add, it is the task of the historian to examine how all past experiences of a person programmed him or her to have the desires, beliefs, abilities he or she has. This leads directly to a consideration in the next chapters of the etiology of desires, beliefs, abilities, and opportunities.

84. Cummins, *The Nature of Psychological Explanation*, 14.
85. Ibid., 90.

9 THE ETIOLOGY OF DESIRE

The child is father to the man.

— Sigmund Freud, quoting William Wordsworth

R. G. Collingwood believed that once the historian had discovered the thought "inside" an action, he or she had thereby completed the task of historical explanation. It was sufficient that the historian had discovered the reasons that had led to the action. There was no need to search for the causes of those reasons. Action, he wrote, "is precisely that which is not caused; the will of a person acting determines itself and is not determined by anything outside itself. Causation has doubtless its proper sphere. . . . But . . . [it] cannot be applied to the activity of the will without explicitly falsifying the whole nature of that activity. An act of will is its own cause and its own explanation; to seek its explanation in something else is to treat it not as an act but as a mechanical event."[1]

Herein Collingwood is surely wrong. No historian of any worth would

---

1. Quoted in Donagan, *The Later Philosophy of R. G. Collingwood,* 231. Michael Oakeshott ("Historical Continuity and Causal Analysis," 198–99) and Alan Donagan ("Social Science and Historical Antinomianism," 437–38) agree that in explaining a human action it is unnecessary to look beyond the choice made.

terminate an explanation with the discovery of the purpose of the agent. The historian would want to know why the agent had that purpose and what desires lay behind the formation of that purpose. Even more, the historian would want to know why the agent chose the particular means to achieve the purpose and why the agent was able and in a position to achieve it. In short the historian would wish to examine the etiology of all the elements in an action scheme.

What Collingwood failed to see is that events, joined with desires, can cause the formation of purpose. The housewife's finding the refrigerator empty of milk, an event, created in her, given her desire for milk, the purpose to drive to the store to get milk. Charles I's coming down to the House of Commons, an event, engendered in members of the Commons, who desired safety, a determination to adjourn to the City. In order to discover what an agent's purpose is, the historian, as argued in the previous chapter, often works backward from the agent's subsequent actions; but to discover the etiology of that purpose the historian must look to what preceded it. "To get beyond the everyday understanding," Finn Collin observes, "we must shift to a causal approach: we must examine the conditions which shape action from behind, as it were, rather than the ends toward which it steers and the rules to which it seeks to conform."[2]

Collingwood would have "events" and "actions" inhabit separate worlds, but he fails to see that what is "an action" to the agent is "an event" to those observing the agent. Charles's coming down in person to the House—an action on his part—was to those observing him as much an event as a fire's breaking out in the lobby. What happens to a person does shape that person's purposes. In fact Collingwood on one occasion nearly admits this. A poor man, he writes, cannot be led to action "by the fact of his children's unsatisfied bellies and wizened limbs, but by his thoughts of that fact." This is undoubtedly true, and W. H. Walsh, in "The Causation of Ideas," persuasively develops this theme of the agent's subjective appreciation of his or her situation; but Walsh, unlike Collingwood, acknowledges that the objective situation plays a role in causing the agent's thoughts.[3] One wonders if even Collingwood would deny that the sight of the unsatisfied bellies and wizened limbs caused the poor man's thoughts, the thoughts that led to action.

The question then arises, by what logic does the historian demonstrate

---

2. Collin, *Theory and Understanding,* 336.

3. Walsh, "The Causation of Ideas," 192–96. Jerzy Topolski ("Towards an Integrated Model of Historical Explanation," 333–34) likewise sees that the causal model is required to explain the origin of motives.

that a particular event led to the formation of a purpose? How does he or she demonstrate that a car crossing into the wrong lane caused the motorist's purpose to swerve in order to avoid a collision and save his life, or that Charles's attempt to arrest the Five Members led the House of Commons to form a purpose to seek a safe haven in the City? One obvious logic is to subsume the explanandum event—forming a purpose to swerve or to seek a safe haven—under an explanans statement, such as "An oncoming car causes all motorists to form a purpose of swerving to avoid a collision and save their lives" or "Threats to arrest its members cause all representative assemblies to form a purpose to seek safety." Because no covering law could be written about Charles I's propensity to arrest five members, the covering law had to be redescribed in a more general manner. The historian would also rely on elimination analysis. What other event that occurred at that moment could have caused members of the House of Commons to form that purpose? Surely not that twelve impeached bishops protested that the votes of the House of Lords were null and void in their absence, though this did occur shortly before the decision to adjourn to the City. Suitably redescribed, and other causes eliminated, this explanans statement carries conviction.

And yet the historian did not actually count the number of instances when "threats to arrest its members caused representative assemblies to form a purpose to seek safety." He or she probably did not even count the number of times that "oncoming cars caused motorists to form a purpose of swerving to avoid a collision and save their lives." Nor did he or she pursue any research to discover these facts. Then how could the historian know that there are such laws? Probably by the following reasoning: Were I the motorist, I would swerve, and were I in the Commons, I would seek safety. I am a rational person; indeed because I am a rational person, I would swerve or seek safety. Most of humankind are rational and therefore most of humankind would swerve or seek safety. Thus the historian arrives at the covering law under which he or she subsumes the two explanandum events. It is my belief that historians constantly reason in this manner, quite instinctively, even unconsciously, but all the time.

The attentive reader may at this point exclaim, "But this is identical with situational analysis, with the rationality principle." And in fact it nearly is. Only the terminology differs. Hermeneuticists use situational analysis to discover what the agent's purpose is. They do so by asking, what would be the likely purpose of a person in this situation who acts in this manner? They could seek to answer this by interviewing countless persons who were in this situation and who acted in that manner, and then establishing a law about their purposes. But they probably would not. Rather, they would reason thus: had I been in that situation and acted in that manner, then my purpose would have been such and such. I am a rational person, therefore it is likely that all rational persons who acted in that manner in that situation had the same purpose. The historian then subsumes the agent under this law. The agent is rational and therefore the agent's purpose must be such and such. Hempelians use the rationality principle in the same way, only they do so to establish the cause of the purpose rather than its nature. Both hermeneuticists and Hempelians have used the rationality principle as a shortcut to the establishment of a law, a law needed in one instance to decode the agent's purpose, in the other to establish the cause of the agent's adopting that purpose. The importance of William Dray's rationality principle, though he might not acknowledge it, is this: it allows both hermeneuticists and Hempelians (and the historian is both) to arrive by a shortcut at the establishment of those laws necessary both to decode and to explain. Dray's rationality principle complements rather than undermines Hempel's covering-law model.

Or, to put it another way, the logic used to determine the cause of the adoption of a purpose so closely resembles the logic used to elucidate that purpose that one can almost dispense with the elucidation of purpose. This is especially true because in hermeneutical analysis the action (swerving) is so closely allied to the situation (a car coming down the wrong side of the highway), which situation includes the event (the car's coming down the wrong side of the highway) that causes the purpose. One can now, therefore, shorten the chain by asserting that the event caused the action, rather than that the event caused the purpose that caused the action. One replaces an action explanation with an event explanation. This allows the historian to describe a causal chain without referring to purpose. Thus the impeachment of Charles's ministers led him to rely upon the secret advice of courtiers; his reliance upon their advice led to the Ten Heads, requiring Charles to consult ministers who enjoyed the confidence of Parliament; that demand led Charles to reject the Ten Heads; his rejection of the Ten Heads caused the Commons to pass the Nineteen Propositions, whose demands led Charles to raise his standard at Nottingham.

In a causal chain such as this, one can, for the sake of brevity, omit purpose, but where the cumulative impact of events heightens a purpose, the historian will not omit purpose. Consider this litany of grievances against the Earl of Strafford: his disrupting the Short Parliament in 1640, his urging that sheriffs be prosecuted for not collecting ship money, his favoring the seizing of silver stored in the Tower, his threatening aldermen who would not loan the King money, his levying charges on the inhabitants of Yorkshire without their consent, his refusal to parley with the Scots, and his raising an army in Ireland that could be used to destroy liberty in England. All of these grievances heightened distrust of Strafford and led an angry House of Commons to impeach him for high treason.

And what about the logic of dispositional traits? Is it applicable both to hermeneutics and to a search for the cause of a purpose. The answer would have to be "Yes, it is applicable to both."

The applicability to the determination of what caused a person to adopt a particular purpose can be illustrated by the problem that arises when one asserts that a second person instigated a first to act. Hart and Honoré have fully discussed the legal problems that arise when a second person instigates a first to commit a crime. They distinguish between "causing" the person to commit the crime, which occurs when threats, lies, and authority are used, and "instigating" the person to act, which occurs when only counseling and persuasion are employed. In the latter case the agent acts voluntarily but only makes up his or her mind to act after the intervention of the second person, whose intervention is a sine qua non condition of the agent's acting as he or she did.[4] Historians are concerned with the problem of instigation, less because they seek to assign responsibility than because they want to discover the origin of the purposes expressed by the act. Neither Henrietta Maria nor Lord Digby were tried for the attempted arrest of the Five Members, but historians have concluded that they instigated Charles I to attempt their arrest. The problem is, by what logic can the historian say that their advice was a sine qua non condition of Charles's action? One obvious answer is to rely upon the avowals of Charles that he only acted in that manner because of the advice of others. But such avowals are rare and cannot be fully trusted. So the historian must fall back on the subsumption of the episode under a covering law. In this case the law would concern the disposition of Charles to heed the advice of others, particularly his wife, a disposition well attested to by his contemporaries. Or the historian might subsume the episode under a law that Charles heeded advice that dovetailed with his prejudices. Even more explanatory power is engineered when the two are combined. A person is most likely to act upon the advice of others if he or she is disposed to listen to their advice and if that advice dovetails with his or her prejudices. It is thus not unreasonable to believe, as Samuel Gardiner and Anthony Fletcher do, that Charles acted on Digby's and Henrietta Maria's advice. On the other hand, no historian would believe that Otto von Bismarck ever acted upon the advice of his wife.

4. Hart and Honoré, *Causation in the Law,* 48–53, 330–39, 404.

Dispositional traits are applicable to hermeneutical analysis because they allow the historian to judge more intelligently what an agent's purpose is, especially if the agent often acted on that same purpose in the past. Even more, dispositional traits are often part of the situation described in situational analysis. Thus the purpose of the suicidal driver who swerved right to save the lives of those in the oncoming car differs from that of the nonsuicidal driver who swerved right to save his own life. Knowledge of dispositional traits is even more necessary when it comes to explaining different responses to the same situation. The suicidal driver might not have swerved at all; only his suicidal nature could explain why he did not. Anthony Fletcher tells us that a few stalwart royalists spoke against adjourning to the City. For them Charles's attempt to arrest the Five Members gave rise to different purposes, perhaps a resolve to stand behind him more firmly than ever, since he had shown courage and determination. Clearly, members of the House of Commons differed in their ultimate purposes. It is even possible to explain the origins of immediate purposes (such as seeking a safe haven in the City) by deriving them from higher purposes, or desires, to which they become means. Thus the historian may derive the wish to secure a safe haven from a desire to redress the grievances of the realm. The historian is led by such derivations to what Alan Donagan calls "the ultimate principles of action." "Most choices," Donagan writes, "are conditioned by logically prior choices; but any logical chain of choices must terminate in a simple choice of an ultimate principle of action."[5] Walsh describes a similar connection between subordinate and dominant ideas, with the subordinate ideas being logically related to the dominant.[6]

The historian who pursues the connection between subordinate and dominant ideas will soon reach an ultimate principle of action. Such ultimate principles are compounded of a person's desires, hopes, fears, ambitions, jealousies, and dreams, on the one hand, and beliefs, values, and prejudices, on the other. A person may *desire* to be free from arbitrary taxes, may *believe* that taxes levied without the consent of Parliament are illegal. The historian is thus inescapably concerned both with the etiology of desire and with the etiology of belief. The etiology of desire (as well as other aspects of personality) falls largely into the realm of psychology. The etiology of belief (as well as other aspects of thought) falls largely into the realm of the history of ideas. By what logic do the practitioners of each seek to explain the genesis of their component?

5. Donagan, "Social Science and Historical Antinomianism," 437.
6. Walsh, "The Causation of Ideas," 190–91.

The Etiology of Personality

Historians have long invoked ambition, love, fear, hate, pride, anger, jealousy, greed, generosity, cowardice, courage, indolence, and pity in their efforts to explain the purposes of a historical actor, but they have rarely sought to explore the genesis of those traits. They will paint the character of a historical actor—the Earl of Clarendon is celebrated for his ability to do so—but they will not seek to explain why he or she possessed the traits that made up that character. Or if they do so, they resort to some brief observations of a mildly speculative nature. But how character is formed is a difficult question to answer. Historians, not possessing a technical vocabulary to explain the development of character, can only fall back on common sense.[7] But common sense seemed unable to discover those correlations between upbringing and character that historians sought. They therefore turned to the generalizing sciences, to physiology, psychology, sociology, and psychoanalysis. This change from commonsense observations to psychological generalizations came with the rise of psychoanalysis, which brought in its wake psychohistory. Psychohistory is an attempt to replace the commonsense observations of historians with the scientific concepts established by psychology, particularly by one branch of psychology, by psychoanalysis. Where traditional historians feared to tread, psychohistorians rushed eagerly in. They tell us that the key to Leonardo da Vinci's achievements and misfortunes lay hidden in a childhood fantasy of a vulture landing on his cradle, or that Luther suffered an identity crisis because he had a malicious and tyrannical father, or that Emily Dickinson's passion for solitude arose from a cruel rejection by her mother, or that Woodrow Wilson's thirst for power was a means of restoring his self-esteem damaged in childhood.[8]

Despite the pleas of William Langer and Peter Gay in favor of psychohistory, very few historians have accepted its validity. Indeed, the whole enterprise has come in for an avalanche of criticism, the most comprehensive expression of which can be found in David Stannard's *Shrinking History*. He charges that psychohistory is crudely reductionist, ahistorical, and unempirical. This is not the place to settle the dispute between psychohistory and its critics, but a review of the course of that debate can usefully illuminate the logic of historical explanation. By what logic

---

7. For a persuasive argument that historians do not employ a technical vocabulary, see Stanley Paluch, "The Specificity of Historical Language," 77–82.

8. For a fuller account of these interpretations, see Runyan, *Life Histories and Psychobiography,* 64, 198, and Stannard, *Shrinking History,* 9, 22.

do psychohistorians seek to validate their explanations, and what faults do psychohistory's critics find in that logic?

The principal form of psychological reductionism is to explain adult behavior solely in terms of childhood experiences. These experiences are seen as determinants of the adult personality. The child is seen as the father of the man. Thus Freud explains Leonardo da Vinci's sublimated homosexuality by the fact that his mother showed him too much tenderness as a child. He even adds that the smile of bliss and rapture on the Mona Lisa is explained by Leonardo's memory of his mother's smile. Freud supports this interpretation by declaring that clinical observation taught him that homosexuals have in early life a very intense erotic attachment to a female person, usually the mother.[9] He is here subsuming Leonardo's case under a covering law, a perfectly legitimate procedure. But it is a covering law much like the macrolaws discussed in Chapter 1. It is broad, timeless, imprecise, and probably wrong. It certainly could not support a detail, such as the Mona Lisa's smile. To be convincing, Freud should have subsumed Leonardo's case under a more precise, firmly established covering law or traced the development of Leonardo's (alleged) homosexuality, validating each step in such a colligatory explanation with an appropriate and convincing covering law.

The charge that psychohistory is ahistorical, and so misleading, is likewise based on the invalidity of universal macrolaws. Psychohistorians employ theories and laws derived from clinical studies made in the present and then impose them upon a past that is different. The assumption is that the etiology of homosexuality in Renaissance Italy is the same as in twentieth-century Vienna, but there is no proof that this is so. In fact David Stannard offers pages of evidence that even so basic a matter as perception is shaped by our culture.[10] Whenever possible the historian should employ theories and laws derived from an exhaustive study of the particular culture itself. With all of this most historians are in agreement, but they should be careful not to make too wide a gulf between the present and the past. Total relativism gives the historian no access to the past. Readers of Homer's *Iliad* will find there the play of emotions—pride, revenge, love, jealousy, heroism, and treachery—that are not unknown today. It is certainly true, as Huizanga and Bloch and a host of other historians have argued, that the past is unlike the present, but that difference may well lie in different values and beliefs, not in different passions. The fault with psychohistory may well lie less in the

9. Stannard, *Shrinking History,* 9–20.
10. Ibid., 124–44.

inapplicability of its theories and laws to the past than in the falseness of those theories and laws both in the present and the past.

It is the hollowness of the theories and laws employed by psychohistorians that lies at the heart of their failure. Their interpretations lack empirical support. This can be understood in two ways: that the historical evidence about the individual is mistaken and that the theories and laws employed want empirical support. The first kind of error, of course, would subvert any model of historical explanation, but it is particularly rife in psychohistory because of the emphasis on early childhood, a period in a person's life about which the historian has the least information. Thus there exists no concrete evidence that Emily Dickinson's mother cruelly rejected her or that Luther's father regularly beat him. To overcome this defect psychohistorians have relied upon the reconstruction of childhood experiences from the facts of adult behavior. Thus John Cody deduces from the clinical study of patients who bore psychological scars similar to Emily Dickinson's the fact that she suffered from maternal deprivation. Erik Erikson has in a similar fashion reconstructed Luther's relationship with his mother from his adult behavior.[11] This procedure smacks of logical circularity—A establishes the existence of B, which then becomes the cause of A—but the procedure is in fact defensible. Consider, for example, Ida Macalpine and Richard Hunter's explanation of George III's madness. From the symptoms that George III displayed in adult life—acute abdominal pain, discolored urine, and mental disturbance—they deduce that he suffered from porphyria, a hereditary ailment. They then assert that porphyria caused his madness. Historians have readily accepted this explanation, though its logic is seemingly circular. They accept it because the covering law employed in its deduction is so convincing. On six different instances the King's physicians observed that his urine was dark or bloody at the height of an attack of madness. His symptoms read like a textbook case of porphyria.[12] It is not the circularity of the logic of psychohistorians that is at fault; it is the lameness of their covering laws.

The main fault of psychoanalytic history is that its laws want empirical support. Having examined numerous studies of the validity of the hypotheses employed by psychoanalysts, David Stannard finds none that is valid. For example, there are no studies that show that the source of the Oedipus complex is sexual jealousy or that there are specific adult personality patterns that arise from the repressed Oedipus complex.

11. Runyan, *Life Histories and Psychobiography*, 198, 206.
12. Ibid., 133.

Likewise, psychologists have found little evidence for such ego defense mechanisms as denial and projection. Most recent works on "repression" have failed to support that key hypothesis. Studies of oral and anal personalities offer no support for the hypothesis that relates such personality syndromes to specific infant care. "Dozens of studies," writes Stannard, "have shown that there is no discernable link between specific child-rearing practices and adult personality patterns." Not only experimental psychology but common sense challenges these laws. If Leonardo da Vinci failed to complete projects because his father abandoned him in childhood, why did Goethe, who was raised by both his parents, also fail to complete projects? And if Luther's attitude toward death arose from his relations with his father, why did Erasmus express the same attitude, though he had a different parental background? Psychohistory fails from a want of correlations to support its explanations. There are no valid covering laws to span the gulf between the initial conditions and the explanandum event. Instead there are leaps of imagination, breathtaking speculations, all based on a psychoanalytic theory that has little or no empirical support.[13]

The failure of psychoanalytic theory has led some psychohistorians to turn to life histories as a superior way to explain the formation of the psychological traits of a historical figure. One of the chief proponents of life histories is William Runyan, who argues that an adult's personality cannot be attributed directly to specific childhood experiences. Rather, these childhood experiences shape early personality, which in turn influences the kind of environment that a person is later likely to encounter, which environment in turn shapes personality, and so on in an interactive cycle. Because the focus is on the life history of a single individual, Runyan calls this an ideographic, as opposed to a nomothetic, approach. But though he eschews laws covering the behavior of many people, he does allow that there are laws that apply to an individual, that one can correlate variables within the behavior of a single individual, even that one can search for causal relations. He cites the example of a young woman whose asthma attacks occurred whenever she met her mother. It is obvious that William Runyan is here proposing a colligatory solution to the problem created by the psychohistorian's reliance on timeless macrolaws. Leap not from childhood experience directly to the adult personality, he urges, but carefully trace the formation of that personality through time.[14] The question then presents itself: can this approach explain the psychological traits of a historical figure?

---

13. Stannard, *Shrinking History*, 26, 77–78, 89–108; the quotation appears on 104.
14. Runyan, *Life Histories and Psychobiography*, 42, 74, 90, 168, 173, 175, 180–81, 212.

Charles Carlton's life of Charles I offers a useful test of this new approach, since Carlton explicitly bases his study on social-learning theory and the belief that an individual's reactions to an experience will mainly be influenced by his or her behavior during the most recent similar experience. Carlton clearly sets forth those psychological traits of Charles I that contributed to the outbreak of civil war: an obstinacy that would not allow him to compromise, a lack of self-confidence that made him dependent first upon Buckingham and then upon the Queen, a duplicity that led his opponents to conclude that he could not be trusted, a lack of judgment that allowed him to dismiss the opposition as a small conspiracy of evil men, and an authoritarianism that found expression in attempts to solve problems by direct action.[15] With this description of Charles's personality few historians would disagree. The problem arises when Carlton seeks to explain the origin of Charles's obstinacy, lack of self-confidence, duplicity, want of judgment, and authoritarianism.

For the most part, Carlton simply describes these traits, but he does seek the etiology of two of them: Charles's lack of self-confidence and his authoritarianism. Carlton traces Charles's lack of self-confidence to the want of a close, warm relationship with his mother or with a substitute mother, such as a nanny. This meant that in later life Charles found it hard to make friends, particularly with women. The inability to make friends with women in turn deprived him of the feelings of a conqueror, of that confidence in success that often induces success. Charles therefore lacked what Freud called "the legacy of a mother's favour." To this basically Freudian explanation Carlton adds others: the public grief at his elder brother's death sapped his confidence, James's refusal to take him to Scotland in 1617 further undermined his confidence, the infanta's rejection of his courtship likewise diminished his self-confidence, and the Duke of Buckingham's insistence that Charles accept responsibility for the defeat at the Isle of Re did nothing to reinforce his confidence.[16] Charles's authoritarianism Carlton traces to James's demanding that Charles kowtow to Buckingham. These were painful and humiliating experiences, but the pain of submission was followed by the pleasure of exercising authority when he became king. As English public schools and United States Marine Corps boot camps have proved, writes Carlton, "humiliation and the painful acceptance of authority, followed by the reward of the grant of authority, make the eventual exercise of that authority all the

15. Carlton, *Charles I*, 20, 83, 99–103, 109; idem, *Royal Childhoods*, 86, 94, 97–98.
16. Carlton, *Charles I*, 7–8, 95, 98; idem, *Royal Childhoods*, 80, 83, 86.

more complete." Because he had found obedience painful yet the product pleasant, Charles when he ascended the throne insisted that others must yield as he had.[17]

This attempt to explain the origin of these psychological traits provokes two comments. The first is that the tracing employed illustrates both linear colligation and cumulative colligation. Linear colligation is evident in the chain of circumstances leading from a want of motherly love to an inability to make friends with women to a deprivation of the feeling of a conqueror to a lack of self-confidence. The cumulative colligation is evident in the progressive sapping of his self-confidence by having to kowtow to Buckingham, by his father's refusal to take him to Scotland, by the infanta's rejection of him, and by Buckingham's loading him with blame for the defeat at the Isle of Re. One suspects that the latter approach will prove more fruitful to the historian than the linear colligation proposed by Runyan. Runyan illustrates the idea of a chain of circumstances by showing how the use of heroin will lead a person to seek the company of other heroin users, which will lead in turn to an addiction to heroin.[18] But this kind of sequence is harder to trace with such characteristics as obstinacy or duplicity.

The second comment is this: the persuasiveness of these explanations depends both on the accuracy of the historical evidence given and the validity of the covering law employed. How certain is it, for instance, that Charles's relationship with his mother was distant and cold. Pauline Gregg finds it to be close and deeply affectionate. The Venetian ambassador found the Queen to be "passionately attached" to Charles.[19] But allow that the relationship was distant and cold. Such a nonaffective relationship, as Lawrence Stone has argued, was typical of the aristocracy in the early seventeenth century.[20] If the lack of a close, warm relationship with one's mother led to a lack of self-confidence, there must have been a legion of shy Englishmen in the seventeenth century. But there was no such legion of shy Englishmen, so one cannot help but regard with suspicion Carlton's explanation of Charles's lack of self-confidence. Likewise a vague reference to English public schools and marine boot camps hardly seems to be the kind of empirical support needed for a covering law that a king's demanding obedience from his son will make the son an authoritarian personality. Since most kings demanded such obedience, one must accept that most of their sons grew

---

17. Carlton, *Charles I*, 59; idem, *Royal Childhoods*, 95–96.
18. Runyan, *Life Histories and Psychobiography*, 86–91.
19. Gregg, *King Charles I*, 23–24.
20. Stone, *The Family, Sex, and Marriage in England*, 5–6, 105–11.

up to be authoritarian personalities. On the other hand, the proposition that a young man lacking self-confidence will have that self-confidence further sapped by being rejected by his father, spurned in love, and wrongly blamed by the favorite strikes one as a platitude. But the very fact that it is a platitude, that is, a commonplace truth, makes it all the more acceptable as a covering law in an explanation.

The same weaknesses that undermine explanations of the origins of individual psychological traits undermine explanations of national character. This is not to deny that there is such a thing as national character—every traveler and every reader of comparative literature knows that there is. Furthermore, the psychological traits of a people do affect the course of history. The character of the English worker differs from the character of the Japanese worker, a fact that does much to explain the economic decline of England and the economic growth of Japan. What is in question is whether historians, anthropologists, or psychologists can explain the origins of those psychological traits that make up a national character. Some have tried. Geoffrey Gorer, for example, sought to show that severe early toilet training led to an emphasis on neatness and tidiness in the adult Japanese. Unfortunately his explanation was undermined when D. G. Haring in 1949 showed that Japanese toilet training was not particularly rigid.[21]

The character of a people can, of course, change through time, and the historian can seek to explain that change. Stone found Englishmen of the middle and upper classes in the seventeenth century to be cold and indifferent in their personal relationships, whereas in the eighteenth century they tended to exhibit warmth and ease in their personal relationships. He attributes the coldness and indifference of the seventeenth-century Englishmen to four factors: the lack of a unique mother figure in the first two years of life, the constant loss of close relatives and friends through premature death, the physical imprisonment of the infant in tight swaddling clothes in early months, and the deliberate breaking of the child's will. All this created a "psychic numbing," which in turn produced adults whose response to others was that of indifference at best and hostility at worst.[22]

To prove this proposition a historian would have to show that psychic numbing is regularly associated with these four factors. In doing so he or she would have to show both that the evidence was accurate and that the covering laws were valid. That Englishmen in the seventeenth century lacked ease and warmth in their personal relations, Alan Macfarlane, for

---

21. Stannard, *Shrinking History*, 74–76.
22. Stone, *The Family, Sex, and Marriage in England*, 101–2.

one has doubted, citing as proof of warmth and depth of feeling the very same diary, the diary of Ralph Josselin, that Lawrence Stone cites as proof of its absence.[23] But for the sake of argument allow that Stone is correct in finding a lack of warmth and feeling in personal relationships in the seventeenth century. How would he prove that the above four factors caused that "psychic numbing." Clearly, he would have to correlate the presence of each of those practices with the creation of "psychic numbing," and the absence of such practices with the failure to create "psychic numbing." Stone offers little such empirical evidence, and it is probable that no such empirical evidence could be discovered for the seventeenth century. The historian could use clinical evidence from today, applying it to the seventeenth century. Stone cites, but does not quote, from several such studies. What he has done, in all probability, and what many historians frequently do, is to fall back on a rational explanation. It seems reasonable to conclude that the lack of a mother figure in the first two years and the loss of relatives and friends in premature deaths would cause psychic numbing. It is not irrational to conclude that swaddling clothes and the breaking of the child's will might contribute to psychic numbing. These are theories that rationally explain the correlation between certain practices and psychic numbing. Lacking empirical proof of the correlation, the historian produces the theory that seems to explain the correlation, and thereby furtively implies that the correlation must exist. This is sloppy history, but a great many historians resort to it—for want of anything better.

Historians have speculated—and will continue to speculate—on how race, topography, soil, climate, and demographic factors have shaped the character of a people, but their speculations should not be regarded as anything more than speculations. I have so speculated myself, arguing in *A History of England* that the English were a pacific people because they, unlike the Prussians, lived on an island defended by the sea and so needed no standing army. But the fact that the Japanese also lived on islands, yet became a militaristic people, greatly weakens my thesis.[24]

The final conclusion must be that most accounts of the etiology of personality are unconvincing. The reason for this is that there are few, if any, convincing theories of personality development. More particularly there are few, if any, covering laws connecting the steps in such a theory. Psychologists of all schools—psychoanalytic, behaviorist, developmental, social, and humanistic—have sought such laws but have largely failed to find them. They have not failed from a want of intellectual acuity or

23. Macfarlane, review of *The Family, Sex, and Marriage in England*, 117.
24. Roberts and Roberts, *A History of England*, 1:1.

from ignorance of the logic by which to proceed. They have failed, rather, because the phenomenon studied—the formation of personality—is so complex, the variables are so many, and the correlations so few that no patterns can be found. There is a want of regularity in the phenomenon being studied, and explanation depends on the principle of regularity. "It is perfectly legitimate," writes May Brodbeck, "to ask why someone is the kind of man he is, why he has the character he has. . . . The quest may well be futile, but there is no logical necessity that it be so."[25]

Such skepticism about the etiology of personality, however, does not damage the historical enterprise too deeply, since the historian does possess knowledge about the nature of the historical agent's personality, knowledge that is helpful in explaining the course of events. Even more, the principal concern of the modern historian is less with the personality of the historical agent than with his or her beliefs and values. It was not always so. Renaissance historians were fascinated with individual motives such as ambition, avarice, pride, cowardice, treachery, and revenge. But this fascination, as Benedetto Croce has observed, led to atomistic explanations, explanations that added up to no clear sum, that produced a chaos of causes.[26] This man sought high office, that man to defend his honor, a third to seek revenge. The picture presented is like a heap of iron filings pointing in all directions. But students of physics know that if one places a magnet beneath that pile of iron filings, they will immediately line up around the two poles of the magnet, in a clear pattern. The magnet that makes sense of history is opinion, that is, widely held, commonly shared beliefs and values. It is this truth that led Leopold von Ranke, in all his many histories, to search for the dominant ideas that shaped events, thereby overcoming the atomism that characterized Renaissance history. Because of this primacy of beliefs and values in explaining the course of events, what counts most in the writing of history is the etiology of beliefs and values, not the etiology of personality.

25. Brodbeck, "Explanation, Prediction, and 'Imperfect' Knowledge," 270.
26. Croce, *History: Its Theory and Practice*, 234–35.

10 THE ETIOLOGY OF BELIEF

It is not the consciousness of men that determines their existence, but, on the contrary, their social existence that determines their consciousness.

— Karl Marx, *A Contribution to the Critique of Political Economy*

The belief that particularly concerns the historian is the historical agent's belief in what ought to be. How should society be organized? How should men and women worship God? How should the economy be regulated? How should criminals be punished? How should children be reared? And so forth. The etiology of such beliefs raises two questions, the first of which is how such beliefs are formed in a single individual. The answer to that will often be that the individual's beliefs are shaped by the society into which he or she is born. This raises the second question: given that such a society (as the historicists insist) is not permanent, how does one explain the changes in belief that occur in society as a whole?

The Beliefs of an Individual

The first question is the easier to answer, and Charles I's authoritarianism offers a useful illustration. It was less a psychological trait than a deeply held political belief that led Charles to act in an authoritarian manner. Charles believed that he ruled by divine right, that he was God's lieutenant on earth, that he was to rule and his subjects to obey, and that it appertained not to his subjects to meddle in the actual government of the realm. Where did he gain these beliefs and by what logic does the historian establish that he did? Both Charles Carlton and Pauline Gregg, the two most recent biographers of Charles, agree that he gained these beliefs from the milieu in which he was educated. His father wrote a textbook for him, *Basilikon Doron*, in which he told him that kings are God's lieutenants on earth. Numerous sermons, the precepts of his tutors, and the flattery of courtiers reinforced this belief. Guicciardini's *Aphorisms*, which made a deep impression on Charles, taught him that the good of the state, as interpreted by the Prince, was the end of good government and that this end justified the means chosen to secure it. Such an exaltation of the monarch was common to the age; Queen Elizabeth herself had done much to advance it.[1]

This explanation carries conviction, but by what logic would one defend it? As is normal with historians, Carlton and Gregg do not display the logic of their argument, but one can guess at it. Basically they subsume Charles's case under a general law that persons, even princes, absorb the beliefs and values inculcated in them by their parents, teachers, and counselors. It is true that the law is not invariable. Sometimes a person rebels. But historians are not predicting; they are explaining. In this instance they know that Charles did not rebel. What is more to the point is the objection that something else may have caused him to adopt these beliefs. This is where Michael Scriven's elimination analysis proves so fruitful. The historian readily offers and the reader readily accepts the above explanation because alternative explanations are so feeble. That he gained the beliefs from a mystical experience or from playing tennis with Buckingham or because the stars were in the right constellation when he was born are easily rejected because any covering law to support them would be absurd. Even Carlton's reference to English public schools and marine boot camps seems unconvincing compared to the influence upon Charles of his milieu, though it is not totally inconceivable that James's humiliation of Charles did make him readier to accept these authoritarian teachings.

A tougher problem of explanation arises when the historian seeks to be more particular. Was it James's *Basilikon Doron*, as Carlton empha-

---

1. Carlton, *Charles I*, 20–21, 86; Gregg, *King Charles I*, 33–34, 52–54.

sizes, or Guicciardini's *Aphorisms*, as Pauline Gregg emphasizes, that had the most to do with shaping his political thought.[2] One solution is to compare the ideas expressed and the rhetoric employed by Charles when king with those of *Basilikon Doron* and of the *Aphorisms*. If they seem to be drawn more from the *Basilikon Doron*, then the historian would be inclined to attribute the greater influence to that work, on the basis of a covering law that a greater resemblance in ideas and rhetoric betokens a greater influence.

The etiology of Charles's opinions in religion present an interesting problem, since his Arminianism and his sympathy for Catholicism ran counter to the Protestant tutor placed over him. The answer lies in part in the greater influence exercised over him by his mother, who heard mass in private; by his secretary, Francis Cottington, who had Catholic leanings; by Endymion Porter, who was brought up in the same household as the Conde d'Olivares; by William Laud, his chaplain; and by his wife, Henrietta Maria, and her friends. But his Arminianism and his sympathy for Catholicism is also in part explained by the fact that those beliefs fit so well with his other beliefs. Charles was attracted to Arminianism for aesthetic and political reasons. The "beauty of holiness" fit the temperament of a connoisseur of painting. Arminian doctrines that urged loyalty to the monarch suited Charles much better than Puritan doctrines that taught that magistrates might punish ungodly princes. The historian may conclude that such considerations led Charles to embrace Arminianism, because experience indicates that human beings, though they do not invariably act logically, often do. They tend not to embrace discordant opinions, such as the opinion that kings rule by divine right, on the one hand, and the opinion that magistrates may punish an ungodly king, on the other. The historian, however, must be careful not to follow the logic of ideas too blindly. Men and women are capable of holding discordant beliefs. What might seem logical to the historian might not seem logical to the historical actor. The historian, therefore, should investigate with care the patterns of thought—or lack of patterns of thought—of the historical actor being studied. In short, the covering law under which the historian subsumes this causal attribution should apply to Charles I, not to humanity in general. Charles did live by a coherent system of thought, and since Arminianism fit better into that system than Puritanism, the historian may validly conclude that he adopted Arminianism in part for that reason.

A conscientious historian, of course, would trace the gradual adoption of a belief by a historical personage. This can be seen in Oliver Cromwell's Puritanism, a belief that was nearly as central to the civil war as

2. Carlton, *Charles I*, 20–21. Gregg, *King Charles I*, 73–76.

Charles's Arminianism. Cromwell was born into a Puritan family that had gained its property from the confiscation of the monasteries. His great-grandfather gained the rich Abbey of Ramsey; his father received a small property that once belonged to the Austin canons. From his mother he gained an earnestness in religion, an earnestness reinforced by school. He attended a grammar school presided over by the fearsomely devout and puritanical Dr. Beard, whose *Theatre of God's Judgment* taught that God's providence for man governs the world. At Cambridge he entered Sidney Sussex College, a hotbed of Puritanism. While there he read Sir Walter Raleigh's *History of the World*, which expounded in far greater detail Dr. Beard's belief that this world was a theater where God punished the wicked and rewarded the virtuous. At twenty-eight, in a typically puritanical fashion, Cromwell regarded himself as the chief of all sinners, but then he experienced a conversion by which God's grace was poured in upon him.[3] This explanation of Cromwell's Puritanism is clearly an example of cumulative colligation, with each step supported by a covering law—for example, that mothers exercise a strong influence on their sons, that one's schooling is a formative experience, and so on. The final explanation is convincing and shows how profoundly one's milieu shapes one's beliefs and values. The much harder problem is to explain how that particular milieu came into being.

The Beliefs of Society

No historian ever showed greater skill than Leopold von Ranke in showing how dominant ideas shape the course of history. In his history of England the dominant ideas were those of Protestantism and parliamentary government; in his history of France, Catholicism and absolutism; in his history of the European state system, the idea of the balance of power. But where did these ideas come from? To this question von Ranke, being the pious Lutheran he was, gave a clear answer: they came from God.[4] To a secular age, such as ours, this answer is as unsatisfactory as R. G. Collingwood's belief that the question should not even be asked. Von Ranke's fellow German Friedrich Hegel gave a very different answer: the ideas that shape history arise from the working out, through a dialectical process, of the cosmic spirit, or Absolute. Neither von Ranke's theology nor Hegel's philosophy has satisfied modern histori-

---

3. Firth, *Oliver Cromwell and the Rule of the Puritans in England*, 1–7.
4. Geyl, *Debates with Historians*, 14–16.

ans, particularly those writing in the English-speaking world. The answer that has had far greater influence, even among liberal historians, is Karl Marx's answer. Marx asserts that the techniques of production in society, and the property relations based upon them, determine the consciousness of people in that society. Narrowly conceived, as a doctrine of strict economic determinism, Marxism has not proved convincing. But broadly conceived, as a sociology of belief and values, a sociology that declares that the circumstances of a people's existence shape their ideas, it is more persuasive.

Even Karl Popper, the scourge of Marxist historicism, admits that Marx's scheme is superior to John Stuart Mill's "psychologism." Popper quotes Marx's proposition, "It is not the consciousness of man that determines his existence—rather, it is his social existence that determines his consciousness."[5] And he comments, "In developing what I believe to be Marx's antipsychologism, I am developing a view to which I subscribe myself." Popper then defines Mill's psychologism. It is the doctrine that all laws of social life must ultimately be reducible to the psychological laws of "human nature." Mill himself, for example, derives the institution of the marketplace from the psychological phenomenon of the pursuit of wealth. Popper denies that this can be done. To psychologism he opposes the institutional view, the view that no action can ever be explained by motive alone. Motive must be supplemented by reference to the general situation. The pursuit of wealth must be supplemented by the sellers' knowledge of the buyers' presence, and the sellers' hope of getting a higher price. But this knowledge and this hope are not ultimate data of human nature; they are only explicable in terms of the social situation, the market situation. Popper's emphasis falls on the role of institutions; he recognizes that the moral values of a society are closely bound up with, cannot survive the destruction of, its institutions and traditions.[6]

To these arguments of the institutionalists the adherents of psychologism retort that the structure of the social environment is manmade and therefore explicable in terms of human nature. In other words, the origin and development of traditions must be explicable in terms of human nature. Were this true, historians should be able, given a knowledge of human nature, to predict the course of history from the

---

5. Popper, *The Open Society*, 2:89. Popper translates Marx's celebrated dictum in the singular; I have adopted a translation in the plural. The German reads, "Es ist nicht das Bewusstsein der Menschen, das ihr Sein, sondern ungekehrt gesellschaftliches Sein, das ihr Bewusstsein bestimmt."

6. Popper, *The Open Society*, 2:89–96.

general circumstances existing at its beginning. But they cannot. The reason they cannot Mill himself saw: "after the first few terms of the series, the influence exercised over each generation by the generations which preceded it becomes . . . more and more preponderant over all other influences." In other words the social environment becomes more dominant than human nature.[7]

Popper rightly sees the defects of psychologism, but how much truth is contained in Marx's dictum? Particularly, can it be shown that the social existence of a people determines their consciousness? One way in which to test the truth of Marx's assertion is to examine the emergence of a new idea. What explanation, for example, can be given for the rise of Puritanism in late-sixteenth-century and early-seventeenth-century England? And more to the point (the point of this book), by what logic does the historian defend his explanation? The most recent historian of English Puritanism, Patrick Collinson, has shown how pervasive Puritanism was, even in Elizabeth's reign, and has explained its pervasiveness by the fact that Elizabeth failed to establish a church as Protestant as many Englishmen desired.[8] This fact forces the historian to ask why Englishmen desired a more Protestant church, in other words, to trace the rise of Protestantism in England. And that story leads back to Martin Luther's break from Rome. Two tasks thus present themselves to the historian: first, to account for Luther's beliefs, the *fons et origo* of the movement; second, to account for the spread of Protestant ideas throughout England.

The Genesis of Luther's Beliefs

Two endeavors to account for the genesis of Luther's ideas have won widespread popularity over the last thirty years: Erik Erikson's psychoanalytical explanation and Roland Bainton's historical explanation. The historical profession has on the whole rejected Erikson's explanation because it finds its logic faulty, and has accepted Bainton's because it finds its logic convincing. For that reason a comparison of the two explanations may cast light on one aspect of the logic of historical explanation—the etiology of belief.

Erikson's argument in *Young Man Luther* is twofold: first, that a somber and harsh childhood precipitated in Martin Luther a severe identity

7. Ibid., 91–92.
8. Collinson, *The Elizabethan Puritan Movement*, 29–44.

crisis, and second, that his efforts to resolve that crisis shaped his religious beliefs.

It was, maintains Erikson, Hans Luther's temper, his anger, his beating his son, and his opposing his entering a monastery that engendered in the adolescent Martin the sadness, the anxiety, the rebelliousness, the hate, and the guilt that added up to an identity crisis. To support this explanation, Erikson cites some dubious evidence about Han's viciousness—there is only one recorded instance of his beating his son—and about the severity of Luther's identity crisis, the alleged incident in the choir. But this merely concerns *what* happened, not *why* it happened, and this present study focuses on the latter. Therefore I shall assume that Luther was regularly beaten and I shall assume he did become an estranged, anxious, rebellious, and guilt-ridden young man. By what logic does one demonstrate that his being beaten by his father was the cause of that anxiety? Erikson principally falls back on clinical experience, though he more often refers in a vague way to the experience of clinicians than he provides statistical generalizations.[9] Had he given clinical evidence that joins symptoms and disease as closely as medical researchers do, his argument would have carried more conviction. In fact critics quickly pointed out that Lincoln, Erasmus, and Calvin had severe fathers but did not make rebellion the center of their careers. To this criticism Erikson replied that Hans Luther represented a deadly combination of driving economic ambition, the concentration of his ambition in his son, and a fierce righteousness.[10] This is fair, but Erikson now has the obligation to provide clinical evidence that such a combination always or usually leads to a rebellious son. He does not. Rather, to the criticism that the caning and whipping of children was common in Luther's time, he replies, "But since we are not making a zoological survey of human behavior we are not obliged to accept what everyone does as natural."[11] And to the criticism that caning and beatings could not explain Luther's sadness and scrupulosity, since all students were caned, he replies, "However, the professor's [Roland Bainton's] statistical approach to a given effect—the assertion that the cause was too common to have an uncommon effect on one individual—is neither clinically nor biographically valid. We must try to ascertain the relationship of caner and caned, and see if a unique element may have given the common event

9. Erikson, *Young Man Luther,* 8, 51, 61, 62, 72, 102.
10. Ibid., 66.
11. Ibid., 68.

a specific meaning."[12] Aside from the fact that Erikson does not identify that unique element, there arises the objection that historians can prove an element to be a cause only if they can show that whenever it is present with other conditions (caning and beating) it leads to sadness and scrupulosity. The unique element presumably occurred only in a single instance (Luther's), and a single instance, as argued elsewhere, cannot be explanatory. Only if there is a covering law that asserts that sadness and scrupulosity will occur whenever the unique element is combined with caning and beating can there be an explanation. To rely upon a single instance in an explanation is to commit the fallacy of *post hoc, ergo propter hoc*. The historian can then pick any event that occurred before the event to be explained and assert that it was the latter's cause. This is what Erikson does when he retreats from a nomothetic explanation to a singular assertion, though elsewhere he offers vague clinical material that is clearly nomothetic.[13] His ego psychology aspires to be a science, but is not.

The second stage in Erikson's argument is the assertion that Luther's efforts to resolve his identity crisis shaped his religious beliefs. Erikson is quite emphatic about this. He asserts that Luther's crisis led to the revelation in the tower that faith is more important than the deed. He argues that Luther's sense of guilt, sensitivity, and power drive led to "a new positive conscience" that "sowed ideological seeds into fresh furrows of historical change." And he writes that Luther's earliest lectures "show that in his self-cure from deep obsessive struggles he came, almost innocently, to express principles basic to the mastery of existence by religious and introspective means."[14] The key question then is this: by what logic does he support these assertions? The answer is that he draws a plausible scenario of Luther's spiritual development that is based on a parallel between an earthly father and a heavenly Father and that is supported by psychoanalytic concepts such as projection, transference, and regression. Thus Luther projected onto the Father in heaven his doubts that his own father, when punishing him, was guided by love and justice rather than arbitrariness and malice. Luther shifted the whole matter of obedience and disavowal to a higher, historically significant plane. He sought in religion what he could not find in his father. He transferred the desperation of his filial position to the human condition vis-à-vis God. Luther finally crowns his struggle by changing God's attributes from

12. Ibid., 63–64.
13. Ibid., 8, 43–44, 57, 61, 65, 72–73, 83, 100, 102–3, 115.
14. Ibid., 158, 221.

those of an earthly father whose moods are incomprehensible to those of a God whose wrath is really compassion. He has now found a faith that was there before doubt, a faith that goes back to the basic trust of early infancy, a trust that his mother had established but that his father had destroyed.[15]

It is apparent that the various pieces of this scenario, like a jigsaw puzzle, fit well together, and this makes the argument appear reasonable. But do the pieces reflect reality? Do we know that Luther projected his own doubts about his father onto God? Do we know that he transferred the desperation of his filial position to the human condition vis-à-vis God? The use of vague psychoanalytical terms such as "projection" and "transference" does not establish the truth of such assertions. The assertions are mere speculations, not true descriptions. It is the want of a covering law to bridge Luther's filial position with his religious thoughts that makes Erikson's scenario, however plausible, ultimately unconvincing. Nor do analogies offer such covering laws. Erikson does rely upon such analogies. Take his observation that "it was probably his father's challenging injunction against the little boy's bond with his mother which made it impossible for Martin to accept the intercession of the holy Mary."[16] This assertion may well strike the reader as reasonable. It does seem reasonable that a boy taught not to seek the intercession of his mother would later not seek the intercession of the mother of Christ. But this only reveals again the dangers of rational explanation. What strikes the historian—in this case Erik Erikson—as reasonable may not have struck the historical agent as reasonable. Numerous Protestants whose fathers had not challenged their sons' bond with their mothers rejected the intercession of the holy Mother. And among Catholics there were certainly many sons whose fathers had forbidden them to seek the intercession of their mothers but who went on in life to seek the intercession of the holy Mary. Luther may well have rejected the intercession of the holy Mary because such an act was part of a mechanical approach to salvation, an approach he rejected. The reasonable, whenever possible, should lead to empirically verifiable laws.

At times Erikson does invoke such laws. Thus he writes that no man could speak and sing as Luther later did if his mother's voice had not sung to him of heaven. Or again, no man would discuss women and marriage in the way Luther often did who had not been deeply disappointed by his mother. Or yet again, wondering why Luther emerged as the greatest orator, publicist, showman, and spiritual dictator of his

15. Ibid., 58, 95–96, 115, 221–22, 255.
16. Ibid., 123.

time, Erikson answers, drawing on "the inner economy of the Man," "We can only account for this fact by assuming a fierce, if as yet quite dumb struggle in him between destructive and constructive forces, and between regressive and progressive alternatives—all in a balance at this time."[17] In these instances Erikson is subsuming Luther's individual case under general laws about human behavior—that only those to whom a mother sang of heaven could later speak and sing eloquently of religion, that only those disappointed by a mother could discuss women and marriage harshly, and that great orators, publicists, showmen, and spiritual dictators were great because a fierce struggle within them between destructive and constructive forces, and between regressive and progressive alternatives, was in balance. The use of general laws in this way is quite legitimate. What raises doubts is the unlikelihood that these general laws are true.

There is also the objection that Erikson's approach represents a severe case of reductionism. Surely considerations other than his father's breaking young Martin's bond of trust with his mother led Luther to reject the intercession of the holy Mary. Erikson does anticipate this objection. He admits that his explanation does not "explain either the ideological power or the theological consistency" of Luther's solution, but only illustrates "that ontogenetic experience is an indispensable link and transformer between one stage of history and the next."[18] True, he does mention the growth of capitalism, the voyages of discovery, the invention of printing, the holy war against Islam, and the suppression of chivalry. Every one of these developments, he writes, "had ramifications for the course of Luther's life."[19] But he does not show how they did. He does not trace in detail how these developments did (or did not) influence Luther. Similarly, he mentions humanism, scholasticism, Occamism, and the influence of Saint Augustine, but he does not spell out how they influenced Luther.[20] In both instances there is a failure of colligation, a failure patiently to trace the development of Luther's thought.

The key event in Roland Bainton's etiology of Luther's beliefs is the tower experience, in which Luther came to believe that salvation is to be gained, not by good works, but by faith in God and the redemptive power of Christ. To explain the genesis of this quintessential Protestant idea Bainton depicts a Luther who is terror stricken by the prospect of

17. Ibid., 72, 99.
18. Ibid., 256.
19. Ibid., 55.
20. Ibid., 89–90, 178–92.

death and damnation, who has tried in vain all Catholic helps to
salvation—good works, confession, monasticism, mysticism—and who
finally discovers in his study of the Psalms and of the Epistles of Saint
Paul that God "justifies" humankind through faith.[21] The convergence of
these three experiences in Luther caused him to discover the idea of
justification by faith alone. By what logic would Roland Bainton, if
pressed, justify this explanation? One cannot know for certain, since
Bainton casts his explanation in the form of a narrative, but one can
surmise. In the first place, Bainton would appeal to Luther's own self-
avowals. Luther himself testified to his terror of death and damnation;
Luther himself recorded the failure of the traditional Catholic paths to
salvation; and Luther himself declared that it was his study of the Psalms
and the Epistle of Saint Paul and his discovery of the dual meaning of
"justice" in Greek (meaning both "justice" and "justification") that led
him to his new insight.[22] It is remarkable how analytical philosophers of
history ignore self-avowal as a mode of explanation, though historians
themselves, dwelling amid documents, texts, letters, and memoranda,
accept it readily. Unless a historian believes that a historical agent has a
reason to lie, the historian will believe the agent's self-avowals. As my
colleague the late Professor William Macdonald once told me, "The only
rule that I rely upon is that a person is telling the truth unless he has a
reason to lie."

Nevertheless, historical agents do on occasion lie and do on occasion
deceive themselves, so the historian must critically examine their self-
avowals. In Luther's case one is inclined to conclude that his self-
avowals are credible because persons wrestling with a problem, who
find traditional solutions inadequate, and who stumble on a new solution are likely to embrace that solution. The historian cannot subsume
Luther's experience in the tower under a covering law about Luther's
responses while in despair at reading the Psalms and Saint Paul, since
that was a unique event. But the historian can, and unconsciously does,
redescribe the event. Thus Luther's experience in the tower is redescribed as that of a person who wrestles with a problem, who finds
traditional solutions to the problem unacceptable, and who then stum-
bles on a solution that strikes him as acceptable. The covering law becomes the assertion that such a person will embrace that solution. Not
only reason, but experience, tells us that such a law is valid.

Such a redescription explains why Luther would embrace any solution

21. Bainton, *Here I Stand*, 22, 32, 40–44, 47–49.
22. Ibid., 22, 34, 38, 43, 49–50.

he found acceptable, but it does not explain why he found that particular solution acceptable. To answer this question one must invoke another covering law, namely, that persons seeking an answer to a problem will accept a solution that fits logically with their other beliefs. "He who believes Q, will also believe P." Luther's rejection of good works and his insistence upon faith in God fit logically with his belief in the innate depravity of humankind, in the initial wrathfulness of God, in the redemptive power of Christ, and in the ultimate mercifulness of God. Bainton follows the development of Luther's thought step by step, in what might be called "logical colligation." Each step in this logical colligation is established upon the assumption that Bainton and the reader, as well as Luther, recognized that one idea was logically connected to another—that humankind's innate depravity, for example, makes the confessional futile. The covering law invoked would be this: a person who believes Q will also believe P. And the assumption is that what the historian sees as a logically compelling step the historical agent likewise saw as a logically compelling step—and therefore took it.

W. H. Walsh, in "The Causation of Ideas," seeks to draw a sharp distinction between explanation by finding intelligible connections and explanation by finding constant conjunctions. The former relies on logical thought and finds expression in the practical syllogism; the latter seeks causal linkages and finds expression in the covering-law model. He then asserts that the former model is appropriate for explaining the connection between dominant and subordinate ideas. We do not, he argues, establish this connection by showing that the dominant idea is found in constant conjunction with the subordinate idea. Rather, we show that someone who believed P could not do so unless be believed Q. He even argues that this mode of explanation is superior to the Humean in explaining the connection between ideas and the situations that gave rise to them. To validate such connections, he writes, we do not look "round for a plurality of similar cases, in order if possible to arrive at some constant conjunction which is not to be denied, but by thinking ourselves into the position as envisaged, reconstituting the background, and then looking at things through the eyes of the agents concerned, in order to represent the development of the idea as natural. There does not need to be a constant conjunction of the two items if the second is to be appropriate in the light of the first."[23] What Walsh fails to see is that finding an intelligible connection is only a shortcut to establishing a constant conjunction. The historian finds it logical that a person

23. Walsh, "The Causation of Ideas," 193.

who believes Q will also believe P, or that a person in situation X will find idea Y appropriate. The historian therefore need not look round for a plurality of similar cases. He or she need only assume that they exist, since all rational agents will make the same logical deductions that the historian made. If all rational agents did not make the same logical deductions that the historian made, explanation by finding intelligible connections would collapse. It would collapse because then there would be no constant conjunction to support the explanation. There would only be chaos. Intelligibility as a guide in the history of ideas has the same status as rational explanation in practical affairs. Both are shortcuts to establishing the constant conjunction that makes explanation possible. Walsh does finally recognize this truth when he writes that rational explanation does not apply to the mentally ill, the obsessive, and those suffering severe brain damage.

The experience in the tower was a key event in the development of Luther's thought, but by no means the only event. In fact the experience in the tower offers an excellent example of convergent colligation in historical explanation. Three lines of thought converged at that time. The first was Luther's mounting terror of death and damnation. The second was his increasing conviction that the usual Catholic helps to salvation were inadequate, if not downright harmful. The third was his belief that God was merciful as well as wrathful and that Christ's anguish on the cross and final resurrection allowed those who had faith in God to be justified. Bainton traces carefully each of these lines of thought, with suitable covering laws (never explicitly given, of course) to bridge the gaps between the steps in these developments. It would be tedious to recite all those steps and the covering laws to bridge them, but one example might be cited. Bainton traces Luther's fear of death and damnation back to the obsession with death and damnation common in late medieval Europe, particularly among peasants, from which milieu Luther's parents came. In his fear of death and damnation Luther was very much a son of his time, no different from others who heard sermons threatening damnation and saw woodcuts of fiends dragging the damned down into hell. He differed from others only in his greater terror, which arose from the fact that he was an extraordinarily sensitive person and subject to recurrent periods of exaltation and depression. Why he was so sensitive and why he suffered from recurrent periods of exaltation and depression Bainton does not try to explain, though he does reject any belief that they arose from gastric or glandular deficiencies. Implicitly invoking a covering law that no one capable of working as indefatigably as Luther did could suffer from gastric or glandular deficiencies, he declares that Luther was too capable of work to suffer from such deficiencies. He finally falls back on the Collingwoodian position that for some phenomena there are no explanations, that Luther simply was extraordinarily sensitive and was subject to oscillations between exaltation and severe depression.[24]

There is also convergence within convergence. Thus in the chain leading to the reading of the Psalms and Saint Paul there converge two developments. One was John Staupitz's command in 1513 that Luther should study theology, earn a doctorate, and become professor of theology at the University of Wittenberg. This set in train a series of events that led him to the tower experience. A second development was Erasmus's translation of the New Testament into Greek with a literal Latin translation printed next to it. Without this translation, as Luther himself avowed, he could not have had the insight he did in his study in the tower at Wittenberg.[25]

Bainton's study of Luther is rich in the logic of ideas, that is, in tracing the logical connections between ideas. This is true of the thoughts leading up to the experience in the tower and likewise true of the thoughts leading away from that insight to his future theology. "Luther's new insight," writes Bainton, "contained the marrow of his mature theology."[26]

But to this exercise in "logical colligation" there is added an exercise in linear colligation. In the beginning Luther envisaged no reform beyond that of theological education, but the extravagant promises made by Tetzel in the sale of indulgences provoked him to nail the "Ninety-five Theses" to the church door. This in turn led the Pope to order Sylvester Prierias to reply, which brought forth a reply from Luther, in which he said that the Pope might err. This led to Cajetan's mission, to whom Luther declared that the Pope was not above Scripture. There followed the debate with John Eck, about which Luther wrote, Eck "may yet drive me to a serious attack upon the Romanists. So far I have been merely trifling."[27] Assertion and counterassertion led Luther to further and further radicalism, or, as Bainton expresses it, "every fresh stage served to elicit the radicalism implicit in Luther's suppositions."[28]

The steps in this linear colligation are often bridged by situational analysis. One example will suffice. In debating with Cajetan, Luther declared that Pope Clement VI, in the bull Unigentus, did not establish

24. Bainton, *Here I Stand*, 19–22, 42.
25. Ibid., 45, 49, 96.
26. Ibid., 51.
27. Ibid., 83.
28. Ibid., 67.

indulgences. Cajetan then read the bull, showing that Pope Clement had established the doctrine of indulgences. This embarrassing situation forced Luther to make a blunt rejection of the bull and of the authority of the pope who formulated it. Cajetan then reminded Luther that the pope was the supreme interpreter of Scripture. This led Luther to declare, "His Holiness abuses Scripture. I deny that he is above Scripture." It is clear that Luther originally intended only to attack indulgences. It was the embarrassing situation in which he found himself that caused him to attack the authority of the pope.[29] The covering law to justify this explanation would run as follows: in such a situation a proud man, convinced that indulgences were wrong and suspicious of Rome, would likely challenge the pope's authority.

There is little in Bainton's study of the genesis of Luther's ideas that could be called a sociology of belief, little that would support Marx's pronouncement that social existence shapes consciousness. Bainton does not argue that because Luther was the son of a petty capitalist he broke from the Catholic Church. Quite the reverse, he emphasizes Luther's medieval and peasant mentality. Yet if one follows Bainton's narrative with care, if one traces back the colligatory chain to Luther's youth, one finds that certain social developments were critical. Two examples spring to mind: the rise of the university and the birth of humanism. Luther's social existence was within the university, and his scholarship was assisted by a humanistic knowledge of Greek. Had Luther been born in the twelfth century, he would never have broken from Rome. The university and humanism were necessary, though certainly not sufficient, causes of Luther's intellectual development. And behind the rise of universities and humanism, as Henri Pirenne has shown, lay the rise of towns and the revival of commerce.[30] A simple sociology of belief, based on correlating a person's beliefs with his or her occupation or class, will not survive the most elementary researches of the historian, but a sociology of belief that shows that certain social circumstances were critical in a person's intellectual development does make sense.

Having, to the best of his or her ability, explained the origin of an idea, the historian's next task is to explain its spread through society. To illustrate how the historian performs that task, I have chosen to analyze the most recent literature on the rise of Puritanism, since Puritans played a central role in the coming of the English Revolution. The historian who would explain the occurrence of the English Revolution must explain the rise of Puritanism.

29. Ibid., 72–73.
30. Pirenne, *Medieval Cities.*

The Rise of Puritanism

Confronted with the task of explaining the rise of Puritanism in England, historians immediately face the task of defining Puritanism, since it is a protean word, forever changing its meaning. Put in a more formal way, historians must exactly define the explanandum event, so that their readers know exactly what they are explaining. William Laud, for example, defined a Puritan as anyone who believed in the Calvinist doctrine of predestination, but this definition makes Archbishop Whitgift, the scourge of the Puritans, a Puritan. Until 1624 nearly all the English believed in predestination.[31] As a result others have defined Puritanism as a belief in the government of the church by presbyters rather than by bishops. But most Puritans in Elizabeth's and James's reigns did not believe in Presbyterianism. Thus Patrick Collinson, the historian of Elizabethan Puritanism, chooses to call Puritans those who sought a further reformation of the church, that is, an end to popish ceremonies and an emphasis on preaching. Indeed, Collinson calls this "moderate puritanism"; a demand for Presbyterianism he calls "extreme puritanism."[32]

Define the explanandum event, then, as moderate Puritanism, which is neither too broad nor too narrow. How does the historian explain its emergence? One hopeful method is by a sociology of belief—correlate the holding of puritanical beliefs with a particular occupation or class or geographical area, in short, with a particular kind of "social existence." Historians have made detailed studies of the social composition of Puritanism. They have found that Puritanism throve in East Anglia, in corporate towns, and among the middling sort of people, but Puritans could also be found in the Southeast, the Midlands, and the West Country, in the villages of England, and among the gentry and nobility. Furthermore, even in East Anglia, in corporate towns, and among the middling peoples Puritans were a minority. As Patrick Collinson writes, "Three recent studies of religion and society in certain villages of the Kent and Sussex Weald have all failed to discover any clear-cut difference of class between the reformed and unreformed elements. . . . We conclude that it is premature simply to equate the godly elite of early Stuart England with the social elite or even with the broad band laying across the middle rungs of the social ladder."[33] This failure of macrocorrelation is not unique to studies of Puritanism. Attempts to correlate English revolutionaries, French revolutionaries, American revolutionaries, and supporters

31. Tyacke, "Puritanism, Arminianism, and Counter-Revolution," 120–21, 134.
32. Collinson, *The Elizabethan Puritan Movement*, 13–27, 131, 208.
33. Collinson, *The Religion of Protestants*, 240–41.

of Nazism with a particular class—merchants, the bourgeoisie, artisans, the lower middle class—have failed. A simple, direct sociology of belief seems out of reach; the correlations are not there, which helps explain why the quantifiers, who search for such correlations, have failed.

Since a simple sociology of belief fails to explain the rise of Puritanism, how then does the historian explain its rise? The answer, as seen in Collinson's *Elizabethan Puritan Movement* and *Religion of Protestants*, is by colligation. In these books Collinson traces the beginnings, growth, vicissitudes, and triumphs of Puritanism. He finds the earliest beginnings in the returning Marian exiles, who had during their years in exile learned habits and ideas different from those that prevailed in the corporate English Church. But their desire for a further reformation of religion promptly ran up against Queen Elizabeth's opposition to a further reformation. The Puritans were, however, able to secure a foothold in the Church because reforming bishops (perhaps named at the behest of Robert Dudley, Earl of Leicester) were reluctant to enforce the Act of Uniformity against them and because lay patrons, both landed and municipal, named Puritans to benefices and lectureships. The capture of the universities paved the way for the most significant achievement of the Puritans, the recruitment of a sizable section of the gentry to the Puritan party. Clerical Puritanism was likewise created in the universities. Between 1565 and 1575 Cambridge produced 228 Puritan clergymen; Oxford, 42. From the universities came the prophesying movement, which in town and country brought the nongraduate clergy to Puritanism. During these years the Protestant nobility and gentry, in the Privy Council and universities, supported the moderate Protestants. In the last years of Elizabeth's reign the press poured out works on "practical divinity" and lives of Puritan saints, works that created a tradition of pastoral Puritan piety. In James's reign this moderate Puritanism became a socially respectable movement. The Puritans held the bishops in high esteem, and the bishops sought a reconciliation with the Puritans. Disaster followed, however, when Archbishop Laud destroyed the high esteem in which bishops were held. By promoting sacramentalism, by suppressing lecturers, by opposing predestination, Laud made a moderate, reconciled Puritanism an extreme, anti-episcopal movement.

Such in rough outline is the colligatory scheme found in Collinson's two works, though in detail the tracing is far more minute—with Chaderton carrying Puritanism from Christ's College to Emmanuel, and with John More and Thomas Roberts carrying it from Cambridge to Norwich. But every step in this colligatory scheme has to be bridged by a covering law, which leads one to ask, What is the nature of the covering laws used by Patrick Collinson? It is impossible to examine them all, but two examples may suffice.

Consider first the assertion that the future leaders of Puritanism came from the cities of Switzerland and Rhineland, where for five years they invented and quarreled over liturgies and church constitutions. "In the course of five years," writes Collinson, "many of the habits and attitudes that belonged to life in an established Church—the habits of centuries— were temporarily discarded."[34] That these clergymen returned with new habits and attitudes, the records amply attest. The problem is to explain why, and the explanation that springs to mind is that the experience of five years free from corporate direction, of five years when these clergymen were forced to improvise for themselves, taught them to think for themselves about liturgies and church constitutions. The historian, of course, could appeal to no law about English clergymen living in the Rhineland and Switzerland. He or she would have to redescribe the event to refer to people in general enjoying five years freedom from direction. To this law the historian would (in this case) add a second, that clergymen who live abroad are often influenced by the clergy native there, in this instance by German and Swiss Calvinists. The historian might even invoke a third covering law, that the close similarity of ideas between those adopted by the exiles and those espoused by their Calvinist hosts proves an influence. Given the dearth of other possible explanations (in short, employing elimination analysis), these explanations carry conviction.

A second example is Collinson's assertion that "many heads of landowning families were now sending their sons to the universities, where many of them would be deeply affected by the influence of their tutors."[35] How does one support the assertion that they were deeply affected by their tutors? Principally, I imagine, by showing that they entered university without puritanical ideas and departed with such ideas. Experience hardly tells us that such ideas came from frequenting taverns or punting on the Backs. Experience tells us that they more likely came from tutors. Evidence from diaries and lecture notes shows that students often gained these ideas from their Puritan tutors.

Collinson traces the growth of Puritanism with great care and caution, but his colligatory scheme leaves one question unanswered: why did the clergymen abroad and the students at the universities find Puritan beliefs congenial? A covering law, as argued in earlier chapters, connects not a single cause but a set of conditions with the explanandum event.

34. Collinson, *The Elizabethan Puritan Movement*, 24.
35. Ibid., 54.

The covering laws mentioned in the two paragraphs above should include among the set of conditions causing the adoption of Puritan beliefs the fact that the clergymen and students found the beliefs congenial. Experience surely teaches us that persons do not adopt beliefs they find uncongenial. So that one is faced with the question why these clergymen and these students found Puritan beliefs congenial. Did their social existence predispose them to hold Puritan beliefs. Collinson is generally silent on this point, though on one occasion he does speak to it. He writes, "The kind of ecclesiastical reform to which the prophesyings and exercises were a pointer was much to the liking of the protestant nobility and gentry. . . . The enthusiasm of the governing class will be all the easier to comprehend if we consider that the effect of these reforms would have been to reduce still further both the powers of the unpopular ecclesiastical courts and the social status of the higher clergy, while exposing spiritual government to lay interference."[36] The explanation invoked here is a rational one. It strikes Collinson as logical that a person hostile to the ecclesiastical courts and the social pretensions of the higher clergy would welcome reforms that reduced the powers of the one and the status of the other. It seems logical to him, a rational person. He would then conclude that numerous Protestant noblemen and gentlemen, also being rational creatures, had reasoned in the same manner. Once again rationality points to a covering law: whoever is hostile to the ecclesiastical courts and the pretensions of the higher clergy will find puritanical ideas congenial. If by chance the Protestant noblemen and gentlemen had not reasoned in that way, the covering law would be false—and the explanation invalid. But in this instance the historian's own experience may have taught him that people often adopt congenial ideas.

Where Collinson is cautious in speculating about the reasons Englishmen embraced Puritanism, William Hunt is bold. He asserts that there were at least four reasons persons of substance in sixteenth-century England found Puritanism congenial, four ways in which their social existence predisposed them to Puritan doctrines: their alarm at the growth of the number of the poor, their anxiety at their own precarious prosperity in an age of change, their hatred of Rome, and their unease at the decline of the village community. "Alarm at the growth of poverty," Hunt writes, "was one cause of the movement for moral reform that gained momentum in the late sixteenth century and that is generally associated with the religious tendency known as puritanism."[37] Preach-

36. Ibid., 187.
37. Hunt, *The Puritan Moment*, 79.

ers were the indispensable allies of a local elite who were grappling with the problems of overcrowding, unemployment, and disorder. But in an age of great upward and downward mobility, the elite were likewise anxious that they might plummet down. "The doctrine of predestination, with its stark division of humanity into the irrevocably and inexplicably saved and damned, must have seemed congruent with the social conditions that the Saints saw around them. . . . to men and women achieving a precarious prosperity in a world of spreading misery, the doctrine of double predestination must have seemed both more plausible and more insistently relevant than most people find it today."[38] To this was added a hatred for the Church of Rome, which "prevented many of the more rigorous English Protestants from resting satisfied with the Elizabethan settlement."[39] Finally, there was the decline of the village community. "One reason for the appeal of Protestantism," writes Hunt, "especially in its more rigorous forms, may have been the fact that the symbols of collective identity had been rendered dysfunctional by widening ethical and economic divisions."[40]

The logic by which Hunt supports these explanations of the growth of Puritanism is the logic of ideas. The ideas that form his logical scheme come from the sermons and books of Puritan preachers, sermons and books from which he quotes extensively. But empirical evidence about the impact of these ideas on persons of substance is thin. Hunt therefore does what countless historians do. He places himself in the situation of these persons of substance. He, a rational person, faced with the problem of a growing number of poor, would find most congenial the preachers' message that poverty was a moral failing and that the way to end poverty was to reform the outlook of the poor. Persons of substance in the sixteenth century were rational people, and so would reason likewise. Such an explanation can be called either the rational model of explanation or situational analysis, depending upon whether the emphasis falls on the rationality of the agent or the description of the situation. But this kind of explanation, where the situation is a body of ideas, can also be called an intelligibility explanation. One could say that Hunt made the Puritanism of the sixteenth century intelligible. Historians seek to understand how a logical scheme of ideas fits together. Once they have understood that scheme, once they have seen that a belief in Q logically entails a belief in P, then by showing that people did believe Q, they have shown why people believed P. In an intelligibility explana-

38. Ibid., 125.
39. Ibid., 90.
40. Ibid., 136.

tion the "situation" is a scheme of ideas, and the purpose is to show that given that scheme a person comes to accept certain beliefs. Like rational explanation, intelligibility explanation is a perfectly legitimate way of proceeding. It is likewise an accurate description of what historians do— especially historians of ideas. It is, however, a dangerous procedure, especially if the historian is unaware of the assumptions upon which he or she acts. In an intelligibility explanation historians assume that because they hold that a belief in Q entails a belief in P, persons of substance in the sixteenth century held that a belief in Q entails a belief in P. This is a dangerous assumption, because men and women do not invariably act logically. Logically the Puritan ministers of Scotland, believing that God had predestined all men and women either to salvation or damnation, should not have exhorted their parishoners to seek salvation by leading a more godly life. Yet they did so, constantly. The logic of ideas points toward possible covering laws (Persons who believe Q will also believe P). But ultimately those covering laws depend for their validity on empirical evidence that persons believing Q did in fact come to believe P. For this reason historians who study the sixteenth century until they know how men and women then thought will be better historians than those who bring their twentieth-century ideas to the writing of that history.

Indeed, historians often differ from one another in the interpretations they give to the logic of ideas within a system of belief. Collinson, for example, differs from Hunt in his interpretation of what the godly preachers said about the poor. "In the literature of complaint," he writes, "there is little evidence of a desire to equate religious and moral reformation with social control or the correction of 'non-respectable society.' Indeed, the poor and disreputable are conspicuous by their absence from the complaints of the moralists."[41] Even more, he is inclined to place the etiology of Puritanism in the personal experience of English men and women. "It is very likely," he writes,

> that the religion of most puritans was anchored in experience, and probable that the experience related in some way to inner dissatisfaction or personal [concerns]. It is rather more apparent that puritan gentlemen and magistrates, having learned to apply to their condition the salves of practical, "experimental" divinity for which they were designed, addressed themselves to a disorder which was external to themselves and to their class and calling, and which they identified with popery, or the ecclesiastical

41. Collinson, *The Religion of Protestants*, 220–21.

hierarchy, or the corruption of the Court, or the machinations of a contrary and evil-minded faction, or the gross sins of the rabble.[42]

For Collinson the concern that Puritan gentlemen and magistrates expressed for the disorder around them was a consequence of their Puritanism, not a cause. The etiology of that practical, "experimental" divinity he places in an inner personal experience, which he does not attempt to explain.

This brings us back to the question: is Karl Marx right to say that social existence shapes consciousness? The answer is probably yes, if one defines "social existence" widely enough. Clearly, defining "social existence" as merely a person's class is too narrow. Even Hunt admits that no correlation can be drawn between belief in Puritanism and class.[43] Social existence needs to be defined more broadly—to include, for example, all the ways in which Tudor and Stuart England differed from thirteenth-century England. It should include the rise of literacy as well as the rise of capitalism, the invention of the printing press as well as the invention of the water-powered mill. It should also include the ideas and institutions inherited from an earlier age. Between substantially different societies meaningful differences in consciousness can be found. Kenneth Stampp points to one such difference in the United States: in the North there were a great many abolitionists among the working class; in the South there were few abolitionists among the working class.[44] Clearly, different social existences had shaped different consciousnesses. But though one can say in general that social existence, broadly defined, shapes consciousness, one must admit that it is difficult to prove that a particular aspect of social existence produced a particular element in consciousness. It is not easy to show what in a particular society produced a particular idea or value. Karl Mannheim spent years trying to specify the ways in which a worldview was the consequence of the social situation of its adherents. But the more he elaborated on the theme, the more mysterious became the nature of the connection.[45]

The historian should certainly seek to carry out such analysis. Stampp did so with conspicuous success, showing that non-slave-owning whites in the South suffered from an intense fear that free Negroes would claim equality with them. "As things stood," writes Stampp, "even in poverty

---

42. Ibid., 181.
43. Hunt, *The Puritan Moment*, 124–25.
44. Stampp, *The Peculiar Institution*, 425.
45. I have borrowed this observation from Robert Brown's review of *The Intellectual Development of Karl Mannheim*, by Colin Loader, *Times Literary Supplement*, 10 January 1986, 27.

they enjoyed the prestige of membership in the superior caste and proudly shared with the slaveholders the burden of keeping black men in their place."[46] But the historian should carry out such an analysis with becoming modesty; it is difficult to find particular connections. Just as the Freudians can assert that the child is father to the man, so can the Marxists assert that social existence shapes consciousness. Both assertions are true, but both truths are so general as to be vacuous. As Peter Medawar once observed, that which explains everything explains nothing. What the Freudians and Marxists need to do is to show exactly how one's childhood shapes one's character and exactly how social existence shapes the consciousness of a people. At this task both have signally failed, largely because they have sought macrocorrelations, and the macrocorrelations—say, between toilet training and stinginess or between capitalism and Puritanism—are not there. The most that the biographer can do is to trace the formation of a person's character, searching along the way for those factors that formed it. And the most that the historian can do is to trace the emergence of a new idea or value, searching along the way for those factors that caused the new idea or value to emerge. The biographer and the historian should push their analyses as far as they can, but they should also be ready to admit that some historical questions cannot be answered, some phenomena not explained. To this extent Collingwood was right.

In his celebrated dictum Marx not only asserted that social existence determines consciousness, he also asserted that the consciousness of people does not determine their existence. In asserting this he was profoundly wrong. The consciousness of people does most palpably determine their existence. Discovering a new productive force is a conscious act that determines the existence of a people. When Henry Newcomen, in order to pump water out of deep mines, invented the atmospheric engine, and when James Watt, having heard Joseph Black's lecture on latent heat, improved that engine by adding a separate condenser, they created the age of steam. "People may not," writes Karl Federn, "always be conscious of the importance and of the consequences of their discoveries, but every discovery, the most primitive contrivance as well as the most surprising invention, was made by the imaginative and reasoning forces of the human mind."[47] In order to explain the development of humankind the historian must investigate the causes as well as the consequences of such inventions. Nor should inventions be limited to the world of engineering. Discoveries and inventions have been made in

46. Stampp, *Peculiar Institution*, 426.
47. Federn, *The Materialist Conception of History*, 8.

finance, administration, medicine, communications, and government. Marx, of course, recognized this, writing in another passage, "Man develops the powers slumbering in nature and subjects the play of her force to his command."[48] But he did not seem willing to incorporate this observation into his philosophy of history. The dialectic that he ought to have seized upon is not the Hegelian dialectic of thesis and antithesis, of essence and existence, but the dialectic between consciousness and social existence. Conscious decisions, through their intended and unintended consequences, shape social existence. Social existence in turn shapes the consciousness of people, especially their values. And so the dialectic continues through human history.

The Etiology of Ideas

The previous pages have been concerned with the etiology of beliefs about what *ought to be*, but historians are also interested in the etiology of beliefs about what *is*, of the ideas men and women have about the nature of the world in which they live. Historians are as interested in the ideas that an age holds as in the values it cherishes. This former concern leads into the realm of intellectual history and raises the question: how do intellectual historians account for the etiology of such ideas.

Keith Thomas's study of belief in witchcraft offers a useful example. He begins by posing the question: how is one to account for the active prosecution of witches from 1550 to 1675?[49] He then asserts that it is wrong to lay the responsibility for these prosecutions on the passage of new statutes against witchcraft. "It must be traced," he writes, "to a change in the opinion of the people themselves."[50] This change in opinion he attributes to the convergence of (at least) four factors: a belief in the reality of Satan, a decline in the protections offered by organized religion against Satan and witchcraft, a need for some people to seek revenge through witchcraft, a need for others to explain the inexplicable and to assuage their guilt through witchcraft accusations. Now, these four factors could be viewed as the initial conditions in a classic Hempelian model of explanation. The covering law would be "Whenever these four conditions are found, people will believe in witchcraft." But Thomas is far too good a historian to

48. Ibid., 12.
49. Thomas, *Religion and the Decline of Magic,* 454. The arguments that follow are contained in chapters 14 through 18.
50. Ibid., 463.

resort to so naïve an exercise in macrocorrelation. Instead he shows how each of these factors is connected logically with a belief in witchcraft. Having described the emphasis placed by Protestantism on the pervasive role of the Devil, Thomas writes, "Thus the belief that witches might make compacts with Satan is readily intelligible as a consequence of the rhetoric of contemporary religion."[51] He then adds, belief in the reality of Satan also made possible the idea of demoniacal possession. Similar intelligible connections are drawn between the other factors and belief in witchcraft: playing down the importance of guardian angels left the way open to the Devil; the desire of the poor for revenge against wealthy villagers who refused charity led them, having no recourse to the law, to employ witchcraft; and the bereaved husbands of wives who had inexplicably died of cancer, already burdened with guilt at refusing charity, found satisfaction in bringing accusations of witchcraft against those they had offended.

With each of these factors it is the logic of ideas that makes the connection intelligible. What makes Thomas's explanation so powerful is his use of the accusations and confessions made by participants in witchcraft trials. From these he reconstructs the logic of seventeenth-century English men and women, the logic that guides their thought. The historian, so to speak, is putting together a giant jigsaw puzzle, and the picture becomes increasingly intelligible as all the pieces fit neatly together. But this is only a metaphor, and philosophers should beware of metaphors. Instead they should describe how, in the thinking of English men and women in the seventeenth century, one proposition leads to another, which, in combination with yet others, leads to a third, and so on. One might call this process logical colligation. And each step in the sequence of thoughts must be bridged with a covering law. Such a law may take several forms: "He who believes Q will be led to believe P" or "He who believes Q will not believe P, which is incompatible with Q" or "He who believes both Q and P will believe R." Now, historians will rarely add up instances of people who believed Q and also believed P (though Thomas's exploitation of proceedings in witchcraft trials carried him close to this). Rather, they will conclude that they, as rational persons, see that believing Q has the consequence of believing P; they will then assume that the historical agent, who was also rational, would have done the same. If the historical agent was not rational in the way that the historians are, then the preferred explanation may well be false.

Thus when historians seek to discover the genesis of a new idea, they proceed much as they do when they seek to discover the genesis of a new belief or value. They do not resort to some grand sociology of

51. Ibid., 477.

knowledge. They do not seek to correlate the emergence of the new idea with some particular circumstance. Rather, they trace minutely the emergence of the new idea. They often do so in a fashion that I have called logical colligation. But each step in that colligatory sequence must be bridged by a covering law. Once again, explanation rests squarely on a marriage between colligation and correlation.

In such a manner does the historian trace the etiology of the beliefs and ideas that men and women hold about the world in which they live. In this and the previous chapter I have examined the logic by which the historian sets forth the etiology of the desires and beliefs that lie behind the historical agent's actions. But schemes of purposive action also include the ability of the historical agent to take the action he or she did and the opportunity to do so. The historian, therefore, must also ask why the agent possessed the ability and why the agent had the opportunity to act as he or she did. It would be tedious to describe the logic by which the historian answers these two questions, since it would be the same logic that is set forth in Chapter 6 on the logic of colligation. Suffice it to say that the historian traces in detail, justifying each step in the explanation with a covering law, how the agent—say Barère—acquired his ability to act and how he came to have the opportunity to act.

Historical explanation begins with an exact description of the aggregate event whose occurrence the historian wishes to explain. It proceeds by the historian's breaking that event into subevents, discovering the authors of those events, elucidating their purposes, relating those purposes to their desires and beliefs, and investigating the origins of those desires and beliefs. When the historian has done all this, he or she has brought the search for a total explanation to an end.

11 THE LOGIC OF HISTORICAL INTERPRETATION

> To know things well, detail must be known, and since detail is almost infinite, our knowledge remains superficial and imperfect.
>
> — La Rochefoucauld, maxim number 106

Imagine for a moment that an eager young student in class or a history buff at a public lecture asks a professor of English history, "What caused the outbreak of civil war in England in 1642?" And suppose further that the professor, imbued with the logic of historical explanation that I have set forth in the previous chapters of this book, replies, "The causes of the outbreak of civil war in England in 1642 may be found in these volumes." Whereupon he produces over one hundred volumes, each with over one thousand pages, volumes that trace in minute detail the many events leading from the introduction of a new service book in St. Giles to the raising of the royal standard at Nottingham, that describe the origins of the social and political structures that prevailed in England in 1640, that investigate the etiology of the beliefs of the English, that rely upon linear and cumulative and convergent and micro- and parallel colligation, and that employ covering laws to bridge every gap in the intricate, complex web of events that led to the outbreak of the civil war. Clearly such an answer would be useless, indeed, quite absurd. That is not what the student or the history buff wants. What they want is a two- or three-minute statement on the principal causes of the civil war, or a reference to a short book on the subject. They want, not an exhaustive account of the coming of the civil war, but an interpretation of the causes of the civil war.

Historians use the word "interpretation" in many different ways; therefore one must define it exactly before proceeding to a discussion of the logic of historical interpretation. In the first place, one should distinguish between "the interpretation of historical evidence" and "the interpretation of a historical event." Historians have long spoken of the interpretation of historical evidence—of a document or an inscription or a coin or a shard. The historian here asks what the document or inscription or coin or shard means. The document or artifact, having been made by a human being, has meaning, a meaning that the historian seeks to discover. This is a legitimate and familiar meaning of "interpretation," and the word will continue to be used by historians in that sense. But it is not what historians mean by "interpretation" when they speak of an "interpretation of a historical event"; that is, it is not what most historians mean. A few historians, it is true, might regard events as having meaning, and historians as having the obligation to elicit that meaning. Cromwell certainly believed that events had meaning, and studied them in order to discover God's providence for humankind. But to believe that events have meaning is to believe that they have an intelligent author, a God, whose purposes are to be read in the course of events. For such a historian the word "interpretation" has the same meaning in the phrase "the interpretation of a historical event" as it has in the phrase "the interpretation of a document." But few historians in this secular age see the hand of God in history and therefore do not interpret events as they would interpret a document. They may see a *pattern* in events, but unless they attribute that pattern to God, as the author of it, they do not attribute *meaning* to the course of events. They may even see a final goal to all history, but unless some God, some Awful Author of Our Existence, has set that goal and shaped events to attain it, it makes no sense to speak of interpreting events in order to discover their meaning.[1]

It is likewise important to distinguish between interpretation and theory, though many social-science historians do not. Thus Peter Burke refers to "four monographs in search of a theory," those by Braudel, McNeil, Ladurie, and Wachtel; but in fact these four monographs offer interpretations, not theories.[2] Similarly, Arthur Stinchcombe, in *Theoreti-*

---

1. J.F.M. Hunter ("On Whether History Has a Meaning," 87–96) likewise finds it bewildering to ask if an event has a meaning.
2. Burke, *Sociology and History*, 94–101.

cal Methods in Social History, under the rubric "theory," discusses what
are in fact interpretations. He entitles one section of his book "The
Theoretical Character of a Narrative." He even declares that the conflict
between "the epochal theories of Marx, De Jouvenal, and Parsons has to
do with how these cumulations of effects over time come about."[3] And
Thomas Cochran, discussing the work of "growth theorists," gives as an
example Habakkuk's interpretation of the rapid industrialization of
America.[4] Even as careful a thinker as Karl Popper confuses theory and
interpretation. In The Poverty of Historicism he has the historicists "interpret the past, in order to predict the future." And he asserts that historicists "interpret history, in order to discover the laws of its development."[5] In Objective Knowledge he even writes:

> Regarded as a third-world object, the interpretation will always
> be a theory; for example a historical explanation, supported by a
> chain of arguments and, perhaps, by documentary evidence.
>   So in every interpretation is a kind of theory and, like every
> theory, it is anchored in other theories and in other third-world
> objects. And in this way the third-world problem of the merits of
> the interpretation can be raised and discussed, and especially its
> value for our historical understanding.[6]

What these scholars fail to see is that "interpretation," as commonly
used by historians, refers to an assertion that some variable or number of
variables are the most important causal agencies in a particular historical
development, that is, in a single sequence of events, whereas "theory"
refers to an explanation of a repetitive phenomenon, that is, an explanation why a sequence of events repeats itself over and over again. Interpretation concerns a single sequence of events; theory, a sequence of
events that repeats itself over and over again. These are two quite different things.
   The difference can be illustrated by looking at Karl Marx's philosophy
of history. Though often called a theory, the main scheme in his philosophy is an interpretation. Marx believed that the movement from a tribal
society to a slave society, from a slave society to a feudal society, from a
feudal society to a capitalist society, and from a capitalist society to a

---

3. Stinchcombe, Theoretical Methods in Social History, 1–9, 13.
4. Cochran, The Inner Revolution, 132–33.
5. Popper, The Poverty of Historicism, 50–52.
6. Popper, Objective Knowledge, 163. In The Open Society, 2:266, Popper calls certain
"untestable historical theories" "general interpretations."

socialist society was relevant to Europe alone. He did not expect Russia or India to follow the Western path.[7] His efforts to find the main variables explaining that Western development represent an effort at interpretation, not a theory. Yet within that scheme there is a theory, the theory of structure and superstructure. The material powers of production shape the economic structure, upon which rises the legal and political superstructure, to which correspond definite forms of social consciousness.[8] It is a theory because it applies to repetitive phenomena; in all societies this will be true. Admittedly it is a theory only in a vague sense, since in each society the way in which the mode of production influences the economic structure and in which the economic structure shapes the legal and political structure and social consciousness has to be spelled out anew, in what closely resembles an interpretation. Marx does make his theory more specific, however, when he writes that the hand mill will give rise to feudalism, the steam mill to capitalism. The argument here, presumably, is that wherever there is an economy that relies on a hand mill, there will be feudal institutions, and wherever an economy based on a steam mill, capitalistic institutions. A moment's reflection, though, will suggest that Marx probably did not mean this. He gives no example of a hand mill leading to feudalism except in medieval Europe, and no example of a steam mill leading to capitalism except in modern Europe. He is really giving an interpretation of medieval and modern European history before, during, and after the French Revolution.[9] When applied to European history during those years Marx's interpretation contains insights that even liberal historians find profound. Only when Marxists treat it as a theory applicable to Asiatic, Arabic, and African history does it appear absurd. The reason for this is clear: at bottom the Marxist philosophy of history is an interpretation, not a theory.

In *The Poverty of Historicism* Popper draws a rather different distinction between interpretation and theory. Theories, which are appropriate to science, can be tested, but interpretations, which are appropriate to history, cannot. An interpretation is "a preconceived selective point of view" that cannot be tested, but it allows historians to write the history that interests them. Though historians should not allow such a point of view to twist or falsify the facts, they will allow it to govern the selection of facts. Further, there may be a plurality of interpretations, correspond-

---

7. Burke, *Sociology and History*, 90–91.
8. Marx, *Contribution to the Critique of Political Economy*, 10–13.
9. David McLellan (*Marx*, 36–49) shows that Marx's so-called theory of history was in reality, and by Marx's own explicit admission in 1881, an interpretation, not a theory.

ing to a plurality of points of view. Each interpretation is equally valid, though some may be more fertile than others.[10] In *The Open Society* Popper elaborates on this same theme, concluding that "there will always be a number of other (and perhaps incompatible) interpretations that agree with the same records."[11]

This view of historical interpretation opens the door to a large element of subjectivity, and though some part of that subjectivity is warranted, the remaining part is not. What is warranted is the assertion that the historian's own interests govern what questions he or she will ask about the past. Before the rise of the Civil Rights Movement and before the emergence of the Women's Liberation Movement, few historians asked about the role of blacks or the role of women in history; afterward many did. In this sense every generation writes its own history. But once having posed the question or questions they wish to answer, historians are not free to select only those facts that interest them. If history is to have any legitimacy as a scholarly discipline, some rules more objective than the point of view and interests of the historian must guide his or her selection of facts. Those rules make up the logic of historical interpretation.

This logic is certainly not that to which Carl Hempel adverts when he writes:

> Closely related to explanation and understanding is the so-called *interpretation of historical phenomena* in terms of some particular approach or theory. The interpretations which are offered in history consist either in subsuming the phenomena in question under a scientific explanation or explanation-sketch; or in an attempt to subsume them under some general idea which is not amenable to any empirical test. In the former case, interpretation clearly is explanation by means of universal hypotheses; in the latter it amounts to a pseudo-explanation which may have emotive appeal and evoke vivid pictorial associations, but which does not further our theoretical understanding of the phenomena under consideration.[12]

The logic of historical interpretation I propose to set forth has little to do with subsuming a phenomenon under a scientific explanation or explanation-sketch. Neither does it have anything to do with subsuming the phenomenon under some general idea, or with discovering a

10. Popper, *The Poverty of Historicism*, 150–51.
11. Popper, *The Open Society*, 2:266.
12. Hempel, "Aspects of Scientific Explanation," 240–41.

pattern in history, or with understanding a series of events holistically.[13] Rather, it is an inductive logic and has to do with generalizing from particulars.

But before describing that logic it would be wise to define "historical interpretation" more precisely. As used in this chapter it means an abbreviation of a complete explanation. In making that abbreviation, certain factors may emerge as dominant—perhaps economic, perhaps demographic, perhaps religious—but the historian has a duty not to give more prominence to those dominant factors than they in fact have in the complete explanation. Indeed, the historian has not given an accurate or fair abbreviation if for reasons of prejudice or bias he or she has emphasized certain factors more than they deserve to be emphasized. The historian may, however, having given an accurate and fair abbreviation, and having noticed that the economic factors were decisive, speak of an economic interpretation.

Before turning to a description of the logic of historical interpretation a second excursus is required, one concerning the problem of selectivity. When historians set out to write the history of the past, they face, as La Rochefoucauld observed, a sea of facts, yet only an infinitesimal portion of that infinity of facts will appear in their final histories. What governs the selection of the facts that do appear? Four steps, at least, can be identified in the process of selection. The first is the selection of a topic, which may well be governed by whim. Historians who set out to write the history of the cultivation of asparagus will have at one stroke sharply delimited the extent of the facts they will use. The second step, also a matter of personal choice, is the historian's decision what kind of history to write, whether a chronicle setting forth what happened or a monograph describing how an institution works or a narrative telling a dramatic story or a history explaining why certain events occurred. Each has its own rules of selection. Assuming that the historian chooses to write explanatory history, the selection of facts will be governed by those rules of colligation and correlation set forth in the previous ten chapters. The fourth step in the process of selection is the drawing up of an abbreviation or abstract of the complete explanation arrived at in the third step. This final step, too, is governed by rules, not whim.

Of all the means of abbreviating a complete explanation perhaps the most often used is that of remaining on a high level of abstraction, of not descending to particulars—or to put it differently, of remaining on a

13. As F. R. Ankersmit would argue. For a valuable discussion of Ankersmit's rejection of "explanation" in favor of "interpretation," see A. P. Fell, " 'Epistemological' and 'Narrativist' Philosophies of History," 72–86.

high level of colligation, of not descending to further and further microcolligation. Thus in reporting a victory in a football game, a journalist might merely write that the Buckeyes marched eighty yards to a touchdown in the fourth quarter, thereby defeating the Michigan Wolverines seven to nothing. The journalist need say nothing about the various plays in that eighty-yard drive. This is an explanation of the Buckeyes' victory, but a brief and superficial one. Or a historian might begin an explanation of the coming of the English Civil War by writing that the introduction of a new liturgy into Scotland precipitated a war between England and Scotland. He or she need not descend to the minute tracing of events to show how the introduction of the liturgy led to war. There is nothing fraudulent about this kind of abbreviation, unless, that is, the historian offers a perverse explanation, an explanation that the historical evidence does not support. But though this kind of abbreviation is legitimate, it is also superficial, as the reading of any textbook in Western civilization will demonstrate. La Rochefoucauld was right: without detail "our knowledge remains superficial and imperfect."[14]

A second means of abbreviating a complete explanation, a means so constantly practiced that one might overlook it, is to omit the covering laws that bridge the gaps in the detailed narrative. As argued in Chapter 4, those laws are implicit, not explicit. They are in the historian's mind but not in his or her narrative. But they, too, just like the omitted detail, must be supported by the historical evidence.

A third means to abbreviate a complete account is to omit any discussion of the origins of structures or of the etiology of desires and beliefs. The journalist, for example, might describe in great detail each play in the Buckeyes' victory over the Wolverines but say not a word about the coaching, the training, or the recruitment of players. Similarly the historian of the English Civil War might trace in minute detail the events leading from the introduction of the new liturgy to the raising of the royal standard at Nottingham, and yet not examine why the Crown's finances were bankrupt or why so many of the King's subjects were Puritans. He may choose to avoid explaining (through cumulative colligation) how the structure and beliefs in place in 1637 came into being. He will mention them, he will describe them, he will assess their role in the shaping of events, but he will not explain how they came to be. Again, this is legitimate—but also superficial. There is no requirement that a historian must explain the origins of the structures and beliefs prevailing in a society at a given moment, but his account will be more profound if he does.

14. La Rochefoucauld, maxim number 106.

A fourth means to abbreviate a complete account—and one that is essential to any interpretation of the past—is to generalize from the results of parallel colligation. The authors of any great historical event may run into the hundreds of thousands, even millions. How can the historian grapple with such complexity? No one saw this dilemma more clearly than Hippolite Taine, who wrote, "What was there in France in the eighteenth century? Twenty million men . . . twenty million threads the crisscrossing of which makes a web. This immense web, with innumerable knots, cannot be grasped clearly in its entirety by anyone's memory or imagination. All we have is mere fragments." But Taine also saw a path out of this dilemma.

> The historian's task is to restore them—he reconstructs the wisps of the threads that he can see so as to connect them with the myriad threads that have vanished. Fortunately in the past, as now, society included groups, each group consisting of men who were like one another—born in the same condition, moulded by the same education, moved by the same interests, with the same needs, same tastes, same *moeurs*, same culture, same basis to their lives. In seeing one, you have seen all. In every science we study each class of facts by means of chosen samples. . . . Let us enter into the private life of a man (typical of his time after we have studied him minutely). . . . We shall understand the force and direction of the current that carries forward the whole of his society. The monograph is the historian's best tool; he plunges it into the past like a lancet and draws it out charged with complete and authentic specimens. One understands a period after twenty or thirty such soundings: only they must be carried out and interpreted correctly.[15]

One need not share Taine's belief that history is a science to recognize that his observations here are shrewd. Historians do solve the problem of dealing with twenty million Frenchmen by observing similarities in the motives and actions of those Frenchmen and by then classifying them into groups, indeed into a fairly small number of groups— royalists, constitutionalists, Girondists, Jacobins, and so forth. Nor can historians describe all members of a group—the want of historical records and the want of space prevent it. Therefore they will study a few whom they regard as a fair sample. Max Weber called such a sample "an

15. Taine, *Histoire: Son present et son avenir*, quoted in Berlin, "The Concept of Scientific History," 28.

ideal type." Taine might not approve how casually historians generalize from one or two cases, but they regularly do so. Anthony Fletcher, for example, in studying the outbreak of the English Civil War, writes, "The pattern of parochial conflict is nicely summarized by the case of Mr. Andrews, vicar of Busbridge in Surrey. . . . There is good reason to think that the Andrews case was by no means an isolated one."[16] Fletcher does not vouchsafe to say how many parochial conflicts he studied, but presumably he studied many and formed the impression that Andrew's case was typical. Were Andrews's case not typical, the writing of the history of the English Civil War would be supremely difficult. If each person who opposed the Crown opposed for a different motive, if it was impossible to classify them according to the similar motives that drove them into opposition, then the ensuing scene would be chaos, and the history of it equally chaotic. Fortunately, such a bewildering variety does not often prevail. The county school of English historians, led by Alan Everitt, once argued for such a variety, once argued that the civil war was fought over myriad local issues, each differing from the other. But the more recent researches of Clive Holmes have shown that a few national issues did dominate in every county.[17] Englishman after Englishman voted to send members to Parliament who would defend his property by condemning ship money. A pattern did appear, thereby allowing the historian to explain the opposition to Charles's personal government without having to inquire into and exhibit the individual motives of every Englishman who voted for a member of Parliament.

Careful historians, of course, will give greater weight to the motives and actions of those in greater authority. The motives and actions of a forty-shilling freeholder counted for more than those of a cottager, just as the motives and actions of a member of the Long Parliament counted for more than those of the forty-shilling freeholder. But once having given the appropriate weight to the participants in the events leading to the civil war, historians will then generalize from all the particulars before them. And these generalizations about the motives that led men to oppose and to favor the King will be part of their interpretation of the English Civil War. It is an inductive process, in which historians have the duty to express in their summations the same proportion of motives— say, between religious and political—that they found in their search for a complete explanation.

Consider, for instance, this example of interpretation by summation,

16. Fletcher, *The Outbreak of the English Civil War,* 219.
17. Holmes, "The County School of English Historians."

written by J. H. Plumb in *The Growth of Political Stability*, after he has described James II's onslaught on local government:

> The universality that permeates the Revolution of 1688 arose not only because of James II's specific attacks on the Anglican monopoly of the Church, the Army, Navy, and universities, but also because of his outright onslaught on the very basis of political power, which if successful would have made the Stuarts as absolute as their French or Spanish cousins. It is this attack on the natural leaders of society in their county neighbourhoods that must be regarded as the most fundamental cause of the Revolution of 1688.[18]

Plumb here gives an interpretation of the Revolution of 1688 that emphasizes James II's attack upon the gentry's and the nobility's control of local government. To sustain that interpretation Plumb would have to show that the natural leaders of society were James's chief opponents (not a difficult matter to show) and that in the minds of a majority of them the fundamental issue was control of local government (a rather more difficult matter to show, but not impossible). What he has done, presumably, is to generalize from numerous statements and actions by English gentlemen and noblemen during James's reign, statements and actions that show that they prized their control over local government above all other concerns.

The historian who deals with election results has a much easier time of it, since the election in itself is a summation of the opinions of numerous persons. But election results tell one little about the motives that led a person to vote for one candidate rather than another. In contemporary elections this is done by exit interviews at the polls (which interviews offer an excellent example of microcolligation in journalism). Exit polls create the possibility that a bewildering variety of motives will emerge, yet in fact there are usually only a few, repeated over and over again. The journalist conducting the exit interviews will then group the many replies under a few rubrics and report them, perhaps quoting one individual for each, as a sample of that opinion. The ensuing newspaper article, no doubt brief, represents generalizations based on many particulars.

Such generalizations are not laws; they are generalizations of fact. A. J. Ayer has drawn the distinction between the two sharply: "whereas generalizations of fact cover only actual instances, generalizations of law

18. Plumb, *The Growth of Political Stability*, 62.

cover other possible instances as well."[19] The journalist is not predicting how future voters will vote or explaining why the present voters voted as they did (other than reporting their self-avowals). He is only summarizing how they did vote and the reasons they gave for voting as they did. Plumb, however, though he is summarizing the attitudes of gentlemen and noblemen toward local government (a generalization of fact) is also claiming that those attitudes were a fundamental cause of the Revolution of 1688 (which explanation rests on a generalization of law, namely, that those who control local government will resist the monarch's attempt to take that control from them.) Herein interpretation differs from explanation. Interpretation depends on generalizations of fact, explanation on generalization of law.

Yet another means to abbreviate a complete explanation is to generalize from the sequence of events that led to the event to be explained. Thus a sports writer will observe a sequence of plays leading to an Ohio State touchdown, but rather than describe each play in his article, he will sum up what he has observed and write that there were seven running plays, gaining fifty-one yards, and two pass plays, gaining nine yards. He then might even offer an interpretation of Ohio State's victory: it was a result of its running game, not its passing attack. The historian who traces the coming of the English Civil War will similarly generalize from a long sequence of events. Consider this example from Fletcher's *Outbreak of the English Civil War:* To secure the passage of the article concerning the militia in the Nineteen Propositions, Pym, Goodwin, and Strode asked the House of Commons what assurance Englishmen would have of their safety if the militia were abandoned. Fletcher then observes, "In their heart of hearts the majority still believed what Pym had told them all along. They were still possessed by the delusion of a Catholic and malignant conspiracy against the state."[20] Indeed, Pym's use of this delusion to persuade the House to make inroad after inroad into the royal prerogative lies at the heart of Fletcher's interpretation of the outbreak of civil war.

A historian may even treat an episode as a sample of many other episodes. David Hart-Dyke, commander of HMS *Coventry,* has recently given such an explanation for Britain's victory over Argentina in the Falklands War. It was not, he argues, superior numbers or superior arms but superior morale that explains the victory. To arrive at this judgment he no doubt observed or heard about or read about many separate episodes in which the valor of the British and the lack of valor among the

---

19. Ayer, "What Is a Law of Nature?" 49.
20. Fletcher, *The Outbreak of the English Civil War,* 274.

Argentinians led to a British victory. But rather than detail every episode, he gives one example of valor upon his own ship and then sums up his other observations. Were he offering a complete explanation, he would need to show why in each instance he believed that superior morale and not superior numbers or superior arms led to victory, but when he offers his interpretation of the victory, he is merely summing up the results of those many individual inquiries.[21]

The historian may similarly generalize from cumulative colligation. He or she may observe that every time Charles I broke a promise, distrust of him mounted, a distrust that finally brought him down. The historian need not give every example of a broken promise leading to distrust, but can sum up his or her observations in a statement that Charles's bad faith was a chief factor in the coming of the civil war.

But not all events in a sequence of events are of equal weight, as the discussion in Chapter 6 showed. Some events are of great consequence, some of little. The sports writer will place less weight on a routine five-yard gain off tackle (though not if it is on the goal line) than on a completed pass made on the third down with seventeen yards to go for the first down, a play critical to keeping the scoring drive alive. Similarly, the historian of the outbreak of the civil war in England will give greater weight to the motives that led men to vote for the Militia Ordinance than to the motives that led them every two months to vote to extend tonnage and poundage. In summing up the various motives that led members of Parliament to oppose the King, the vote on the Militia Ordinance clearly deserves greater weight.

The requirement that the historian give greater weight to one event rather than another or to one motive rather than another points to the single most important means by which a historian can abbreviate a complete explanation: he or she can emphasize the more important causes. In fact, as commonly understood, an interpretation is more than an abbreviation of a complete explanation; it is an abbreviation that emphasizes the more important causes. As Charles Frankel observes, "An interpretation may assert that some variable or group of variables—e.g. economics, geography, technology—are the most important causal agencies in history."[22]

The search for "the most important causal agencies in history" is, of course, a complicated one. It is complicated because there are so many ways in which an initial condition or a cause or a factor may be more

21. Hart-Dyke, "HMS Coventry—the Day of Battle," *Manchester Guardian Weekly*, 27 July 1986, 17.
22. Frankel, "Explanation and Interpretation in History," 419.

important. There are at least ten ways that I have described in this and previous chapters:

1. An initial condition may be more important because it is abnormal, as the introduction of the liturgy into St. Giles, because abnormal, was more important than the Protestant zeal of the congregation.
2. A cause in a causal chain may be more important because it is unusual, as the movement of Marlborough's troops to the center in the afternoon of 13 August 1704 was more important than the assault on Blindheim in the morning, an assault that was but a means to the later action.
3. A cause in a causal chain may be more important because so many consequences flowed from it, as from Charles's decision to summon the Long Parliament.
4. A cause may be more important because it is not overdetermined, as a vote for Labour in a marginal constituency in Essex is a more important cause of a Labour Party victory in a general election than a vote for Labour in a Welsh mining community.
5. A purpose may be more important than another purpose because it is predominate, as when a man votes Tory because he trusts Tories to manage the economy, rather than Labour, though he trusts the Labourites to protect the National Health Service.
6. A weakness in the structure of society may be a more important cause than a triggering event, as the fierce nationalism in the European state system in 1914 was a more important cause of the First World War than was the assassination of Archduke Ferdinand at Sarajevo.
7. A cause may be more important because it is repeated many times over in a causal chain, as disputes over taxation occurred far oftener than disputes over commerce in the chain of events leading to the American Revolution.
8. A cause may be more important because in a web of events it occurs more often than other causes, as superior morale rather than superior numbers or superior arms led to victory on numerous occasions in the Falklands War.
9. One purpose may be a more important cause than another because it is held by many people, while the other is held by few, as when many Ukrainians desired to separate from Russia and few desired to remain.
10. A cause may be more important because in so many instances it is the principal cause of an event, as speed is the most important cause of road accidents.

A careful reading of the above ten "more important" causes will show that numbers one through five concern a cause that occurred but once, while numbers seven through ten concern causes that are important because they occurred often. In the latter cases historians usually refer to them as important factors in the explanation of a complex event. Number six is a hybrid, since the assassination of the Archduke is a singular event but the repeated expressions of a fierce nationalism in the next two months a plural event. It is the number of times that nationalism found expression in the chain of events that leads historians to say it was a more fundamental cause of the First World War than was the assassination.

The above ten possible meanings of "more important than" arise out of the arguments of this book. It would certainly be useful to see what meanings other philosophers of history have given to the phrase. At least five philosophers have wrestled with the problem: Ernest Nagel, Murray Murphey, Behan McCullagh, Raymond Martin, and Richard Miller.

Ernest Nagel, in *The Structure of Science*, gives six possible meanings of "more important" in historical explanation.[23] To begin with, he asserts that A can be said to be a more important determinant of C than is B if variations in A (with consequent variations in C) occur more frequently than variations in B, which hardly ever occur. Thus xenophobia and a need for markets may both have caused a nation to adopt an imperialistic policy, but if xenophobia had always been present in a country, whereas the need for markets was recent, then the historian will deem the need for markets more important than the presence of xenophobia as a determinant of the adoption of an imperialistic policy. Nagel has resorted here to the doctrine of abnormalism and used it in a deductive model of explanation at the macrolevel. His conclusion, incidentally, exposes the weakness of the deductive model applied at the macrolevel, for in fact the pursuit of national greatness was a more important cause of imperialism than the pursuit of markets. Historians of imperialism have studied in detail the Italian seizure of Tunisia in 1881, the British seizure of Egypt in 1882, the German seizure of German Southwest Africa in 1884, and the German seizure of German Southeast Africa in 1885. They have read the letters of secretaries of state, scrutinized parliamentary debates, analyzed editorials in the press, and examined the extent of trade and investment in those areas. And they have concluded that the search for markets was peripheral. Nagel's conclusion probably owes more to the theories of J. A. Hobson and V. I. Lenin than to an examination of the historical facts.

---

23. Nagel, *The Structure of Science*, 584–86.

Nagel then turns to the second meaning of "more important." A is more important than B in causing C if changes in A give rise to greater changes in C than do equal changes in B. Thus if a 10 percent increase in the trained labor force yields a larger volume of goods than is obtained by a 10 percent increase in the supply of coal, then a trained labor force is more determinant of industrial productivity than the availability of coal. Barring any physical description of how the increase in each factor led to greater production, one must reason from a covering law: whenever, *ceteris paribus*, one increases the trained labor force by 10 percent, one gains X increase in production; whenever, *ceteris paribus*, one increases the availability of coal by 10 percent, one gains Y increase in production, with X always being greater than Y. This makes sense, but one suspects that this is more an exercise in model building than a reflection of reality.

The third meaning Nagel gives to "more important" declares A to be more important than B in causing C because B is merely one part of a set of conditions K. Though A is less consequent than K it is more consequent than that part of K denominated B. He illustrates this by making A stand for discontent with the political and economic conditions in a country, K for one of many precipitating events (loss of employment, news of brighter prospects elsewhere, acquisition of funds for travel, and the like), and B for the acquisition of travel funds alone. As factors causing emigration, discontent with political and economic conditions is thus more important than the acquisition of funds for travel, but not more important than all of the precipitating events put together. Here Nagel has deserted the deductive model for an inductive one; one can only assume that the reasoning leading to this conclusion came after countless interviews with emigrating men and women.

The fourth meaning of "more important" shows that Nagel has completely left the deductive-nomological model. He now supposes that the joint presence of A and B is not a necessary condition for the occurrence of C, but that C occurs either when A is present conjointly with X or when B is present conjointly with Y (with X and Y being unspecified determining factors). If A in conjunction with X occurs much more frequently than does B in conjunction with Y, then A is the more determinant of C. Thus negligence is "a more important factor" than mechanical failure in causing automobile accidents, since the frequency with which mechanical failures cause accidents is less than the frequency with which negligence does. The reasoning here is inductive, which Nagel signals by using the term "factor."

The fifth meaning supposes that the joint presence of A and B is not necessary for the occurrence of C, but that C occurs more often when A is realized and B is not than when B is realized and A is not. Thus if the relative frequency with which juvenile delinquents come from broken homes that are not poor is greater than the frequency with which delinquents come from poor homes where the parents live amicably together, then broken homes may be said to be a more fundamental cause of juvenile delinquency than poverty. This conclusion is clearly based on generalizations from many particulars, an example of inductive reasoning.

The sixth meaning propounded by Nagel is a search for a basic cause, a cause of causes. Suppose, writes Nagel, that A is a basic notion in a theory T (he could have said in an interpretation) but B is not, and also that T can account for a large class of phenomena, including C. Suppose, further, that in order to explain C a specialized assumption referring to B must be introduced, though most of the other phenomena accounted for by T may be accounted for without reference to B. Thus factor A may be said to be more important than B because it accounts for more phenomena. "Something like this sense of the phrase," writes Nagel, "appears to be intended by those who claim that the relations of production and distribution of wealth operative in a society constitute more basic determinants of its legal institutions than do its religious practices and beliefs."[24] Dogma might lead one to this conclusion, but more persuasive would be numerous instances wherein legislators and judges fashion laws and make judgments in favor of existing relations of production, set against the few instances in which they did so in favor of religion.

Murray Murphey, like Nagel, emphasizes the variety of senses of "more important than another" and offers some of those different senses. One of them is the following: "A and B are not necessary conditions for C, so C can occur if A does and also if B does, and A occurs more frequently than B." And another: "Joint occurrence of A and B is not a necessary condition for C, and C occurs relatively more frequently when A occurs and B does not than B occurs and A does not."[25] Since neither of these examples concerns the problem of determining which of the two necessary conditions is the more important, one can examine a large number of Cs (say accidents) and determine whether A (speed) or B (mechanical failure) is the more important factor in causing Cs (accidents). Murphey does offer an example in which A and B are both necessary conditions for C, but a greater change in C is associated with a proportional change in A than with an equal proportional change in B.[26] Thus (my example) both A (fuel) and B (a flame) are necessary for C (a fire), but changing A from a wastepaper basket to a tinder-dry forest will

24. Ibid., 586.
25. Murphey, *Our Knowledge of the Historical Past*, 129.
26. Ibid., 129.

cause a greater change in the magnitude of C (the fire) than changing B from a lighted cigarette to a lighted match. Clearly, Murphey is more interested in important factors than in important initial conditions.

Behan McCullagh's formula for discovering the more important cause, say, between cause A and cause B, is to ask what would have happened in the absence of A and what would have happened in the absence of B. By embracing this formula McCullagh clearly departs from the deductive-nomological model, with its attempt to find the more important of two necessary conditions, for if A were a necessary condition of C, C would not happen in the absence of A, and the same would be true for B. What McCullagh's formula does require is counterfactual reasoning. His first example makes this clear. He gives Robert Fogel's argument that railroads were not an important cause of growth of wealth in America in the nineteenth century, and Albert Fishlow's that they were.[27] Fogel supported his case by estimating the extent to which the GNP in 1890 would have been different had other methods of transport been developed instead of railroads. Albert Fishlow proceeded somewhat differently. He proceeded railroad by railroad, calculating exactly the transport services performed by each and reallocating these to the most efficient existing alternative routes. The difference between the total costs incurred is a measure of the benefit conferred by the least expensive method of transportation. Using an aggregative method of analysis, Fishlow found that the savings resulting from the use of railroads in 1859 was not great, since extensive water transport was available at little extra cost. But by 1890 railroads had grown more efficient, with no comparable increase in the efficiency of road and water transport. The loss of the GNP in 1890 had railroads not been used would have been 15 percent; Fogel estimated 5 percent.

Both historians addressed the question: what would have happened in the absence of railroads? To answer this both described, measured, and calculated the actual contribution of railroads. Where they differed was in the extent of their counterfactual reasoning. Albert Fishlow limited his to what was likely in 1859, knowing all we do about the world in 1859, and to what was likely in 1890, knowing all we do about the world in 1890. His calculations were not based so much on lawlike generalizations about the world of 1859 and the world of 1890 as on information about existing costs of transportation by rail, road, and canal in 1859 and 1890. Robert Fogel's counterfactual reasoning was more breathtaking, as he considered what improvements were likely in road and canal transport during the nineteenth century. Since it is undeniably true that the longer a chain of counterfactuals, the greater the chance of a mistaken

27. McCullagh, *Justifying Historical Descriptions*, 196–98.

conclusion at the end, Fogel has taken a dangerous path. Yet Albert Fishlow's reasoning is likewise based on such a chain, namely, the assertion that there would have been no improvement in land and water transport between 1859 and 1890.

McCullagh's second example concerns A. J. Youngson's judgment that a 17 percent decline in the level of industrial production was a more important cause for the fall in the production of coal between 1929 and 1933 (it fell from 262 million tons in 1929 to 210 in 1933) than was the pegging of the price of coal (by act of Parliament) at a time when the general price level fell by 15 percent.[28] To support his assertion Youngson must show that in the absence of the act of Parliament pegging the price of coal, the fall of production of coal would have been little, but that in the absence of the decline in industrial production, it would have been great. The first assertion Youngson defends by demonstrating that a decline in the price of coal would have made little difference because the demand for coal was inelastic, a generalization he must have made from observations of the sale of coal at different prices upon various occasions. The second assertion Youngson defends, not by a lawlike generalization, but by a measurement or estimate of the amount of coal that various industries did not order. In both cases Youngson relies on counterfactual reasoning, but in the former he appeals to a lawlike generalization and in the latter to a measurement or estimate.

McCullagh gives other examples of the search for the more important causes—for the American Civil War, for the success of the Yorkshire woolen industry, for the outbreak of the First World War.[29] In every case the historian asks, what would be the probability of the effect occurring if this particular cause were absent? But how does the historian estimate that probability? Of the outbreak of the First World War, McCullagh writes, "Thus if the probability of war, given imperial rivalry was, say about 30%, and the probability of war given imperial rivalry plus fierce national feeling was very high, say 80% then national feeling was a more important cause than imperial rivalry, contributing 50% to its 30%." But McCullagh, alas, does not say how the historian arrived at the judgment that the probability of war, given imperial rivalry, was 30 percent, but with both imperial rivalry and fierce national feeling, 80 percent. If there were many examples of wars breaking out where there existed both imperial rivalry and fierce national feeling, and only a few where there existed only imperial rivalry, the historian could subsume the First World War under such a generalization and arrive at such probabilities. But

28. Ibid., 199–200.
29. Ibid., 200–205.

there are not many such examples, and historians do not proceed in this manner. Yet McCullagh does describe P. J. Perry doing something very like this. Perry observed that the managers in the Yorkshire woolen industry possessed a pushing, hardworking attitude (which led to the introduction of machinery) and concentrated on cheaper, coarse goods, for which there was a market. As a result the Yorkshire woolen industry flourished, while the woolen industry in East Anglia and the West of England, not driven by this attitude or concentrating on coarser cloth, declined. Though a covering law based on only three instances seems insecure, the reasoning here is probably based on covering laws of a far wider provenance, such as "Hard work leads to success," "The adoption of machinery lowers costs," and "Goods for which there is a market sell."

But it is in his discussion of slavery as the most important cause of the American Civil War that McCullagh makes his most fruitful suggestion. "Basic causes," he writes, "are usually causes which were common to the causal antecedents of each of a cluster of activities being regarded by an historian as a whole."[30] He then cites David Potter's judgment that in the events leading to the Civil War slavery was such a cause. This is an important observation. The historian traces the sequence of events from the Compromise of 1850 to the outbreak of war in 1861 and finds that slavery—not tariffs, not the bank, not public lands—repeatedly lay at the heart of disputes. McCullagh seeks to distinguish between "basic cause" and "most important cause," but the distinction seems artificial. One might say that "the most important cause" is the one that emerges most often in the colligatory chain leading to an event, and "the basic cause" is the cause of that and other causes. Thus a Marxist might say that the plantation system was the basic cause of the Civil War, since it was the cause of Southerners' adherence to slavery, of their opposition to tariffs, of their loyalty to state banks, and of their fear of cheap public lands. On the other hand, if a desire to protect slavery caused these other attitudes, it might be characterized as basic.

Raymond Martin defines "more important" in the following manner: A is a more important cause of p than is B when, had B not occurred, something would have occurred more closely approximating p (the event to be explained) than had A not occurred. The example Martin gives makes clear the meaning of "more closely approximates p": the barbarian invasions are a more important cause of the fall of the Roman Empire than were uninventiveness and lack of enterprise, since the barbarian invasions would have led to something like the fall of the Roman

30. Ibid., 204.

Empire even had the Romans in the West been inventive and enterprising.[31] The reasoning here is the same that McCullagh proposes: what is the probability of the effect occurring in the absence of cause A, all the other causes being present? And what is the probability of the effect occurring in the absence of B, all the other causes being present? Once again, counterfactual reasoning is required. One could ask how many empires have fallen for lack of inventiveness and enterprise, with no barbarian invasions threatening, and how many, though inventive and enterprising, have fallen because of barbarian invasions. But the sample of fallen empires being small, only an Arnold Toynbee would follow that path. Another possibility would be, in a grand exercise in counterfactual history, to trace the history of the Roman Empire, assuming at every step the presence of inventiveness and enterprise and the presence of barbarian invasions, then to trace the history of the Roman Empire, assuming at every step the absence of barbarian invasions and the absence of inventiveness and enterprise. Most historians would eschew this daunting task. Instead they would trace the web of events leading to the collapse of the Roman Empire, observing how often barbarian invasions played a crucial role, how often a lack of inventiveness and enterprise played a crucial role. The more important cause would be that which was more often crucial to the unfolding of events.

Richard Miller introduces two new concepts: depth-as-necessity and depth-as-priority.[32] He defines depth-as-necessity as follows: a cause X of Y is too shallow to explain why Y occurred, if Z would have produced some causal substitute for X, bringing Y about in some other way. Thus, even had President Hindenburg not named Hitler as chancellor, the political needs and powers of German business and of the military would have forced Hindenburg or his successor to have installed a Nazi government anyway. McCullagh would have put it this way: the absence of Hitler's nomination would have increased the probability of the Nazi's coming to power far less than the absence of the needs and power of German business and the military. Yet Miller's way of expressing it has the advantage that it emphasizes the importance of overdetermination in historical interpretation. Hindenburg's nomination of Hitler is of less importance because (counterfactual reasoning upon the world of politics in Germany in 1933 tells us) there existed so many other ways that German business and the military could have installed a Nazi government.

Miller defines depth-as-priority as follows: Z has depth-as-priority, and X is too shallow to explain the occurrence of Y, if X brings about Y

---

31. Martin, *The Past Within Us,* 64–83.
32. Miller, *Fact and Method,* 98–105.

only in circumstances in which Z is present and in which Z also caused X. Thus the circumstances in which the rightward drift of the middle class produced the Nazi seizure of power might have to include the dominance of the German elites, which was present in 1933 and which was also responsible for that rightward drift. On close examination, depth-as-priority is only another way of describing the basic cause, the cause of causes. The cause of causes here is the dominance of the German elites, which brought about both the rightward drift of the middle classes and the immediate seizure of power by the Nazis.

The principal conclusion that arises from this survey of what philosophers of history have said about discovering "the more important causes" is that the task is a complicated one. It is not simply a matter of finding the more abnormal condition among the initial conditions causing an event. Indeed a second conclusion that arises from this survey is that the deductive model at the macro level is useless in the search for the more important causes. Somewhat more useful is counterfactual reasoning, though if this is used on a long causal chain, it becomes suspect. The best solution is to look for those causes that emerge again and again in the web of events that leads up to the explanandum event, especially those that emerge at crucial junctures in that web and those that might be regarded as the cause of other causes. This is what Charles Beard did in his *Economic Interpretation of the Constitution of the United States*, and a careful examination of his arguments shows both the fruitfulness and the pitfalls of this approach.

Beard begins by boldly announcing his thesis, namely, that "economic motives were behind the movement for a reconstruction of the system" and that one form of property, personal property, was "the dynamic element in the movement for the new Constitution."[33] Having declared his thesis, he now faces the need to prove it, which he does in the first place by tracing the major events that led to the establishment of the Constitution: the growth of dissatisfaction with the Articles of Confederation, the movement leading to the election of delegates to a constitutional convention, the proceedings in the convention, the decision to seek ratification of the new constitution by state conventions, the election of delegates to the state conventions, and the proceedings in those conventions. Within each of these six steps, which collectively are an exercise in linear colligation, Beard proceeds in a manner I have chosen to call analytical colligation; that is, he proceeds from the event to the author of the event, from the author of the event to the author's motives and purposes, and from the author's motives and purposes to the etiol-

33. Beard, *Economic Interpretation*, 51, 73.

ogy of those motives and purposes. Readers of *The Economic Interpretation of the Constitution of the United States* will know that Beard devoted great labors to discovering the authors of those events. In doing so he proved a master of the art of parallel colligation. With a great wealth of information he seeks to show that throughout all these steps the propertyless were largely excluded from participation, the owners of land (realty) opposed change, and the owners of personal property (money, public securities, manufacturing capital, and commercial capital) favored change. This careful identification of the authors of the Constitution is the most convincing part of his interpretation.

He then seeks to discover the motives that led the owners of land (mostly small farmers in debt) to oppose the Constitution and owners of personal wealth (especially those holding public securities) to favor it. Here he relies heavily on rational explanation or situational analysis. Reason tells us that creditors—merchants, manufacturers, holders of public securities—would be the beneficiaries of a strong federal government that could secure the western lands, protect manufacturing and shipping, maintain a sound currency, and repay the public debt. Reason tells us that farmers in debt might fear a strong federal government that would prevent the inflation of money and suppress Shay rebellions. Beard, of course, is not aware of the extent to which he is relying upon rational explanation; nor, for that matter, does he rely solely upon it. He cites some empirical evidence showing that economic motives played a role in these men's actions—petitions from merchants and manufacturers asserting the need for tariffs, and arguments in *The Federalist Papers* about the need to protect property.

He devotes less space to a study of the etiology of these motives, since it is so apparent to him that people will always act to promote their own economic well-being and that their class defines their economic well-being. He finds the most convincing testimony to the truth of this observation to be the fact that people in identical economic situations, that is, in the same class, form identical political beliefs. Thus he observes that the debtor class in the several states had developed common political interests, such as advocacy of paper money and opposition to imprisonment for debt.[34] It is this assumption, that economic interests shape political beliefs, that makes the economic element "basic" in Beard's interpretation. It is not merely that economic interests appear in his explanatory scheme more often than political interests; economic interests shape those political interests. Here one is back to the logic of explanation, not the logic of interpretation, and Beard's task is to prove that economic interests

34. Ibid., 28.

shape political ones. This he does primarily by establishing a correlation between certain economic interests and certain political beliefs. Members of the debtor class always favor paper money; members of the propertied class (holders of personalty) always favor sound money. He even has a theory to explain the correlation, namely, that people invariably support policies of which they are the beneficiaries.

The explicitness of Beard's economic interpretation of the Constitution allows one to see clearly many elements of the logic of historical interpretation. The fallacies in his interpretation likewise tell us much about the logic of historical interpretation. There are three fallacies that particularly permeate his work: an arbitrary reduction of the explanandum event, a failure to summarize the debates in the convention, and a capricious attribution of motives. Though I treat each separately, each is but a variant of one egregious fallacy—source mining.

Beard purports to offer an interpretation of the Constitution, which thus becomes the explanandum event of the complete explanation, of which his interpretation is an abbreviation. But he defines that explanandum event in a remarkably narrow manner, reducing a complex and varied document to a mere economic document. "The Constitution," he writes, "was essentially an economic document based upon the concept that the fundamental private rights of property are anterior to government and morally beyond the reach of popular majorities."[35] And he thereupon discusses those clauses that prohibit the emission of paper money, forbid the states to impair the obligation of contract, and grant the federal government the power to regulate interstate commerce. The other seventy-eight clauses in the Constitution he either ignores or depicts as serving an economic purpose (thus the new government should have an army to guard against "desperate debtors" but not, presumably, to guard against foreign enemies).[36] True, he has explained a part of the Constitution, but only a small part.

The second fallacy is a failure to trace in detail the debates in the convention or, rather, to summarize fairly the concerns that emerge from a detailed tracing of those debates. Beard acknowledges that he ought to trace the debates over every clause, but pleads "that an entire volume would scarce suffice to present the results of such a survey and an undertaking of this character is accordingly impossible here."[37] Yet when it serves his purpose, he descends to such detail. He describes how on 26 July Mason and Pinckney favored a landed qualification for members of

35. Ibid., 324.
36. Ibid., 88.
37. Ibid., 153.

Congress. Gouverneur Morris was on his feet in an instant. King sagely remarked that there might be a danger in imposing a landed qualification, because "it would exclude the monied interest, whose aid might be essential in particular emergencies to the public safety."[38] The historian who offers an interpretation of the making of the Constitution has a duty to examine in detail the debates on every clause. And though he cannot fit that detail into a single volume, he should present a summary in which all concerns expressed in those debates are proportionately stated. Otherwise he is guilty of source mining, that is, of mining his sources for only that information that will support his thesis.

The third fallacy committed by Beard is to search only for the economic concerns that motivated the authors of the Constitution. He is quite candid in stating that this will be his method. On pages 53 and 54 he declares that he will "study the economic forces," "inquire into their economic sources," describe "the economic interests of all the members," "describe the economic forces in the community," and make a minute study "of the economic interests of the leading spirits in Congress and the state legislatures and outside of legislative chambers." He says not a word about investigating other forces and interests—religious, political, legal, moral—and their sources. He is a prospector mining for gold, and only gold will he find. Further, he is true to his announced method of illustrating his thesis. Again and again he attributes to their possession of public securities the support that members of the convention and of the state legislatures gave to the Constitution.[39] Never does he discuss other possible motives; about them he is silent. This is source mining with a vengeance.

I have borrowed the concept of source mining from J. H. Hexter, who used it in a celebrated review of Christopher Hill's *Change and Continuity in Seventeenth-Century England*.[40] There is no need here to enter into the controversy that arose over Hexter's criticism of Hill, since I only wish to borrow the concept, not to defend or to oppose its application to Hill. Furthermore, I have extended the use of the concept beyond Hexter's use of it. For Hexter source mining "is the examination of a corpus of writing solely with a view to discovering what it says on a particular matter narrowly defined," and he cites as an example the cultivation of asparagus. Source mining of this kind Hexter regards as appropriate and legitimate. What he regards as inappropriate and illegitimate is to examine a corpus of writings solely with a view to advancing a thesis. I have

38. Ibid., 166–67.
39. Ibid., 74–151.
40. *Times Literary Supplement*, 24 October 1975, 1250–52.

chosen to apply source mining also to the construction of an interpretation. A historian constructing such an interpretation would be guilty of
source mining if he or she abbreviated a total explanation solely with a
view to advancing a thesis. This is what Beard appears to have done. He
is not alone, of course. Many historians do it. John Morrill, for example,
presented an interpretation of the English Civil War entitled "England's
Wars of Religion."[41] By concentrating on the religious issues leading to
the civil war and ignoring the political one's, by mining sermons, broadsides, and tracts for arguments about episcopacy and the Book of Common Prayer, and by ignoring pamphlets, broadsides, and tracts written
about Strafford's impeachment, the Militia Ordinance, and the Nineteen
Propositions, he presented a plausible case that the civil war was indeed
a war of religion. But a historian ought not to follow whim in the construction of an interpretation, Karl Popper notwithstanding. He or she
must follow certain rules, among them the injunction not to ignore
events, issues, motives, and structures that occupy a central place in the
web of events leading to the phenomenon to be explained. These events,
issues, motives, and structures should bear the same proportionate
weight in the interpretation as they do in the explanation.

Hexter also accuses Hill of being a "lumper," which he contrasts with
being a "splitter." "Lumpers" do not like untidiness. Rather than noticing
differences, they see connections. They want to put the past into boxes,
and not too many of them. "Splitters," on the other hand, accept untidiness, differences, and separateness.[42] In this dichotomy, "lumpers" is the
pejorative term, but it is hard to see how any interpretation of the past
could be constructed without "lumping." As Taine observed, there were
twenty million Frenchmen whose myriad activities led to the French Revolution. The mind of the historian cannot begin to comprehend this movement without putting people and events into boxes, and not too many of
them. Hexter does realize this, hinting that "splitting historians" were
"willing to leave the Temple of Clio in a shambles." And he soon distinguishes between "compulsive lumpers" and the "more moderate variety."[43] The compulsive lumpers are the great system builders like Hegel,
Marx, Spengler, and Toynbee; the more moderate variety may be permitted, for example, to lump historians into two boxes, labeled lumpers and
splitters. The issue is not whether historians shall lump; it is whether they
shall lump accurately and whether they shall lump productively. One

41. John Morrill, "England's Wars of Religion," a paper read before the Conference on
British Studies, Toronto, October 1984.
42. *Times Literary Supplement*, 24 October 1975, 1251–52.
43. Ibid., 1252.

may lump apples and oranges together as fruit, but one may not lump apples and carrots together as fruit. Merchants and tradespeople may be grouped together as bourgeoisie, but not merchants and gentry. Likewise apples and carrots may be classified as food, but this would be of little help to the botanist. Taine once said that all history is explained by three factors—race, *milieu*, and the moment—but this lumping of historical factors into three boxes is far too abstract to be of any use.[44]

The conclusion that flows from these considerations is that historians are not free to construct whatever whimsical interpretation they wish. In constructing an interpretation they are governed by rules, rules that are objective, "objective" in the sense that they are accepted by nearly all historians. Historians, though they instinctively rely on these rules, have given little thought to them. There is practically no literature on the rules of interpretation. This being so, it would be foolhardy to attempt to give a systematic statement of those rules. It would be useful, however, to give a preliminary statement about what some of those rules might be. In the first place, all classifications should be accurate and meaningful. Second, samples should be truly representative. Third, summations made from steps in a linear sequence or from instances from parallel colligation or from purposes revealed by action explanation or from factors in the etiology of purpose should reflect the true proportions of those steps, instances, purposes, and factors found in the total explanation. Where possible—as in parallel colligation—that summation should be stated in quantitative terms. Where difficult to state in quantitative terms—as with episodes in linear sequences or the purposes of the authors of an action or the factors shaping those purposes—the ensuing impressionistic summation should not be idiosyncratic. The best control on such idiosyncratic summations is the impressions formed by other historians who have worked through the same material. And finally, in making such summations, the historian should give more weight to the crucial or critical episodes, that is, to those which are abnormal rather than routine and to those which are consequential rather than inconsequential.

It is the difficulty in distinguishing between the critical and the routine conditions among the initial conditions causing an event that led Karl Popper to declare that interpretation must be personal.

> The attempt to follow causal chains into the remote past would not help in the least, for every concrete effect with which we might start has a great number of different partial causes; that is

---

44. Quoted in Gooch, *History and Historians in the Nineteenth Century,* 239.

> to say, initial conditions are very complex, and most of them have
> little interest for us.
>
> The only way out of this difficulty is, I believe, consciously to
> introduce a *preconceived selective point of view* into one's history;
> that is, to write *that history which interests us.* This does not mean
> that we may twist the facts until they fit into a framework of
> preconceived ideas, or that we may neglect the facts that do not
> fit. On the contrary, all available evidence which has a bearing on
> our point of view should be considered carefully and objec-
> tively. . . . But it means that we need not worry about all those
> facts and aspects which have no bearing upon our point of view
> and which therefore do not interest us.[45]

If interpreted in one way this muddled excerpt presents no difficulties. If
a *preconceived selective point of view,* which Popper later calls a historical
interpretation, only governs the historian's choice of topic, then his
analysis is quite unexceptionable. He who is interested in the history of
the cultivation of asparagus will naturally select facts about the cultivation of asparagus. But if he means that a *preconceived selective point of view*
should govern which facts are chosen to explain the occurrence of a
phenomenon, then it is a highly dangerous doctrine. And the final sentence in his first paragraph suggests that this is his meaning. Such a
proposition reduces an interpretation to the expression of the whims of
the historian.

There is one form of subjective interpretation that is acceptable—if
carefully labeled "a personal interpretation." This is an interpretation in
which a historian traces a long chain of causation through initial conditions that are necessary, though not sufficient, to explain what they
purport to explain. James Burke has done this in an episode entitled
"The Long Chain," which formed a part of his television series called
Connections: A Personal Interpretation. In order to show that the growth of
trade in the seventeenth century led to the creation of the German dye
industry in the nineteenth century, Burke takes the viewer on the following breathtaking romp through history: the growth of trade led to the
invention of the Dutch *fluyt,* which led the English to seek better ships,
which led to the painting of the hulls of ships with tar, which led to a
demand for tar, which led Dundonald to seek to produce tar as a by-
product of turning coal into coke, which led to the production of the
waste product naptha, which led Macintosh to purchase naptha to clean
his dyeing machines, which led him accidentally to discover that naptha

45. Popper, *The Poverty of Historicism,* 150.

dissolved rubber, which led to the invention of the waterproof mackintosh and other products, which led William Perkin in 1856 to discover that one chemical compound in the sludge, remaining after naptha was extracted, resembled quinine, which led Perkin to seek to make quinine from the sludge, which led others to see what dyes could be made from coal tar, which led to the German dye industry.[46] In fairness to Burke, it must be said that he occasionally introduces other necessary conditions. Yet his choice of necessary conditions remains largely personal and differs from those other historians might choose. As Ernest Nagel has observed, "though the explanations that historians propose for a given event frequently differ, they are not necessarily incompatible. Accounts only differ in mentioning different necessary conditions."[47] He goes on to observe that though historical explanations do not state the sufficient conditions for a given happening, neither do scientific explanations always do so.

Nevertheless, Burke's long chain strikes one as a *jeu d'esprit*. It certainly reveals the simplicity of such an explanation. There must certainly be a better way to explain and to interpret the rise of the German dye industry, or any other historical phenomenon. And there is. A more traditional historian would pursue a multicausal approach, as does Lawrence Stone in *The Causes of the English Revolution*. Having more than one cause to discuss, having perhaps four or five or six, Stone frequently falls into the habit of listing them, a habit for which other scholars have chided him. To this chiding Stone has quite rightly replied that he believes in a multicausal approach to historical explanation.

> All my work has been based on two fundamental hypotheses about how the historical process works. The first is that great events must have important causes, and not merely trivial ones. The second is that all great events must have multiple causes. This eclectic approach towards causation has given rise to a certain amount of negative criticism. Many scholars whose judgment I respect have described the assemblage of a multiplicity of causes for any given phenomenon as "a shopping list," the mere unweighted enumeration of a whole series of variables of widely different types and significance. This is true, but an argument for multiple causation can be made on the grounds used by Max Weber. They are convincing, provided that they form a set of

46. Burke, *Connections*, 185–206 (in the book arising from the television series, Burke drops the subtitle *A Personal Interpretation*).
47. Nagel, *The Structure of Science*, 581–82.

"elective affinities," held together not by mere random chance but by a system of logical integration that points them all in the same direction and makes them mutually reinforcing.[48]

But a careful reading of *The Causes of the English Revolution* shows that Stone does not list the initial conditions that, subsumed under the appropriate covering law, explain the occurrence of an event. Rather, what he lists are the principal factors that emerge from tracing the web of events leading to the phenomenon to be explained, in this case the English Revolution. Thus he asserts that Puritanism "provided an essential element in the Revolution," that "the ideology of the common law had become a powerful independent force" and led to the abolition of the prerogative courts, and that "the bottomless duplicity of King Charles" played "a decisive part" in the coming of the revolution.[49] These are generalizations from linear colligation; he also generalizes from parallel colligation. Though his search for the authors of the revolution is not methodical, he does focus on members of Parliament and justices of the peace; does discuss the role of the clergy, barristers, and merchant oligarchies; does declare that 25 percent of the peers opposed the King; does note that the Catholic gentry tended to support the King, and the Puritan gentry, Parliament; does assert that small merchants, tradesmen, and artisans supported Parliament; and does observe that the laboring poor played no part except as cannon fodder for each side.[50]

Stone is particularly interested in the motives of the opponents of the King, about which he generalizes boldly at times, cautiously at other times. Thus of the peers who supported Parliament he declares, "What they all had in common was a sympathy to religious reform, and a traditional medieval hostility to royal constitutional autocracy." But of the gentry he can only write, "The motives for the alignments of the gentry when the war began are still not wholly clear." On the other hand, he says confidently of the English troops at Newburn that the suspicion that the King intended a union with Rome "was the main cause of the refusal of the troops to fight the Scots"—a generalization about the motives of numerous troopers (though one suspects that an observer at the scene made the generalization).[51] But what interests Stone even more than a characterization of these motives is their etiology. This is evident in the section entitled "Precipitants," in which he shows how the "ruthless and

48. Stone, "A Life of Learning," 19.
49. Stone, *The Causes of the English Revolution*, 100, 105, 138.
50. Ibid., 95–97, 143–45.
51. Ibid., 122, 143–144.

uncompromising nature of the royal policies after 1629 steadily drove more and more of the silent majority into the arms of the opposition."[52] He then describes how a religious, a political, a social, and an economic reaction drove people into opposition. Though he gives details about Laud's ecclesiastical policies and Charles's fiscal policies, he does not mention particular persons who were offended by particular policies. But presumably he is generalizing from separate investigations into why persons were driven into opposition.

In the section entitled "Preconditions" Stone turns his attention to those changes in structure that helped cause the English Revolution. What follows is not a detailed narrative of those changes, explaining them by resort to cumulative colligation, but rather a series of generalizations about the factors that emerge from such a detailed study. He lists six such factors: economic growth, social changes, a decline in foreign and domestic threats, a loss of confidence in the leaders of society, the rise of an opposition, and the emergence of new ideas and values (though in some sense these are merely a description of the changes in structure). He then describes the factors that led to each of these changes, and in many instances the causes for the emergence of those factors. In Stone's complex view of past developments there are factors within factors within factors. It would be tedious to summarize all his arguments, but one illustration will help to illuminate his method. A principal social development was the rise of the gentry. Three factors led to their rise: an increase in numbers, an increase in wealth, and a different attitude toward the local magnates and toward the state. The different attitude toward the local magnates, in turn, arose because of five factors: the absenteeism of the magnates, the substitution of economic rents for customary rents, the extension of the role of the central government in local affairs, the education of the sons of gentlemen at school and university rather than in the households of noblemen, and service by the gentry as justices of the peace rather than in noble households.[53] In all of this Stone is generalizing from particulars with which he is familiar but which he does not describe for the reader.

Scholars have, as Stone remarks, criticized him for assembling a multiplicity of causes, a mere "shopping list," "an unweighted enumeration of a whole series of variables of widely different types and significance."[54] This seems unfair, since in *The Causes of the English Revolution* he does explicitly point to the most important preconditions, the most im-

52. Ibid., 118.
53. Ibid., 58–117, esp. 71–74.
54. Stone, "A Life of Learning," 19.

portant factors, the critical events. Thus he singles out four preconditions as "the most salient elements in the manifold preconditions,"
namely, the want of a standing army and paid bureaucracy, the decline of
the aristocracy and rise of the gentry, the spread of Puritanism, and the
erosion of confidence in holders of high office. Indeed, he declares that
the rise of the gentry "is politically the single most important social development of the age."[55] He likewise singles out factors within such developments. Thus he writes of the gentry's becoming Puritan, "Education in
the universities, studying the works of Calvin and Beza under the direction of Puritan dons, was undoubtedly a most important, perhaps critically important, factor."[56] What makes these events critical is the fact that
momentous consequences flowed from them. What makes the Puritan
dons an important factor is the fact that they influenced so many gentlemen. What makes the rise of the gentry so important is the major role the
gentry played in the coming of the English Revolution.[57] It is part of the
task of an interpretation to emphasize important factors and critical
events, as well as to abbreviate the total explanation of that event. Indeed,
an accurate abbreviation should illuminate the important factors.

If there is a criticism of Stone's interpretation, it is not that he fails to
assign weight to the more important factors and events in his interpretation. Rather, it is that he fails to demonstrate, through narrative, that
these factors were in fact the forces that shaped events, and that certain
events were in fact critical. He does not, through a careful tracing of the
web of events, show why he came to the conclusion that these were the
important factors and critical events. Stone is aware that such a web of
events exists, calling the web "multiple helix chains of causation more
complicated than those of DNA itself."[58] (His metaphor marks a triumph
of rhetoric over truth; the web resembles a cone, not a multiple helix.)
Furthermore, in his researches he has certainly traced this complex web
and has generalized honestly from it. But the undergraduate who reads
his book and who has never traced that web can only accept it on faith.

To this charge Stone might answer that space did not allow him to
include such a narrative. Given that I have argued that an interpretation
is an abbreviation, such a defense carries considerable weight. But need
he abbreviate so severely? The narrative in *The Causes of the English
Revolution* is very thin, with Stone skipping from the introduction of an
English liturgy into Scotland to the defeat of England in war to the City's

55. Stone, *The Causes of the English Revolution*, 75, 116.
56. Ibid., 100.
57. Ibid., 122, 128, 138.
58. Ibid., 146.

refusal of a loan to the settlement of 1641 to the Irish Rebellion to the attempted arrest of the Five Members to the Militia Ordinance and so to the outbreak of war. Episodes in between are not described. The historian has an obligation to show that a particular factor, say Charles's duplicity, did occur over and over again and did lead many persons to distrust him. This can only be done with a full narrative of events. There is reason to believe that Stone now realizes this, for in 1979 he wrote an article praising the revival of narrative.[59] It is no accident that historians are returning to narrative. The reason lies in the principal argument of this book, namely, that explanation requires colligation as well as correlation and that the proper literary form for colligation is narrative.

This is less true for interpretation than for explanation. When historians seek to explain, they tear apart, they deduce, they analyze, they trace minutely. When they set out to interpret, they put together, they add up, they synthesize, they generalize from particulars. What microcolligation tears apart, interpretation puts together again. Imagine that a carpenter builds a splendid house, a frame house with many alcoves and closets and dormer windows. Many years later another carpenter, admiring the house and wondering how it is constructed, attacks it with a crowbar and claw hammer, taking it apart board by board. When he is finished the various boards lie there in disarray. But then he puts together what he has torn apart—only in a different way. He piles all the two-by-fours in one pile, the two-by-sixes in another, the shingles in a third, the window frames in a fourth. And he carefully counts and records how many there are of each. This is what historians do when, having torn the past apart, they put it back together again. The analogy is, no doubt, imperfect, but it is also illuminating. It points to the fact that the logic of historical interpretation is inductive rather than deductive. The historian is generalizing from particulars, not tracing a sequence of events ever more minutely or subsuming events under covering laws.

The fact that the logic of historical interpretation is inductive rather than deductive helps to explain the absence of laws in historical works. In fashioning an interpretation the historian generalizes from initial conditions, causes, and factors discovered while pursuing a total explanation. His or her conclusions therefore take the form of a generalization of fact, not a generalization of law. May Brodbeck has suggested that a generalization of fact does not have explanatory power. A law, she observes, "goes far beyond the evidence. If it did not, but was just a summary of observations, it would have neither explanatory nor predic-

---

59. Stone, "The Revival of Narrative."

tive power."[60] She is certainly correct that generalizations of fact have no predictive power, since the moment one grants them predictive power, they become generalizations of law. But do they have no explanatory power? Given the nature of a total explanation, leading through an almost infinitely complex web of events, surely generalizations about the initial conditions, causes, and factors at work within that web contribute to the clarity of the explanation. Were a person able to comprehend this total web of events, to comprehend the totality of the actions of twenty million Frenchmen in 1789, then May Brodbeck would be correct in saying that mere generalizations have no explanatory power. But the human mind is not able to do so. It follows, then, that if historians are to explain rightly the course of events, they must both tear apart the past through the minutest colligation and build it up again by generalizing from the particulars thus laid bare.

---

60. Brodbeck, "Explanation, Prediction, and 'Imperfect' Knowledge," 247.

12 CAUSAL EXPLANATION AND THE USES OF HISTORY

Therewith the saying *Historia vitae magistra* takes on a higher yet a humbler sense. We wish Experience to make us, not shrewder (for next time), but wiser (for ever).

— Jacob Burckhardt, *Reflections on History*

The argument of this book appears to give little support to the proposition that the study of history has a practical value. If macrocorrelation is a failure, then where will one find those laws that allow the historian to draw lessons from the past? If one explains the occurrence of an event by tracing the unique sequence of events leading up to it, then how does that explanation help the historian to learn from the past? If one employs in that explanation covering laws that are so trivial as to be platitudinous, how do those laws help to instruct the statesman, the legislator, or the citizen? Since the logic of historical explanation depends heavily upon colligation, it does appear that we cannot draw lessons from the past that will allow us to guide our conduct in the future.

Skepticism about the practical utility of the study of history has existed for some decades. Throughout most of the twentieth century historians have doubted that one could draw lessons from the study of the past. In 1898 Charles Langlois and Charles Seignobos declared, in what was long regarded as the authoritative manual for the writing of history, "It is an obsolete illusion to suppose that history supplies information of practical utility in the conduct of life."[1] Geoffrey Barraclough, a distinguished English historian, concurs. "It is well," he writes, "that the illusion that history has a direct, positive, assessable contribution to make to the conduct of current affairs has been jettisoned."[2] Arthur Schlesinger Jr., reflecting on the American scene, paints a similar picture. Referring to the proposition that the knowledge of yesterday provides guidance for tomorrow, he writes:

> This is a point, it should immediately be said, on which professional historians, on the whole, have few illusions among themselves. They privately regard history as its own reward. . . . Many professional historians—perhaps most—reject the idea that generalization is the goal of history. We all respond, in Marc Bloch's phrase, to "the thrill of learning singular things." Indeed, it is the commitment to concrete reconstruction as against abstract generalization—to life as against laws—which distinguishes history from sociology.[3]

Such skepticism about the practical utility of the study of history has not always prevailed. The Greeks and the Romans certainly did not share it. Polybius believed that "a knowledge of history is the most satisfactory training and education for affairs," and Cicero declared that "history is a storehouse containing all the countless lessons of the past."[4] At the Renaissance this belief in the pragmatic value of history was revived and prevailed until the end of the eighteenth century. From Machiavelli through Voltaire historians regarded the past as an arsenal of lessons, maxims, errors, and follies, from which the statesman could profitably learn. As Edmund Burke put it, "In history, a great volume is unrolled for our instruction, drawing the materials of future wisdom from the past errors and infirmities of mankind."[5]

What finally brought this belief in the practical utility of the study of history to an end was the rise of historicism during the late eighteenth and early nineteenth centuries. Historicism undercut the pragmatic use of history both by denying that the past resembled the present and by insisting that whereas science deals with the abstract aspects of phenom-

1. Langlois and Seignobos, *Introduction to the Study of History*, 319.
2. Quoted in a *Times Literary Supplement* editorial for 27 February 1953.
3. Schlesinger, *Bitter Heritage*, 81–82.
4. Quoted in Milburn, *Early Christian Interpretations of History*, 3.
5. Quoted in Schlesinger, *Bitter Heritage*, 82.

ena, phenomena that are repeated, history deals with events that are unique. Historians from Tacitus to Hume had indeed believed that the past resembled the present, that nothing new appeared under the sun. The Roman emperor Marcus Aurelius believed that if a man attained the age of forty he would have seen all that has happened or could happen in the future, and David Hume voiced similar sentiments.[6] The historicists, abetted first by the Romantic revolt and then by Darwinian evolutionary thought, held that the essence of reality was change and that the duty of the historian was to reconstruct a past society on its own terms and to trace how the present grew out of a profoundly different past. Even human nature changes—thus Marc Bloch explicitly rejects Machiavelli's and Hume's belief that man is changeless.[7] But if the past is unlike the present, what use, aside from satisfying our curiosity about the past, does the study of history have? Imagine a society wholly unlike ours, say the society of a colony of ants. Would a statesman look to the conduct of ants for guidance in the world of people? Obviously not. This raises the question, what then is the use of studying history? The answer that the nineteenth century gave was the genetic use of history. We study the past in order to discover how the present grew out of the past. "History," argue Langlois and Seignobos, "enables us to understand the present in so far as it explains the origin of the existing state of things."[8] Hugh Trevor-Roper echoes this sentiment when he declares, "We study it [history] not merely for amusement—though it can be amusing—but in order to discover how we have come to where we are."[9]

The genetic use of history certainly helps us to understand how we came to be what we are. Only by studying the rise of Parliament can one understand why Britain today is governed by a Parliament. But does such an understanding have any practical utility? Those who espouse the genetic use of history suggest that it does, in three ways at least. Tracing how the present grew out of the past allows us (1) to understand the present better, (2) to understand the process of change itself, and (3) to extrapolate into the future. It is worth looking at each of these three propositions to see what truth attaches to each.

To the question, Does an understanding of how we came to be what we are help us to understand ourselves better? the answer must be both yes and no. It must be no because often the study of the origins of an

6. Black, *The Art of History*, 95–96.
7. Bloch, *The Historian's Craft*, 41.
8. Langlois and Seignobos, *Introduction to the Study of History*, 319.
9. "The Rise of Christian Europe: The Great Recovery," *Listener Magazine*, 28 November 1963, 871.

institution or habit or custom says nothing about its nature today that we did not already know. Bloch, celebrating the search for origins, gives the example of the custom of farming long, narrow fields in northern France. He then asks, "How do we account for it?" And answers the question by tracing the existence of long, narrow fields back to prehistorical times.[10] This explanation undoubtedly satisfies our curiosity about the origins of this practice, but offers no practical advice to the farmer or agronomist. Or take the example of the fire in the alley filled with trash. A historian imbued with the genetic impulse might search into the origins of the alley, why it was there, why it was narrow. He or she might discover in the municipal records who built the buildings enclosing the alley, when they built them, and why they built them. Such information would satisfy our curiosity, but would be of no practical use to the fire chief charged with preventing fires in the city. To believe that an understanding of origins invariably promotes an understanding of the present may be called the genetic fallacy.

But it is only a fallacy to believe that a knowledge of origins *invariably* promotes an understanding of the present. It is no fallacy to believe that on some occasions it does. Take again the example of the fire in the alley. The fire chief might want to know why the local inhabitants dumped their trash in the alley. Had they only done it on this one occasion? Or was it a custom? If a custom, how old was it? and how deeply entrenched? These are questions a historian could answer. The historian might discover that it was a deeply entrenched habit, even that it had arisen some years ago during a strike of garbage collectors and had continued after the strike had ended. To the fire chief the origin of the custom in a strike is of little importance, but the fact that it was a deeply entrenched custom is of great importance. He or she must make an energetic effort to eradicate it. The fire chief is here dealing with a tradition, and it is upon tradition that the historicists focus their attention. Through tradition the past lives in the present, in the pattern of our lives, in our habits, customs, institutions. "But suppose," writes R. G. Collingwood,

> the past lives on in the present; suppose, though incapsulated in it, and at first sight hidden beneath the present's contradictory and more prominent features, it is still alive and active; then the historian may very well be related to the non-historian as the

10. Bloch, *The Historian's Craft*, 39–40. But Bloch does not approve of an obsessional concern with origins, especially in cases where it is inappropriate, as in the study of remote origins. He urges that one not confuse "ancestry" with explanation.

trained woodsman is to the ignorant traveller. "Nothing here but trees and grass," thinks the traveller, and marches on. "Look," says the woodsman, "there is a tiger in that grass." The historian's business is to reveal the less obvious features hidden from a careless eye in the present situation. What history can bring to moral and political life is a trained eye for the situation in which one has to act.[11]

By showing how the past still lives in us, historians increase our knowledge of ourselves, of our present character. They have deepened our consciousness of ourselves, which is the reason that Collingwood wrote elsewhere that "history is but human self-knowledge," and why Droysen wrote that "history is humanity's knowledge of itself."[12]

In a similar vein, history is praised for giving a person or a group a sense of identity. This is well illustrated in the rise of black history and perhaps never more eloquently expressed than by Eldridge Cleaver in *Soul on Ice.* Chiding those blacks who would decline to look into the past, he wrote, "Rather the past is an omniscient mirror; we gaze and see reflected there ourselves and each other—what we used to be, what we are today, how we got this way, and what we are becoming."[13]

But a careful examination of this language shows that it merely conceals the pragmatic use of history. What is being discovered is the habitual conduct of persons. Because that conduct has been what it has been in the past, one predicts that it will be so in the present and the future. Because blacks in the past have created great art, ruled kingdoms, shown courage, made scientific discoveries, written books, commanded troops, served in legislatures, and fought for freedom, one may conclude that they can and will do so in the present and future. People, of course, have exhibited vices as well as virtues, and one can predict they will continue to do so. Because the inhabitants of Ulster have exhibited sectarian strife in the past, politicians and statesmen predict that they will exhibit it in the future. This truth is often expressed in the observation that the past weighs heavily upon the present, which indeed it often does. And the more heavily it weighs on the present, the greater the ability of the politician to predict, if not alas to control, the vicious behavior. But this ability to predict is based on a basic postulate of the pragmatic use of the study of history, namely, that the present resembles the past.

11. Collingwood, *Autobiography*, 100.
12. Collingwood, as quoted by G. R. Beasley-Murray, in "Rudolph Bultman and Demythologizing," *The Listener,* 13 October 1965; Droysen, *Outline of the Principles of History,* 49.
13. Cleaver, *Soul on Ice*, 207.

Such behavior is not wrought in granite. Behavior changes, values change, institutions change, society changes. The more profound the change, of course, the less chance that one can reason from the past. Yet this limitation can be transcended if one focuses on the nature of the process of change itself. A biologist, equipped with a knowledge of the theory of natural selection and living in the age of dinosaurs, could not have predicted the emergence of humankind. He could, however, have predicted that life would evolve through a process of variation, struggle for existence, the survival of the fittest, and the transmission of favorable characteristics. The process that explains change does not itself change. Thus Christian historians have sought to describe the hand of God in change, philosophic historians (from Ibn Khaldun to Arnold Toynbee) to describe the process by which civilizations rise and fall, and liberal historians (chiefly Crane Brinton) to describe the process of revolutionary change. But undoubtedly the most ambitious attempt to describe the process of change is that of the Marxists. Recently the Marxist Jerzy Topolski, in his *Methodology of History*, has declared that the task of historical research is to explain the development of systems (i.e., societies) by describing the means and causes of that development. There are laws of social development, and it is the historian's task to elucidate them. Needless to say, Topolski finds that it is dialectical materialism that is the mechanism of that development.[14] Most historians, I believe, would dismiss all such attempts to describe the process of change as failures, but at a much more modest level historians do identify more or less permanent factors that lead to cumulative changes, as, for example, industrialization leads to urbanization. Any careful study in cumulative colligation will discover certain factors promoting change. But what needs to be said here is that the practical knowledge that arises from such an exercise is based on the main postulate of the pragmatic use of history, namely, that the present will continue to resemble the past.

A third practical use of the genetic approach to history is extrapolation, predicting the future on the basis of trends perceived in the past. Extrapolation should be distinguished from laws of development. A law of development cannot predict the appearance of something wholly new in the future, since a law is by definition a description of a correlation that holds in the present. A law declares that whenever A occurs, B will happen. The historian or scientist who propounds such a law has obviously already observed that both A and B exist. He or she may even wish to explain why such a correlation exists, and discover a theory that does indeed explain it. The theory may show how A leads to x, which leads to

14. Topolski, *Methodology of History*, 2–6, 208–13, 674–76.

y, which leads to *z*, which leads to B. But all stages in this development, each and every phenomenon, already exist. Auguste Comte's "law of three stages" illustrates this. He argues that humankind developed from a theological stage through a metaphysical stage to a scientific stage.[15] He does not, however, propose that this law predicts the appearance of a fourth stage. He brings the cognitive development of humankind to a close with the scientific stage. For that matter, Comte's "law of three stages" is not really a description of a process of change; it is a description of a unique development, the development by which humanity acquired its cognitive powers. Comte does not suggest that this process will continue in the future.

Karl Marx, on the other hand, believed he had discovered the mechanism of change: the law of superstructure. Assuming that there is such a law—a very great assumption—it resembles Darwin's theory of natural selection, which describes the mechanism or process that governs change in the natural world. Each species adapts to its environment, as the various species of turtles on the Galapagos islands adapted to the various environments on the several islands. The great difference between Darwin's theory and Marx's is that the processes of change Darwin described are known to operate throughout the natural world, whereas the process of change that Marx described does not in fact operate throughout the human world. Knowing the process of change has not allowed the Marxists to predict. The law of the superstructure was supposed to dictate that socialism would come in the advanced industrial societies. "History," writes Schlesinger, "thus far has refuted the central proposition in Marx's system of prediction."[16]

It is not by laws of development that one can predict the future, but by extrapolating from existing trends. One traces developments from an earlier time to the present, draws the curve of those developments on a graph, then continues the line, now a dotted line, into the future. Demographers thus forecast an increase in population, and planners plan according to that forecast. Such trends are to tradition (to make a fanciful comparison) what acceleration is to velocity in physics. What really matters is the fact that such trends, though they predict change, are dependent on factors that do not change. Thus demographers in the 1950s in the United States predicted a doubling and trebling of the population, but they no longer do so, since the United States now approaches a zero population growth. What happened was a feminist

15. For a perceptive analysis of Comte's thought, see Richard Vernon, "Auguste Comte and 'Development,' " 323–26.

16. Schlesinger, *Bitter Heritage*, 85.

revolt and a determination on the part of young women to have no family or a small one in order to be able to pursue a career. The factors operating in the 1950s—for example, a desire to marry and have four children—no longer operated. Marx sought to extrapolate when he predicted that the rich would grow richer and the poor grow poorer under capitalism. It was not an absurd prediction, since the real wages of the working class in Great Britain did fall between 1780 and 1820 and property owners did grow wealthier, but with the end of the heavy taxation accompanying the Napoleonic wars and with the end of the early demands for heavy capitalization, real wages began a slow, then a rapid, rise. Extrapolation, then, is a hazardous undertaking, but not an illegitimate one.

It should, however, be based on more recent, rather than more remote, trends, as the example of Marx's prediction shows. There is more rhetoric than truth in Winston Churchill's remark that "the further you can look back, the further you can see forward."[17] For highly abstract trends he may be right. From the history of the growth of disbelief from the twelfth century to the present, despite outbreaks of religious fervor in Puritan and Victorian England, one can hazard the prediction that religious belief will continue to decline in the future. But for less abstract trends, more recent history is a better guide than remote history because the factors shaping the more recent trends are more likely to operate in the future. What is patent is the fact that extrapolation depends on the future being like the past. The same factors that cause a trend now must continue in operation. Thus once again a practical application of the genetic use of history rests upon the main postulate of pragmatic history, namely, that the future will resemble the past.

It should occasion no surprise that the genetic use of history, divorced from the pragmatic uses concealed within it, has no utility. It should occasion no surprise because the principal postulate propounded by the advocates of the genetic use of history is that the past is unlike the present, that earlier societies were unique, that the duty of the historian is either to reconstruct those societies in their own terms or to trace how contemporary society grew out of those earlier, different societies. In moments of unbridled enthusiasm they even argue that all events are unique. The discordance between this postulate and that of the pragmatists' poses a fundamental question: is the past like or unlike the present? And the only sensible answer is that it is both, both like and unlike the present. How this is possible is well illustrated by Montaigne's observation that the human face is both unique and universal. When one

17. Quoted in Schlesinger, *Bitter Heritage,* 95.

looks at a friend, one knows instantly that he is Peter and no one else, and yet one also knows that he is a human being, a member of *Homo sapiens*, and not an ape or chimpanzee. Similarly, a historian studying the past knows that a particular society, say, that of the early Hebrews, is unique and yet at the same time that it exhibits features that are common to ours. Of these early Hebrews, whose society differs so profoundly from ours, C. S. Lewis could nevertheless observe, "In the Psalmists' tendency to chew over and over the cud of some injury . . . most of us can recognize something we have met in ourselves. We are, after all, blood-brothers to these ferocious, self-pitying, barbaric men."[18] And he goes on to argue that in the maledictory Psalms we can learn much that is relevant to our own lives. We can see how the memory of an injury may sour the soul of even the best of people, and that forgiveness is never an easy business. The basic truth is this: inasmuch as the past exhibits features that are common to our age, the study of its history can instruct us today.

Yet professional historians remain skeptical that the past can instruct us, remain skeptical that there is a pragmatic use to the study of history. Why should this be so? The answer, I believe, lies in the historian's exasperation at the abuse of the pragmatic use of history. Politicians, journalists, moralists, preachers, and propagandists ransack the past for lessons universally applicable to the present. What historian has not winced upon hearing a preacher declare that all history proves that blasphemy, drunkenness, and fornication lead to the downfall of kingdoms, or a politician assert that history shows that appeasement always fails, or a commencement orator declare that history shows that any person who believes in himself and works hard may reach the top. Such preachers, politicians, and orators, often guided by their prejudices, draw neat "lessons" from the past, which they then apply indiscriminately to the present. It was probably such abuses of the pragmatic use of history that led Jacob Burckhardt to declare that history teaches us wisdom, not lessons.

But how does one distinguish wisdom from lessons? An analogy drawn from bridge helps to answer this question. A tournament bridge player may play a particular hand brilliantly, but he does not play that hand brilliantly because he remembers how he played that same hand once before. The chances that he will ever be dealt the same thirteen cards are small and that his partner and opponents will be dealt identical hands even smaller. He has learned no "lesson" from playing that particular

---

18. Quoted in the *Times Literary Supplement*, review of C. S. Lewis, *Reflections on the Psalms*, 12 September 1959.

hand before. Yet he is a far better player than a beginner, and he is better because he is more experienced. He has learned "wisdom" from playing thousands of hands of bridge in the past, and that wisdom consists of a huge repertoire of rules, maxims, probabilities, strategies, and hunches. These rules, maxims, probabilities, strategies, and hunches he applies whenever new circumstances resemble older circumstances.[19] Similarly the politician, statesman, publicist, legislator, or citizen is wiser for his or her study of the past if he or she garners from that study a repertoire of rules, maxims, probabilities, strategies, and hunches and applies them in the appropriate circumstances.

The difference between lessons and wisdom can be vividly illustrated by listing some of the more foolish lessons drawn from the past. Thomas Macaulay describes one of them, James II's monotonous complaint, "I will make no concessions, my father made concessions, and he was beheaded." Such a lesson of history, as Macaulay observes, rests on two misconceptions. The first is a misreading of the causes of Charles's downfall. The second is drawing a lesson from a single instance. As Macaulay writes:

> Even if it had been true that concessions had been fatal to Charles the First, a man of sense would have remembered that a single experiment is not sufficient to establish a general rule even in a science much less complicated than the science of government; that, since the beginning of the world, no two political experiments were ever made of which all the conditions were exactly alike; and that the only way to learn civil prudence from history is to examine and compare an immense number of cases.[20]

Mistakes also occur when change overtakes the past. Thus it has become a truism that generals mistakenly fight the present war as if it were the previous war. Even diplomats make this mistake. Harold Nicolson has observed that Viscount Castlereagh in 1815 believed that France, not Prussia, threatened the liberties of the nations of Europe, even though Talleyrand urged the opposite. Castlereagh therefore favored placing a strong Prussia in the Rhineland. "In which illusion," writes Nicolson, "he was surrendering to the all too common error of estimating the

---

19. I have borrowed this analogy from Joseph R. Strayer and Hans Gatske, *The Mainstream of Civilization Since 1500*, viii.
20. Macaulay, *History of England*, 2:52.

factors of future stability in terms of those factors which had caused and influenced the recently concluded war."[21]

If it is a mistake to draw a lesson from a single instance and a mistake to draw a lesson from a different past, it is doubly a mistake to draw a lesson from a single instance from a different past. The most egregious recent example of this compounded error is the Munich analogy. The politicians and generals who have invoked the Munich analogy are legion. Schlesinger has suggested that someday a graduate student might write a doctoral dissertation on the influence of the Munich analogy on subsequent history. Schlesinger admits that Munich was a tragic mistake and that its lesson was that the appeasement of a highly wound-up and heavily armed totalitarian state makes further aggression likely. But it does not follow from this that all attempts to avert war by negotiations will lead to further aggression.[22] Churchill himself saw this when he rejected President Eisenhower's invocation of the Munich analogy in order to secure British backing of the French in Indochina. Churchill, unfortunately, was not in office two years later when his successor, Anthony Eden, invoked the lessons of Munich in the Suez crisis. Eden's mistake was to fail to see that Colonel Nasser was not Adolph Hitler, that 80 million impoverished Egyptians were not 150 million prosperous, educated, well-armed German chauvinists. He applied the lessons of Munich to a case that it did not fit. Churchill saw this danger.

> It may be well here to set down some principles of morals and action which may be a guide in the future. No case of this kind can be judged apart from its circumstances. . . . Those who are prone by temperament and character to seek sharp and clear-cut solutions of difficult and obscure problems, who are ready to fight whenever some challenge comes from a foreign power, have not always been right. On the other hand, those whose inclination is to bow their heads, to seek patiently and faithfully for peaceful compromise, are not always wrong. On the contrary, in the majority of instances, they may be right, not only morally but from a practical standpoint. How many wars have been averted by patience and persisting good will![23]

So persuaded is Schlesinger of the danger of drawing false lessons from history that he proposes to reverse Santayana's famous aphorism; in-

21. Nicolson, *The Congress of Vienna,* 121.
22. Schlesinger, *Bitter Heritage,* 88–90.
23. Churchill, *The Gathering Storm,* 285–86.

stead of saying that those who cannot remember the past are condemned to repeat it, we should declare that those who can remember
the past are condemned to repeat it.[24]

Burckhardt was by no means the only person to assert that the study
of history makes men wiser. "Histories make men wise," said Sir Francis
Bacon. The study of history, wrote Lord Acton, "Fulfills its purpose even
if it only makes us wiser." "One cannot doubt," asserts Schlesinger,
"that the study of history makes people wiser." And Gordon Wood
recently declared, "History does not teach lots of little lessons. . . . History is like experience and old age: wisdom is what one learns from it."[25]
But none of these authors says a word about how learning lessons from
the study of history differs from gaining wisdom from the study of
history. Since this distinction is central to a defense of the pragmatic use
of history, it ought to be made, not just rhetorically, but explicitly. It
seems to me that wisdom can be distinguished from lessons in at least
seven ways.

In the first place, lessons tend to be drawn from a single instance in
the past, whereas wisdom arises from the experience of, or study of,
many instances. The one is anecdotal, the other statistical. The Munich
analogy, for example, offends professional historians because it is rarely
accompanied by other examples of appeasement provoking further aggression. Yet the historian is not offended by de Gaulle's remark that
dictatorship is an adventure that history has shown is bound to end in
ruin and disaster.[26] He is not offended, because the instances of dictatorship ending in ruin and disaster are so numerous.

Second, politicians and publicists often apply lessons indiscriminately,
to situations that differ widely from the situation that gave rise to the
lesson. The war in Korea taught Americans that resolute military action
could prevent aggression, but when they applied that lesson to Vietnam
they discovered that it did not apply. In Vietnam the Communists had
captured the nationalist movement, the government in Saigon was incompetent, and the struggle was a civil war, not a war of aggression.
Even Toynbee, who is second to no one in his love of historical analogies, remarked that the comparable units of history "remain inconve-
niently few for the application of the scientific technique, the elucidation
and formulation of laws."[27] It is this fact that led Schlesinger to observe

24. Schlesinger, Bitter Heritage, 91.
25. Bacon, Essays, 473; Acton, Essays on Freedom and Power, 10; Schlesinger, Bitter Heritage, 92; Wood, "The March of Folly," 8.
26. Quoted in Thomas Cadett, "Portrait of General de Gaulle," The Listener, 5 June 1959.
27. Toynbee, A Study of History, abridged ed., 1:47.

that historical insight is not comparable to the mathematical equations of the physicist but rather to the diagnostic judgments of the doctor.[28]

Third, lessons tend to be universal, whereas wisdom is usually parochial. During the Vietnamese war political scientists put forward lessons based on models of counterinsurgency, models thought to be universally applicable, but those lessons proved mistaken. Those who saw deeper into the problem of Vietnam were the historians of Southeast Asia, whose advice was based on a parochial knowledge of Vietnamese character, values, and society. As Herbert Butterfield has observed, "The eliciting of general truths or of propositions claiming universal validity is the one kind of consummation which it is beyond the competence of history to achieve."[29] Yet a caution must be drawn. Where the wisdom is of a highly abstract character, it may be applicable universally—for example, the remark that generals, to their cost, tend to fight the present war as if it were the last war.

Fourth, lessons drawn from a distant past, and so from a society unlike ours, are less likely to be valid than those drawn from the recent past. This explains why historians wince when they hear a person say that *all* history proves a point. It also explains why Lord Acton urged the study of modern history because it treats of problems now before us. Every part of modern history, he continued, "is weighty with inestimable lessons that we must learn by experience and at a great price, if we know not how to profit by the example and teaching of those who have gone before us, in a society largely resembling the one we live in."[30]

Fifth, those who draw lessons from history seldom allow for the role of chance, of the contingent, of the unpredictable. He who appreciates the role of chance in history has learned wisdom. He deals with probabilities, even possibilities, not certainties. He does not pretend that he can predict, much less control, what others do. Who could have predicted the Nazi-Soviet Pact of 1939 or the recent collapse of Communism in the Soviet Union? Yet this does not mean a complete surrender to chance. There are probabilities, such as the probability that national interests will triumph over revolutionary ideology in most nations. This has led Friedrich Hayek to suggest that the concept of orientation replace that of prediction.

> The service of theory which does not tell us what particular events to expect at a definite moment, but only what kinds of events we

---

28. Schlesinger, *Bitter Heritage*, 92.
29. Butterfield, *The Whig Interpretation of History*, 65.
30. Acton, *Essays on Freedom and Power*, 10.

are to expect within a certain range, or on complexes of a certain type, would perhaps be better described by the term *orientation* than by speaking of prediction. Although such a theory does not tell us precisely what to expect, it will still make the world around us a more familiar world in which we can move with greater confidence not to be disappointed because we can at least exclude certain eventualities.[31]

A corollary to this fifth distinction provides a sixth, namely, that history teaches the wise person what is impossible. The lessons of history are essentially negative. History, A. L. Rowse suggests, gives one a lively sense of what is impossible, as Napoleon and Hitler discovered when they attempted to conquer the whole of Europe.[32] Whether such megalomania can ever be cured by reason is problematic, but reason can and does condemn such ventures. The same may be said of the utopian schemes of revolutionaries, who would transform human nature over night. The Chinese would have escaped much suffering had the impossibility of the aims of the Cultural Revolution been glimpsed earlier. But though one can agree that history is a better guide to what not to do than to what to do, the statesman or legislator or voter must decide what he or she shall do in the place of that which he or she has decided not to do.

Seventh, those who draw lessons from history tend to draw specific lessons; those who seek wisdom arrive at general truths. From past experience it is possible to predict what in a general way will be true of the future; it is difficult to predict in detail what will happen. Thus those generalizations from history that carry most credibility tend to be general truths, such as I. F. Stone's observation that "history teaches us that old enmities between nations usually are resolved only in the rise of new ones," or Sir Edward Appleton's that "history teaches us that many of the outstanding achievements of our modern civilization can be traced back through technology to basic scientific discoveries which at first gave no hint of their practical import."[33] Napoleon, for example, ridiculed those who would gain success by imitating his strategy, yet he also declared that he who would understand the art of war must read and reread the campaigns of the great commanders.[34] The difference lies in the fact that reading and rereading the campaigns of the great command-

31. Hayek, "Degrees of Explanation," 225.
32. Rowse, *The Uses of History,* 102
33. *I. F. Stone's Bi-Weekly,* 6 September 1971; Sir Edward Appleton, "Science for Its Own Sake," *The Listener,* 29 November 1956.
34. Quoted in Quentin Bell, "The Painter as Critic," *The Listener,* 10 November 1960.

ers informs one about the principles of military strategy, not about the details of a single battle. As S. W. Roskell argues, a careful analysis of naval engagements reveals the continuing validity of the historical principles underlying any true maritime strategy despite changes in technology or foe.[35]

The distinction between particularity and generality should not be confused with the distinction between short-run and long-run predictions, though Schlesinger does. "Most useful historical generalizations," he writes,

> are statements about massive social and intellectual movements over a considerable period of time. They make large-scale, long-term predictions possible. But they do not justify small-scale, short-term prediction. For short-run prediction is the prediction of detail and, given the complex structure of social events, the difficulty of anticipating the intersection or collision of different events and the irreducible mystery, if not invincible freedom, of individual decision, there are simply too many variables to warrant exact forecasts of the immediate future. History, in short, can answer questions, after a fashion, at long range. It cannot answer questions with confidence or certainty at short range.[36]

This would be true if short-run predictions were always detailed predictions, but they are not. A forecast of the population of the United States for next year is more dependable than for fifty years hence. Nor are long-run predictions always a matter of generality. Schlesinger himself mentions that leading political figures in Washington in 1966 were shaping their actions by calculations with regard to who should win the Democratic presidential nomination in 1972.[37] The valuable distinction, as Schlesinger's own elaboration of his argument shows, is not between short-run and long-run, but between detailed predictions and general truths.

The enterprise of predicting the consequences of one's decisions and actions cannot be extended too far into the future. Immediate consequences can be predicted far more accurately than ultimate consequences. In a long chain of events too many variables intervene to make the prediction of ultimate consequences accurate. One must distinguish here between a prediction based on a long causal chain and a prediction

---

35. Roskell, *The Strategy of Sea Power*, 7–8, 237.
36. Schlesinger, *Bitter Heritage*, 92.
37. Ibid., 94.

based on a simple generalization. It is, for example, hazardous to predict that a vote of military aid to the Contras will lead to the overthrow of the Sandinistas, since the causal chain between the vote and ultimate victory is so long. It is less hazardous to predict that no insurgent movement can succeed that does not win the support of the local population. But though one cannot predict how a long causal chain will turn out—say, whether a vote of military aid to the Contras will lead to victory—one can predict failure for a decision that flouts a general truth, such as the general truth that no insurgent movement can succeed that does not win the support of the local population.

The attentive reader may by this time have observed that my analysis of the pragmatic use of history often mirrors my earlier analysis of the logic of historical explanation and the logic of historical interpretation. The parallels are numerous. Consider the following: The insistence that lessons be based on many and not one instance corresponds to an insistence that explanations be based not on a single instance but on a covering law. The insistence that lessons not be applied universally reflects the failure of macrocorrelation to discover such truths. The belief that lessons are more dependable when parochial than when universal corresponds to the belief that parochial covering laws are more dependable than universal covering laws when used in historical explanation. Just as probable, not invariant, laws are used in explanation, so the lessons of history are probable, not certain. Likewise, negative lessons carry more conviction than positive lessons, just as negative counterfactuals carry more conviction than positive counterfactuals. Similarly, general lessons are more dependable than particular lessons, just as generalizations about the important factors in a complex web of events are more dependable than a generalization about such factors drawn from a single event. And finally, the admonition to combine many lessons in the face of a difficult situation reflects the fact of multiple causation in human affairs. None of this should cause surprise. It is quite reasonable that the uses of history should grow out of the logic of historical explanation and the logic of historical interpretation.

This applies, of course, only to the pragmatic use of history. History has many uses other than the pragmatic, some of them trivial, some profound. The study of history satisfies our curiosity about the past. It allows us to validate customs and practices by finding precedents for them. It allows us to pass judgment on men and women for the crimes and wrongs they have perpetrated in the past. Above all, it allows us to propagate common values in the community. Indeed, I suspect that this last use is the chief use of the teaching of history in the schools. Through anecdote and biography the historian propagates patriotism, love of

liberty, belief in democracy, toleration of dissent, admiration for heroism, devotion to justice, and many other values. To those who object to
the use of history to propagate values there are two answers. The first is
contained in Louis Gottschalk's remark that the use of history to promote patriotism is valid only if the historian does not falsify the past. The
historian must tell children the truth about their heroes.[38] The second
answer is that the values that weld a community together must be propa-
gated in some way. What better way than by holding up for imitation
those who have fought for justice, for liberty, for tolerance, for love of
country. This is largely done, however, by arresting anecdotes and dramatic narratives and vivid portraits, and therefore this use of history
operates independently of one's theory of causation. Since this chapter
only concerns causal explanation and the use of history, nothing more
need be said about these uses of history.

To return to the pragmatic use of history, one devastating objection
has been made to it, stated most powerfully by Friedrich Hegel. "The
one thing one learns from history," declared Hegel, "is that nobody ever
learns from history."[39] Pierre Bayle was equally despairing: "No! The
world is too unteachable to profit by the follies of past ages. Every age
behaves as if it were the first."[40] Subtract the rhetoric from these ex-
postulations, and there is still a kernel of truth in them. The philosopher
may demonstrate that it is possible to learn, if not lessons, at least wisdom from the study of history, but will statesmen or legislators or voters
learn that wisdom and, having learned it, heed it? The answer is that,
though they often do not, they sometimes do. History, for example,
taught the German people to stop hankering after hegemony in Europe.
As Chancellor Adenauer remarked in 1950 when accepting Jean Mon-
net's plan for an iron and steel community, "In accepting it, my Government and my country have no secret hankering after hegemony. History
since 1933 has taught us the folly of such ideas. Germany knows that its
fate is bound up with that of Western Europe as a whole."[41] What taught
the German people this lesson, however, were events, not history
books, which led Alan Bullock to observe, "The historian will reflect that
change of heart, he may even contribute to it, but he cannot initiate it."[42]

When it comes to matters as fundamental as a change of heart of a
people, Bullock is certainly right to say that historians can only contrib-

---

38. Gottschalk, *Understanding History*, 1.
39. Quoted in A. L. Rowse, *The Uses of History*, 29.
40. As quoted in Howard Robinson, *Bayle the Sceptic*, 179.
41. Quoted in the *New Yorker*, 30 March 1981, 79.
42. Bullock, "Mirrors of German History," *Encounter*, September 1954, 74.

ute to it. But with lesser matters they may make a more direct contribution. Historians of the Second World War could have told President Lyndon Johnson that the effect of strategic bombing is to raise morale rather than to lower it, thus saving him from a major blunder of his administration—the attempt to bomb North Vietnam into submission. This is not to suggest that Lyndon Johnson should have majored in history in college (though it would have done him no harm); it is to suggest that he ought to have sought to inform himself about the consequences of strategic bombing. And those on whom he called to advise him should have studied the effects of strategic bombing in Europe during the Second World War. Either be guided by that experience or trust to chance. As Peter McClelland puts it, "For all their imperfections, causal generalizations have been, and will remain, an invaluable guide for human action. We mortals are, as Max Born noted, invariably committed to playing dice for our little purposes of prognosis. Those players who rely upon available generalizations do better in the long run than those who do not—or so we believe, and much in our personal experience supports the belief."[43]

To this eminently sensible conclusion that it is wise to rely upon "available generalizations" in guiding human conduct, one can add a second truth. Those "available generalizations" will be more dependable, more useful, more profitable if they are based upon a right understanding of the causes of events in the past, which right understanding depends in large measure upon a right understanding of the logic of historical explanation and of the logic of historical interpretation.

43. McClelland, *Causal Explanation and Model Building*, 41.

Glossary

analytical colligation. The procedure by which an historian proceeds from the description of an event to the discovery of its authors, from the discovery of its authors to the discovery of their purposes, desires, and beliefs, and from the discovery of their purposes, desires, and beliefs to the causes of those purposes and the etiology of those desires and beliefs.

classification. The grouping of events under appropriate conceptions, for example, "a renaissance."

colligation. The tracing of the steps (i.e., causal connections) by which an event came about.

correlation. A relation between initial conditions and an event, such that they occur together more often than would be expected on the basis of chance alone. This repeated relation may be either causal (low pressure causing rain) or epiphenomenal (the barometer falling as the rain comes in). Throughout this work "correlation" refers to the causal relation, unless modified by "epiphenomenal."

covering-law model. A model of explanation in which the event to be explained is subsumed under a law correlating the occurrence of events of that kind with a set of initial conditions.

cumulative colligation. Tracing the steps by which changes in the structure of society come about.

deductive-nomological explanation. A more technical name for the covering-law model; sometimes reserved for covering-law models that employ invariable laws.

divergent colligation. The tracing of the manifold consequences of a significant event.

elimination analysis. The procedure by which the historian isolates the cause of an event by eliminating, as unlikely, other possible causes.

enthymeme. A syllogism in which one of the premises is implicit.

explanandum (pl. explananda). The event to be explained in a covering-law model; also called "explanandum event."

explanans. The two premises (i.e., the statement of initial conditions and the statement of the covering law) in a covering-law model; also called an "explanans statement."

explanatum (pl. explanata). The explanandum redescribed so as to remove particular designations.

explicandum (pl. explicanda). Another word for explanandum.

explicans. Another word for explanans.

factor. Those causes that appear often in the explanation either of a complex event ("national enmities were a factor in the coming of the First World War") or of many like events ("speed is an important factor causing auto accidents").

generalization, of fact, summative. A description of a contingent fact *after* the determination of all cases, no prediction of any of its instances being based upon it.

generalization, of law, lawlike. A description accepted as true, though many cases remain to be determined, the further, unexamined cases being predicted to conform with it. Wherever "generalization" is used in this book without a modifier, it means a lawlike generalization.

hypothesis. A generalization made by induction that might yet be proved false.

hypothetical. A description of the covering law that is contained in the explanans statement.

intelligibility explanation. A species of rational explanation in which the situation is a scheme of ideas, an explanation whose purpose is to show that a rational person, holding that scheme of ideas, will come to accept certain beliefs. That person's coming to hold those beliefs then becomes intelligible.

interpretation. An abbreviation or summary of a complete explanation, an abbreviation in which certain factors (economic, religious, etc.) are said to be dominant.

invariable laws. Laws to which there are no exceptions (sometimes called universal laws, though that phrase can also mean "not parochial").

linear colligation. The tracing of a sequence of events through the more abnormal conditions found in each set of initial conditions.

logical colligation. Tracing a sequence of ideas, in which the holding of one idea leads a rational person to hold a second, and so forth.

macrocorrelation. Establishing a relation between certain initial conditions and a complex event, such as a revolution.

microcolligation. Tracing the steps in a colligatory chain or web ever more minutely, searching for steps within steps.

microcorrelation. Establishing a relation between certain initial conditions and the occurrence of a discrete event.

nomological explanation. A deductive explanation in which one explains the occurrence of an event by subsuming it under an appropriate covering law.

nomothetic explanation. Another term for a nomological explanation.

parallel colligation. Tracing similar, parallel sequences of events, as in the tracing of a growing fear of popery among many Englishmen.

parochial laws. Laws applicable only to a specific time and place or to a particular person or persons.

probable laws. Laws to which there are exceptions, though the law, to be a law, must describe a relation between initial conditions and events that is greater than chance.

rational explanation. Explaining an action by discovering the reasons that led the agent to perform the action, a discovery made by sympathetically identifying oneself with the agent in his or her particular situation.

redescription. The act of redescribing an event so that all particular designations are omitted and the event can be subsumed under a covering law.

regularity principle. Another term for the covering-law model of explanation.

repetitive colligation. Tracing a sequence of events that exactly repeats itself over and over again (as in the sequence of events that occurs when one turns on the ignition in a car).

scenario. The sequence of events, not repeated, that leads up to the singular event to be explained.

sentential facts and events. Facts and events denominated by a sentence.

singular hypothetical. A lawlike generalization describing a single individual and used in a covering-law explanation.

situational analysis. The reconstruction of the problem situation that confronts the historical agent, which reconstruction allows the historian to understand the agent's action or, more particularly, to see why the action was appropriate.

theory. A description of a repeated sequence of events that explains the existence of a given correlation or law.

universal law. A law that applies through all time and space and to all persons (though some philosophers use the term to apply to an invariant law).

Bibliography

Abel, Theodore. "The Operation Called *Verstehen.*" In Herbert Feigl and May Brodbeck, eds., *Readings in the Philosophy of Science.* New York, 1953.

Abelson, Raziel. "Cause and Reason in History." In Sidney Hook, ed., *Philosophy and History: A Symposium.*

Achinstein, Peter. "The Problem of Theoretical Terms." In Baruch A. Brody, ed., *Readings in the Philosophy of Science.*

Acton of Aldenham, John Emerich Edward Dalberg Acton, First Baron. *Essays on Freedom and Power.* Boston, 1948.

Allison, Paul D. *Event History Analysis: Regression for Longitudinal Event Data.* Beverly Hills, 1984.

Alston, William P. "The Place of the Explanation of Particular Facts in Science." *Philosophy of Science* 38 (1971).

Anscombe, G.E.M. *Intention.* Oxford, 1958.

Ashton, Robert. *The English Civil War: Conservatism and Revolution, 1603–1649.* New York, 1978.

Atkinson, R. F. *Knowledge and Explanation in History: An Introduction to the Philosophy of History.* London, 1978.

Aydelotte, William O. "Quantification in History." In Robert P. Swierenga, ed., *Quantification in American History: Theory and Research.*

Ayer, A. J. "Meaning and Intentionality." Chap. 3 in *Metaphysics and Common Sense.* San Francisco, 1970.

———. "What Is a Law of Nature?" In Baruch A. Brody, ed., *Readings in the Philosophy of Science.*

Bacon, Sir Francis. *Essays.* Edited by Franklin Fiske Heard. Boston, 1873.

Bailyn, Bernard. "The Problems of the Working Historian: A Comment." In Sidney Hook, ed., *Philosophy and History: A Symposium.*

Bainton, Roland. *Here I Stand: A Life of Martin Luther.* New York, 1950.

Ball, Terence. "On 'Historical' Explanation." *Philosophy of the Social Sciences* 2 (1972).

———. "Popper's Psychologism." *Philosophy of the Social Sciences* 11 (1981).

Bambrough, Renford. "Comment: Ideology and the Modes of Explanation." In Stephan Korner, ed., *Explanation.*

Barker, Evelyn. "Rational Explanations in History." In Sidney Hook, ed., *Philosophy and History: A Symposium.*

Barraclough, Geoffrey. *Main Trends in History.* New York, 1979.

Bartley, W. W. "Achilles, the Tortoise, and Explanation in Science and History." *British Journal for the Philosophy of Science* 13. (May 1962–February 1963).

Beard, Charles A. *An Economic Interpretation of the Constitution of the United States.* New York, 1913.

Beer, Samuel H. "Causal Explanation and Imaginative Re-Enactment." *History and Theory* 3 (1963).

Belford, Lee A. "Observations on History." In Sidney Hook, ed., *Philosophy and History: A Symposium.*

Benson, Lee. "On the Logic of Historical Narration." in Sidney Hook, ed., *Philosophy and History: A Symposium.*

———. "Quantification, Scientific History, and Scholarly Innovation." In Robert P. Swierenga, ed., *Quantification in American History: Theory and Research.*

———. *Toward the Scientific Study of History: Selected Essays by Lee Benson.* Philadelphia, 1972.

Berkhofer, Robert. *A Behavioral Approach to Historical Analysis.* New York, 1969.

Berlin, Isaiah. "The Concept of Scientific History." In William H. Dray, ed., *Philosophical Analysis and History.*

Black, John Bennett. *The Art of History: A Study of Four Great Historians of the Eighteenth Century.* London, 1926.

Blalock, Hubert M., Jr. *Causal Inference in Nonexperimental Research.* Chapel Hill, 1964.

Bloch, Marc. *The Historian's Craft.* New York, 1953.

Bogue, Alan G. "United States: The 'New' Political History." Reprinted in Robert P. Swierenga, ed., *Quantification in American History: Theory and Research.*

Braithwaite, R. B. "Laws of Nature and Causality." In Baruch A. Brody, ed., *Readings in the Philosophy of Science.*

———. "Models in the Empirical Sciences." In Baruch A. Brody, ed., *Readings in the Philosophy of Science.*

Brand, Myles. *Intending and Acting: Toward a Naturalized Action Theory.* Cambridge, Mass., 1984.

Brandt, R. B. "Personality Traits as Causal Explanations in Biography." In Sidney Hook, ed., *Philosophy and History: A Symposium.*

Bratman, Michael. "Davidson's Theory of Intention." In Bruce Vermazen and Merrill B. Hintikka, eds., *Essays on Davidson: Actions and Events.*

Braudel, Fernand. *The Mediterranean and the Mediterranean World in the Age of Philip II.* London, 1972.

———. *On History.* Translated by Sarah Matthews. Chicago, 1980.

———. "Personal Testimony." *Journal of Modern History* 44 (December 1972).

Brodbeck, May. "Explanation, Prediction, and 'Imperfect' Knowledge." In Herbert Feigl and Grover Maxwell, eds., *Minnesota Studies in the Philosophy of Science,* vol. 3, *Scientific Explanation, Space, and Time.*

———. "Meaning and Action." In May Brodbeck, ed., *Readings in the Philosophy of the Social Sciences.*

———. "Methodological Individualism: Definition and Reduction." In William H. Dray, ed., *Philosophical Analysis and History.*

———. "Models, Meaning, and Theories." In May Brodbeck, ed., *Readings in the Philosophy of the Social Sciences.*

———, ed. *Readings in the Philosophy of the Social Sciences.* London, 1968.

Brody, Baruch A., ed. *Readings in the Philosophy of Science.* Englewood Cliffs, N.J., 1970.

Bromberger, Sylvain. "Why-Questions." in Baruch A. Brody, ed., *Readings in the Philosophy of Science.*

Brown, Robert. *Explanation in Social Science.* Chicago, 1963.

———. *The Nature of Social Laws: Machiavelli to Mill.* Cambridge, 1984.

Brunton, Douglas and D. H. Pennington. *Members of the Long Parliament.* London, 1954.

Buckle, Henry Thomas. *The History of Civilization in England.* London, 1972.

Buckley, Walter, ed. *Modern Systems Research for the Behavioral Scientist: A Source Book.* Chicago, 1968.

Bullock, Alan. "Mirrors of German History." *Encounter,* September 1954.

Burckhardt, Jacob. *Reflections on History.* Indianapolis, 1979.

Burke, James. *Connections.* Boston, 1978.

Burke, Peter. *Sociology and History.* London, 1980.

Burston, W. H. "Laws, Generalization, and the History Teacher." In W. H. Burston and D. Thompson, eds., *Studies in the Nature and Teaching of History.*

Burston, W. H., and D. Thompson, eds. *Studies in the Nature and Teaching of History.* New York, 1967.

Butterfield, Herbert. *History and Human Relations.* New York, 1952.

———. *The Whig Interpretation of History.* London, 1931.

Butters, H. C. *Governors and Government in Early Sixteenth-Century Florence, 1502–1519.* Oxford, 1985.

Campbell, N. R. "What Is a Theory?" In Baruch A. Brody, ed., *Readings in the Philosophy of Science.*

Carlton, Charles. *Charles I: The Personal Monarch.* London, 1983.

———. *Royal Childhoods.* London, 1986.

———. "Three British Revolutions and the Personality of Kingship." In J.G.A. Pocock, ed., *Three British Revolutions: 1641, 1688, 1776.*

Carnap, Rudolph. "Theories as Partially Interpreted Formal Systems." In Baruch A. Brody, ed., *Readings in the Philosophy of Science.*

Carr, David. *Time, Narrative, and History.* Bloomington, Ind., 1986.

Cebik, L. B. "Colligation and the Writing of History." *The Monist* 53 (January 1969).

Chambers, J. D. *Population, Economy, and Society in Pre-industrial England.* London, 1972.

Chisholm, Roderick. "The Structure of States of Affairs." In Bruce Vermazen and Merrill B. Hintikka, eds., *Essays on Davidson: Actions and Events.* Oxford, 1985.

Churchill, Winston. *The Gathering Storm.* New York, 1961.

Churchland, Paul M. "The Logical Character of Action-Explanations." *Philosophical Review* 79 (April 1970).

Clark, Peter. *English Provincial Society from the Reformation to the Revolution: Religion, Politics, and Society in Kent.* Hassocks, Sussex, 1977.

Clarke, Simon. *The Foundations of Structuralism.* [Brighton], 1981.

Cleaver, Eldridge. *Soul on Ice.* New York, 1968.

Climo, T. A., and P.G.A. Howells. "Possible Worlds in Historical Explanation." *History and Theory* 15 (1976).

Cochran, Thomas C. "Historical Use of the Social Sciences." In Thomas C. Cochran, *The Inner Revolution: Essays on the Social Sciences in History.*

──────. *The Inner Revolution: Essays on the Social Sciences in History.* Gloucester, Mass., 1970.

Cohen, L. Jonathan. "Comment." In Stephan Korner, ed., *Explanation.*

Cohen, Michael. "The Same Action." *Proceedings of the Aristotelian Society*, n.s., 70 (1969–70).

Cohen, Morris R. "Causation and Its Application to History." *Journal of the History of Ideas* 3 (January 1942).

Coles, Harry. *The War of 1812.* Chicago, 1965.

Collin, Finn. *Theory and Understanding: A Critique of Interpretive Social Science.* Oxford, 1985.

Collingwood, R. G. *An Autobiography.* London, 1939.

──────. *An Essay on Metaphysics.* Oxford, 1940.

──────. *The Idea of History.* Oxford, 1956.

Collinson, Patrick. *The Elizabethan Puritan Movement.* Berkeley and Los Angeles, 1967.

──────. *The Religion of Protestants: The Church in English Society, 1559–1625.* Oxford, 1982.

Conkin, Paul K. "Causation Revisited." *History and Theory* 13 (1974).

Coward, Barry. *The Stuart Age.* London, 1980.

Croce, Benedetto. *History: Its Theory and Practice.* New York, 1960.

Cummins, Robert. *The Nature of Psychological Explanation.* Cambridge, Mass., 1983.

Danto, Arthur C. *Analytical Philosophy of History.* Cambridge, 1965.

──────. *Narration and Knowledge* (including the integral text of *Analytical Philosophy of History*). New York, 1985.

Danto, Arthur, and Sidney Morgenbesser, eds. *Philosophy of Science.* Cleveland, 1960.

Davidson, Donald. "Actions, Reasons, and Causes." In May Brodbeck, ed., *Readings in the Philosophy of the Social Sciences.*

──────. "Adverbs of Action." In Bruce Vermazen and Merrill B. Hintikka, eds., *Essays on Davidson: Actions and Events.*

──────. *Essays on Actions and Events.* Oxford, 1980.

──────. "Freedom to Act." In Ted Honderich, ed., *Essays on Freedom of Action.*

──────. "Hempel on Explaining Action." In *Erkenntnis: An International Journal of Analytic Philosophy* 10 (October 1976).

Deane, Phyllis. *The First Industrial Revolution.* 2d ed. Cambridge, 1979.

Degler, Carl N. "Do Historians Use Covering Laws?" In Sidney Hook, ed., *Philosophy and History: A Symposium.*

Dennet, D. C. "Mechanism and Responsibility." In Ted Honderich, ed., *Essays on Freedom of Action.*

Dickerson, Oliver M. *The Navigation Acts and the American Revolution.* New York, 1974.

Diderot, Denis. *Pensées sur l'interprétation de la nature.* In J. Lough, ed., *Diderot: Selected Philosophical Writings.* Cambridge, 1953.

Dilthey, Wilhelm. "The Understanding of Other Persons and Their Life-Expressions." In Patrick Gardiner, ed., *Theories of History.*

Dollar, Charles M., and Richard J. Jensen. *Historian's Guide to Statistics, Quantitative Analysis, and Historical Research.* Huntington, N.Y., 1971.

Donagan, Alan, "Alternative Historical Explanations and Their Verification." *The Monist* 53 (January 1969).

———. "Explanation in History." In Patrick Gardiner, ed., *Theories of History.*

———. *The Later Philosophy of R. G. Collingwood.* Oxford, 1962.

———. "The Popper-Hempel Theory Reconsidered." In William H. Dray, ed., *Philosophical Analysis and History.*

———. "Social Science and Historical Antinomianism." *Revue Internationale de Philosophie* 11 (1957).

Dray, William H. "Colligation Under Appropriate Conceptions." In Leon Pompa and William H. Dray, eds., *Substance and Form in History: A Collection of Essays in Philosophy of History.*

———. "Concepts of Causation in A.J.P. Taylor's Account of the Origins of the Second World War." *History and Theory* 17 (1978).

———. " 'Explaining What' in History." In Patrick Gardiner, ed., *Theories of History.*

———. "Explanatory Narrative in History." *Philosophical Quarterly* 4 (January 1954).

———. "The Historical Explanation of Actions Reconsidered." In Sidney Hook, ed., *Philosophy and History: A Symposium.*

———. "Historical Understanding as Re-Thinking." *University of Toronto Quarterly* 27 (January 1958). Reprint in Baruch A. Brody, ed., *Readings in the Philosophy of Science.*

———. *Laws and Explanation in History.* Oxford, 1957.

———. "Narrative Versus Analysis in History." In J. Margolis, M. Kraus, and R. M. Burian, eds., *Rationality, Relativism and the Human Sciences.* Dordrecht, 1986.

———. *On History and Philosophers of History.* Leiden, 1989.

———. "On the Nature and Role of Narrative in Historiography." *History and Theory* 10 (1971).

———. *Perspectives on History.* London, 1980.

———. *Philosophy of History.* 2d ed. Englewood Cliffs, N.J., 1993.

———. "R. G. Collingwood and the Acquaintance Theory of Knowledge." *Revue Internationale de Philosophie* 11 (1957).

———. "R. G. Collingwood and the Understanding of Actions in History." In William H. Dray, *Perspectives on History.*

———. "Singular Hypotheticals and Historical Explanation." In Llewellyn Gross, ed., *Sociological Theory: Inquiries and Paradigms.*

———. "Toynbee's Search for Historical Laws." *History and Theory* I (1960–61).

———, ed. *Philosophical Analysis and History.* New York, 1966.

Droysen, Johann Gustav. *Outline of the Principles of History.* New York, 1967.

Dusinberre, William. *Henry Adams: The Myth of Failure.* Charlottesville, Va., 1980.

Dussen, W. J. van der, and Lionel Rubinoff, eds. *Objectivity, Method, and Point of View: Essays in the Philosophy of History.* Leiden, 1991.

Eberle, Rolf, David Kaplan, and Richard Montage. "Hempel and Oppenheim on Explanation." *Philosophy of Science* 28 (October 1961).

Eckstein, Harry. "On the Etiology of Internal Wars." *History and Theory* 4 (1965).

Eliot, George. *The Mill on the Floss.* Oxford, 1980.

Ellis, B. "On the Relation of Explanation to Description." *Mind*, n.s., 65 (1956).

Elster, Jon. *The Cement of Society: A Study of Social Order.* Cambridge, 1989.
———. *Logic and Society: Contradictions and Possible Worlds.* Chichester, 1978.
———. *Making Sense of Marx.* Cambridge, 1985.
———. *Nuts and Bolts for the Social Sciences.* Cambridge, 1989.
———. *Solomonic Judgments: Studies in the Limitations Rationality.* Cambridge, 1989.
———. *Sour Grapes: Studies in the Subversion of Rationality.* Cambridge, 1983.
———. *Ulysses and the Sirens: Studies in Rationality and Irrationality.* Rev. ed. Cambridge, 1984.
Erikson, Erik H. *Young Man Luther: A Study in Psychoanalysis and History.* New York, 1958.
Fain, Haskell. *Between Philosophy and History: The Resurrection of Speculative Philosophy Within the Analytical Tradition.* Princeton, 1970.
Farr, James. "Hume, Hermeneutics, and History: A 'Sympathetic' Account." *History and Theory* 17 (1978).
———. "Popper's Hermeneutics." *Philosophy of the Social Sciences* 18 (1983).
———. "Situational Analysis: Explanation in Political Science." *Journal of Politics* 47 (1985).
Federn, Karl. *The Materialist Conception of History: A Critical Analysis.* Westport, Conn., 1971.
Feigl, Herbert, and May Brodbeck, eds. *Readings in the Philosophy of Science.* New York, 1953.
Feigl, Herbert, and Grover Maxwell, eds. *Minnesota Studies in the Philosophy of Science.* Vol. 3, *Scientific Explanation, Space, and Time.*
Fell, A. P. " 'Epistemological' and 'Narrativist' Philosophies of History." In W. J. van der Dussen and Lionel Rubinoff, eds., *Objectivity, Method, and Point of View.*
Feyerbrand, P. K. "How to Be a Good Empiricist: A Plea for Tolerance in Matters Epistemological." In Baruch A. Brody, ed., *Readings in the Philosophy of Science.*
Fielding, Henry. *The History of Tom Jones, a Foundling.* New York, [1940].
Firth, C. H. *Oliver Cromwell and the Rule of the Puritans in England.* London, 1900.
Fischer, David Hackett. *Historians' Fallacies: Towards a Logic of Historical Thought.* New York, 1970.
Fischoff, Baruch. "Intuitive Use of Formal Models: A Comment on Morrison's 'Quantitative Models in History.' " *History and Theory* 17 (1978).
Flanigan, William H. "The Conduct of Inquiry in Social Science History." *Social Science History* 8 (fall 1984).
Fletcher, Anthony. *The Outbreak of the English Civil War.* London, 1981.
Fogel, Robert William. *Railroads and American Economic Growth: Essays in Econometric History.* Baltimore, 1970.
Fogel, Robert William, and G. R. Elton. *Which Road to the Past? Two Views of History.* New Haven, 1983.
Frankel, Charles. "Explanation and Interpretation in History." In Patrick Gardiner, ed., *Theories of History.*
Fryer, W. R. "The Study of British Politics Between the Revolution and the Reform Act." *Renaissance and Modern Studies* 1 (1957).
Gallie, W. B. "Explanations in History and the Genetic Science." *Mind*, n.s., 64 (1955). Reprint in Patrick Gardiner, ed., *Theories of History.*
———. *Philosophy and the Historical Understanding.* 2d ed. New York, 1968.

Gardiner, Patrick. *The Nature of Historical Explanation*. Oxford, 1952.
——, ed. *Theories of History*. Glencoe, Ill., 1959.
Gardiner, Samuel Rawson. *History of England from the Accession of James I to the Outbreak of the Civil War, 1603–1642*. 10 vols. London, 1883–84.
Gay, Peter. *Art and Act: On Causes in History: Manet, Gropius, Mondrian*. New York, 1976.
Gellner, Ernest A. "Explanations in History." *Aristotelian Society*, supplementary vol. 30 (1956).
——. "Holism Versus Individualism in History and Sociology." In Patrick Gardiner, ed., *Theories of History*.
Gershoy, Leo. "Some Problems of a Working Historian." In Sidney Hook, ed., *Philosophy and History: A Symposium*.
Geyl, Pieter. *Debates with Historians*. Cleveland, 1958.
Giddings, Franklin H. "A Theory of History." *Political Science Quarterly* 35 (December 1920).
Ginsberg, Morris. "The Character of a Historical Explanation." *Aristotelian Society*, supplementary vol. 21 (1947).
Goldman, Alvin I. *A Theory of Human Action*. Englewood Cliffs, N.J., 1970.
Goldstein, Leon J. *Historical Knowing*. Austin, Tex., 1976.
Gombrich, E. H. "On Frances Yates." *New York Review of Books* 30 (3 March 1983).
Gooch, George Peabody. *History and Historians in the Nineteenth Century*. London, 1913.
Goodman, Nelson. *Fact, Fiction, and Forecast*. 3d ed. Indianapolis, 1973.
Gorman, J. L. *The Expression of Historical Knowledge*. Edinburgh, 1982.
——. "A Review of Leon J. Goldstein's *Historical Knowing*." *History and Theory* 16 (1957).
Gottschalk, Louis. *Understanding History: A Primer of Historical Method*. New York, 1969.
Goubert, Pierre. *Louis XIV and Twenty Million Frenchman*. New York, 1970.
Graham, Gordon. *Historical Explanation Reconsidered*. Aberdeen, 1983.
Grant, C. K. "Collingwood's Theory of Historical Knowledge." *Renaissance and Modern Studies* 1 (1957).
Gregg, Pauline. *King Charles I*. London, 1981.
Grice, Paul, and Judith Baker. "Davidson on 'Weakness of the Will.' " In Bruce Vermazen and Merrill B. Hintikka, *Essays on Davidson: Actions and Events*.
Gross, Llewellyn. *Sociological Theory: Inquiries and Paradigms*. New York, 1967.
Gruner, Rolf, and W. H. Walsh. "The Notion of an Historical Event." *Aristotelian Society*, supplementary vol. 43 (1969).
Gustavson, Carl G. *The Mansions of History*. New York, 1976.
Haag, Ernest van den. "History as Factualized Fiction." In Sidney Hook, ed., *Philosophy and History: A Symposium*.
Hampson, Norman. *The Enlightenment*. Harmondsworth, Middlesex, 1968.
Hanson, N. R. "Causal Chains." *Mind* 64 (July 1955).
Harrison, Ross. *Rational Action: Studies in Philosophy and Social Science*. Cambridge, 1979.
Hart, H.L.A., and A. M. Honoré. *Causation in the Law*. Oxford, 1959.
Hay, Cynthia. "Historical Theory and Confirmation." *History and Theory* 19 (1980).
Hayek, F. A. "Degrees of Explanation." *British Journal for the Philosophy of Science* 6 (May 1955–February 1956).

Hays, Samuel P. "Scientific Versus Traditional History: The Limitations of the Current Debate." *Historical Methods* 17 (spring 1984).

Hempel, Carl G. "Aspects of Scientific Explanation." In Carl G. Hempel, *Aspects of Scientific Explanation and Other Essays in the Philosophy of Science.*

———. *Aspects of Scientific Explanation and Other Essays in the Philosophy of Science.* New York, 1965.

———. "Deductive-Nomological vs. Statistical Explanation." In Herbert Feigl and Grover Maxwell, eds., *Minnesota Studies in the Philosophy of Science,* vol. 3, *Scientific Explanation, Space, and Time.*

———. "Explanation and Law." In Patrick Gardiner, ed., *Theories of History.*

———. "Explanation in Science and in History." In William H. Dray, ed., *Philosophical Analysis and History.*

———. "Explanatory Incompleteness." In May Brodbeck, ed., *Readings in the Philosophy of the Social Sciences.*

———. "The Function of General Laws in History." In Patrick Gardiner, ed., *Theories of History.*

———. "The Logic of Functional Analysis." In May Brodbeck, ed., *Readings in the Philosophy of the Social Sciences.*

———. "A Logical Appraisal of Operationism." In Baruch A Brody, ed., *Readings in the Philosophy of Science.*

———. "Postscript (1964) to Studies in the Logic of Explanation." In Carl Hempel, *Aspects of Scientific Explanation and Other Essays in the Philosophy of Science.*

———. "Probabilistic Explanation." In Baruch A. Brody, ed., *Readings in the Philosophy of Science.*

———. "Reasons and Covering Laws in Historical Explanation." In Sidney Hook, ed., *Philosophy and History: A Symposium.*

———. "Studies in the Logic of Confirmation." In Carl Hempel, *Aspects of Scientific Explanation and Other Essays in the Philosophy of Science.*

———. "The Theoretician's Dilemma: A Study in the Logic of Theory Construction." In Carl Hempel, *Aspects of Scientific Explanation and Other Essays in the Philosophy of Science.*

Hempel, Carl G., and Paul Oppenheim. "The Logic of Explanation." In Herbert Feigl and May Brodbeck, eds., *Readings in the Philosophy of Science.*

Hexter, J. H. "Fernand Braudel and the Monde Braudellien." In J. H. Hexter, *On Historians.*

———. *The History Primer.* New York, 1971.

———. *On Historians: Reappraisals of Some of the Masters of Modern History.* Cambridge, Mass., 1986.

———. *Reappraisals in History.* Evanston, Ill., 1961.

———. "Reply to Mr. Palmer: A Vision of Files," *Journal of British Studies* 19 (fall 1979).

———. "Storm over the Gentry." In J. H. Hexter, *Reappraisals in History.*

Hill, Christopher. "The English Revolution." In Christopher Hill, ed., *The English Revolution.* London, 1940.

Hofstadter, Albert. "The Philosophy in History." In Sidney Hook, ed., *Philosophy and History: A Symposium.*

Hofstadter, Richard. "History and Sociology in the United States." In Seymour Martin Lipset and Richard Hofstadter, eds., *Sociology and History: Methods.*

Hollis, Martin. "Comment: Ideology and Metaphysics." In Stephan Korner, ed., *Explanation.*

Holloway, John. *Narrative and Structure: Exploratory Essays.* Cambridge, 1979.
Holloway, S.W.F. "History and Sociology: What History Is and What It Ought to Be." In W. H. Burston and D. Thompson, eds., *Studies in the Nature and Teaching of History.*
Holmes, Clive. "The County School of English Historians." *Journal of British Studies* 19 (spring 1980).
Honderich, Ted. "One Determinism." In Honderich, ed., *Essays on Freedom of Action.*
————. *Essays on Freedom of Action.* London, 1973.
Hook, Sidney. "Objectivity and Reconstruction in History." In Sidney Hook, ed., *Philosophy and History: A Symposium.*
————, ed. *Philosophy and History: A Symposium.* New York, 1963.
Hospers, J. *An Introduction to Philosophical Analysis.* 2d ed. London, 1967.
Humphreys, R. Stephen. "The Historian, His Document, and the Elementary Modes of Historical Thought." *History and Theory* 19 (1980).
Hunt, William. *The Puritan Moment: The Coming of Revolution in an English County.* Cambridge, Mass., 1983.
Hunter, J.F.M. "On Whether History Has a Meaning." In W. J. van der Dussen and Lionel Rubinoff, eds., *Objectivity, Method, and Point of View.*
Hurst, B. C. "A Comment on the Possible Worlds of Climo and Howells."
Hutton, W. H. *William Stubbs, Bishop of Oxford.* London, 1906.
James, Susan. Review of *Philosophy and Methodology in the Social Sciences,* by Barry Hindness. *History and Theory* 17 (1978).
James, William. *Pragmatism.* Cambridge, Mass., 1978.
Jeffrey, R. C., *The Logic of Decision.* New York, 1965.
Jordan, W. K. *Men of Substance.* New York, 1967.
Joynt, Carey B., and Nicholas Rescher. "On Explanation in History." *Mind* 68 (1959).
————. "The Problem of Uniqueness in History." *History and Theory* 1 (1961).
Kamarck, Andrew M. *Economics and the Real World.* Oxford, 1983.
Kaplan, Abraham. *The Conduct of Inquiry: Methodology for Behavioral Science.* San Francisco, 1964.
Kaplan, David. "Explanation Revisited." *Philosophy of Science* 28 (October 1961).
Kemeny, John G., and Paul Oppenheim. "On Reduction." In Baruch A. Brody, ed., *Readings in the Philosophy of Science.*
Koch, Sigmund. "The Logical Character of the Motivation Concept, I and II." *Psychological Review* 48 (1941).
Kocka, Jurgen. "Theories and Quantification in History." *Social Science History* 8 (spring 1984).
Korner, Stephan, ed. *Explanation.* New Haven, 1975.
Kousser, J. Morgan. "The Agenda for 'Social Science History.' " *Social Science History* 1 (spring 1977).
Krieger, Leonard. "Comments on Historical Explanation." In Sidney Hook, ed., *Philosophy and History: A Symposium.*
Kublick, Bruce. Review of *Theoretical Methods in Social History,* by Arthur Stinchcombe. *History and Theory* 18 (1959).
Kuhn, Thomas S. "The Function of Dogma in Scientific Research." In Baruch A. Brody, ed., *Readings in the Philosophy of Science.*
————. *The Structure of Scientific Revolutions.* Chicago, 1962.
Ladurie, Emmanuel Le Roy. *The Mind and Method of the Historian.* Chicago, 1981.

Landes, David S., and Charles Tilly. "What Is History?" In David S. Landes and Charles Tilly, eds., *History as Social Science*. London, 1973.
——, eds. *History as Social Science*. Englewood Cliffs, N.J., 1971.
Landesman, Charles A. "Actions as Universals: An Inquiry into the Metaphysics of Action." *American Philosophical Quarterly* 6 (July 1969).
Langlois, Charles Victor, and Charles Seignobos. *Introduction to the Study of History*. London, 1898.
Latham, Robert. "English Revolutionary Thought, 1640–60." *History*, n.s., 30 (March 1945).
Leach, James J. "The Logic of the Situation." *Philosophy of Science* 35 (March 1968).
Lefebvre, Georges. *The Coming of the French Revolution*. Princeton, 1967.
Leff, Gordon. *History and Social Theory*. Tuscaloosa, Ala., 1969.
Leuthy, Herbert. "Once Again: Calvin and Capitalism." *Encounter* 22 (January 1964).
Lewis, David. "Causation." In Ernest Sosa, ed. *Causation and Conditionals*.
Lipset, Seymour Martin. "History and Sociology: Some Methodological Considerations." In Seymour Martin Lipset and Richard Hofstadter, eds., *Sociology and History: Methods*.
Lipset, Seymour Martin, and Richard Hofstadter. *Sociology and History: Methods*. New York, 1968.
Lloyd, Christopher. *Explanation in Social History*. Oxford, 1986.
Louch, A. R. "History as Narrative." *History and Theory* 8 (1969).
Loyn, Henry Royston. *Anglo-Saxon England and the Norman Conquest*. London, 1962.
Lucas, P. G. "Explanations in History." *Aristotelian Society*, supplementary vol. 30 (1956).
Macaulay, Thomas Babington. *A History of England*. 5 vols. London, 1931.
MacCaffrey, Wallace. *The Shaping of the Elizabethan Regime*. London, 1969.
Macfarlane, Alan. Review of *The Family, Sex, and Marriage in England, 1500–1800*, by Lawrence Stone. *History and Theory* 18 (1979).
MacIver, A. M. "The Character of a Historical Explanation." *Aristotelian Society*, supplementary vol. 21 (1947).
——. "Levels of Explanation in History." In May Brodbeck, ed., *Readings in the Philosophy of the Social Sciences*.
MacIver, R. M. *Social Causation*. New York, 1942.
Mackie, J. L. *The Cement of the Universe: A Study of Causation*. Oxford, 1974.
——. "Ideological Explanation." In Stephan Korner, ed., *Explanation*.
Macklin, Ruth. "Norm and Law in the Theory of Action." *Inquiry* 11 (1968).
Mackreel, Rudolf. Review of *Wilhelm Dilthey: The Critique of Historical Reason*, by Michael Ermath. *History and Theory* 19 (1980).
Mandelbaum, Maurice. *The Anatomy of Historical Knowledge*. Baltimore, 1977.
——. "Causal Analysis in History." *Journal of the History of Ideas* 3 (January 1942).
——. "The Distinguishable and the Separable: A Note on Hume and Causation." In Maurice Mandelbaum, *Philosophy, History, and the Sciences: Selected Critical Essays*.
——. "Functionalism in Social Anthropology." In Maurice Mandelbaum, *Philosophy, History, and the Sciences: Selected Critical Essays*.
——. "G. A. Cohen's Defense of Functional Explanation." In Maurice Mandelbaum, *Philosophy, History, and the Sciences: Selected Critical Essays*.

————. "Historical Explanation: The Problem of 'Covering Laws.' " *History and Theory* 1 (1961).

————. "History and the Social Sciences." In Patrick Gardiner, ed., *Theories of History*.

————. "Objectivism in History." In Sidney Hook, ed., *Philosophy and History: A Symposium*.

————. *Philosophy, History, and the Sciences: Selected Critical Essays*. Baltimore, 1984.

————. *The Problem of Historical Knowledge: An Answer to Relativism*. New York, 1938.

————. "Societal Facts." In Patrick Gardiner, ed., *Theories of History*.

————. "Societal Laws." In William H. Dray, ed., *Philosophical Analysis and History*.

Manning, Brian. *The English People and the English Revolution*. London, 1976.

Marshall, Peter. *The Impeachment of Warren Hastings*. London, 1965.

Martin, Michael. "Situational Logic and Covering Law Explanations." *Inquiry* 11 (1968).

Martin, Raymond. *The Past Within Us: An Empirical Approach to Philosophy of History*. Princeton, 1989.

Martin, Rex. *Historical Explanation: Re-enactment and Practical Inference*. Ithaca, N.Y., 1977.

Marwick, Arthur. *The Nature of History*. New York, 1971.

Marx, Karl. *A Contribution to the Critique of Political Economy*. Chicago, 1904.

Maxwell, Grover. "The Ontological Status of Theoretical Entities." In Baruch A. Brody, ed., *Readings in the Philosophy of Science*.

Mazlish, Bruce. "On Rational Explanation in History." In Sidney Hook, ed., *Philosophy and History: A Symposium*.

McClelland, Peter D. *Causal Explanation and Model Building in History, Economics, and the New Economic History*. Ithaca, N.Y., 1975.

McCullagh, C. Behan. "Colligation and Classification in History." *History and Theory* 17 (1978).

————. *Justifying Historical Descriptions*. Cambridge, 1984.

————. "Narrative and Explanation in History." *Mind*, n.s., 78 (April 1969).

McLellan, David. *Marx*. [London], 1975.

Meiland, Jack. *The Nature of Intention*. London, 1970.

Melden, Abraham Irwin. *Free Action*. London, 1961.

Mellor, D. H. "Comment." In Stephan Korner, ed., *Explanation*.

Milburn, R.L.P. *Early Christian Interpretations of History*. London, 1954.

Miller, David, ed. *A Pocket Popper*. Oxford, 1983.

Miller, Richard. *Fact and Method: Explanation, Confirmation, and Reality in the Natural and the Social Sciences*. Princeton, 1987.

————. "Methodological Individualism and Social Explanation." *Philosophy of Science* 45 (September 1978).

Mink, Louis O. "The Autonomy of Historical Understanding." In William H. Dray, ed., *Philosophical Analysis and History*.

————. *Mind, History, and Dialectic: The Philosophy of R. G. Collingwood*. Bloomington, Ind., 1969.

Montefiore, Alan. "Professor Gallie on Necessary and Sufficient Conditions." *Mind*, n.s., 65 (1956).

Moore, Barrington. *Social Origins of Dictatorship and Democracy: Lord and Peasant in the Making of the Modern World*. Boston, 1966.

Morrison, Rodney J. "Franklin D. Roosevelt and the Supreme Court: An Example of the Use of Probability Theory in Political History." *History and Theory* 16 (1977).

Morrow, Glen. "Comments on White's 'Logic of Historical Narration.' " In Sidney Hook, ed., *Philosophy and History: A Symposium.*

Murphey, Murray G. *Our Knowledge of the Historical Past.* Indianapolis, 1973.

Nadel, George H. "On the Logic of Historical Narration." In Sidney Hook, ed., *Philosophy and History: A Symposium.*

Nagel, Ernest. "Determinism in History." In William H. Dray, ed., *Philosophical Analysis and History.*

———. "The Logic of Historical Analysis." In Herbert Feigl and May Brodbeck, eds., *Readings in the Philosophy of Science.*

———. "Mechanistic Explanation and Organismic Biology." In Baruch A. Brody, ed., *Readings in the Philosophy of Science.*

———. "Probability and Degree of Confirmation." In Arthur Danto and Sidney Morgenbesser, eds., *Philosophy of Science.*

———. "Relativism and Some Problems of Working Historians." In Sidney Hook, ed., *Philosophy and History: A Symposium.*

———. *The Structure of Science: Problems in the Logic of Scientific Explanation.* New York, 1961.

———. "Teleological Explanations and Teleological Systems." In Baruch A. Brody, *Readings in the Philosophy of Science.*

Namier, Sir Lewis. *The Structure of Politics at the Accession of George III.* 2d ed. London, 1957.

———. *Vanished Supremacies: Essays on European History, 1812–1918.*

Neustadt, Richard E., and Ernest R. May. *Thinking in Time: The Uses of History for Decision-Makers.* New York, 1986.

Newman, Frederick Delano. *Explanation by Description: An Essay on Historical Methodology.* The Hague, 1968.

Nicolson, Harold. *The Congress of Vienna: A Study of Allied Unity, 1812–1822.* San Diego, 1970.

Neilsen, Kai. "Rational Explanation in History." In Sidney Hook, ed., *Philosophy and History: A Symposium.*

Nowell-Smith, P. H. "Are Historical Events Unique?" *Proceedings of the Aristotelian Society,* 14 January 1957.

———. "History as Patterns of Thought and Action." In Leon Pompa and William H. Dray, eds., *Substance and Form in History: A Collection of Essays in Philosophy of History.* Edinburgh, 1981.

Oakes, Guy. "The Verstehen Thesis and the Foundations of Max Weber's Methodology." *History and Theory* 16 (1977).

Oakeshott, Michael. *Experience and Its Modes.* Cambridge, 1933.

———. "Historical Continuity and Causal Analysis." In William H. Dray, *Philosophical Analysis and History.*

O'Conner, D. J. "Causal Statements." *Philosophical Quarterly* 6 (January 1956).

Ossorio, Peter G. *"What Actually Happens": The Representation of Real-World Phenomena.* Columbia, S.C., 1978.

Palmer, William G. "The Burden of Proof: J. H. Hexter and Christopher Hill." *Journal of British Studies* 19 (fall 1979).

Paluch, Stanley. "The Specificity of Historical Language." *History and Theory* 7 (1968).

Passmore, J. A. "Explanation in Everyday Life, in Science, and in History." *History and Theory* 2 (1962).

———. "Law and Explanation in History." *Australian Journal of Politics and History* 4 (November 1958).

———. "The Objectivity of History." In William H. Dray, ed., *Philosophical Analysis and History.*

Peacocke, Christopher. *Holistic Explanation: Action, Space, Interpretation.* Oxford, 1959.

———. "Intention and Akrasia." In Bruce Vermazen and Merrill B. Hintikka, *Essays on Davidson: Actions and Events.*

Pears, David. "Rational Explanation of Actions and Psychological Determinism." In Ted Honderich, ed., *Essays on Freedom of Action.*

Pearson, Karl. *The Grammar of Science: Part I—Physical.* 3d ed. New York, 1911.

Perry, L. R. "The Covering Law Theory of Historical Explanation." In W. H. Burston and D. Thompson, eds., *Studies in the Nature and Teaching of History.*

Peters, Richard S. *The Conception of Motivation.* London, 1960.

Pirenne, Henri. *Economic and Social History of Medieval Europe.* London, 1936.

———. *Medieval Cities: Their Origins and Revival of Trade.* Translated by Frank D. Halsey. Princeton, 1952.

Pitt, J. "Generalizations in Historical Explanation." *Journal of Philosophy* 56 (4 June 1959).

Plumb, John Harold. *The Growth of Political Stability in England.* Harmondsworth, Middlesex, 1969.

Pollard, A. F. *The Evolution of Parliament.* London, 1926.

———. *Henry VIII.* New York, 1966.

Pompa, Leon. "Truth and Fact in History." In Leon Pompa and William H. Dray, eds., *Substance and Form in History: A Collection of Essays in Philosophy of History.*

Pompa, Leon, and William H. Dray, eds. *Substance and Form in History: A Collection of Essays in Philosophy of History.* Edinburgh, 1981.

Popper, Karl. *The Logic of Scientific Discovery.* London, 1968.

———. *Objective Knowledge: An Evolutionary Approach.* Oxford, 1972.

———. *The Open Society and Its Enemies.* 2 vols. Princeton, 1966.

———. "Popper's Psychologism: A Reply to Ball." *Philosophy of the Social Sciences* 12 (1982).

———. *The Poverty of Historicism.* New York, 1964.

———. "The Rationality Principle (1967)." In David Miller, ed., *A Pocket Popper.*

Porter, Dale H. *The Emergence of the Past: A Theory of Historical Explanation.* Chicago, 1981.

Railton, Peter. "A Deductive-Nomological Model of Probabilistic Explanation." *Philosophy of Science* 45 (June 1978).

Randall, John Herman, Jr. *Nature and Historical Experience.* New York, 1958.

Ratner, Sidney. "History as Inquiry." In Sidney Hook, *Philosophy and History: A Symposium.*

Rescher, Nicholas. *Scientific Explanation.* New York, 1970.

Richardson, Lewis. *Statistics of Deadly Quarrels.* London, 1960.

Ritter, Harry. *Dictionary of Concepts in History.* New York, 1986.

Roberts, David, and Clayton Roberts. *A History of England.* 2 vols. Englewood Cliffs, N.J., 1985.

Robinson, Howard. *Bayle the Sceptic.* New York, 1931.
Rosenblueth, Arturo, and Norbert Wiener, "Purposeful and Non-purposeful Behavior." In Walter Buckley, ed., *Modern Systems Research for the Behavioral Scientist: A Source Book.* Chicago, 1968.
Rosenblueth, Arturo, Norbert Wiener, and Julian Bigelow. "Behavior, Purpose, and Teleology." In Walter Buckley, ed., *Modern Systems Research for the Behavioral Scientist: A Source Book.* Chicago, 1968.
Roskell, S. W. *The Strategy of Sea Power.* London, 1962.
Rotenstreich, Nathan. *Philosophy, History, and Politics: Studies in Contemporary English Philosophy of History.* The Hague, 1976.
Rowse, A. L. *The Use of History.* London, 1946.
Runyan, William McKinley. *Life Histories and Psychobiography: Explorations in Theory and Method.* New York, 1982.
Russell, Bertrand. *Mysticism and Logic.* London, 1921.
Russell, Conrad, ed. *The Origins of the English Civil War.* London, 1973.
Ryle, Gilbert. *The Concept of Mind.* New York, 1949.
————. " 'If,' 'So,' and 'Because.' " In Max Black, ed., *Philosophical Analysis: A Collection of Essays.* Englewood Cliffs, N.J., 1963.
Salmon, Wesley C. *Statistical Explanation and Statistical Relevance.* Pittsburgh, 1971.
————. "Theoretical Explanation." In Stephan Korner, ed., *Explanation.*
Scheffler, Israel. *The Anatomy of Inquiry: Philosophical Studies in the Theory of Science.* New York, 1963.
————. "Explanation, Prediction, and Abstraction." In Arthur Danto and Sidney Morgenbesser, eds., *Philosophy of Science.*
————. "The Fictionalist View of Scientific Theories." In Baruch A. Brody, ed., *Readings in the Philosophy of Science.*
————. "Theoretical Terms and a Modest Empiricism." In Arthur Danto and Sidney Morgenbesser, eds., *Philosophy of Science.*
Schlesinger, Arthur M., Jr. *The Bitter Heritage: Vietnam and American Democracy 1941–1966.* Boston, 1967.
Scriven, Michael. "Causes, Connections, and Conditions in History." In William H. Dray, ed., *Philosophical Analysis and History.*
————. "Explanations, Predictions, and Laws." In Herbert Feigl and Grover Maxwell, eds., *Minnesota Studies in the Philosophy of Science,* vol. 3, *Scientific Explanation, Space, and Time.*
————. "New Issues in the Logic of Explanation." In Sidney Hook, ed., *Philosophy and History: A Symposium.*
————. "Truisms as the Grounds for Historical Explanations." In Patrick Gardiner, ed., *Theories of History.*
Searle, John Rogers. *Intentionality: An Essay in the Philosophy of Mind.* Cambridge, 1983.
Sellars, Wilfrid. "The Language of Theories." In Baruch A. Brody, ed., *Readings in the Philosophy of Science.*
Shoemaker, Robert G. "Inference and Intuition in Collingwood's Philosophy of History." *The Monist* 53 (January 1969).
Skinner, Quentin. "Meaning and Understanding in the History of Ideas." *History and Theory* 8 (1969).
Smart, J.J.C. "Davidson's Minimal Materialism." In Bruce Vermazen and Merrill B. Hintikka, eds., *Essays on Davidson: Actions and Events.*

Smelser, Marshall, and William J. Davisson. "The Historian and the Computer: A Simple Introduction to Complex Computation." In Robert Swierenga, ed., *Quantification in American History: Theory and Research.*

Sosa, Ernest, ed. *Causation and Conditionals.* Oxford, 1975.

Spector, Marshall. "Models and Theories." In Baruch A. Brody, ed., *Readings in the Philosophy of Science.*

Stampp, Kenneth. *The Peculiar Institution.* New York, 1956.

Stannard, David E. *Shrinking History: On Freud and the Failure of Psychohistory.* New York, 1980.

Stenson, Sten H. "History as Spirit." In Sidney Hook, ed., *Philosophy and History: A Symposium.*

Stinchcombe, Arthur. *Theoretical Methods in Social History.* New York, 1978.

Stoianovich, Traian, *French Historical Method: The Annales Paradigm.* Ithaca, 1976.

Stoll, Marion Rush. *Whewell's Philosophy of Induction.* Lancaster, Pa., 1929.

Stone, Lawrence. *The Causes of the English Revolution, 1529–1642.* London, 1972.

———. *The Crisis of the Aristocracy, 1558–1641.* Abridged ed. Oxford, 1967.

———. *The Family, Sex, and Marriage in England, 1500–1800.* New York, 1977.

———. "A Life of Learning." *ACLS Newsletter* 36 (winter–spring, 1985).

———. *The Past and the Present.* Boston, 1981.

———. "The Revival of Narrative: Reflections on a New Old History." In Lawrence Stone, *The Past and the Present.*

Stover, Robert. *The Nature of Historical Thinking.* Chapel Hill, 1967.

Strawson, Peter F. "Causation and Explanation." In Bruce Vermazen and Merrill B. Hintikka, eds., *Essays on Davidson: Actions and Events.*

———. Review of *Laws and Explanation in History,* by William H. Dray. *Mind* 68 (April 1959).

Strayer, Joseph R., and Hans Gatske. *The Mainstream of Civilization Since 1500.* 4th ed. San Diego, 1984.

Sutherland, N. S. "Motives as Explanations." *Mind* 68 (April 1959).

Swierenga, Robert P., ed. *Quantification in American History: Theory and Research.* New York, 1970.

Tannenbaum, Edward R. Review of *Methodology of History,* by Jerzy Topolski. *History and Theory* 18 (1979).

Taylor, A.J.P. *The Trouble-Makers: Dissent over Foreign Policy, 1729–1939.* London, 1969.

Taylor, Charles. *The Explanation of Behaviour.* London, 1964.

Taylor, Richard. "Comments on a Mechanistic Conception of Purposefulness." In Walter Buckley, ed., *Modern Systems Research for the Behavioral Scientist: A Source Book.*

———. "Purposeful and Non-Purposeful Behavior." In Walter Buckley, ed., *Modern Systems Research for the Behavioral Scientist: A Source Book.*

Teggart, Frederick J. "Causation in Historical Events." *Journal of the History of Ideas* 3 (January 1942).

———. *Rome and China: A Study of Correlations in Historical Events.* Berkeley, 1939.

———. *Theory and Processes of History.* Berkeley and Los Angeles, 1960.

Tennessen, Herman. "History Is Science." *The Monist* 53 (January 1969).

Thernstrom, Stephen. "Quantitative Methods in History: Some Notes." In Seymour Martin Lipset and Richard Hofstadter, eds., *Sociology and History: Methods.*

Thomas, Keith. *Religion and the Decline of Magic.* London, 1971.

Thompson, D. "Colligation and History Teaching." In W. H. Burston, and D. Thompson, eds., *Studies in the Nature and Teaching of History.*

Tilly, Charles. *As Sociology Meets History.* New York, 1981.

Tillyard, Eustace Mandeville Wetenhall. *The Elizabethan World Picture.* London, 1943.

Tolstoy, Count Leo. *War and Peace.* Translated by Constance Garnett. New York, n.d.

Topolski, Jerzy. *Methodology of History.* Dordrecht, 1976.

———. "Towards an Integrated Model of Historical Explanation." *History and Theory* 30 (1991).

Toynbee, Arnold. *A Study of History.* 12 vols. London, 1934–1961.

———. *A Study of History.* Abridged ed. 2 vols. Edited by D. C. Somervell. New York, 1946.

Trevor-Roper, Hugh R. "The Acts of the Apostles." *New York Review of Books*, 12 May 1983.

———. "Fernand Braudel, the *Annales,* and the Mediterranean." *Journal of Modern History* 44 (December 1972).

———. *The Gentry, 1540–1640.* London, [1953].

———. "Religion, the Reformation, and Social Change." *Historical Studies*, vol. 4, *Papers Read Before the Fifth Irish Historical Conference of Historians* (1963).

———. "The Rise of Christian Europe: The Great Recovery." *The Listener*, 28 November 1963.

Tyacke, Nicholas. "Puritanism, Arminianism, and Counter-Revolution." In Conrad Russell, ed., *The Origins of the English Civil War.*

Vermazen, Bruce, and Merrill B. Hintikka, eds. *Essays on Davidson: Actions and Events.* Oxford, 1985.

Vernon, Richard. "Auguste Comte and 'Development': A Note." *History and Theory* 17 (1978).

Wallace, Carol. Review of *Has History Any Meaning? A Critique of Popper's Philosophy of History,* by Burleigh Taylor Wilkins. *History and Theory* 18 (1972).

Walsh, W. H. "The Causation of Ideas." *History and Theory* 14 (1975).

———. "Colligatory Concepts in History." In W. H. Burston and D. Thompson, eds., *Studies in the Nature and Teaching of History.*

———. "Historical Causation." *Proceedings of the Aristotelian Society,* n.s., 63 (1962–63).

———. "The Intelligibility of History." *Philosophy* 17 (April 1942).

———. *An Introduction to Philosophy of History.* London, 1967.

———. "The Limits of Scientific History." In William H. Dray, ed., *Philosophical Analysis and History.*

———. " 'Meaning' in History." In Patrick Gardiner, ed., *Theories of History.*

———. "The Notion of an Historical Event." *Aristotelian Society,* Supplementary vol. 43 (1969).

———. Review of *Kant and the Problem of History,* by William A. Galston. *History and Theory* 16 (1977).

Walzer, Michael. "Puritanism as a Revolutionary Ideology." *History and Theory* 3 (1963).

Watkins, J.W.N. "Historical Explanations in the Social Sciences." In Patrick Gardiner, ed., *Theories of History.*

———. "Ideal Types and Historical Explanation." In Herbert Feigl and May Brodbeck, eds., *Readings in the Philosophy of Science.*

———. "Methodological Individualism and Social Tendencies." In May Brodbeck, ed., *Readings in the Philosophy of the Social Sciences*.

Webb, Walter Prescott. *The Great Frontier*. London, 1953.

Wedgwood, C. V. *The King's Peace, 1637–1641*. New York, 1955.

Weingartner, R. H. "The Quarrel About Historical Explanation." In May Brodbeck, ed., *Readings in the Philosophy of the Social Sciences*.

Weiss, Paul. "It's About Time." In Sidney Hook, ed., *Philosophy and History: A Symposium*.

Wernham, R. B. *Before the Armada*. London, 1966.

Whewell, William. *The Philosophy of the Inductive Sciences, Founded upon Their History*. 2 vols. London, 1840.

White, Hayden. *Metahistory: The Historical Imagination in Nineteenth-Century Europe*. Baltimore, 1973.

———. *Tropics of Discourse: Essays in Cultural Criticism*. Baltimore, 1978.

White, Morton. *Foundations of Historical Knowledge*. New York, 1965.

———. "Historical Explanation." In Patrick Gardiner, ed., *Theories of History*.

———. "The Logic of Historical Narration." In Sidney Hook, ed., *Philosophy and History: A Symposium*.

Wiener, Jonathan. "The Barrington Moore Thesis and Its Critics." *Theory and Society* 2 (fall 1975).

Williams, Donald C. "Essentials in History." In Sidney Hook, ed., *Philosophy and History: A Symposium*.

Winch, Peter. *The Idea of a Social Science and Its Relation to Philosophy*. New York, 1958.

Windelband, Wilhelm. "Rectorial Address, Strasbourg, 1894." *History and Theory* 19 (1980).

Wisdom, J. O. "General Explanation in History." *History and Theory* 19 (1980).

Wittfogel, Karl. *Oriental Despotism*. New Haven, 1957.

Wollheim, Richard. Review of *Art and Act*, by Peter Gay. *History and Theory* 16 (1977).

Wood, Gordon. "The March of Folly." *New York Review of Books*, 29 March 1984.

Wright, Georg Henrich von. *Explanation and Understanding*. Ithaca, N.Y., 1971.

Wright, Quincy. *A Study of War*. 2 vols. Chicago, 1942.

Zagorin, Perez. "The Social Interpretation of the English Revolution." *Journal of Economic History* 19 (September 1959).

Index

DATE D